1972

This is the first detailed survey of democratic ideas on the British Left in the period leading to 1914. Socialists of the late nineteenth century inherited assumptions about the priority of democracy from a long tradition of British Radicalism. However, the advent of the Fabians, who rejected this tradition as primitive, and of an ILP leadership more concerned to enter than reform parliament, meant that the movement was split between 'strong' and 'weak' views of democracy. 'Strong' democracy characterised an attempt to weld unions into a 'fighting federation' during the late 1890s. Its collapse sheds light on the reception of syndicalist ideas a decade later.

By the eve of the First World War a consensus was emerging that might have formed the basis for a more realistic *and* more radical approach to democracy than has actually been pursued by the Labour Party and the Left during the twentieth century. *Democratic Ideas and the British Labour Movement* assesses an important debate in the history of socialist ideas and in the formation of the British Labour movement.

Democratic ideas and the
British Labour movement, 1880–1914

Democratic ideas and the British Labour movement, 1880–1914

Logie Barrow
University of Bremen

Ian Bullock
Brighton College of Technology

CAMBRIDGE
UNIVERSITY PRESS

Published by the Press Syndicate of the University of Cambridge
The Pitt Building, Trumpington Street, Cambridge CB2 1RP
40 West 20th Street, New York, NY 10011-4211, USA
10 Stamford Road, Oakleigh, Melbourne 3166, Australia

© Cambridge University Press 1996

First published 1996

Printed in Great Britain at Redwood Books, Trowbridge, Wiltshire

A catalogue record for this book is available from the British Library

Library of Congress cataloguing in publication data
Barrow, Logie.
Democratic ideas and the British Labour Movement, 1880–1914 /
Logie Barrow, Ian Bullock.
    p.   cm.
ISBN 0 521 56042 X (hc)
1. Labor movement – Great Britain – History. 2. Trade-unions – Great
Britain – Political activity – History. 3. Socialism – Great Britain –
History. 4. Democracy – Great Britain – History. 5. Labour Party
(Great Britain) – History. 6. Great Britain – Politics and
government – 1901–1936. 7. Great Britain – Politics and
government – 18937–1901. I. Bullock, Ian, 1941– . II. Title.
HD8390.B274 1996
331'.0941–dc20   95-32842   CIP

ISBN 0 521 56042 X

WD

Contents

Acknowledgements

Logie Barrow gratefully acknowledges the help of librarians and archivists at Aberdeen, Birmingham, Bolton, Bradford, Glasgow, Halifax (Calderdale), Huddersfield, Leeds, Leicester, Liverpool, Manchester, Newcastle and Nottingham public libraries; at the British Library, the Irish Congress of Trades Unions, the National Library of Ireland, the National Library of Scotland, the Public Record Office, and, not least, the Modern Records Centre (University of Warwick). The latter now houses some of the documents that, at the time, were kindly made available by the AUEW (Peckham), the GFTU, the GMBTU (Thames Ditton), and the Lancashire Miners (Bolton) to all of whom thanks are due. To this, Ian Bullock would like to add thanks to the Library of the University of Sussex, particularly the Document Section, and to the British Library of Political and Economic Science, and the libraries of the universities of Hull, Manchester, Reading and Sheffield

Individuals who have assisted with access, helpful criticism, active support, typing and encouragement include Sue Bullock, Tony Carew, John Harrison, Walter Kendall, Victor Rabinovitch, Siân Reynolds and John Simpson, in the case of Ian Bullock, and Kate Caute, Nils-Finn Christiansen, Barbara Dabrowski, Marjorie Hanlon, Julian Harber, James Hinton, Richard Hyman, Selma Leydesdorff, Dorle Partenie, Richard Price, Alice Prochaska, Richard Storey, Siep Stuurman and the late Harry Wicks in the case of Logie Barrow. Both authors wish to acknowledge the help of Bob Holton and Stephen Yeo.

Introduction

Readers fresh to this area of history will find this book relatively easy and be amazed to be told that much or even most of it is new to specialists. Until recently, historians had time and again picked over some vital features of the area while either blind or indifferent to those others whose relevance this book argues. True, during the last decade or so there has been work that touches on some aspects of our themes, but this has focused mainly on single organisations and particular regions – such as Dylan Morris's study of the ILP – or on very different problems – such as Duncan Tanner's important contribution to the debate on why and how Labour replaced the Liberal Party as the main alternative to the Conservatives. Like some other recent authors, such as Jon Lawrence, Tanner emphasises the overlaps between socialist and non-socialist radicalism. While these are hardly absent from our book, we focus almost entirely on the 'Labour movement' as traditionally understood – socialist organisations and trade unions: a different perspective.[1]

With concern over low participation in US elections, over the European Union's 'democratic deficit', with Central and Eastern Europe launching half-built parliamentary hulls into an economic hurricane blowing towards the whirlpool of authoritarian nationalism, with the uncertainties of post-apartheid South Africa, and a host of other developments worldwide, discussion of the nature and forms of democracy has never been more vital.

---

[1] Dylan Morris, 'Labour or Socialism? Opposition and Dissent within the ILP, with special reference to Lancashire', PhD thesis, Manchester University, 1982. Duncan Tanner, *Political change and the Labour Party 1900–1918* (Cambridge, 1990). Jon Lawrence, 'Popular Radicalism and the Socialist Revival in Britain', *Journal of British Studies*, 31, April 1992, 163–86.

Other recent work in the general areas of our concern includes Mark Bevir, 'The British Social Democratic Federation 1880–1885. From O'Brienism to Marxism', *International Review of Social History*, 37, 1992; David Howell, *British Workers and the Independent Labour Party 1888–1906* (Manchester, 1983); and Eugenio F. Biagini and Alastair J. Reid (eds.), *Currents of Radicalism and Party Politics in Britain, 1850–1914* (Cambridge, 1991), especially the contributions of Duncan Tanner and Pat Thane.

In Britain from the later 1970s, the ideas of citizenship and universally available public services – even the validity of the concept of 'society' itself – were under attack from a new Right that combined free market dogmas with 'public order' authoritarianism. Why was resistance so feeble for so much of this time? Why was the Right allowed to hijack the rhetoric of popular accountability and conflate it with the rights of shareholders in privatised industries and more recently with the 'consumer rights' of the Citizen's Charter? Why was the Left so ineffective in counterposing democratic control to 'popular capitalism'? Why did it only belatedly – and still hesitantly – begin again to speak the language of democracy and 'enablement'? Partly because the Left had for so long abandoned the field that, during the period covered by this book, had formed a vital part of its territory.

Since 1918, as the *New Statesman* noted seven decades later (26 August 1988), there have been two main currents on the Left – ' "reformers" and "revolutionaries" '. 'The first place faith in, the other pit [their] faith against, the traditional constitution. The first rejects and the second scorns constitutional change.' These twin exclusions are surely remarkable, given how wide the recognition now is that the British state is among the least democratic in the Western world.

This stalemate began to break up precisely with such late-1980s arguments. Within Labour there was an upsurge of concern reflected in a growing *Labour Campaign for Electoral Reform*, in motions on the annual conference agenda and in the Plant Report. More widely, there was the start of *Charter 88* addressing people of all parties or none. By the mid-1990s, with the Labour Party committing itself to 'an open democracy, in which Government is held accountable by the people', to devolution (known before 1914 as 'home rule all round'), and even the Conservatives appointing a 'minister for open government', the issues examined in this book are at least starting to reappear on the political agenda.

By contrast, during the two decades in which the research for this book was undertaken, interest in such matters was widely regarded on the Left as – at best – whimsy. Our concern with debates on representation or delegation, with ideas for making democracy more 'direct', with attempts to rid trade unions of bureaucracy and to place decision-making directly in the hands of their members, was, for one reader, to 'reify political theory'. The equivalent nineteenth-century verdict was more blunt: it was all disruption and 'mere politics'.

Such a response is far less likely today. Instead, the criticism is more likely to be that *circum*-1900 socialists and trade union activists (not all socialist) are irrelevant for our generation, however worthy in their own.

For some, the spectacular collapse of 'actually existing socialism' in Eastern and Central Europe demonstrates conclusively that socialism – of whatever variety – is no longer an 'ism' but a 'wasm'.

Conceivably, in fifty years time, socialism will seem as strange and mystifying as the doctrine of the Muggletonians. Yet there are reasons for doubt. Even at the height of the twin-hegemony of Stalinism and of social democracy (or, as the latter's British version became, bureaucratic welfarism and nationalisation combined with constitutional do-nothingism) there were those ready to protest that both of these were travesties of socialism. Real socialism would be, above all, infinitely more democratic than either. Even for this reason alone, socialism, seen once more as a movement for ever greater democracy, may yet confound the sceptics.

'Democracy or reforming the structure of the state never ranked high on the socialist wish list', claims Will Hutton in his best-selling *The State We're In*.[2] This he rightly sees as a central weakness of Labour. While his criticism has been true, until very recently at least, of the 'head office' socialism he is discussing, it is not at all true of very many of the socialists who appear in this book. Here, our intention is to demonstrate that before 1918 the trade union and socialist movements were, in Britain as elsewhere, major arenas – indeed *the* major arenas – for arguments about democracy. This was not simply because commitment outside these movements – with the exception of Cooperators who overlapped with them overwhelmingly – was by comparison variable, reluctant and sometimes unreliable. It was also because democratisation – of existing working-class and socialist organisations as well as of the political processes of the state – was, for many decades, central for most socialist and many trade union activists. True, into the early 1900s, democratisers were repeatedly marginalised. We see this as partly their fault, conceptually as well as tactically. But by the 1910s, many activists had, consciously or not, left some of their mistakes behind. This time the forces for marginalisation came on a world scale: war and Bolshevism.

These changed not only working-class radicalism but also working-class moderation. On the Continent the impact was complex enough. But in Britain one further factor was at work. Eager, during the post-1918 generations, to 'win power' within the existing mechanisms, British Labour differed from many of its Continental cousins not, as universally assumed, in never having shared their concerns to widen and deepen democracy, but in forgetting that it ever had. That so much important evidence has until very recently been largely overlooked or ignored is remarkable. Only paranoids would imagine a vast conspiracy of suppression embracing several generations of historians, from Tories to Trotskyists. The likelier reasons are to do with the problems of writing history at all, within a first-past-the-post prime-ministerial absolutism which petrifies all 'less urgent' issues into eternal irrelevance.

Although, as we will note, oppositional voices were never quite stilled after 1918, they cried for the most part unheeded in the wilderness. Most historical work, naturally enough, took place within the new framework which, since it allowed disagreement or even bitter denunciation, did not seem restrictive. None the less, the last thirty or forty years have seen a gradual growth of perspectives 'from below' which helped bring about the collapse of that world of discussion in the late 1980s. Despite feeling isolated (and perhaps a trifle smug about this) we turned out unexceptional: none of us ever writes from outside history.

This has intensified our motivation to try recreating those aspects of the past with which we are concerned – with all its not-yet-discussed dead-ends and, above all, its confusions as open and fluid as they were at the time. We try to treat the preoccupations of the time from 'inside' that moment. We therefore try not to import anachronistic terminology. Our tariff-barrier carries, of course, a price. Our typical historians' preference for 'ordinary' language constantly risks blurring distinctions between meanings 'then' and 'now'. We hope to stay close to the usages of the time or, when we do import 'historians' words', to make this clear.

We begin by tracing the legacy of democratic ideas and practice in the late nineteenth century, focusing on the views held by working-class socialists in the 1880s about their democratic grandparents, the Chartists of the 1830s and 1840s, and how these views interacted with ideas on democracy. We go on to consider more broadly the range of strategies for increasing working-class power during the late nineteenth century. Parts 2 and 3 deal with two brief hinge-periods – around 1900 and 1910 respectively – in the development of democratic ideas among socialists and trade unionists.

The trade union movement during the 1890s saw a growing unease as to the effectiveness and justice of existing institutional arrangements. By the end of the decade, the 'employers' counter-attack', climaxing in the 1897–8 engineering struggle, produced a panic-fear in the unions that the basic structure of British industrial relations was to be swept aside. This panic was short-lived, but it reverberated long enough to help power two responses, one almost totally forgotten. This was the brief attempt to revolutionise the structure of the unions by absorbing them into an ultra-democratic 'fighting Federation'. The other was the strategy of independent Labour representation: sending working-class men to the

Commons independent of the non-working-class Tory and Liberal parties. These two efforts began side by side, but the first has been all but expunged from memory whereas the second – as the Labour Representation Committee – is well-known as the ancestor of today's Labour Party.

We have therefore dealt with the 'Federation' phenomenon in rather more detail than the 'political' because it was here that, most clearly, the would-be democratisers, represented in this case by the proponents of the *Clarion* Federation, came up against what the less sanguine would have called 'reality'. Here more than anywhere else, the conceptual and practical weaknesses of the 'ultra-democrats' were remorselessly tested to destruction.

But it was not, and is not, the end of the debate. There were signs of a more viable approach emerging by 1914 which drew on the most radical strains of democratic socialism. What might have developed subsequently is impossible to say. Within the British structures, the shocks of war and revolution changed almost everything. But perhaps only for the twentieth century.

Part 1

1 The survival of Chartist assumptions

This chapter discusses one small and one tiny organisation: the Social Democratic Federation (SDF) and its short-lived child, the Socialist League. The importance of these organisations, into and beyond the 1900s, lies for us in the growing influence of those they helped to form. Originating in the 1880s – thus encouraging historians to talk of a socialist revival – they were self-consciously in the shadow of Chartism.

Just as the 1940s remain vital for many on the Left today, so the Chartist movement of around the 1840s remained the reference point for generations afterwards. Most relevant for this book, it had aimed to democratise parliament as a precondition for whatever social reforms working people (or rather working men) might next demand.

Into the new century, the SDF weekly *Justice* saw SDFers as Chartism's 'legitimate heirs and successors'.[1] Some of them had themselves been Chartists, among whom James Murray was on the SDF executive in the 1880s still demanding proportional representation and other democratic measures as a way towards the 'socialisation of production'.[2]

Not that these had necessarily stood still during the intervening decades. The Birmingham-based John Sketchley had gone through Owenism, freethought and republicanism. On the one hand they were open to Continental influences; Sketchley's 1879 *Principles of Social Democracy* is credited by E. P. Thompson with introducing European and particularly German socialist ideas to many future British socialists.[3]

---

[1] *Justice*, 1 August 1903.
[2] For James Murray and his brother Charles see Stan Shipley, *Club Life and Socialism in Mid-Victorian London*, History Workshop Pamphlet No. 5 (London, 1971), E. P. Thompson, *William Morris, Romantic to Revolutionary*, 2nd edn (London, 1977), pp. 280–3, Alfred Plummer, *Bronterre, A Political Biography of Bronterre O'Brien, 1804–1864* (London, 1971), pp. 269–70. Two Northern SDFers imprisoned for Chartism: see *Justice*, 27 February 1885 (W. H. Chadwick) and 12 May 1888 (William Bell). For old Battersea Chartists, see William Stephen Sanders, *Early Socialist Days* (London, 1927), p. 21.
[3] Thompson, *William Morris*, p. 280.

The French Revolution and 1848 both figured prominently in the socialist calendar. The Paris Commune of 1871 was celebrated as a socialist 'Easter', not least for showing how democracy inherently gravitated towards socialism.[4] On the other, the SDF itself had begun as a federation of London working-class Radical clubs, the Democratic Federation, and its programme had been mainly Chartist with only the demand for land nationalisation pointing towards the socialism of its main animator, the flamboyant stockbroker H. M. Hyndman. Hyndman had intended it as a revival of Chartism, or so he told Marx.[5] True, as early as 1883–4, it became officially socialist and added the word 'Social' to its title. But it never relinquished such concerns.

So, when historians talk of the 1880s socialists as distinctive 'precisely' because of their interest 'in social *rather than merely* political reform'[6] the words here italicised are tricky. By definition, socialists saw a new social system as fundamental, but democratisation remained crucial in principle and strategy.

Yet not for all of them. The leading lights in the Fabian Society, the third socialist organisation founded during the 1880s, quickly put away such things – not quite as 'childish' but certainly, in the words of Beatrice and Sidney Webb in the 1890s as 'primitive'. During the same period, their fellow-Fabian Bernard Shaw enjoyed sneering at the SDF as Chartism 'risen from the dead'.[7] Unlike most early local activists who understandably left, many of Fabianism's London intellectuals were inexperienced in plebeian democratic traditions, and proud to be.

The traditions, both British and Continental, to which the SDF most readily related were 'political' as distinct from 'industrial'. They were also predominantly male. When, in December 1888, *Justice* asserted that 'All history shows that it is *the organised force behind the ballot box* that puts the fear of man into the hearts of the oppressors'[8] (original emphasis) it seems odd in retrospect that, after a successful strike by 'matchgirls' at Bryant and May and at the end of a year which had seen the beginning of a major trade union upsurge, there is no hint that 'organised force' might take the form of industrial strength.

This is itself a sign of Chartist influence. Henry Collins has suggested

---

[4] *Justice*, 10 April 1886.
[5] Chushichi Tsuzuki, *H. M. Hyndman and British Socialism*, ed. Henry Pelling (London, 1961), p. 33.
[6] Willard Wolfe, *From Radicalism to Socialism: Men and Ideas in the Formation of Fabian Socialist Doctrines, 1881–1889* (London, 1975), p. 64.
[7] George Bernard Shaw (ed.), *Essays in Fabian Socialism* (London, 1889), p. 186. See also *Labour Leader*, 31 May 1902.
[8] *Justice*, 8 December 1888.

that the SDF's low estimate of trade union potential may be attributed to the influence of the leading Chartist Bronterre O'Brien, transmitted through the Murrays.[9] More recently, Mark Bevir has traced the SDF's emphasis on the political, as distinct from social and economic, specifically to this source. He argues that, 'The socialism of the D.F. still embraced O'Brien's political strategy according to which the immediate need was political reforms which once introduced would enable the workers to initiate social reforms.' And though old O'Brienites modified their position to accept 'the need to collectivise the means of production', they 'retained much of their O'Brienism.'[10] Certainly, the SDF claimed O'Brien as a precursor. In 1889 *Justice* described him as

the first man in Europe who used the name of Social-Democracy and more than fifty years ago, before Marx and Engels began to write, practically put in popular form, in conjunction with his colleagues, the views which the great German thinker placed on a scientific basis.[11]

In part this was an argument to ward off chauvinistic attacks on the SDF's apparent 'importation' of doctrines perceived as foreign. Yet, to its protagonists, Social-Democracy was not simply an alternative term for socialism. It had a definite meaning to which O'Brien's earlier formulations were crucial.

This can be demonstrated from a much later article by Hyndman in the SDF's monthly journal *The Social-Democrat*. Here, he defended the term 'Social-Democratic'; 'Socialist' was too vague and did not 'necessarily carry with it the notion of a democrat':

Socialists are, indeed, frequently accused of wishing to impose their arbitrary will on the whole population. This is not true, as I believe, of the great majority of them . . . But nobody can truly say that State or Bureaucratic Socialism is not a danger of the immediate future in more than one country.

'Social-Democracy', he went on, had originated with O'Brien, 'in some respects the ablest and most far-seeing of the Chartists.' O'Brien had believed that trade unions 'being composed of what he called "the aristocrats of labour" . . . with a distinct desire to constitute a privileged

---

[9] Henry Collins, 'The Marxism of the Social Democratic Federation', in A. Briggs and J. Saville (eds.), *Essays in Labour History* (London, 1971), pp. 47–69. For the influence of O'Brien and O'Brienites in the metropolitan ultra-radical milieu out of which the SDF emerged, see Shipley, *Club Life and Socialism in Mid-Victorian London*; Logie Barrow, 'The Homerton Social Democratic Club, 1881–1882', *History Workshop*, 5, Spring 1978, and Mark Bevir, 'The British Social Democratic Federation 1880–1885. From O'Brienism to Marxism', *International Review of Social History*, 37, 1992, pp. 207–229.

[10] Bevir, 'British Social Democratic Federation', pp. 223 and 219.

[11] *Justice*, 6 April 1889. See also similar statement in *Justice*, 14 November 1885.

class among the workers' would develop into a 'more or less reactionary force.' Had not his fears been to a large extent justified?

A Social Democrat, then, according to O'Brien, was a man who regarded social questions as of paramount importance, and desired to solve them by collectivist and democratic action. Democratic action might not by any means be collectivist; and collectivist action might not by any means necessarily be democratic . . .

O'Brien took and used the term Social-Democrat to express the views of those who wished to bring about a complete social reconstruction under democratic forms.[12]

The SDF, thus, not only remained more at home in the Paris sections of the 1790s or among the radical artisans and depressed outworkers of Chartist days or of the Paris Commune than within an organised working class whose long-term leverage was growing. More specifically, it saw itself as inheriting an approach, crystallised by O'Brien in the term Social-Democracy, which was equally democratic and collectivist. If most Social-Democrats believed they were the true custodians of this tradition, in what ways did they seek to interpret, develop and embody the 'democratic forms' of which Hyndman wrote with such emphasis?

The development of Social-Democratic forms

Hyndman's assertive personality and his perceived 'dominance' of the SDF have tended to obscure the way his own ideas developed *within* the organisation into a pretty clear statement of what most of its members meant by Social-Democracy. We can see this by retracing Hyndman's own statements and the policy statements and programmes of the Federation in its formative years. In particular, we can see very significant changes of both language and substance when we compare his book, *England For All* (1881) with the manifesto *Socialism Made Plain* (1883)

The programme adopted in June 1881 at the foundation of the Democratic Federation comprised the following: (1) Adult Suffrage; (2) Triennial Parliaments; (3) Equal Electoral Districts; (4) Payment of MPs and official election expenses out of the rates; (5) Bribery, Treating and Corrupt Practices to be made acts of Felony; (6) Abolition of the House of Lords as a Legislative Body; (7) Legislative Independence for Ireland; (8) National and Federal Parliaments; (9) Nationalisation of Land.[13]

The demand for universal suffrage in point 1 was already more radical

[12] H. M. Hyndman, 'Social-Democrat or Socialist?', *The Social-Democrat*, 8, August 1897, pp. 228–31.
[13] Tsuzuki, *H. M. Hyndman*, p. 41.

than the more qualified and tentative proposal in Hyndman's *England For All* which he had distributed to the conference delegates. There he had hummed and ha'd. On the one hand, he had attacked the 'present restricted franchise' and concluded that 'manhood or adult suffrage' – a significant 'or' – was a prerequisite to social reform. On the other, he had considered the 'dilemma' that without universal suffrage 'a minority unjustly controls the country', while with it there was a risk of 'wholesale corruption' and the danger that 'ignorance should become the ultimate court of appeal'.[14] Hyndman gave the impression of arguing himself into support for universal suffrage through many misgivings. Yet even this was an advance; as recently as 1880 when standing for parliament in Marylebone as an independent, he had demanded merely an extension of 'household' suffrage to the counties – essentially what was soon achieved by the 1884 Reform Act. By 1883 he was helping to draft *Socialism Made Plain* which demanded 'complete adult suffrage for every man and woman in these islands'.[15] He had moved swiftly.

The same is true of his views on parliament. *England For All* claimed that 'Triennial parliaments, or better still a retirement of one-third of members each year, could keep the House of Commons thoroughly in harmony with the constituencies.' Equal electoral districts and payment of MPs and election expenses had been 'demanded in 1848 by a powerful organisation and now here we are in 1881 without them.' In more radical language the 1883 manifesto declared support for 'paid delegates and annual conventions because by these means alone can the people control their representatives.'[16] This echoed the demands of the People's Charter and earlier radical attempts to achieve greater control over MPs. Calls for annual or triennial parliaments, the enforcement of election pledges and for the constituents' right to recall MPs had been made during the Reform Bill crisis of 1830–1832. 'The ballot, shorter parliaments, pledges and compulsory resignations all had one object', as Norman Gash has said: 'the transfer of initiative and decision from the floor of the Commons to the polling booth'.[17] Such a transfer

---

[14] H. M. Hyndman, *The Textbook of Democracy: England for All* (London, 1881; rpt. Brighton, 1973), pp. 88–91.

[15] H. W. Lee and E. Archbold, *Social-Democracy in Britain* (London, 1935), p. 275, appendix 1. Address to the Electors of Marylebone. 'Socialism Made Plain', 1883, in Henry Pelling (ed.), *The Challenge of Socialism* (London, 1954), p. 130.

[16] Hyndman, *England For All*, pp. 48–9, and 'Socialism Made Plain', p. 131.

[17] Norman Gash, *Politics in the Age of Peel: A Study in the Techniques of Parliamentary Representation, 1830–1850* (London, 1953), p. 31. An interesting application of this principle is found in Helen Taylor's proposal for shorter terms of office for members of school boards in order to ensure that they remained 'responsible to their constituents'. See *Justice*, 26 December 1885.

was to remain the common thread in all the demands of radical democrats in and outside the British socialist movement.

The 'early' Hyndman of *England For All* (1881) is relatively conservative in both language and ideas. His proposals involve modification rather than replacement of existing institutions. Assemblies for Ireland, Wales and Scotland 'can scarcely be organised until there is a more active demand for them'. Local authorities' powers should be increased, but continue to operate in the 'old, well-understood divisions, county, municipality and township'. The House of Lords is unacceptable in its present form, but 'to sweep away an institution is . . . scarcely our English way . . . What we need in place of the House of Lords is a Great Council' to conduct foreign affairs and regulate 'the policy towards our great colonies, in conjunction with direct representatives from them'. Such statements must have contributed to the early suspicions 'as to the thorough-going character of Hyndman's democratic sentiments' that the veteran Social-Democrat, Ernest Belfort Bax, was to recall in 1918.[18] But there is already strong emphasis on positive and convinced mass support. However desirable, Scottish and Welsh assemblies will only be practical politics when, as in Ireland, there is sufficient demand. More frequent elections will 'quicken the general interest in public affairs'.

By contrast the language of *Socialism Made Plain* (1883) is more radical – if also more ambiguous. It went beyond the 1881 programme not only by calling for the nationalisation of all means of production, distribution and exchange, but also in demanding the 'abolition of all hereditary authority' and 'direct reference of all grave issues to the country at large'. It is quite wrong to view the evolution of the Democratic Federation into the SDF in terms of radical political demands being relinquished for a socialist commitment to public ownership. Radical political democracy remained integral to the SDF's conception of socialism.

A leader in *Justice* by Hyndman in June 1884 shows us the further evolution of his own thought and the position of the, now, Social-Democratic Federation. Headlined *Our Republic*, it begins by asking what socialists mean when they say they care nothing for the forms of government:

Surely a republic must be preferred to a monarchy and parliamentary government to dictatorship. Certainly, we answer, we wish to have a republic and when we declare that forms of government are indifferent to us we speak only of such forms as exist and are chiefly advocated today.

---

[18] Hyndman, *England For All*, pp. 96–9, 109. Ernest Belfort Bax, *Reminiscences and Reflections of a Mid and Late Victorian* (London, 1918), pp. 94–5.

He goes on to describe 'the Government we intend to have instead of the decaying system of today'. The services of the Royal Family should be dispensed with 'in a polite manner and in the handsome way that will become us as a nation. They have the right to stay here as long as the majority of Englishmen choose, not a moment longer.' Moreover,

we desire that the Republic that will follow shall be one that really means government of the people, for the people, by the people. To this end we necessarily claim the entire abolition of the House of Lords or any Second Chamber, and call for the adequate representation of the whole adult population, by means of paid delegates, in a National Convention annually elected. The numbers in the Convention should be far less than in the present unwieldy House of the middle classes and there should be no President . . . From this Assembly of Delegates of the Democracy, Committees should be elected to conduct our Foreign Affairs, our Commerce, our Legislature, our Railways and other departments of State; but no laws should be made, no treaties concluded, no warlike action taken, without direct reference to the vote of the entire people.

This is a much more radical Hyndman. Unlike the Hyndman of *England For All*, he has no hesitation about abolishing the Lords, and the 'Great Council' has given way to a committee elected by the Convention. But the practical concern has remained. The article is more explicit than *Socialism Made Plain*, and we are given some idea of how the annually elected convention might work. Again, the republican implication is spelt out, as are the sorts of 'grave issues' appropriate for decision by referendum. Here too, Hyndman had moved swiftly; in 1881 according to Bax he had opposed the inclusion of the abolition of the monarchy in the Democratic Federation's programme.[19]

Proposals for socialisation are integrated into this conception of democracy.

As control of the land, machinery, capital, communications and credit would be vested in townships, municipalities and the State; as centralisation and decentralisation . . . would go on simultaneously, the whole people would have a direct interest in securing the best administration of their own affairs.[20]

One of *Justice*'s earliest issues demanded 'direct paid delegation' in addition to universal suffrage and proportional representation.[21] Delegation, as distinct from representation, was a major feature of the

[19] Bax, *Reminiscences and Reflections*, pp. 94–5.
[20] *Justice*, 14 June 1884. Hyndman was to reiterate the position he had taken in the 'Our Republic' article many times over the years. It is particularly interesting to compare it with his views more than twenty years later in *Justice*, 29 July 1905; 13 June 1908; 6 November 1909; and with his opening address to the first British Socialist Party conference reported in *Justice*, 1 June 1912.
[21] *Justice*, 2 February 1884.

SDF's vision of the future system of government. The lack of control of electors over the elected was constantly emphasised. Helen Taylor in 1884 demanded that 'men getting into Parliament should go there as delegates of the people'. (As step-daughter and intellectual sister of the late John Stuart Mill, Taylor surely needed no prompting on late-nineteenth-century democratic deficits.) For Hyndman during the same weeks, 'the very traditions of [Westminster] are anti-democratic and the policemen who continually cry "step back" in the lobby only represent the attitude of the House of Commons itself to the people it is supposed to represent'. And what was the alternative? A statement issued by the Democratic Federation Executive that summer when the Liberal government introduced what became the third Reform Act insisted that

> you must have Paid Delegates from your own class, not time-serving unpaid representatives from the classes which rob you. You must put your servants, not your masters, at Westminster; you must have a National Convention of the People, not a House of the Confiscating Classes.
> But your delegates will need definite orders . . . [22]

There was a, perhaps deliberate, ambiguity about the phrase 'National Convention'. Was it an entirely new and revolutionary body, initially contesting power with Parliament? Or was the 'Convention' a House of Commons purged by the electorate, with paid delegates of the workers taking the place of the representatives of the 'Confiscating Classes'? In part at least, this ambiguity reflected the differing opinions of SDFers on the question of participation in parliamentary politics. This was to be the main *political* cause of the 'split' which led to the setting up of the Socialist League.

The need for *delegation* continued to be pressed by the SDF. A clear, if crude, distinction was made when *Justice* insisted that 'We must have delegates whom we can kick out if we wish, not representatives who can kick us', or when Hyndman called for 'the fullest direct democratic representation of, or rather delegation from, the people'.[23]

The Democratic Federation, then, began as a conscious revival of Chartism, and for Social-Democrats the sense of being heir to this tradition lasted well beyond the 1880s. From the Chartists, the Federation inherited both a programme of democratic political demands which it maintained and extended, and a strain of 'barricades mentality'

22 *Justice*, 19 January 1884; *Justice*, 29 March 1884; 12 July 1884.
23 *Justice*, 16 April 1887; 9 July 1887; 11 April 1885; 1 January 1887.

which was only partly siphoned off into the uncompromisingly
revolutionary Socialist League. Crucially, Social-Democrats did not
identify democracy with the parliamentary system – not even a parliamentary system elected on the basis of universal suffrage and purged of
anomalies such as the House of Lords. This was evident from *Justice*'s
denunciations of 'Parliamentary dictatorship' and the 'Unconstitutional
Cabinet'.[24] Control of the elected, and active participation in decision-
making through various means including the referendum, were essential
features of what the SDF meant by Social-Democracy.

'True democracy' and the Socialist League

Internal tensions arose early in the newly formed SDF, partly about
disagreements on policy and strategy and partly from personality
conflicts centring on alleged domination by Hyndman. They culminated
in a 'split' and the formation of the Socialist League at the very end
of 1884. From the following February *Commonweal* – monthly until
May 1886 and after that weekly – appeared as the organ of the new body.
It was edited by William Morris. The League's suspicions of SDF
'opportunism' and its own complete rejection of electoral politics were
greatly strengthened by the revelation that the Federation had accepted
'Tory Gold' to finance candidates in the general election of November
1885.

The split

Before the split, collective statements by the SDF often tried to accom-
modate a wide range of views even though this could lead to apparent
self-contradiction, as in the January 1884 statement of 'The Principles of
Justice' which was signed by Hyndman, William Morris and Jonathan
Taylor. It began by stating baldly that 'We look for no improvement
under the present parliamentary system'. But this was soon followed by
a claim that

Universal suffrage, annual parliaments, payment of members, equal electoral
districts and proportional representation are useful only in so far as they may help
to put an end to the daily confiscation of labour. For this object only we shall urge
such political reforms.[25]

[24] *Justice*, 26 September 1885; 6 February 1888.
[25] *Justice*, 19 January 1884. Since 1881 'annual parliaments' and 'proportional representation' had replaced 'triennial parliaments' and 'equal electoral districts' in the
Democratic Federation's programme.

Many of the group soon to form the Socialist League saw in the advocacy of parliamentary reforms the acceptance of a political system whose democratic legitimacy they had rejected. Some, like Frank Kitz, believed that 'the mere dropping of pieces of paper in ballot boxes by wage slaves only results in the legalisation of their bondage'.[26] Hyndman and those who remained in the SDF, although almost as scathing about the existing political system, were developing a notion of socialist democracy that went beyond a representative system based on universal suffrage plus state ownership. They supported any means which might achieve more active participation by the citizen and more 'directness' – more frequent elections, delegation, the referendum. For them, a much fuller political democracy was one condition for socialism. Socialisation *meant* the effective control by citizens of the means of production, distribution and exchange through a democratic state. Real progress *might* be made, they believed, by means of thorough-going parliamentary reform and electoral politics.

No clear distinction was made between proposals that could be carried out within the system and ones which meant replacing it. But at the 1884 Conference a new attempt was made to commit the SDF exclusively to the second kind of change. A drafting committee was given the task of reformulating the programme. Three of the four members of this committee, which included William Morris, were future Socialist Leaguers.[27]

From the new programme disappeared – temporarily as it turned out – most of the points that had comprised the platform of the Democratic Federation – such as proportional representation and abolition of the Lords. The first three points of the new programme were:

1. All officers or Administrators to be elected by Equal Adult Suffrage and to be paid by the Community.
2. Legislation by the people in such wise that no project of law should become binding till accepted by the majority of the people.
3. The Abolition of Standing Armies and the Establishment of a National Citizen Force: the people to decide on Peace or War.[28]

These seem to have had a similar status to the call in the final point of the programme for 'The means of Production, Distribution and Exchange to be declared Collective or Common Property'. They were all for the future: part of the socialist transformation rather than measures that might, conceivably, be implemented piecemeal within the existing

---

[26] *Justice*, 3 May 1884.
[27] *Justice*, 9 August 1884. Tsuzuki, *H. M. Hyndman*, p. 58.
[28] *Justice*, 25 October 1884.

system. As such, they satisfied the anti-parliamentary attitudes of the future members of what was about to become the Socialist League. Nevertheless, the 'split' had taken place by the end of the year. After this the SDF retained the programme which had been adopted in 1884, but 'short-term' political demands reappeared together with other 'stepping stones'. Direct decision-making by the people was frequently advocated. For *Justice*, there was 'no more important article in the whole of our programme than [the "Peace or War" referendum]. If it were carried out we should never "drift into war", and when we did fight we should fight to some purpose'.

The 'political' part of the programme adopted by the 1884 SDF conference was seen as a rough blueprint for government in a socialist future when all office-holders would be elected and accountable, and major policy issues would be settled by referendum. This was a victory for the anti-parliamentary group.[29] The more modest demands of the old programme, such as annual parliaments and proportional representation were perceived as attainable under capitalism. Their presence, or temporary absence, came to be symbolic of the SDF's stance on electoral politics.

To his anti-parliamentary opponents, Hyndman seemed determined to drag the Federation into reformist electoral politics. He was already on the defensive against the accusation that he was bent on personal domination. In the first issue of *Justice* (January 1884) he felt obliged to insist that 'As Democrats they had no faith whatsoever in personal supremacy', and that as 'the annually elected chairman of the Executive Committee' he 'had no more power or permanent authority than any other member of that Committee'.[30]

But at this time it was Hyndman's editorship of *Justice*, as much if not more than his rôle on the Executive, which enabled him to exercise influence. Short unsigned articles on the front page of the paper were bound to be taken as speaking for the SDF. Towards the end of November after the issue of whether socialists should take part in conventional politics had seemingly been settled in the negative by conference decision, the following appeared:

at elections we ought to lose no opportunity of bringing our views before the electors . . . political control . . . is essential *before* economical freedom can be hoped for . . . though we should oppose political action at this time, we are

[29] Morris to Scheu, 13 August 1884, in Philip Henderson (ed.), *The Letters of William Morris to his Family and Friends* (London, 1950), p. 211. Tsuzuki, *H. M. Hyndman*, p. 58.
[30] *Justice*, 19 January 1884.

strongly of the opinion that we should be making ready by organisation, in every constituency, for the time when payment of members and universal suffrage will give us the opportunity of putting forward distinct revolutionary Socialist labour candidates for the National Convention with every chance of success.[31] (original emphasis)

We can almost hear Hyndman's critics, their worst suspicions confirmed, muttering angrily as they read this. They believed they had established the Federation's abstention from electoral politics as a *matter of principle*, and here was Hyndman, with his editorial 'we', presenting it as, at best, a short-term tactic.

The disagreements and mistrust engendered by this issue were a major factor in bringing about the 'split' by the end of that year. But by then it had become mingled with personal conflicts and passing events, so that it was not a split on clear lines of policy difference. Morris and the other dissidents set up the Socialist League, but the seceders included people whose position on the question of parliamentary participation was closer to that of Hyndman. At the other end of its spectrum were people like Frank Kitz whom Morris described as 'somewhat tinged with anarchism or perhaps one may say destructivism'.[32]

Most significantly for our present purposes, the League also became the home of a strain of thought, most clearly represented by John Sketchley, that can best be described as a Rousseauesque variant of plebeian radical democracy. Its watchword was 'direct sovereignty.'

'Direct sovereignty' and the 'Commune'

Sketchley's ideas on democratic government can be found in many of his articles and pamphlets from *Principles of Social Democracy* in 1879 through to and beyond his *Shall the People Govern Themselves?* in the later 1890s. His starting point was to ask what constituted legitimate authority and to reject all claims based not only on Divine Right, hereditary succession and conquest but also on election.

The latter was based 'on the theory that a people can alienate, or transfer their rights to a single individual'.[33] But, as Rousseau had insisted in the *Social Contract*, sovereignty was not transferable, 'being

---

[31] *Justice*, 22 November 1884. For another statement at this time of Hyndman's belief in the *chronological* primacy of democratic political change, see *Justice*, 13 December 1884.

[32] Morris to Joynes, 3 February 1885. Quoted in Thompson, *William Morris*, p. 376.

[33] John Sketchley, *The Principles of Social-Democracy. An Exposition and a Vindication* (Social-Democratic Party, 6 Rose Street, Soho, 1879), pp. 17–18.

only the exercise of the general will'. In the words of 'the immortal and incorruptible Robespierre', whom Sketchley was for ever quoting, '*Will* cannot be represented'. There was therefore no legitimate basis for representative government, however broad the franchise. Sketchley also mobilised in his support, not only Rousseau and Robespierre, but also such figures as Anacharsis Cloots, and several revolutionaries of the 1848 generation including Ledru-Rollin, Moritz Rittinghausen and, especially, Victor Considérant, the Fourierist socialist.

The latter, Sketchley explained, had argued in *The Difficulty Solved* for the 'direct government of the people', suggesting popular assemblies in each local section and the referendum as the means for accomplishing it. The referendum should be introduced in Britain, Sketchley's argument continued,

to put an end to political intrigue, political jobbery, political corruption, and as the only means by which the people can free themselves from . . . the curse of officialism . . .
By it, as Victor Considérant said in 1850, we shall be able to distinguish between those who still desire to govern and plunder the people and those who wish to see the people govern themselves.[34]

Sketchley's strong opposition to all forms of representative government was to lead to accusations of anarchism, particularly from the SDF.[35] Unlike Sketchley, other Social-Democrats saw 'direct legislation' as not, or not necessarily, the negation of representative government. Not *every* issue could be decided by referendum.

From Sketchley's position it was indeed easy to move unambiguously into anarchism. Frank Kitz and even more his close associate Joseph Lane did so. In the words of Lane's *Anti-Statist Communist Manifesto* (1887), 'If it be admitted that individual man has no right to govern we cannot admit that a number of men should'.[36]

---

[34] John Sketchley, *Shall the People Govern Themselves?* (Hull, Sketchley's People's Bookshop, n.d.), pp. 10-13. Although not dated, this seems to have been published in the spring of 1896. It was reviewed in *Justice*, 30 May 1896. A second, very hostile review in which Sketchley's views are attacked for being 'anarchist' appeared on 12 September the same year. The Webbs mention the influence in Britain in the 1850s of pamphlets by Rittinghausen and Considérant. See Sidney and Beatrice Webb, *Industrial Democracy* (1902 edn), p. 21. Rittinghausen's attempts to promote 'direct government' in Prussia in 1848 are touched on in Robert Michels, *Political Parties: A Sociological Study of the Oligarchical Tendencies of Modern Democracy* (1915; rpt. New York, 1959), p. 23.

[35] See *Justice*, 30 March 1901. As late as this Sketchley was indignantly rejecting such accusations.

[36] Joseph Lane, *An Anti-Statist Communist Manifesto*, International Revolution Library, 1 (London, 1887). For Kitz, see *Justice*, 3 May 1884.

Against them, William Morris, the dominant figure in the Socialist League before it went anarchist, envisaged some form of direct majority rule after the transition to socialism. But if this 'true democracy' would begin on the morrow of the revolution, partial approaches to it – though perhaps necessary and even in their own way desirable – were shams. Socialists should not waste their time pursuing 'a long string of "stepping stones", measures which no bourgeois Parliament would pass and which yet would be out of date in the very first days of a Revolution, promises not capable of fulfilment, nor worth fulfilment'.[37] Instead, 'I say for us *to make Socialists* is *the* business at present, and at present I do not think we can have any other useful business'[38] (original emphasis).

How, then, would society make its collective decisions *after* the revolution? This was not entirely regarded as a matter that could or should be left till then. A *Statement of Principles* by the Socialist League council foresaw that 'people would manage their own affairs in communities not too large to prevent all citizens from taking part in the administration necessary for the conduct of life, so that party politics would come to an end'.[39] This implied a very decentralised system. As Morris explained in the course of reviewing Edward Bellamy's *Looking Backward* in 1889,

there are some Socialists who do not think that the problem of the organisation of life and necessary labour can be dealt with by a huge national centralisation working by a kind of magic for which no one feels himself responsible; but on the contrary that it will be necessary for the unit of administration to be small enough for every citizen to feel himself responsible for its details, and be interested in them; that individual men cannot shuffle off the business of life on the shoulders of an abstraction called the State, but must deal with it in conscious association with each other.[40]

In Morris's own utopia in *News From Nowhere*, written in part at least in reaction to Bellamy, affairs are managed by general meetings – or 'Motes' – of the commune, ward or parish. Every effort is made to arrive at a consensus, or failing that to win at least the acquiescence of the minority. Then, as 'old Hammond' is made to explain, 'when the matter is of common interest to the whole community, and doing or not doing something affects everybody, the majority must have its way; unless the minority were to take up arms and show by force that they were the effective or real majority'. This interesting notion of the 'effective

[37] *Commonweal*, 25 June 1887.   [38] *Commonweal*, 15 November 1890.
[39] *Commonweal*, 5 October 1889.   [40] *Commonweal*, 22 June 1889.

majority' is not explored further because in a 'society of men who are free and equal . . . the apparent majority *is* the real majority'.[41]

'We are very well off as to politics', says old Hammond, 'because we have none.' In this respect, Morris's utopia *is* very like Bellamy's 'Nationalist' United States in the year 2000, for as Dr Leete – the equivalent figure to old Hammond in *Looking Backward* – explains, 'We have no politicians and as for demagoguery, and corruption, they are words having only an historical significance.'[42] But in Morris's world, unlike Bellamy's, the nation-state has also disappeared.

The Paris Commune was seen as the – very imperfect – forerunner of the commune of the future. In 1886 at a meeting to mark its 15th anniversary, *Commonweal* reported 'Pierre Krapotkine' – the Russian 'anarchist prince', Peter Kropotkin – as saying:

> After all the Commune did but little, but the little it did sufficed to throw out to the world a grand idea and that idea was the working class governing through the intermediary of a Commune – the idea that the State should rise from below and not emanate from above.[43]

It may be that Kropotkin's apparent approval of a 'state' – even one rising from below – owed something to translation: he had addressed the meeting in French. But there is a relationship between his ideas and those of Morris and the Socialist League. The commune would be the basic unit. Its size could not be arbitrarily fixed but 'it will not be merely a senseless geographical or diplomatic expression like "Great Britain", "Italy", "Austria" but a definite community within definite limits, fulfilling a definite function in the world federation of such communities.'[44] In such a decentralised system, it is difficult to see what functions the world federation would fulfil or how it would be controlled. The League's *Statement of Principles* spoke simply of 'One harmonious federation through the whole of civilisation,' while even Belfort Bax, usually more precise than most Socialist Leaguers, could only predict that 'the centralised state of today will eventually be merged in a federation of all socialised communities. The *centre* of the larger (as opposed to the smaller or communal) social organisation will be shifted from the nation to the group of nations constituting the socialised world.'[45]

[41] William Morris, *News from Nowhere: or an Epoch of Rest, being some chapters from a Utopian Romance*, 5th edn (London, 1897), p. 97.

[42] Morris, *News from Nowhere*, p. 94. Edward Bellamy, *Looking Backward, 2000–1887*, ed. John L. Thomas, 2nd edn (1888: rpt. Cambridge, MA, 1967), p. 130.

[43] *Commonweal*, April 1886.

[44] *Commonweal*, 1 May 1886.   [45] *Commonweal*, 5 October 1889; 11 June 1887.

The attractiveness of these ideas was not necessarily lessened by their generalised nature. For the Socialist League, then, democracy was not to be looked for until socialism had been achieved. During the more or less lengthy period of transition, the main rôle of conscious socialists was to keep alive the ideal of classlessness and virtually stateless communism. If reality was ever to match up to their egalitarian and democratic principles, and given that any form of representation would be flawed, democratic decision-making would have to operate at the face-to-face level of the general meeting. This could only be possible with very small units, so the logic of this view of democracy led to an extreme decentralisation.

Members of the Socialist League would have seen themselves as democrats – perhaps the only true democrats. But from the perspective of a century later it is possible also to detect some germs of authoritarian élitism. The unqualified rejection of politics, the a priori assumption that socialist society would be – must be – 'harmonious', the assumption that socialism would have to be achieved by a violent seizure of power, and Morris's hint in News From Nowhere that a minority might legitimate itself as an 'effective majority' by successful resort to violence can all be seen in this light. Nor was there any challenge to Paul Lafargue's Commonweal article 'The Morrow of the Revolution', which predicted that

> The revolutionary government would constitute itself by simply taking possession, and it would not be till it was the master of the situation that it could think of ratifying its acts by so-called universal suffrage. The bourgeois have so long kept the non-possessing classes out of the suffrage, that they must not be over astonished if all ex-capitalists are disenfranchised until the revolutionary party is absolutely victorious.[46]

But by the end of the 1880s the League was in greater disarray. The withdrawal in 1888 of the 'parliamentary' faction allowed control to slide decisively to the opposite – anarchist – end of the League's spectrum. In May 1890 an anarchist majority was elected at the 6th annual conference which also removed Morris from the editorship of Commonweal. He and his immediate following in the Hammersmith Branch left the League the following November.

The Socialist League and the SDF: a comparison

More than the SDF, the League was the heir of 'physical force' Chartism; not from any preference for violence but from a conviction

---

[46] Commonweal, 9 July 1887.

that there was no alternative to eventual insurrection as a means of achieving socialism. The SDF was less certain. Social-Democrats tended to believe, with Hyndman, that 'the coming struggle between landlords, capitalists and wage slaves *could* be peaceably settled by a democratic vote'. The use of *defensive* force was sometimes envisaged as in James Blackwell's judgement that, 'A majority of Revolutionary Social-Democrats in the House of Commons would make the capitalists hesitate about fighting. They would fight all the same if they had half a chance of winning.'[47]

At other times, SDFers presented violence as a question of expediency. 'It is a great mistake to suppose that we are in the least opposed to physical force', warned *Justice* in 1888. 'On the contrary we are entirely in favour of it and should resort to it tomorrow if we were strong enough to have a fair chance of success.'[48] But this was a semi-defensive, semi-defiant gesture to the barricades tradition, made in the context of a repudiation of anarchism and *individual* violence. There was no foreseeable 'chance of success'. Had one arrived, many Social-Democrats would have argued that the very strength of popular support that made a successful resort to force possible, made it unnecessary. It is unlikely that Helen Taylor was alone in believing that socialism would be achieved 'by the people getting the voting power and not through force which always produces a reaction as it did in France'.[49]

Generally, in the SDF, the belief was that violence would be unleashed by the other side. The winter of 1885–6 saw the beginning of the Federation's unemployment agitation in London. 'Black Monday' – a West End riot in February 1886 – led to the unsuccessful prosecution at the Old Bailey of Hyndman, Jack Williams and John Burns for sedition. The SDF and the League alike were involved in 'Bloody Sunday' the following year. In November 1887, during an attempt to defy a ban on public meetings in Trafalgar Square, Socialist Leaguer Alfred Linnell was killed. Burns and Cunningham Graham, the Radical MP for NW Lanark, were briefly imprisoned for their part in these events. As Harry Quelch, now editor of *Justice* wrote soon after 'Bloody Sunday':

If the classes are prepared to use [force] . . . with the most contemptuous disregard of law and public right, simply in order to shut the people out of Trafalgar Square; what will they not do to defend their right to rule the workers whenever and however it may be assailed.[50]

---

[47] *Justice*, 30 June 1888.   [48] *Justice*, 8 December 1888.
[49] *Justice*, 19 January 1884. Report of her lecture to the Nottingham branch of the Democratic Federation.
[50] *Justice*, 31 December 1887. Quelch edited *Justice* from March 1886 until his fatal illness in 1913.

The Socialist League was, in the 1880s, no more likely than the SDF to advocate the use of force in the foreseeable future, but fewer members of the League shared Hyndman's guarded optimism about an eventual peaceful transition to socialism. There was a fair amount of adolescent rhetoric and bravado on the subject of violence, but it is clear that members of both League and Federation were far too insistent on the maintenance of internal democracy to be any good as Blanquist conspirators. *Justice* maintained that conspiratorial organisation was unnecessary, fraught with dangers, and played into the hands of the government.[51]

Unlike the League, the SDF was, on occasions, prepared to see some merit in non-socialist politics and politicians, particularly 'advanced radicals' who supported elements of the Federation's 'stepping Stones'. Thus the candidates of Deptford Liberal and Radical Club were praised for promising to resign from office if so instructed, as were Fenwick, the Lib-Lab miners' MP, for supporting payment for MPs and Labouchère for his general democratic radicalism and in particular for his commitment to abolish the House of Lords.[52]

Participation in electoral politics led the SDF into local government, which, especially in London, proved a more rewarding field than the parliamentary. Candidates for the London School Board in 1881 were run in co-operation with other groups, notably the Metropolitan Radical Federation, under the umbrella of a Central Democratic Committee. Annie Besant, an SDF member, and Stewart Headlam, an unusually democratic Fabian, were elected.

Under socialism the SDF favoured 'the fullest possible decentralisation consistent with the socialised system of production' in order to maximise democratic control, and in the meantime believed that if socialists could take charge of the local administration of laws – if not yet their making – they could at least ensure the fullest implementation of reforms beneficial to the working class.[53] Hyndman's *Commune for London* (1887) was accompanied by articles in *Justice* calling for 'Home Rule for London'. In one of these James Blackwell called for 'complete control of the police' by the new London government and for *elected* magistrates, and in 1888 Hyndman argued – in an article headed 'The Whitechapel Murders and the Maniacs of the Yard' – that the lack of

[51] *Justice*, 21 January 1888.
[52] *Justice*, 12 November 1887; 14 July 1888; 17 March 1888.
[53] *Justice*, 7 January 1888; 8 June 1889. See also Paul Thompson, *Socialists, Liberals and Labour. The Struggle for London, 1885–1914* (1967). For relative success by the SDF in London School Board elections 1885–1891, see pp. 118–19.

progress in the 'Jack the Ripper' inquiry highlighted the urgent need for democratic control of the Metropolitan Police.[54] At a time when local government reform was in the air – the Local Government Act of 1888 established elected county and county borough councils – the Socialist League had little to say except to note that, as Morris put it, 'Local self-government may mean something considerably short of free communes'.[55]

On one thing both SDF and Socialist League were equally adamant; there must be no 'hero worship' of the living or the dead. 'Democracy while it lasts', wrote Morris in 1886, 'will never free us from this hero worship, and all the traps which the heroes (poor devils) wittingly and unwittingly lead their worshippers into.'[56] In later years Hyndman, in particular, inveighed from time to time against the deplorable tendency – which he detected among some SDFers – to 'deify' Marx or to 'regard his teachings as authoritative'.[57]

Thus, democracy also applied internally. After the 1884 'split', both sides justified themselves by appeals to it, and both SDF and Socialist League went to considerable lengths to try to democratise themselves further. The first Socialist League conference determined that 'The Executive Committee shall be bound to carry out the resolutions and instructions of the Annual Conference' which elected it, while at the SDF annual conference, held at the same time, the change was made to an Executive made up of branch delegates with the proviso 'All branches to have the power to remove their delegate if he does not carry out their wishes.'[58]

When, later, the SDF claimed to be more democratic because the League's national body was 'an Executive not a Delegate Council' so that 'the policy [was] therefore fixed for twelve months', Morris retorted that the Federation's delegate council was 'bogus' since many branches could not afford to send their delegate and thus branches fell back on the expedient of electing well-known metropolitan figures to represent them – Hyndman, for example, represented the Salford Branch at the 1888 annual conference.

But even if some way could be found to overcome the gap between radical democratic theory and hard-up reality, there would still have been

---

54 *Justice*, 3 December 1887; 6 October 1888.
55 *Commonweal*, 16 October 1886.
56 *Commonweal*, 8 May 1886. Similarly, before the split in *Justice*, 6 September 1884.
57 *Justice*, 24, 31 January 1903; 13 August 1904; 30 June 1906. J. B. Askew and John E. Ellam were criticised by Hyndman for their 'deifying' tendencies. Similarly, much earlier, protesting against the 'canonisation' of Marx, *Justice*, 15 March 1884.
58 *Commonweal*, August 1885. *Justice*, 8 August 1885.

a problem of reconciling accountability to the branches with the need for prompt action. This problem was debated at length at the 1888 SDF conference. One branch proposed a return to an Executive elected by the annual conference, complaining that the Delegate Council was 'nothing but a fraud' since 'when any energetic action had been taken it had been done by riding roughshod over the delegate system without any reference to the branches at all'. Others disagreed, arguing that a conference-elected Executive would necessarily favour those most widely known, to the detriment of local activists. In the end, the conference squared the circle by retaining the (delegate) General Council while adding an Executive Committee elected by it.[59]

1888 was, in fact, a year of internal conflict in the SDF. Hyndman was convinced that another prominent SDFer, H. H. Champion, was being manipulated by the Tory 'spy' Maltman Barry. While deputising as editor during Quelch's illness, he used *Justice* to attack the two, in an unsigned article. The General Council publicly censured Hyndman 'for having prostituted the paper of the Federation by using it to circulate a one-sided expression of personal opinion on a matter affecting the reputation of a well-known member of the SDF'. Hyndman claimed that this motion had been 'carried by a snatched vote'. The point of the episode for us is to weaken the widely held view that he dominated the SDF. Not only was he censured, but at no time did he challenge the *right* of the General Council to do so.[60]

Accountability of the elected was central to the Social-Democratic notion of Democracy. In May 1885, Eleanor Marx-Aveling drew *Commonweal* readers' attention to the recently elected German Social-Democratic deputies who had challenged the right of the party press to criticise them:

The immense and unexpected success at the last elections seems to have turned the heads of a few of the elected, who seem to think that the voice of the people has invested them with quite unusual powers. This appears to be especially the case with what might be termed the right wing of the Parliamentary Party.

Here, *Justice* agreed entirely. In a similar situation it would 'take precisely the same course'.[61] True, even so libertarian a socialist as Andreas Scheu, the Austrian refugee, conceded that 'the notions of leadership and command, of office and subordination seemed insepar-able from organisation'. But he believed they could be modified. 'If we

59 *Justice*, 11 June 1887. *Commonweal*, 18 June 1887. *Justice*, 11 August 1888.
60 *Justice*, 13, 20, 27 October 1888.
61 *Commonweal*, May 1885. *Justice*, 2 May 1885.

delegate the power of command to a person among ourselves, let it only be for a spell of time, for a distinct purpose, and out of necessity.'[62] The democratic ethos of the majority of socialists of the 1880s – whether members of the League or the SDF – is exemplified by Quelch in *Justice* during 1889.

It is necessary that we should impress this truth persistently on our readers. A man may be abler than his fellows . . . [Such] qualities are most valuable, and will surely secure him leadership in some shape. Reason the more to have some control over him . . . a man or woman who cannot submit to any discipline is generally on the lookout to dominate others.[63]

[62] *Commonweal*, September 1885.   [63] *Justice*, 3 August 1889.

2   Democracy and socialism in the 1890s

During the 1880s the SDF and the Socialist League disagreed about how the strong democratic values they shared should be put into practice either within the existing socialist organisations or in the socialist society of the future. They also discussed how far it was proper for socialists to participate in the existing electoral system. But neither had any doubt that the system was so far from democratic as to require wholesale replacement, not partial reform.

It was in the 1890s that an alternative version of socialist democracy emerged to challenge this stance. For the Fabians explicitly, and for Keir Hardie and the leadership of the Independent Labour Party (ILP) less stridently, the system needed some reforming in a democratic direction but was generally satisfactory. This judgement applied both in the here-and-now and also for the forseeable and, it was hoped, socialist future.

Fabian democracy and its Social-Democratic critics

The Fabian Society appeared during the years that saw the formation of the SDF and the secession from it of the Socialist League. By the mid-1890s, this self-consciously middle-class body had evolved its own distinctive version of socialism. A central feature was a conception of democracy at variance in spirit and in almost all details with that of the SDF which it sneered at as 'primitive'.

The evolution of Fabian democracy

This distinctive Fabian view did not crystallise at once. In the mid '80s the Society had experienced a parallel with the Socialist League/SDF split. Mrs Charlotte Wilson, a Kropotkinite anarchist and a member of the Fabian Executive, mustered enough support among 'anti-parliamentary' Fabians to worry the 'possibilists'. *What Socialism Is*, the only Fabian Tract published in 1886, comprised expositions of the 'two

30

distinct schools, Collectivist and Anarchist', with the latter written by Wilson.[1]

By 1888 the anarchist variant was in decline. Meanwhile the anti-anarchists, organised as the Fabian Parliamentary League, had demanded adult suffrage, and payment for MPs in *The True Radical Programme*. 'But in order that they may be called to account for their work at short intervals, there must be no seven year sinecures', they added, with a to us by now familiar radical-democratic stress on account-ability and 'directness', 'No Payment of Members without Annual Parliaments.'[2]

The *Fabian Essays* of 1889 had little to say on democracy. Sidney Webb called for the usual radical reforms, including annual parliaments and the abolition of the House of Lords. He also advocated the second ballot, a demand which also found its way into the revised version of the *True Radical Programme* which appeared in 1890 as Tract No. 11 under the title *The Workers' Political Programme*. Although the call for payment of MPs to be contingent on the introduction of annual parliaments had vanished by 1891 when the Fabian Tract on *The New Reform Bill* appeared – the demand was now for 'triennial parliaments' – the earlier stress on accountability remained: the key was seen as 'the fullest control over [MPs'] actions'.[3]

But soon there was a change. Increasingly, Fabians stressed the adequacy of 'constitutional' means for the achievement of socialism. This shift was conscious. Shaw in 1892 contrasted 'the Constitution-alism which now distinguishes us with the "revolutionary" attitudes of 1884 and 1885'.[4] He might have had in mind the *Manifesto* he himself had written in the earlier year. It had ended with a fine piece of insurrec-tionary rhetoric:

> That the Government has no more right to call itself the State than the smoke of London has to call itself the weather.
> That we would rather face a Civil War than such another century of suffering as the present one has been.[5]

---

[1] *What Socialism Is*, Fabian Tract No. 4 (1886).
[2] *The True Radical Programme*, Fabian Tract No. 6 (London, 1887), p. 7.
[3] *The New Reform Bill*, Fabian Tract No. 14 (1891). The main reforms advocated in this Tract reappeared later that year as means to secure 'Democratic Political Machinery' in Fabian Tract No. 24, *Questions for Parliamentary Candidates* (London, 1891).
[4] Shaw's paper was published initially as *The Fabian Society: What It Has Done and How It Has Done It*, Fabian Tract No. 41 (1892) and later as *The Early History of the Fabian Society*.
[5] *A Manifesto*, Fabian Tract No. 2 (1884). Pease records that he objected to Shaw's last proposition, as quoted above, but was 'assured by the author that it was all right since in fact no such alternative would ever be offered!' Edward R. Pease, *The History of the*

In contrast to the SDF, the Fabians came to see the parliamentary system – indeed, the 'British Constitution' in general – as basically sound, albeit with anomalies in need of reform. In 1896, a *Report on Fabian Policy*, drafted by Shaw, explicitly rejected the 'direct democracy' on which contemporary Social-Democrats – and, as we shall see, *Clarion* supporters – placed such importance:

Democracy, as understood by the Fabian Society, means simply the control of administration by the freely elected representatives of the people. The Fabian Society energetically repudiates all conceptions as to a system by which the technical work of government administration and the appointment of government officials shall be carried out by referendum or any other form of popular decision.[6]

This seemed to confirm that the Fabians really did take the view which Robert Blatchford, founder of the *Clarion*, attributed to Shaw, that 'true democracy does not mean that the people are to rule themselves, but only that they should have the power to choose who rules them'.[7]

The 1896 *Report* was aimed at the Congress of the Socialist International, which took place in London that year. It contained model 'resolutions' which the Fabians hoped would win approval. One, which ran to more than 500 words, detailed the arguments for 'Fabian Democracy'. Voters could 'only judge political measures by their effect' and were, therefore, unable to 'give precise instructions to their representatives'. Socialists and 'intelligent reformers' were always in a minority and would never be able to do more than gain the general sympathy of the ordinary voter' uninterested in – and uncomprehending of – 'the dry detail'. For these reasons, the referendum was 'in practice the most reactionary' proposal, and 'strenuously advocated in England by noted leaders of anti-Socialist opinion'.

Similarly, the 'election of public officials by the general vote' made the official 'independent of the representatives of the people' and 'practically unremovable'. This had 'been absolutely proved by the experience of English Trade Unions . . . the sole exception being those unions in the cotton industry in which the officials are controlled by a representative body and not by the mass of the members'. The 'Resolution' concluded

---

Fabian Society (London, 1916), p. 43. See the footnote on p. 62 for Shaw's insistence that 'the Fabians were at first as bellicose as the others'.

6 *Report on Fabian Policy and Resolutions presented by the Fabian Society to the International Socialist Workers' and Trade Union Congress, London, 1896*, Fabian Tract No. 70 (July 1896), p. 5.

7 *Clarion*, 24 November 1894.

by urging study of 'democratic institutions in the light of practice and not theory alone' and declaring opposition to

the Referendum, the Initiative, the election of officials by universal suffrage, and the reduction of representative bodies to meetings of delegates . . . in all cases where their effect would be to place the organised, intelligent and class-conscious Socialist minority at the mercy of the unorganised and apathetic mass of routine toilers . . . [8]

In fact, the Fabians made little impact on the Congress which was side-tracked by wrangles about anarchist participation. Beatrice Webb's view of this 'hideous fiasco' may have been coloured also by the defeat of her husband on the report of the Education Commission, when the ILPer Keir Hardie and the SDFer Herbert Burrows combined to persuade the delegates to delete all reference to scholarships for able pupils.[9] From his side, the delegate from Bristol Socialist Society described the Fabians as 'already in the grip of Liberalism and middle-class interestism'. He was pleased to be able to report that their 'verbose modifications of Socialist principle and distrust of democracy' had no influence on the Congress's debates.[10]

The Political Action Committee of the Congress did indeed endorse demands for the referendum and initiative as well as for equal adult suffrage and the second ballot. Its report seems to have been adopted without challenge. The referendum also figured in the report of the War Commission which advocated its use when war threatened and when the governments concerned refused to accept arbitration.[11]

Fabian ideas may have evoked some private sympathy among the delegates, but they were plainly out of step with the declared views of the international movement on issues of 'direct' democracy. This was to remain so, as can be seen from the survey of the programmes of European socialist parties in the 1900s by R. C. K. Ensor, himself a Fabian. Most of them – the SPD, the Belgian Labour Party, the French Tours Programme, the Austrian Social Democrats – included the referendum and initiative.[12]

Undaunted by the failure to persuade the International Congress of the virtues of 'Fabian democracy', Sidney Webb delivered a series of

[8] *Report on Fabian Policy*, p. 13.
[9] Beatrice Webb, *Our Partnership* (London, 1948), p. 134. *Justice*, 1 August 1896. Report of International Congress.
[10] *Justice*, 15 August 1896. Report of Robert Gilliard to the Bristol Socialist Society.
[11] *Labour Leader*, 8 August 1896. Supplement on International Socialist Congress. Later reprinted as *Report on the Proceedings of the Workers' Congress held in London in July 1896*.
[12] R. C. K. Ensor, *Modern Socialism as set forth by Socialists in their Speeches, Writings and Programmes*, 3rd edn (NY, 1910).

lectures in the autumn of 1896 entitled 'The Machinery of Democracy' which dismissed as 'primitive expedients' the mass meeting, rotation of offices, direct legislation, popular election of executive officials, and mandatable and recallable delegates. Instead, Webb advocated the representative system with administrative experts permanently appointed on the basis of performance in relevant examinations – in other words the sort of administrative reforms advocated by many middle-class ideologues throughout the century.

The same themes and arguments appeared again in the Webbs' *Industrial Democracy* the following year (1897). Like the present book, they sought to link industrial and political structures. Their work became something of a bible for opponents of many of the strands unravelled in ours. The Webbs' model for government – whether of trade union or state – was the British system of cabinet and parliament. The cotton spinners' union, presented as the exemplar of the best features of 'modern' trade union government and the harbinger of evolution towards 'representative institutions', was praised for 'being free of all the early expedients for securing 'popular government' and for the substitution 'both in fact and in name of the representative for the delegate'. Moreover, the Cottonspinners' Association had become

a fully-equipped democratic state of the modern type. It has an elected parliament exercising supreme and uncontrollable power. It has a cabinet appointed by and responsible to that parliament, and its chief executive officer, appointed once for all on grounds of efficiency, enjoys civil service permanence of tenure.

The Webbs traced what seemed to them the transition from 'primitive democracy' into 'representative institutions':

As the union developed from an angry crowd unanimously demanding the redress of some particular grievance into an insurance company of national extent, obliged to follow some definite trade policy, the need for administrative efficiency more and more forced itself on the minds of the members.

Efficiency meant specialisation, and loss of popular control as 'an official governing class, more and more marked off by character, training and duties from the bulk of the members' emerged.[13] 'Primitive' devices

---

[13] Sidney and Beatrice Webb, *Industrial Democracy* (London, 1902), pp. 48, 59, 16. For a very different view of the workings of the 'Cotton Spinners' Parliament', see H. A. Turner, *Trade Union Growth, Structure and Policy: A Comparative Study of the Cotton Unions*, 1963 – especially p. 277. For interesting comments on the persistence of what the Webbs called 'primitive expedients' into the second half of the twentieth century, see Anthony Carew, *Democracy and Government in European Trade Unions* (London, 1976).

proved inadequate for retaining democratic control. 'At each particular crisis the individual member found himself overmatched by the official machinery he had created' and a future of bureaucratic rule seemed inevitable. But, fortunately, 'democracy found yet another expedient' in the shape of a specialised 'legislature' of elected representatives to balance the specialised executive.

As the Webbs saw it, 'primitive democracy' instead of ensuring control by the members had, in fact, strengthened the power of officials. Annual elections of general secretaries, for instance, 'invariably resulted in permanence of tenure exceeding even that of the English civil servant'. Likewise, 'when the right of putting questions to the vote came practically to be confined to the executive, the Referendum ceased to provide members with any effective control' and became instead yet another element in the power of the officials.

The Webbs saw delegation – as distinct from representation – as an illogical compromise between direct government by means of the referendum and the, much superior, 'modern' representative system. The referendum, they argued, was at least cheaper and 'more thorough-going', while the complexity of the issues to be dealt with meant that in practice the delegate was compelled to move from being the mouthpiece of constituents, putting forward the decisions already agreed, and to exercise more personal judgement: to become a representative rather than a delegate.

The 'lessons' of the trade unions applied equally to democracy in general. Echoing the 1896 Fabian 'Resolution', the Webbs asserted that 'In the democratic state, as in the Trade Unions, the eventual judgement of the people is pronounced not upon projects but upon results'. This meant that the referendum was logically futile since '*What Democracy requires is assent to results; what the Referendum gives is assent to projects*' (original emphasis).[14] The Webbian analysis confirmed the virtues of the British system of a Cabinet responsible to a Parliament of representatives governing through a permanent, expert, civil service. 'Fabian democracy' required neither the destruction nor radical restructuring of the existing state. It did, however, assume its continued evolution.

In one of the most interesting parts of *Industrial Democracy*, the Webbs gave their views on what they called 'the further evolution of the representative'. These views, which modified significantly the essential conservatism of their position on democratic reform, must be seen in the context of the earlier Fabian statements on the role of MPs. Despite the emphatic linking of payment of members to the achievement of

[14] S. and B. Webb, *Industrial Democracy*, p. 60.

annual parliaments in 1887, this demand had been dropped by 1891, though *The New Reform Bill*, as we have seen, had supported 'the fullest control over their legislative action.'

Something of this earlier emphasis on control and accountability reappeared in *Industrial Democracy*. For all their belief in the superiority of representation over delegation, the Webbs, in that book at least, explicitly rejected the conventional view they are so often seen as supporting.

At present it is a point of honour in a member of Parliament not to express his constituents' desires when he conscientiously differs from them. To the 'gentleman politician' the only alternative to voting as he himself thinks best is resigning his seat.

This attitude, said the Webbs, was the outcome of the amateurism that characterised British politics, for 'This delicacy is unknown to any paid professional agent'. The trade union representative acted in an entirely different manner:

It is his business not only to put before his constituents what he believes to be their best policy and to back up his opinion with all the argumentative power he can bring to bear, but also to put his entire energy into wrestling with what he conceives to be their ignorance and to become for the time a vigorous propagandist of his own policy. But, when he has done his best in this way to get a majority over to his view, he loyally accepts the decision and records his vote in accordance with his constituents' desires.

The Webbs were aware that this account might 'seem to indicate a return of the professional representative to the position of a delegate'. As always, it was a matter of definition. The Webbs – like Edward Carpenter in an attack on delegate democracy which will be discussed later – seem to have interpreted delegation to mean that the elected had an 'imperative mandate' on each and every issue which they simply carried out in a robot-like way. On this definition, what the Webbs were describing here is clearly not delegation. They argued that since constituents would only in a minority of cases have a clear and firm view of how they wished their representative to act, they would be content most of the time to leave him to 'act in a manner which, in his opinion, will best serve to promote their general desires'.

Yet it is very doubtful if anyone seriously advocated delegation in this sense. As the columnist 'Tattler' had put it in *Justice* a couple of years previously: 'I believe in delegation, and in a mandate being given to the delegate, but if there is no deliberation whatever, only mechanical voting, there will be no need to send delegates at all. A central office, at which the decisions arrived at by various societies may be registered, is all that will be required.'[15] And, as we shall see, Robert Blatchford's description of how the delegate should behave is remarkably similar to the Webbs' account of the 'professional representative'.

If the essential difference between representation and delegation is that, in the latter system, constituents must bind those elected on every issue, the Webbs were correct to say they were not advocating a 'return' to that position – a position that virtually nobody was likely to support. If, on the contrary, the crucial distinction lies in the constituents' *right* to give binding instructions when this seems necessary or desirable, the Webbs' 'representation' is difficult to distinguish from what was realistically meant by 'delegation'. On the question of the right of constituents to exercise control, *Industrial Democracy* is quite clear:

once it came to be understood that the final command of the constituency would be obeyed, the representative would run no risk of losing his seat merely because he did his best to convert his constituents.[16]

Nevertheless, and despite the prophecy that 'the typical representative assembly of the future will . . . be as far removed from the House of Commons of today as the latter is from the mere Delegate Meeting', the overall impression of *Industrial Democracy* is one of endorsement of a view of democracy which, relative to the rest of the socialist movement, was conservative.

This was certainly the view of the reviewers of the book in *Justice* and the *Clarion*. In *Justice* it was reviewed by 'Sandy MacFarlane' – William Nairn – who concluded that 'Mr and Mrs Webb professing to believe in democracy, describe the system, in effect, as a congregation of idiots.' Writing in the *Clarion*, Alex Thompson was scornful of the Webbs' lack of logic. They had amply demonstrated that the 'natural reluctance' of full-time officials to act contrary to their personal career interests was an obstacle to otherwise desirable trade union amalgamation:

Progress is delayed and working class interests are hindered by the natural reluctance of place-hunters to abandon any scrap of power, yet, seeing this, the Webbs would still multiply and magnify the professional place-grabbers . . . Surely a remarkable remedy. But to be a good Fabian, *n'est ce pas*, one must be more or less funny.

Thompson went on to contrast his own ideas for using the initiative and referendum to prepare the people for democratic self-government with the Webbs' preference for 'the establishment of a new class of

[15] *Justice*, 29 June 1895.
[16] S. and B. Webb, *Industrial Democracy*, pp. 68–9.

legislative experts, who will continue to boss, flatter and exploit . . . the people'.[17]

This hostile reception given to the treatment accorded to 'primitive democracy' in the book contrasts markedly with Keir Hardie's favourable review in his weekly paper, *Labour Leader*. He was content to paraphrase its conclusions.[18] That Hardie, in contrast to the hostility of *Justice* and the *Clarion*, so completely accepted the Webbs' account is indicative of the division within the British socialist movement on the question of democracy and democratic forms. This division became clear in the 1890s.

The SDF versus 'Fabianistic caesarism'

As the distinctively Fabian conception of socialism became more clearly defined, so SDF hostility to it grew. The issues which separated the two organisations most clearly and decisively were the closely connected questions of the referendum and the role of officials. It was here that the conflicting meanings of social democracy were most readily apparent: much more so than in divisions on theories of value or other economic complexities. For many socialists, issues of economic theory were not necessarily matters of fundamental principle. Issues of democracy were.

When, in 1896, the Fabian Society specifically repudiated direct election of officials and direct legislation – the first two 'planks' of the SDF's platform – Social-Democrat hostility to the Society became intense. During the years when 'Fabian Democracy' became clearly defined, the SDF *strengthened* its commitment to the referendum, while other factors like the Fabian pursuit of 'permeation' reinforced Social-Democrats' impressions that Fabianism was an elitist heresy whose socialism really meant government of, for, and by the professional politician and bureaucrat.

Back in the 1880s there had been a fair amount of overlap in membership, though most Fabians left the SDF at the time of the 'Tory Gold' scandal at the end of 1885. Articles by well-known Fabians had still appeared occasionally in *Justice*. True, as early as 1891, one writer in *Justice* described the Fabians as 'the last vertebra in the tail of the Liberal Party'. Yet the paper remained friendly while grumbling at 'the tendency to "water down" Socialism to suit the tastes of middle class people, which is characteristic of some Fabians'.[19]

---

[17] *Justice*, 29 January 1898. *Clarion*, 12 February 1898.
[18] *Labour Leader*, 8 January 1898.
[19] *Justice*, 28 April; 19 December; 22 August 1891.

SDF regard for the Fabians declined sharply after November 1893. Following the formation of the ILP earlier that year, there was an abortive 'socialist unity' attempt involving the Fabians, the SDF, and William Morris's Hammersmith Socialist Society. An article by Webb and Shaw, 'To Your Tents, Oh Israel!' in the *Fortnightly Review* attacked the Liberals and advocated independent Labour representation. Yet within a fortnight, while one page of *Justice* was conceding that the Fabians were 'not a bad lot', another was reporting that they had voted not to renew their delegation to the Joint Socialist Committee. The writer now interpreted the recent Fabian interest in socialist unity and the manifesto in the *Fortnightly* as a 'game of bluff with the Liberals'.[20]

Meanwhile, *Justice* itself was busy promoting the referendum. It saw a shining example in Switzerland, where the 'means for a peaceful transformation', including the referendum and initiative, were now almost complete. It applauded when the foundation programme of the Australian Social-Democratic Federation called for the Referendum to replace the Upper House;[21] 'It would effectively dispose of the arguments in favour of a second chamber, and it would give the people a much more real voice in the management of their affairs than they can get under any system of delegation'.[22]

In 1893, at about the time that the Zurich Congress of the Socialist International was endorsing the demand for direct legislation, *Justice* posed the choice; 'Democracy or Parliament?'

We do not believe in the parliamentary system, and any event that tends to throw discredit upon it tends to direct public opinion towards the need for a system of pure democracy by means of the 'Initiative' and 'Referendum'.

Issues of principle would be put to a direct vote. This done, legislation could be drafted in line with referendum results and subsequently submitted to the electorate for final endorsement. There should also be a right of initiative; a certain proportion of the electorate, perhaps 5 per cent, should be able to refer a legislative proposition to the general vote. The article concluded that: 'If we had the 'Initiative' and 'Referendum' our members of Parliament would no longer be representatives but delegates.'[23] The issue was important enough to find its way into the Federation's manifesto for the general election of 1895, which urged that

---

[20] *Justice*, 18 November 1893.   [21] *Justice*, 11 July 1891; 19 August 1893.
[22] *Justice*, 2 July 1892.   [23] *Justice*, 5 August 1893.

A single assembly of paid delegates elected by complete universal suffrage must replace the present effete parliament, and instead of the bogus cry against the House of Lords the initiative and referendum should be demanded by the whole people.[24]

Opponents of direct legislation were highly suspect. This was particularly the case with 'that trimming gentleman', Ramsay MacDonald, who became a *bête noire* for the SDF when he stood in the 1895 election as an Independent Labour candidate after having, it was alleged, been turned down by the Liberals. Later the same year, an article by MacDonald in the *Weekly Times and Echo* triggered off an extraordinary front-page broadside from *Justice* against what it christened 'Fabianistic Caesarism'. MacDonald, it said, was

opposed to referring all projects of law to the ultimate decision of the people . . . That according to Mr MacDonald is reaction. His most exquisite reason? Because in Switzerland where the referendum exists, certain reforms, which most socialists would like to see carried, had been rejected! His alternative proposal? That a coterie of 'experts' should be appointed to draw up and enforce certain laws in the interests of the people, having received a general mandate to that end. Socialism and the referendum we understand and appreciate . . . But a caucus of Fabian Caesars posing as 'experts' and dictating laws to Englishmen without recourse – it makes us for to laugh! . . .

Mr MacDonald has kindly shown us what the opponents of the Referendum really aim at – a sort of Directory of Mediocrities.

The great dangers between which socialists had to steer were, *Justice* continued, 'an unorganised and therefore reactionary Democracy' on the one hand, and on the other a 'too completely organised and therefore still more reactionary Caesarism.' There would always be the temptation to seek 'a Socialist Caesar' as a short cut, but this would prove a longer route to socialism in the end.

We prefer to follow the course our name indicates – namely that of Social-Democracy. And we are sparing no pains to educate the people up to the standard of their responsibilities. The referendum is an important part of that education.[25]

The SDF and the Fabians had moved in opposite directions in the 1890s: the Social-Democrats were emphasising support for the referendum and adding the demand for the initiative at precisely the time leading Fabians were rejecting these and other forms of 'primitive democracy'. One result was *Justice*'s campaign against 'caesarism'. In

---

[24] *Justice*, 29 June 1895.   [25] *Justice*, 23 November 1895.

November 1896 it attacked Sidney Webb's lectures on the 'Machinery of Democracy':

> Mr Webb holds that you must not in any sense trust the whole body of the people to decide on the laws they are willing to obey. This must be settled by experts . . . Yet [we say] education and agitation are beginning to tell . . . To decide on a social or political question is itself an education . . .
> Organisation and democratic delegation in executive affairs there must be. But . . . laws should be accepted by the majority of people before becoming binding on them; [as] also the crucial question of peace and war . . . – these seem to be the essential bases of any true democratic system whatever. It is better even to play at democracy for a time and to discount defeats, than to build on a completely wrong foundation from the start . . . We have always said that the Fabians are no more democrats than they are Socialists.[26]

Social Democrats were certainly to say so continually from then on. Fabians were a 'thoroughly bourgeois little set':

> a declaration against the referendum is a declaration against democracy. It is an open avowal that our little Fabian clique wishes to impose on the mass of Englishmen legislation which they either do not understand, or understanding do not accept.[27]

Justice continued to promote the notion of direct legislation whenever possible in the late 'nineties. It suggested a referendum on free maintenance for school children and congratulated the Gadney School Board for holding a local referendum on the need for a new school, and its proposed siting, despite the possible illegality of the Board's action.[28]

Admittedly, with the approach of the South African War *Justice*'s tone became more cautious. Two months before its outbreak 'Tattler' warned that 'The principle of the referendum is right enough. The people who have to pay the piper should call the tune; but it is a mistake to suppose that they would be always wise in their musical selections.'[29] As Walter Kendall says, that war 'was the first occasion on which the [SDF] found itself standing like a rock against a tide of war-time hysteria'.[30] This experience was likely to inhibit campaigning for democratisation. This was the case with the SDF as we shall see later.

---

[26] *Justice*, 7 November 1896.
[27] *Justice*, 27 March 1897.
[28] *Justice*, 17 April 1897; 26 March, 2 April 1898; 21 January 1899.
[29] *Justice*, 5 August 1899. 'Tattler's' column was almost certainly written by the paper's editor, Harry Quelch.
[30] Walter Kendall, *The Revolutionary Movement in Britain, 1900–1920: The Origins of British Communism* (London, 1969), p. 26.

But the Social-Democrat case for the referendum – and for democracy generally – did not presume *necessarily* welcome results. The SDF's challenge to the government on the eve of war was on principle:

If Mr Chamberlain and his fellow conspirators think they have the people behind them in this nefarious business let them take a vote on it. We do not believe the majority is always right and wise; but we hold that it is the right of the people to decide on peace and war. If they are foolish enough to vote for war they have to pay and suffer for it; but they should not be rushed into an unjust and criminal war of aggression without being consulted at all.[31]

Complementing the Fabians' rejection of the referendum was their trust in experts – or in irresponsible bureaucrats as the SDF saw it. Such functionaries had long been *Justice*'s regular targets, along with their allegedly ineffectual 'masters':

When a permanent official in any one of our great departments dies, straight away we are told by the press that these are the men who do the real work of the country, and that the political chiefs in the house of Parliament are mere figure-heads . . . These personages are simply 'bonnets' for the permanent officials . . . Let us have these permanent manipulators of the State business into court in their own impressive personalities.[32]

In the course of an article in *Justice* criticising Eduard Bernstein as 'Our German Fabian Convert', Belfort Bax attacked an article by Ramsay MacDonald which Bernstein had translated and published:

Mr MacDonald among other evidences of his 'practical' intelligence as a democrat (?) defends the bureaucracy in the public services on the grounds that the placing of these services directly under popular control would be undesirable as causing them to reflect too faithfully the fluctuations of public opinion. Out of the dread of allowing the democracy to fulfill a political function Mr MacDonald would perpetuate an official body . . . who have already emasculated and in some cases rendered inoperative every legislative and administrative reform which has passed through their hands. A nice democrat truly!

When Bernstein attempted to defend himself, Bax insisted MacDonald had

questioned the desirability of abolishing the most flagrant and infamous administrative abuse in this country, i.e. the institution of permanent heads of departments. For this reason alone not only all Socialists, but all Democrats and even Radicals with any respect for consistency, must regard Mr MacDonald as an enemy.[33]

---

[31] *Justice*, 9 September 1899.
[32] *Justice*, 13 January 1899.   [33] *Justice*, 7, 14, 21 November 1896.

Bax, who argued for the need for a 'clean sweep' of all the higher state officials as soon as the Social-Democrats were in power,[34] was not always a typical SDFer. His anti-feminist views seriously embarrassed the organisation in the 1900s. But on this issue he was at one not only with other SDF members, but also, as we shall see, with many socialists outside the Federation's ranks. By the late 1890s no Social-Democrat protest against the 'Impudence of the Official' was complete without a jibe at the expense of the Fabians. For example, the 'power of the State official (him who the Fabians would bless as the "expert")' was attacked in the context of the 'flogging question' when

the Home Secretary thought fit to announce to the Commons elect that he did not think those responsible for prison administration would sanction (!) the abolition of flogging! The implication is that the will of 'those responsible for prison administration' is a power before which the body which we are so often assured is the Palladium of British liberties, the House of Commons, must eat humble pie![35]

By the end of the 1890s Fabianism was firmly identified in the minds of Social-Democrats not merely as middle class with tendencies towards liberalism and intellectual élitism, but more precisely as the ideology of the senior civil servant. In 1901 it was Bax, again, who made this point most explicitly. 'Fabianism', he wrote, 'is the special movement of the Government official, just as militarism is the special movement of the soldier, and clericalism of the priest.'[36]

'Real democracy': the *Clarion* version

The *Clarion*'s guiding spirit was Robert Blatchford. As a twenty-year-old runaway brushmaker's apprentice he had joined the army for about six years, leaving in 1877 with the rank of sergeant. Blatchford remained proud of his marksmanship, wrote humorous stories of army life, and was, as his attitude to the South African War was to show, incapable of taking an 'anti-war' position once hostilities had begun: this would betray his old comrades. He had come to journalism in his early thirties, working part-time for various papers until becoming a leader writer for the new Manchester paper, the *Sunday Chronicle*.

In 1891 Blatchford agreed to stand as the parliamentary candidate of the newly formed Bradford Labour Union. To what extent this

---

[34] E. Belfort Bax, 'Socialism: What It Is and What It Is Not', in *Essays in Socialism New and Old* (London, 1907).
[35] *Justice*, 9 July 1898.
[36] *Justice*, 9 March 1901.

'independent Labour' candidature cost him his well-paid job is not clear, but it certainly contributed to his move to Joseph Burgess's *Workman's Times* in October 1891. Here he contributed a series on socialism. In one of the articles he asked:

> How is practical socialism to be brought about? Partly by education; partly by Parliamentary action. We want *real* democracy in place of the sham Party-ridden democracy now existent. To get real democracy we must have some few democratic measures made law. Chief amongst them are Universal Suffrage, payment of members and the second ballot. Once these measures are made law we have a democratic country and we are within measurable distance of practical socialism.[37] (original emphasis)

Thus for Blatchford, at this stage, the kind of reforms advocated even by the Fabians were enough to secure 'real democracy'. This was soon to change.

In December 1891, he left Burgess to launch the *Clarion* with his brother Montagu and fellow journalists Alex Thompson and Edward Fay. The new paper weathered a libel writ from a railway company and played a key role in the formation of the ILP. When the survival of his paper was threatened by the legal action, Blatchford withdrew from the Bradford candidature. He was never to stand for public office again. To 'make socialists' and to educate by discussion and debate of the broadest kind was the declared object of the *Clarion*. Contemporaries and historians all agree with Stanley Pierson's description of Blatchford as 'by far the most effective recruiter for Socialism in England'.[38]

During 1892 the *Clarion* supported the formation of the Manchester and Salford ILP and unsuccessfully campaigned during the following year for the adoption by the new national ILP of the 'Manchester Fourth Clause'. This committed members to abstaining in all circumstances from supporting non-socialist candidates. For a socialist newspaper, the *Clarion* had a large circulation which, in this period, never fell below 30,000 and was at times at double or even treble this figure. The sales of Blatchford's socialist pamphlet *Merrie England* were phenomenal and worldwide. The advance demand for the cheap, penny, edition in October 1894 was such that the initial print order had to be doubled to 200,000.

---

[37] *Workman's Times*, 14 November 1891.
[38] Stanley Pierson, *Marxism and the Origins of British Socialism: The Struggle for a New Consciousness* (London, 1973), p. 272.

'On leaders'

Against this background of influence in the ILP and the socialist movement generally, the *Clarion* began, in 1894, to campaign for a 'real
democracy' very different from that Blatchford had demanded three
years earlier. Keir Hardie's *Labour Leader* was now in the field and the
two papers quickly became rival mouthpieces for those involved in ILP
internal disputes. An apparently chance remark of Blatchford's in June
1894 ('I have always urged the people to watch their leaders – since they
will have leaders – closely and call them sharply to account') triggered
some articles on 'Real Democracy' which were widely construed as
attacking Hardie.[39]

A Liverpool reader charged Blatchford with advocating the writings of
Carlyle and Ruskin while inconsistently denying the need for leaders,
which both insisted on. In reply Blatchford conceded that his own
attitude was not shared 'by any socialist as far as I know', not even close
friends like his brother and Leonard Hall. Carlyle, he maintained, had
confused guidance and government, whereas he, Blatchford, believed
'we must have *guides* but we must resist *rulers*'. By a 'leader' was meant
a commander, whether 'a usurper or the elect of a democracy'. And
Blatchford was always ready, in Walt Whitman's phrase, 'to rise against
the never-ending audacity of elected persons'.

Blatchford also differentiated himself from Hyndman who, he said,
had recently ridiculed 'the idea of a popular movement without leaders'.
Advocating rule by a 'council of three' Hyndman had also said: 'Let the
three be chosen by the people and let the people have power at any time
to supersede them. And then while they hold office let them be obeyed.'
Hyndman had indeed asserted in *Justice* that 'To say that we will have
"no leaders" is childish.' And the council of three idea can also be found
in one of Belfort Bax's essays: executive functions analogous to those of
a ship's captain were to be democratised by replacing one-person rule
with a committee of three.[40]

Blatchford rejected Hyndman's claim that he, Blatchford, was a
'leader' himself. In spite of all the pressures put upon him, he had refused
to become a 'leader' of the Manchester and Salford ILP:

Like Edward Carpenter and William Morris, I am counsellor, and nothing more.
I will have neither pay, nor office, nor power from the people. I am no more a
'leader' than is the scientist who pleads for better sanitation . . .

---

[39] *Clarion*, 9 June 1894.
[40] *Justice*, 1 April 1893. Bax, 'Democracy and the Word of Command', in *Essays in
Socialism: Old and New*.

Having refuted by definition the unmerited charge of leadership, Blatchford went on to protest against the notion that MPs and other elected persons were there to govern:

These men should not be 'masters', they should be delegates. In council let them give their advice and opinion honestly and earnestly, and let that advice be accepted or rejected as the majority deems fit. But in Parliament and in all executive positions their duty is not to command but to obey.

It is interesting to compare this account of how delegates should function with the account we have already examined of the representative of the future in *Industrial Democracy*. Both Blatchford's *delegate* and the Webbs' *representative* have the right, 'in council' with their constituents, to campaign for their own views; and both must, in the end, accept the majority decision of those they represent. Blatchford ended the article by reiterating that

As a Democrat I will agree to no attempt to coerce the people for their own good. If some men have more talent or more wisdom than the general average, let them use that talent and wisdom to 'guide', to 'persuade', to 'instruct' the people, but not to coerce them.[41]

Blatchford stayed with the theme of real democracy during the following two weeks. Claiming to be 'one of the few real democrats amongst the English Socialists', he added 'managers of works and other functionaries' to the list of those who should be delegates rather than 'masters'. He argued that the 'governing classes' deliberately mystified the 'science of government'. When a Liverpool correspondent challenged the distinction between 'guidance' and 'government', Blatchford dismissed his 'very foolish letter' as expressing 'very pointedly the old feeling of Tory distrust of the people':

Speak about the masses, and of handing over the Government of the country to the masses, and the Tory conjures up in his mind a picture of the basest and most foolish amongst the masses. A drunken navvy, a loafing corner-man, a noisy public-house orator, an ignorant farm labourer pass before his mental vision . . .

The greatest obstacle to democracy was, on the contrary, the 'apathy' and lack of 'self-reliance' found in the average man. Guidance was certainly needed. It would be

the average mind, guided by the superior mind that would really sit in judgement upon any act or proposition of a wise or great man in a Democratic State.

It is quite true that a great many minds – perhaps the majority of minds – lack initiative and inventiveness and it may well seem at first sight that minds which

41 *Clarion*, 16 June 1894.

lack inventiveness are unfit to judge the merits of inventions. But this is not so. For there is a difference between the qualities of originality and judgement . . . We have few men in England today who would be capable of *inventing* Scientific Socialism. But Scientific Socialism is so simple a thing in itself, that, when inventive minds have originated it, the masses are quite competent to judge it.

Conversely, an 'originator' might be quite hopeless as an administrator, he concluded.[42]

Others now joined in the debate. John Lister, the national Treasurer of the ILP and soon to be the centre of acrimonious debate himself, thought that, though democratic control was necessary:

a large amount of individual freedom must be left to the selected ones. This, not in the interest of the leaders themselves, but of those they represent and guide. To me the essential thing seems to be that really the fittest men for any special work be selected.[43]

By contrast, a letter from Leonard Hall was much more supportive of Blatchford. It was better to 'go wrong' on democratic principles, Hall argued, with the ultimate certainty of 'going right' as long as those principles were maintained, than to risk 'going wrong, keeping wrong and getting more wrong under caucus cookery or one-man Providence.' He was particularly concerned that the ILP should maintain and exemplify its democratic principles in the running of its own affairs.

Another correspondent was Enid Stacy who had a little earlier taken Alex Thompson to task for the 'Man's Logic' displayed in his condescending attitude towards women's emancipation. She observed that the problem lay in 'Labour leaders' being few in number and having to perform two distinct roles:

they are agitators, educators, stirring up men's minds and raising their energies . . .
But they are also striving to carry out, either in Parliament or on local bodies, the wishes of those who have sent them there . . . And the Labour 'leader' at once a *delegate* of those already mindful of their true interests, and also an agitator and educator of those not yet converted, naturally confuses the two rôles; and in consequence complaints arise that he is trying to control and boss the movement . . . As delegates we must obey the voice of those whom we represent . . .

For Blatchford, there was a real danger that ' . . . unless our English Socialists are sound and sane upon the question of true Democratic Government, the whole Socialist movement will be endangered and perhaps ruined by a few ambitious men'.[44]

---

[42] *Clarion*, 23, 30 June 1894.
[43] *Clarion*, 21 July 1894. [44] *Clarion*, 28 July 1894.

Or as John Trevor, founder and ideologue of the Labour Church movement, warned, the result would be 'an elected Aristocracy' rather than a democracy.[45] Margaret McMillan, on the other hand, believed 'heroes' to be permanently out of fashion. The only function of the modern 'leader' was to ascertain the will of the people and to carry it out. 'Of course, there remains one daring feat for the modern Knight of Labour, viz. to anticipate the *unfolding desire of a people just emerging into manhood*. A fearsome task' (original emphasis).[46]

Blatchford returned to the theme with renewed intensity in November, (1894), when the behaviour of John Lister at Halifax seemed to epitomise 'never ending audacity'. The facts of the case were hotly disputed, but, as initially presented in the *Clarion*, concerned suspicions of dealings with the Liberals by ILP town councillors Lister and James Beever. Whether or not they were guilty of this, Blatchford maintained that it was 'quite clear that they were guilty of another and equally serious offence and that is insubordination', Lister by refusing 'to act according to the direction of his constituents when on the Council', and Beever by refusing publicly to deny charges of Liberalism. They were both prominent, popular people who had been useful to the movement in the past but, according to Blatchford, this made it even more clear that the 'only course open to the Halifax Labour Union as a Democratic body is to expel both these members from the ILP'.

A heated controversy followed, with Keir Hardie defending Lister. But to Blatchford it was less a matter of a particular case than of the dangers that threatened socialism unless the democratic practice of the movement prefigured the future socialist society:

Socialism without Democracy would be a state of abominable tyranny. Democracy means that people shall manage their own affairs, and that their officials shall be public servants, or delegates deputed to put the will of the people into execution.

If the people were not capable of this, then democracy was impossible and socialism undesirable. It was crucial that the working class acquired experience and self-confidence, and it would be a serious mistake to allow middle class recruits to monopolise the management of the socialist movement.[47]

If members of socialist organisations refused to take on their share of the work, Blatchford continued into the following week, those 'left to bear the burden' had the democratic duty to refuse to make up the

[45] *Clarion*, 4 August 1894.
[46] *Clarion*, 16 August 1894.   [47] *Clarion*, 3 November 1894.

deficiency. 'A man is foolish and wrong if he attempts to carry the whole branch upon his back. Let him speak up and tell his comrades that they must help in the work or be content to let it go undone.'[48]

A debate ensued with Edward Carpenter – ironically enough, a disciple of the very Walt Whitman whom Blatchford was so fond of citing as a steadfast democrat. Carpenter attacked what he called

the dancing doll theory. You know what I mean. The constituents (or . . . more often a caucus of the constituents) pull the strings; the delegate holds up his hand. They slacken, and he drops it. He is a mere penny-in-the-slot automatic machine figure. Now, I think no self-respecting or really competent person would accept such terms, or should accept them . . . Very well then, fix your man on the fundamental points; be sure that he is fair and square on these (and it will be very easy to see if he isn't) and then for goodness sake *leave him free* to exercise some judgement and manhood on the minor details. (original emphasis)

Otherwise, Carpenter went on, why have elections at all? Why not manage public affairs by means of postcards from every elector?

I do not say that the *Referendum* is not a good idea, indeed I think it decidedly is for big questions, and will probably before long have to be adopted. But as long as we have councils at all (and I suppose we must always have such for minor questions), our men must take their heads with them and not be decapitated before they go.

Carpenter complained that in Sheffield and elsewhere ILP branches were asking their officials and representatives to sign their resignations before taking office. He supported Keir Hardie against Blatchford over the Halifax affair, eulogised John Lister, and protested against Blatchford's over-simplification of issues. What was needed, Carpenter maintained, was

the common-sense delegate not the superior-person delegate, nor the dull-delegate, but the man who is delegated to hold firm, on pain of death, to the great bases of the party he represents, and to certain definite mandates and measures, but is given power and is trusted to use his good sense and discretion on points of detail subject of course to free criticism from his constituents but not necessarily on that account withdrawal of their trust in him.[49]

In response, Blatchford protested that neither he nor 'any sensible Democrat' wanted to tie down delegates on points of detail. But the elected should represent those who elected them, not themselves. All he asked was for representatives on public bodies to be delegates, 'with delegated powers and instruction just as are the delegates sent by the

---

[48] *Clarion*, 10 November 1894.   [49] *Clarion*, 24 November 1894.

Trade Unions to the Congress'. If anyone was asked to sign his resignation in advance it was his own fault:

He should say before the election 'I shall be ready to consult with you when you think necessary; I will always obey the orders of the party, or if I do not agree with the orders, I will resign; and I am willing to give up my post at any time should the majority of my constituents desire it.' That is what I told the men in Bradford when I stood as a candidate for the Eastern Division.[50]

In theory, the differences between Blatchford and Carpenter were merely ones of emphasis, with both agreeing that delegates should be subject to control but should not – indeed, could not – be instructed on every detailed matter. And, as we noted earlier, the same was true of the Webbs' version of how the 'new model' representative should operate.

On this issue, though, small differences of emphasis tended to become gulfs. Blatchford's strictures 'On Leaders' were repeated from time to time for the next twenty years, but 1895 was to be the year that the emphasis of 'Clarion Democracy' switched from Blatchford's insistence on delegation to Alex Thompson's advocacy of the referendum; a cause which the *Clarion* was to make its own.

'The only way to democracy'

The logic of demanding that participation in decision-making should be as broad and as direct as possible led towards 'direct legislation': the initiative and referendum. But Thompson it was, rather than Blatchford himself, who now took the lead. During the 1894 debate on 'Real Democracy', Blatchford had written that he would

put the people into the place of the House of Peers, so that every measure of importance should, after passing the House of Parliament, be referred to the nation for refusal or acceptance.[51]

The following week, Thompson went much further. He suggested a system of direct legislation which 'would absolutely annihilate Parliament and the whole tribe of politicians'. During a recent visit to Paris he had met the prominent French socialist, Jean Allemane who coincidentally had commanded the barricade at the corner of the street where the young Thompson had lived during the Paris Commune. Allemane, as distrustful of 'leaders' as the *Clarion*, had outlined his ideas of how a democratic socialist state might work.[52]

---

[50] *Clarion*, 1 December 1894.   [51] *Clarion*, 23 June 1894.
[52] Allemane's 'system' was, in fact an important part of the programme of his party, the Parti Ouvrier Socialiste Révolutionnaire. For this, and direct legislation in French

I would abolish all Legislative Chambers, Senates and Councils of State, substituting for these clumsy political wheels within wheels a number of purely administrative Commissions, corresponding to the general divisions of our present Ministries and annually elected by the people. I would divide the population into sections of one thousand each, and every citizen aged 21, unless certified insane, should be registered in his section with full rights of sovereignty – either to vote upon the law proposals of others *or to initiate laws himself.* Removals would be instantly registered in a new section on production at the *Mairie* of the voter's old certificate. Each section would have a president, secretary and four scrutineers elected for three months by the members of the section, and to these would be entrusted the task of counting the citizens votes on every legislative proposal. The results, centralised by districts, would be communicated to the general secretary in the capital who would immediately instruct the Administrative Commissions to execute the people's will.[53] (original emphasis)

Thompson could have referred to the recent endorsement of the referendum and initiative by the Socialist International at the 1893 Congress in Zurich – in which Allemane had played a significant rôle – or to the SDF's support for these devices. In 1895 he produced the first of his pamphlets on direct legislation, *Hail Referendum!*

Far from being a route to democracy, Parliament was, he now claimed, 'a barricade across our road'. For most people, the parliamentary system was 'calculated to discourage them from ever thinking about anything', and conventional electoral reform would do little to 'make the electorate more thoughtful, more sensible of their needs': the results of male suffrage in the United States and in France were not encouraging. Allemane's ideas, though a 'large order', held more promise. They could be implemented by means of the Referendum and Initiative which operated well in Switzerland and were advocated in Britain by the Radical MP for East Edinburgh, Robert Wallace. (Wallace wrote to the *Clarion* supporting Thompson and describing himself as being, no socialist, but a 'thorough-going democrat'.)

Thompson claimed two special advantages for 'direct legislation'. In the first place, by separating issues, it would overcome the problem of those whose 'ancient prejudices render it impossible for them to support a Socialist candidate' but who would 'cheerfully vote for any legislative

---

socialism during this period generally, see Ian Bullock and Siân Reynolds, 'Direct Legislation and Socialism: How British and French Socialists Viewed the Referendum in the 1890s', *History Workshop Journal*, 24, August 1987. For Thompson's childhood experience during the Paris Commune, see his *Here I Lie, The Memorials of an Old Journalist* (London, 1937), ch. 3, and 'What I saw in the Commune', *Clarion*, 11 and 18 March 1893.

[53] *Clarion*, 30 June 1894.

proposal that offered the prospect of alleviating human suffering.'
Secondly, if voting were to be compulsory as demanded at Zurich, it
might be possible to 'achieve the most urgent necessity of our time, that
of forcing men to *think* about the laws that govern them, and of saddling
them, willy-nilly, with their share of national responsibility' (original
emphasis).[54]

Hail Referendum! was reported to be 'selling very rapidly' in early
October 1895, and Thompson was able to cite many letters of support.
'The people have concluded', one optimistic correspondent claimed,
'that making laws by proxy is even more unsatisfactory than making love
by proxy, and so will soon proceed to make laws as they make love, in
person, which is simply the Initiative and Referendum.' Another thought
the referendum 'the logical outcome of the tendency of constitutional
development during the last century . . . for it only puts into logical form
principles already accepted'.[55]

Support for the referendum was welcomed, even from unlikely
quarters.[56] Like the SDF, the *Clarion* would applaud support on such
issues even from reactionaries – in contrast to the Fabians, who used
the existence of Conservative referendum-supporters to bolster their
argument that direct legislation itself was reactionary.

In reply to queries from readers, Blatchford made it clear that he,
too, supported government by referendum and initiative in place of
Parliament.[57] In mid-1896 he suggested that the Reign of Terror 'by
gangs of elected scoundrels' during the French Revolution had been the
'price "the people" paid for their folly in delegating their public duties to
the rascals who made the most noise.'[58]

By this time he had quite abandoned his former belief that 'Real
Democracy' could be secured through a correctly conducted delegate
system. When a Clarion Cycling Club annual conference was mooted, he
wrote:

I should object very strongly to a conference of delegates. I do not believe in the
delegate system. It is not representative; and it breeds all manner of evils.
Parliament, the ILP and the TUC are all worked on the delegate theory and they
all fail for that reason.
What we want is government by the whole people.

---

[54] A. M. Thompson, *Hail Referendum! The Shortest Way to Democracy*, Clarion pamphlet
     No. 7, 1895, pp. 3, 6, 8 and 12. *Clarion*, 19 October 1895.
[55] *Clarion*, 19 October 1895.
[56] *Clarion*, 30 November 1895; for *Justice*'s welcome for Conservative flirtations with the
     referendum, see, *inter alia*, 14 May 1892, 27 March 1897.
[57] *Clarion*, 7 December 1895.
[58] *Clarion*, 11 July 1896.

The only wise, just and practical form of government is government by means of the Referendum and Initiative.[59]

That 'government of the whole people' would transcend majority rule as normally understood had already emerged from an exchange between Thompson and a reader who had sought his endorsement for the formula, 'Government by the *majority*, with as much liberty for the *minority* as is consistent with the liberty of the majority.' Thompson demurred:

Government by 'majority' implies party and consequently chicanery and oppression.
If there were no 'party' there would be no fixed 'majority' which would wield the government.
But in a *government of the whole people* which is what I contend for in my Referendum pamphlet, it would be misleading to say that 'the majority' ruled, for the 'majority' would be as indefinite, as brief, as intangible as a wave of the ocean which is a separate wave for only one moment, and is immediately merged again in the general mass to form part again of many other waves . . . Therein lies the distinction of direct from representative government. A delegate must of necessity represent a whole cluster of ideas; hence, candidates divide themselves into parties – 'for short' – as the children say.
But if there were no delegates, there would be no fixed parties. The voter would exercise his individuality and his judgement on each separate part of politics that cropped up, and he would hardly ever agree three times in succession with the same person.[60] (original emphasis)

Inevitably, the *Clarion* was unimpressed with the Fabian arguments. Reviewing the Webbs' *Industrial Democracy* in 1898, Thompson contrasted their conclusions with those of Professor Georges Renard of the *Revue Socialiste* who had denounced the 'parliamentary system' as

the natural expression of an aristocratic or bourgeois society wherein a portion of the citizens are rightly or wrongly held to be incapable of managing their own affairs. But in any democracy where the people have truly reached their majority and mean to exercise real not nominal sovereignty in the realm of the laws, the Parliamentary system is no longer in harmony with the ruling principle . . .

The apparent disadvantages of direct legislation should not discourage socialists unduly, Thompson concluded. Nobody was suggesting its immediate substitution for the parliamentary system, but merely as

checks and correctives to uncontrolled Parliamentarism. As for the silly legislative propositions which loom so large in the fears of the Webbs in connection with the . . . Power of the Initiative, I have so much faith in their common sense

---

[59] *Clarion*, 27 May 1897.   [60] *Clarion*, 5 September 1896.

that I would trust them to devise half-a-dozen effective plans for sifting the serious from the frivolous or foolish Bills. I am sure they could do it – *if they tried*.[61] (original emphasis)

Thompson was to produce two further pamphlets advocating direct legislation – *The Referendum and Initiative in Practice* in 1899 and *The Only Way to Democracy* in 1900. Much of the material had already appeared in the *Clarion*. The 1899 pamphlet was concerned to show that direct legislation in Switzerland had led to results that were 'exceedingly encouraging to the Democratic faith' rather than ones which were conservative or reactionary, as opponents of the referendum – particularly the Fabians – often claimed. Direct legislation was not, he conceded, a panacea; but, since the 'substitution of Demagoguery for Aristocracy or Plutocracy will butter no parsnips', neither was Labour representation.

The ILP was making modest but continued progress under Keir Hardie's leadership towards the 'labour alliance' with the trade unions, which materialised as the Labour Representation Committee at the beginning of 1900. From the *Clarion*-democratic viewpoint, this meant dangers as well as opportunities. With the founding conference of the Labour Representation Committee in the offing, Thompson seems to have increasingly seen Labour representation and direct legislation as alternatives:

Even if we had payment of members and the fullest electoral reform it would take fifty years to get a majority of Labour leaders in Parliament, and a Parliament of Labour members would develop just the same tendency as any other to division into parties commanded by rival ambitions, between which the democratic vote would, as always, annul itself.

And for Thompson the explanation for opposition to the referendum and initiative was simple.

Those who object to direct legislation object in their hearts to every popular vote.
What is plainly the matter with them is that they distrust the people.[62]

Yet even Thompson's trust stopped short of proposing to transfer 'the whole government of the country – finances, the question of peace . . . as well as ordinary legislation in one fell swoop to the inexperienced direct control of the Democratic mass'. We may note in passing, that questions of peace and war had been precisely what the SDF had favoured putting

---

[61] *Clarion*, 12 February 1898.
[62] A. M. Thompson, *The Referendum and Initiative in Practice*, Clarion pamphlet No. 31 (London, 1899), pp. 4, 16, 13.

to a referendum since its earliest days. Thompson was prepared to concede not only that some subjects might be reserved from the scope of direct legislation but also that it

> might be needful at first, in order to secure the rights of minorities against the tyranny of faddists, to provide that if a popular initiative had failed to secure the actual support of half, or say even two thirds of the electorate, it should not become law without the acceptance of Parliament: and in every case of Initiative it might be allowed to the parliamentary majority to submit simultaneously an alternative proposal.[63]

'Before everything we were Democrats and believed . . . most thoroughly in popular government', wrote Blatchford summing up, at the beginning of 1899, the *Clarion*'s work since its foundation. Representative government was unsatisfactory because, among other things, it was more difficult to judge candidates than policies, because the elected tended to be ambitious and self-seeking, and because the process gave advantage to oratory rather than to honesty or wisdom. By contrast,

> Really popular government under the Initiative and Referendum would inspire the citizens with self-respect and civic zeal, train them to think, habituate them to bear responsibility and decide all questions of public importance with serious care and would do away with . . . superior persons on the make.
> Therefore we are in favour of popular government, I for one regarding it as of supreme importance, feeling as I do that without Democracy there is no Socialism, and without popular government there is no democracy.[64]

Direct legislation was, then – as in the title of Thompson's 1900 referendum pamphlet – *The Only Way to Democracy*. Its rôle as an educator for self-government, as a way of preparing and prefiguring socialism, was its greatest merit. But it would also mean fewer, shorter and more comprehensible laws, would substitute serious political discussion for party-political mud-slinging, would act as a safeguard against corruption and would provide a perfect system of proportional representation. Or so Thompson claimed. It would make it possible to 'introduce reforms *just as fast as the people are ready for them*' (original emphasis).

As in his pamphlet of the previous year, Thompson was concerned to stress the practicality of his proposals. He now placed far less emphasis on the total supercession of the parliamentary system than he had during the mid-90s, and more on ways in which direct legislation could be 'grafted on' to it. The referendum meant, he now argued, that legislation passed by Parliament could be suspended on the requisition of a

---

[63] *Clarion*, 3 December 1898.   [64] *Clarion*, 21 January 1899.

reasonable percentage of voters and submitted to a direct vote. The necessary corollary, the initiative, might mean that the same proportion of the electorate could submit a Bill to Parliament to be either passed in the normal way or, if rejected, put to a direct vote at the next general election. He now presented direct legislation more as a safeguard within the existing system than as its revolutionary replacement. 'The exercise of these two functions by the people is optional, and would only occur when Parliament failed to provide legislation suitable to popular needs.'

Having argued a general case from first principles, there was by 1900 a need to demonstrate its practicality. But other factors also account for the change of emphasis. The attempts of the *Clarion* and its supporters to implement their conception of democracy had met serious setbacks. This must have encouraged Thompson to lower his sights. He hoped that the emerging Labour Party would at least commit itself to promoting a cautious experiment in direct legislation. He may well have tailored his presentation with this in mind. Certainly, for him, a crucial turning point had been reached:

> Our representatives of Labour and our professional agitators are, I believe, the most sturdy and honest in the world. Why? Because their service has been disinterested. Because there has hitherto been no inducement in Britain to go into democratic politics for profit.
>
> The British Labour representatives are, most of them, men who have worked at the bench, at the loom, or in the mine. The French, Italian and German Socialist leaders are mostly lawyers and writers.
>
> This is a distinction which makes a very great difference. We stand in England at the parting of the ways. One way leads to the Payment of Members and the creation of a class of political adventurers; the other leads to the Initiative and Referendum, which I have been advocating for the last few years . . . [65]

[65] Thompson, *The Only Way to Democracy*, Clarion pamphlet No. 35 (London, 1900).

3   Democracy and the industrial struggle

So, historians have underestimated the extent to which the 'socialist revival' of the 1880s was influenced by concerns – reminiscent of Chartism – with constitutional and electoral reform. Thus, aspirations for democracy remained no less central to socialism than the apparently more novel aims of social and economic transformation. We will now see that an analogous mix of 'old' and 'new' was to be found in the trade unions. Thus, there was not simply 'Old' (craft) unionism versus 'New' (unskilled) unionism, or even established 'moderation' versus socialist-influenced militancy. There was also the appearance of seemingly new but in fact old dreams of effective industrial unity.

These usually meshed with the belief that the old, particularistic, structures of the trade union movement served the interests of leaderships and officials better than – or even rather than – those of the membership: the 'rank and file' of militant rhetoric. We have already found SDF, Socialist League and *Clarion* socialists systematically assuming that greater democracy and full-blooded socialism were but two sides of the same coin. We will now find their union equivalents – not infrequently the same individuals – seeing anything but conflict between maximising democratic control of the movement and propelling it into more effective action.

There was an important difference between the industrial and political arenas. Trade union action, being a matter of the most direct and immediate concern for those involved, had far less room for postponing any potential conflict of aims. Possible conflicts between democracy and socialism were at least a little way over the horizon, even on the most optimistic assessment. Trade union effectiveness, on the other hand, could not be left to sort itself out on the morrow of some Grand Turning Point. Democratic aspirations were, in this arena, more inextricably and immediately intertwined with the full range of everyday concerns.

There were many initiatives within particular unions to increase both the control of the membership over their organisations and the success of these organisations as effective 'fighting' bodies. But the first major attempt to transform the movement as a whole in our period was the campaign for 'trades federation' in the late 1890s and, in particular, the federation scheme of P. J. King, which was so closely associated with the *Clarion* newspaper that it became known as the '*Clarion* scheme'.

The campaign resulted in the setting up of the ill-fated National and International General Federation of Trade and Labour Unions (NIGFTLU). This is far less well-known, even among specialists, than the later attempts at wholesale democratic restructuring which were to occur during the period from 1909 to 1914 and which were and are labelled 'syndicalism'. This would justify even by itself our focusing on the NIGFTLU episode with particular attention. Whatever the exact linkages between it and 'syndicalism' during the intervening decade of the 1900s, it somewhat dims the latter's novelty.

Like the socialist ideas of democracy with which it was closely connected, 'trades federation' did not arrive out of the blue. True, it was partly a response to the immediate situation of the time, and in particular to the shattering defeat of the engineers – sometimes called the Grenadier Guards of the trade union world. But the events of the late 1890s marked also a convergence between the assertion of democratic aspirations and the hope for effective fighting unionism. The two had often gone together.

The background to trades federation during the nineteenth century

'Since the advent of the modern trades union, some seventy years ago there [had] been an ever present desire among large sections of trade unionists for federation', according to one leading 1890s trade unionist, Clem Edwards.[1] Historians of almost every aspect of nineteenth-century working-class life have, understandably, tended to emphasise the breaks, jumps and leaps. Many such did occur; but not necessarily to the exclusion of slower, often more sinuous – perhaps less researchable – rhythms. Ideas of federation were part of something older and looser: of those aspirations for united action by all working people – however labelled – unionised or not.

Ideas of what today would be called a general strike to overthrow the existing order are known to have reached print during 1801 from the pen of the autodidact and pioneer socialist, Thomas Spence, a former Tynesider based in London.[2] Spence had very few followers, but one

---

[1] Clem Edwards, 'Labour Federation', *Economic Journal*, 111, 1893, 206.
[2] Olivia Smith, *The Politics of Language, 1791–1819* (London, 1984), pp. 96–109.

or two of those who managed to escape execution for a treasonable conspiracy were influential. One at least partial Spencean was John Gast, key leader of London's artisans for a generation. During 1831–2, amid the crisis over the passing of the first Reform Act, the shoemaker and former – or perhaps not so former – Spencean, William Benbow, published plans for a 'Grand National Holiday' which were obviously Spencean in many ways. For example, the people, on strike, were to take over the land: ideas for some sort of land reform were to recur in association with schemes for united action, in ideological contexts far from Spencean two generations later.[3]

What such recurrence implies is harder to argue with any confidence. Certainly we cannot rely on the persistence of a widespread memory. During the late-1890s federation agitation, a sympathetic writer in the ILP's *Bradford Labour Echo*, for example, went only 'as far back as 1846', thereby omitting the largest inter-union ever associated with socialism, the Owenite, Grand National Consolidated Trade Union (GNCTU) of the early 1830s. Nor was there any mention of the schemes associated with the International Working Men's Association (IWMA) nearly forty years later.[4]

There was no necessary association between ideas for a general strike and for a permanent inter-union alliance. But either might – in the minds of advocates or onlookers – come to imply the other. The first major attempts at an inter-union – John Doherty's National Association of United Trades for the Protection of Labour (NAUTPL) of 1830–1 and, even more, its larger successor the GNCTU were associated for a time with hopes for united industrial action. These were vaguely formulated by the heterodox mystic J. E. Smith, and much less vaguely by the building trade unionist James Morrison and – in 1836 in a desperate attempt to save the GNCTU's last considerable remnant – by Gast.[5]

Such ideas remained sufficiently actual during the immediately following years to become, as the 'Sacred Month', a major option among Chartists, particularly during 1839 around the time of their first national

---

[3] P. Mary Ashraf (or Kemp), *The Life and Times of Thomas Spence* (Newcastle upon Tyne, 1983), pp. 137–9. See also I. Prothero, *Artisans and Politics in Early 19th century London: John Gast and his Times* (London, 1979), pp. 286–90.

[4] 'R.E.N.' in the *Bradford Labour Echo*, 11 June 1898 (Bradford City Library). This writer seems to have shared some sources with Clem Edwards, notably George Howell, *Conflict between Capital and Labour*. Edwards did go further back – to the 1820s.

[5] G. D. H. Cole, *A Short History of the British Working Class Movement, 1789–1947* (London, 1952), pp. 71ff. J. Saville, 'J. E. Smith and the Owenite Movement', in S. Pollard and J. Salt (eds.), *Robert Owen, Prophet of the Poor* (London, 1971), pp. 126, 128–34, 137. Prothero, *Artisans and Politics*, pp. 316ff.

Convention, in connections with plans for a rising – plans which were to come to fruition in South Wales – and during 1842 which saw a general strike involving nearly half a million workers: proportionally more general than that of 1926.[6] The defeat of these efforts helped to bring more modest ideas to the fore more frequently. A second NAUTPL began in 1845. This was a mere 'loose defensive alliance', as Cole describes it, though 'clearly modelled' on its earlier namesake. It was also open to ideas associated both with the GNCTU and, later, with the NIGFTLU: that of producers' and consumers' cooperation.[7] A National Association for the Organisation of Trades (NAOT), formed in 1849, also busied itself for a time with co-operation, as did some of the groups affiliated to the United Kingdom Alliance of Organised Trades (UKAOT) of the late 1860s – which had a membership of, allegedly, 200,000 during 1869 – though the UKAOT as a whole was more interested in setting up a central fund for the support of locked-out trades. It is seen as 'one of the forerunners of the TUC' – if only because the TUC began during 1867–8.[8]

True, such pairs of mutually echoing names often concealed dwindling purposes or perhaps even forgotten ones – as with the National Association which survived until 1867 little more than vestigially.[9] But even the merest indirect echoes, let along the wrangles over personalities, aims, strategy and organisational pre-eminence which bedevilled attempts at inter-union unity during the 1860s, may occasionally have provoked thoughts among some activists.

And some of these would have participated or been interested in organisations affiliated to the 'First International' – the International Working Men's Association (IWMA). This as early as 1868 had 'adopted a resolution for a common strike fund', and in 1873 the Association's British Federal Council issued an 'address to the Trades Unionists of Great Britain and Ireland' in which it advocated 'an international trades union'.[10] It argued that this plan was nothing visionary but 'only an extended application of [basic trade union] principle'. Indeed, the well-known dissensions between the supporters in Britain of John Hales, who was also for forming a union-based political Labour

---

6 Dorothy Thompson, *The Chartists* (London, 1984), pp. 73, 138, 192. David J. V. Jones, *The Last Rising: The Newport Insurrection of 1839* (London, 1985), pp. 86, 92f. Mick Jenkins, *The General Strike of 1842* (London, 1980).
7 Cole, *Short History*, pp. 172, 114.
8 Prothero, *Artisans and Politics*, pp. 334f. Cole, *Short History*, p. 199. S. Pollard, *A History of Labour in Sheffield* (Liverpool, 1959).
9 Cole, *Short History*, p. 198.
10 In an unnamed newspaper. Jung Collection, no. 168, dated 8 May [1873], International Institute of Social History, Amsterdam (IISH).

Party at this time, and of Karl Marx do not seem to have affected the views of any on the question of union federation. For, on the one hand, the British Federal Council that issued this address included a number of Marx's allies alongside his current and future opponents, and on the other similar if windier proposals had been heard during the previous year's 'British Federal Congress' which had been more dominated by the latter.[11]

The plan was:

1. That all unions of one trade in a country combine in electing an executive central body of that trade in that country.
2. That the central bodies of the various trades in the different countries elect a general council of all trades in all countries.[12]

Whether the interest of some IWMA trade unionists had received more impetus from the rise of the short-lived UKAOT or gave more to the revival of federation-discussion at the TUC may be impossible to determine. For the UKAOT had been collapsing just when the TUC was becoming permanent. The reasons adduced for this collapse include economic depression and the hysteria triggered by the 1867 'Sheffield outrages'. More ominously for attempts at Federation later, they had also included 'failure to pay the levies', lack of a nationally representative structure and wrangles over member organisations' eligibility for benefits.[13] Similarly, the IWMA had, by the early 1870s, become a divided and dwindling organisation. By contrast, the TUC's very survival – and relative novelty – helped deflect pressure towards Federation until the late 1880s.

There was one further connection which, being so speculative, would be worth no mention at all had it not involved the future originator of the *Clarion* scheme – the somewhat mysterious P. J. King. During the 1890s the *Labour Annual* spoke of him as having 'come to England for the first time from Belgium in '73' and 'immediately' becoming 'connected with the Liverpool dockers and warehouse labourers'. According to Henry Collins, there is 'no record of British workers approaching the International for aid after the Hague Congress of 1872'.[14] Four pages

[11] Rules and Resolutions of the British Federal Congress (Nottingham, 20–22 July 1872). Unsigned MS Minutes: Jung Collection, no. 116, IISH, Amsterdam, minute-taker's page nos. 4 (universal strike fund) and 12f. (trade unions). The latter entry seems not to occur in H. Collins and C. Abramsky, *Karl Marx and the British Labour Movement* (London, 1964).
[12] As in note 10 above.
[13] 'R.E.N.' as in note 4 above. Cole, *Short History*, p. 199.
[14] *Labour Annual*, 1899 (Liverpool), p. 156. There is also a photograph of P. J. King on p. 104 of the same volume. Henry Collins, 'English Branches of the First International', p. 270.

earlier, though, Collins mentions an exception. Around the time of this meeting, the International's Liverpool branch 'was publicising the appeal of the local dockers against the attempt to introduce non-unionism by importing Belgians'.

We may be fairly confident that King was Irish: his politics certainly were. We can note the news given to the International's General Council in April 1872 that 'an Irish branch' was being formed in Liverpool and the report four weeks later that the Liverpool secretary had lost contact with it.[15] So, if King really did arrive from Belgium, his 'immediate' connection with Liverpool dockers seems likely to have arisen from some task he was performing on behalf of one of the Irish branches of the International, or of its remnants – whether based in Liverpool or elsewhere.[16] Just conceivably, this may indicate some small and very long-term contribution to the developments of King's ideas from a milieu linked, however tenuously, with the IWMA. From 1889, King was leading the Lancashire Chemical and Copper Workers' Union, and, some years later the socialist journalist Joseph Burgess spoke of him and of many of his fellow members in St Helens, where the union once centred, as Irish. King, he remembered, 'had a connection with the Irish Nationalist movement, in which he had spent some time as an organiser'. Likewise, two postwar historians have reported from the local press that King 'had come to St Helens as a Liberal registration agent' – hardly incompatible at the time with Nationalist activities.[17]

The 1890s

We have just seen how ideas for Federation had been around – however tenuously – for two generations before the TUC had come into being. It remains to try to identify the factors that helped spread these ideas during and after the crucial period of the 1890s.

However 'new' the unionisation around 1890 may or may not have been, it was flimsy – and rather manic. Historians have concentrated on the fundamental reasons for this: the insecure situation of the unskilled and the resulting need to strike or at least organise swiftly before the economic situation became hostile again. But there was also an

[15] General Council of the First International, Minutes, 9 April 1972, p. 148; 14 May 1872, p. 194; IISH.
[16] First International, Minutes, 16 January 1872, p. 77; 28 May 1872, p. 212; 11 July 1872, p. 220. The International had another 'Irish Branch' in the steel port of Middlesborough – another town where 'work could be found for refugees'.
[17] *Manchester Weekly Times*, 22 July 1898. T. C. Barker and J. R. Harris, *A Merseyside Town in the Industrial Revolution: St Helens, 1750–1900* (London, 1954), p. 457.

insecurity of mood; and this was bound, for some activists, to widen the appeal of ideas of federation.

Thus, late in 1889, during the germination of what became the General Railway Workers' Union (GRWU), John Ward of the Navvies' Union, and John Burns – hero of Bloody Sunday and of the recent London Dock Strike – were 'much applauded' by two or three thousand, mostly railwaymen, at Battersea Park Gates. They had urged 'all trades . . . [to] federate as rapidly possible and all stand by each'.

The report of this meeting appeared in *Labour Elector*, a weekly founded in 1888 by the now ex-SDFer, H. H. Champion, to prepare the way for an 'Independent Labour Party'. Only a fortnight earlier this paper had pleaded the urgency of federation:

> At present trade unionism is popular because the people believe it will do much for them. A few defeats, and it will vanish, and with it the opportunity for a Federation of Labour that may not come again in our generation. Every genuine trade unionist desires . . . such a combination.

A week after reporting the Battersea meeting, it was urging the speedy convening of an inter-union conference. This should proceed to elect 'an Executive to form a Federation of Trades and Labour Unions'.[18]

During these weeks at least, a 'Mr P. J. King' seems to have been looking to this paper – judging from a short report on his having organised 'the Chemical Workers of Widnes and St Helens'. According to the *Labour Elector*, the Chemical Workers expressly quoted the example of the Gasworkers' Union.[19]

Little more than a year later, in March 1891, the *Labour World*, a paper close to the Irish agrarian nationalist and semi-socialist, Michael Davitt, printed a long appeal from a self-consciously 'unskilled' and blacklisted 'Dock-side Labourer' of Hull, John O'Connor. It was typical of this moment that O'Connor used vaguely messianic rhetoric to stir his fellow unskilled.

> We have been . . . and are being . . . looked upon as the most illiterate of the population of the country, and consequently we have been made slaves of other classes . . . But an era of light has dawned upon us, and we begin to feel that we are a power in the land, but to use that power we must be combined together as one man, trusting in ourselves for our emancipation.

His 'advice' foreshadowed the ideas of radical federationists later in the decade. Existing national executives should be induced to transform themselves and to lessen their rôle.

---

[18] *Labour Elector*, 23, 9, 30 November 1889.   [19] *Labour Elector*, 14 December 1889.

I would advise that at the branch meetings of the various unskilled labour unions or societies, resolutions . . . be carried calling upon their executives to arrange a convention of executives of the unskilled labour organisations with delegates from each section of unskilled labour. Such convention to draw up a scheme of federation or amalgamation, elect one central council to control the whole, subject to the voice of the rank and file of the members.

There should be a low, uniform entrance fee and contribution.

O'Connor had 'no doubt' that 'such resolutions will meet with opposition from some in official positions, and who, no doubt will use their power to frustrate the carrying out of such'. But his remedy for the anticipated opposition to democratic unity was merely a dose of anti-leadership rhetoric – very much of the kind that featured later in the decade:

> But as it is from the rank and file all power is derived, therefore they must see to it that that power must be used in the interest of all, and not made the stepping stone for would-be dictators . . . at the expense of those to whom they are but servants.

One expected benefit was an end to 'the many different organisations whose rules in some respects conflict'. Under his proposed dispensation, 'directed by one authority, there will be no clashing of interests'. This would boost recruitment and lessen blacklegging, 'for I take it that no labouring man possessed of one grain of common sense will remain outside such a combination'. This would in turn bring virtual invincibility, fewer strikes but swifter escalation. Indeed, faced with 'the forces of the Crown', workers could 'say to the government . . . "Surrender that power which has been given to you to use in the interests of the people." We will not only be able to say this, but we will be in a better position to enforce it.'[20]

Most weeks, including this week, a Dr John Moir contributed a medical column in the *Labour World*. Four weeks later, in May 1891, he began to propose federation in the first issue of the *Workers' Cry – the 'Advocate of the Claims of the Labour Army'* – drilled, or rather edited, by the ex-Salvation Army Commissioner and future socialist, Frank Smith. O'Connor was the only thinker Moir praised; and Moir too was concentrating on 'the Emancipation of Unskilled Labour'. Implicitly, he redoubled O'Connor's emphasis on the rank and file by loading his proposals with extravagant comparisons: O'Connor's was, for Moir, 'the constitution of the US of A' (amongst other things) 'supplemented and improved by the Referendum', a description that might equally well become applicable to King's *Clarion* scheme a few years later. While

---

[20] *Labour World*, 29 March 1891.

detailing O'Connor's proposals for a convention, Moir was more concrete, and arguably more conciliatory to the TUC. He envisaged the new federation as 'affiliated' to the TUC, or

. . . amalgamated in some way with it, but federated with it in any case in one chamber like the old Scottish Parliament, but with election direct from the people, a second ballot and no coopted delegates.

It may be fruitful to note how frequently ideas for union federation overlapped with support for a wide-ranging list of working-class demands in which land reform figured prominently, along with a hunger for thorough democracy. The exact phrasing and context of these and other elements varied, but their content recurs throughout the nineteenth century. This content was the ideological compost for the socialisms that began to grow up from the 1880s onwards.

The *Workers' Cry* was to help accelerate the growth from this subsoil of organisations such as the Independent Labour Party (ILP). And from Dr Moir's pen, reform-proposals – some specific, some flowery, and some plain gaseous – sprouted abundantly. The inaugural *Workers' Cry* had opened similarly with a twenty-point programme which combined the traditional Radical-Republican preoccupations – land, single tax, a republic, 'the UnNational Debt', 'the Second Ballot' and curbs on 'wirepulling' – with new Labour and Socialist ones.[21] Such shopping lists blurred demands for social reforms – to be carried out in the first instance by the existing state – with other demands for the democratisation of that very state. In many a working-class scheme of things these two aspects might be compatible. But with hindsight they underline the potential unpopularity of Fabianism's reliance on existing state-institutions – as also of the Fabian-influenced 'New Liberalism' which was to dominate home policy from the late 1900s.

Such reliance was to be particularly tricky, given that part of these Liberals' price for co-opting trade union officials was an emphasis on the state – increasingly, the hope was, a Liberal state. This emphasis jarred with working-class radicals' still fundamental emphasis on democracy. The bigger the suspicion of the Great or 'Servile' State, the less stable would be the attitude towards this New Liberalism and towards its Labour hangers-on in the House of Commons after 1906.

Just a few weeks after Moir, in June 1891, the *Navvies' and Labourers' Guide* gave as its seventh and final reason for joining the Navvies', Builders' Labourers' and General Labour Union its belief that 'Labour Unions' were

---

[21] *Workers' Cry*, 2, 9 May.

the cradle of that great Labour Party of future English politics which will, by scientific use of that most powerful of our weapons – the Boycott – and the *self-chosen* periodical *General Holiday* [i.e. in this definition, rolling strikes, nationally coordinated] and by massing its organised Vote at every election (both local and parliamentary), at the back of a bread and butter, work and wages shorter hours programme – the main planks of which will be the replacing of the present private monopolies and cannibal competition, by Public Services, the Cooperative Commonwealth, and Social Equality and Freedom for all.[22] (original emphasis)

This alliterative language sounds like Leonard Hall's. Hall was prominent in the Navvies' Union – and profiled in its *Guide* of March of that year.[23] In fact, he was both a 'labour agitator' and a prominent socialist in the North West. In his 1894 *Clarion* pamphlet, *The Old and New Unionism*, Hall was to foreshadow concepts which many were to exaggerate as syndicalist when he gained a major following in the British Socialist Party in the 1910s.

Also in 1894, while acknowledging the 'class war' and demanding a 'General Strike' to secure shorter hours for the miners, Hall was talking of his 'Ideal State' as

practically constitut[ing] a National Union of Trade and Labour Unions of the country, of which every citizen will, of natural necessity, be a member. For as the industries of the nation evolves [sic] from private to public ownership and from class dictation to general control, so the due representation of the special needs and powers of each section of the workers . . . will become more and more a necessity and a sign of . . . truly democratic organisation.[24]

On the same page, he demanded 'Trade Federation, the Trade Union strike, the Trade Union boycott'. In 1894, he placed such conceptions in tandem with independent working class political action.

While hardly typical, equally he was hardly isolated. In the same paper at the start of 1891, for example, another writer was calling on 'the new unions' to 'force the powers that be' to accelerate a New Unionist equivalent of the strategies favoured for decades by some advocates of producer co-operation:

the organising of town workshops and country farms under *Public Control and Ownership* and the taking over and managing by the social authorities of all public works with a view, firstly, of employing the 'out of works', secondly, to provide an alternative . . . livelihood and, thirdly, an alternative supply of goods.

---

[22] *Navvies' and Labourers' Guide*, June 1891.
[23] Much of the profile is repeated in the *Workman's Times* of 25 September 1891.
[24] Leonard Hall, *The Old and New Unionism*, Clarion Pamphlet (1895), pp. 4, 6, 9.

These 'new Public Industries' would rescue employees and customers from 'the tender mercies of private greed'.[25]

It may well be that a version of Co-operative strategy may have been one route towards syndicalism. Many co-operative strategies had assumed that the bad old society would die of desertion if the working community could be persuaded to separate itself from it in one way or another. But this *Navvies'* writer, while pointing to the 'Class War' as 'the ABC fact necessary for everybody to grasp', was willing additionally to call in the State to reverse the laws of the economic 'struggle for existence'.

As we shall see, the various federation schemes were disputed and dissected by people of unusually differing strategies. But the inaugural 'Federal Labour Parliament' of the *Clarion* federation – that is to say, of NIGFTLU – 'passed *nemine contradicente*' among its 'Objects' the establishing of 'workshops and factories, trading concerns and insurance companies for the benefit of those connected with' the organisation. While the 'Objects' also at once mentioned 'whatever political or other action may be necessary in the workers' interests', King himself, prefacing the Minutes, spoke mainly of an alliance at the ballot-box between workers and employers against the landlords and 'royalty footpads' – absentees such as the owners of mining property. He saw these two groups as strangling the prosperity of *both* sides of industry, and quoted to this effect a speech made to the Scottish Land Restoration League.[26]

So far, we have treated these discussions as if they simply arose out of the first two or three years of the New Unionism. But there are hints of the earlier 'new unionism' associated with the British activities of the Knights of Labor. During the middle 1880s the glassworkers' component of this American organisation had tried to organise its fellow-workers in Europe. Its impact had lasted only a few years. In Britain, apart from the glassworkers, there was an enthusiastic response among some groups of organised workers in the Midlands, Merseyside and Clydeside.

Even though nothing so far mentioned indicates direct involvement of any identifiable individuals with the Knights, the similarities are worth listing. After all, the organisation had peaked in Britain as recently as 1888–9 with, allegedly, more than 10,000 members in fifty branches.[27]

[25] 'D.E.F.', 'The Way Out', *Navvies' and Labourers' Guide*, 1 January 1891.

[26] Minutes of the Federal Labour Parliament, 1898, pp. 32, 6.

[27] Henry Pelling, 'The Knights of Labour in Britain, 1880–1901', *Economic History Review*, 2nd series, 9 (1956–7), 325.

And there is at least one indication that it may have influenced 'youthful' workers disproportionately.[28] Most 'labour agitators' in the early '90s must have had at least a rough knowledge of its industrial and political principles.

Firstly, the Knights preached the boycott in preference to the strike. From both Hall and King we have noted talk either of the boycott as supplementary to the strike or as an alternative to it. Secondly, they advocated arbitration in preference to either of these forms of conflict.[29] Thirdly, in America at least, the Knights were a loose form of trades federation, which attempted to organise both 'men of all trades or none' and 'craft societies of an exclusive type'. In the British context, Pelling, in a particularly significant phrase, sees the Knights as 'corresponding more closely to Robert Owen's Grand National [Consolidated Trades Union] than to anything more recent'.[30] He notes how 'some small local unions' when hard-pressed 'regarded the Knights as a trades federation which they might look to for support'.[31]

Fourthly, while it is rather difficult to produce instances of the Knights preparing the way for later developments,[32] there are a few places where this may have occurred. One would be Sunderland. Here the Knights were important among the glassworkers. By 1898 the main glassworks had closed but the Sunderland Trades Council sent a delegate to the NIGFTLU's founding 'Federal Labour Parliament'; his claimed representation was the highest of any single trades council on this occasion. A second area where the Knights had made some impact – this time, a rather diffuse one – was the West Midlands. Here, during 1886 and 1887, West Bromwich's *Labour Tribune*, 'which circulated fairly widely among Midland miners and ironworkers', gave 'much publicity' to the Knights.[33] Later, in 1898, some miners were said to be organising special lodge meetings of the West Bromwich District Association, one enthusiast for the *Clarion* scheme informing King that 'those who have heard me explaining [the scheme], because of their inability to read it, are

---

[28] See report of a Smethwick meeting in the London *Star*, 14 May 1888.

[29] E.g. Isaac Cline at the international Glass Workers' meeting at Charleroi, reported in the *St Helens Newspaper and Advertiser*, 21 June 1884; or John Richards of Smethwick speaking at a 'mass meeting of working men at Darlaston' for federation, reported in the West Bromwich *Labour Tribune*, 1 May 1886: something that we shall note of P. J. King among others.

[30] Pelling, *A Short History*, p. 95.

[31] Pelling, 'The Knights of Labour', p. 323.

[32] This would require, among other things, visiting the Knights of Labour documents which are housed at the Catholic University of America at Washington DC.

[33] Pelling, 'The Knights of Labour', p. 321 (quoting the Knights' district secretary, Richard Hill) and p. 320.

unanimous in their approval', as were also 'the men who have read the scheme themselves'.[34]

There may, earlier, have been a national carry-over from the West Midlands. At the 1889 TUC, the mover of a successful motion which instructed the Parliamentary Committee 'to draw up some system of federation for the consideration of the next Congress' was Richard Juggins of the Amalgamated Nut and Bolt Makers of the Midland Counties Trades Federation. Three years previously, Juggins had also spoken powerfully from the chair at a 'mass meeting of working men . . . at Darlaston, for the purpose of considering a system of federation for all Trade Societies or [an ambiguous 'or'] the advisability of joining the Knights of Labour in America'. In 1886, he had traced the 'idea of federation' only 'as far back' as the 1879 TUC.[35] He was to be a TUC delegate during at least two of the same Congresses as King: those of 1890 and 1891.

Fifthly, at the Darlaston meeting, Juggins also brought in the question of producers' cooperation – a pre-eminently British invention which, as noted, King was to raise in his own particular context. 'If the various trade unions in the United Kingdom were federated, they might be [by?] taking a strike – when a strike was legitimate – utilise the surplus labour by starting cooperative workshops, thus claiming their fair share of the Capital to which Labour is justly entitled.' Like the Knights, Juggins – 'for over twenty years until his death in 1895, in a very real sense the voice of the Black Country craftsman' – preferred conciliation if at all possible.[36]

Politically, the Knights had a particularly warm friend in Michael Davitt, who had been present at their 1887 General Assembly in Minneapolis and who spoke for them, the next year, at a very large public meeting in Smethwick. Coincidentally or not, we have mentioned Davitt's *Labour World* as hosting O'Connor's appeal for national federation. The same year in which O'Connor made this appeal, the Knights – at least at national and international levels – began a more active political agitation. As a result the British locals of the Knights affiliated to the 'Lib-Lab' Labour Electoral Association.[37] The question of working-class representation had come up earlier at the 1887 Darlaston meeting, and elsewhere in the area.[38] At the other end of the

---

34 *Clarion*, 24 December 1898.
35 *Labour Tribune* (West Bromwich), 1 May 1886.
36 *Dictionary of Labour Biography*, vol. 1.
37 Pelling, 'The Knights of Labour', pp. 321, 327.
38 *Labour Tribune*, 1 May 1896; 18 September 1896.

trade union spectrum, a number of socialists were in leading positions in some of the Knights' local branches.

Among individuals, one definite overlap is Ben Turner, the West Riding textile workers' leader, who had a brief association with the Knights during their earliest days in Britain.[39] However, his rôle here is as ambiguous as his later association with the NIGFTLU. There is also King himself. It is possible that he had some experience of the Knights – direct or not.

King represented his union, the short-lived Chemical and Copper Workers' Union, at a number of Congresses of the TUC. At that of 1890 he would presumably have heard the Parliamentary Committee's report on a scheme for a Federation of Trades – a report resulting from a probably very brief discussion on the subject at the previous year's Congress. And at that of 1893, a committee was appointed which drew up a vague scheme for a federation of kindred trades, whose member unions would appoint an executive committee. There were also to be local district committees 'arranged and controlled by the executive of the various groups'.[40] Most of the fourteen on the committee are to be met with in this book. One was Pete Curran of the Gasworkers. Curran had been among those at the 1893 Congress urging the formulation of a scheme, and the example he quoted had been the 'American Labour Federation' – a mainly 'skilled' outfit: ironic from a New Unionist.

Just at this time, with his union smashed, King himself – perhaps partly because no longer with a union of his own to occupy his time – became more active on the question. He claimed subsequently to have written to Sam Woods in 1895 'offering the [Parliamentary] committee [his] scheme, and pledging himself that no one should know from whom it emanated, but [his] letter was not even acknowledged'.[41]

What might be called the 'generation of 1910' might have recognised the core of Hall or O'Connor as vaguely syndicalist. But, unlike syndicalists, these two also had an avowedly political dimension. So, how important was federation during its late-1890s heyday to those socialists who supported it?

The *Clarion* devoted much space and energy to propagating King's ideas, but saw federation as a more limited aim than its own socialism. Blatchford claimed from the beginning to offer federation to trade unionists 'not as a Socialist' but merely as a friend.[42]

His close colleague, A. M. Thompson, could be heard off-handedly explaining to fellow socialists that King's scheme 'was not Socialism . . .

---

[39] Ben Turner, *About Myself* (London, 1930), p. 131.   [40] TUC Minutes, 1893.
[41] Minutes of Federal Labour Parliament, 1898, p. 3.   [42] *Clarion*, 4 January 1897.

but we decided that its adoption would probably benefit the workers'.[43] In the end, this off-handedness was to have disastrous results for King. When the *Clarion*'s continued support for him threatened to become too divisive, Blatchford was to issue a long statement in the name of the *Clarion* Board – which he twice misspelt brazenly as 'Bored' – 'leaving the British workman . . . to do as to him seems best', thus leaving King in the lurch.[44] But at the beginning *Clarion* writers had seen federation as not merely a more elementary aim, but also as one which might involve wider numbers than – to the Board's regret – the propagation of '*Clarion* Socialism'.

The campaign for the 'Clarion Federation' – Blatchford's and Thompson's disclaimers notwithstanding – marked the high-water mark of the paper's influence in the trade union movement: its eventual failure was the last of a series of defeats for *Clarion* democracy in the late 1890s. To understand both how powerful a force was the *Clarion* conception of democratic socialism and the hostilities it generated among socialists which contributed to the failure of the NIGFTLU, we must now turn to the way rival versions of democracy increasingly split that movement in the 1890s.

[43] *Clarion*, 3 January 1898.   [44] *Clarion*, 14 October 1899.

Part 2

4   Conflicts in the ILP

The Independent Labour Party (ILP) was founded in Bradford in January 1893. A growing sense of commitment to a sometimes vague but always intensely experienced socialism, among growing numbers of trade union activists and middle-class converts alike, had combined with the experience of 'new unionist' successes and failures during the previous few years. Liberalism seemed bankrupt and perhaps doomed to disintegration; and the hostility of so many Liberal employers and local authorities to working class demands had eroded support among trade unionists.

As we have seen, there was already tension among socialists between, on the one hand, 'realists', who expected to attain short-term goals both via electoral politics at every level and via pragmatic trade union action, and, on the other hand, 'idealists' for whom compromise threatened the ultimate socialist goal. The ILP's disappointing performance in the 1895 election, increased the appeal of Keir Hardie's 'Labour alliance', whereby socialist weakness would be bolstered by trade union funds and organisation. But for others the same disappointments reinforced the need for a more radical approach. The pattern remains familiar today. What was different about the 1890s is that the major issues that divided the movement were, explicitly and directly, about democracy.

In part, the clash took the form of struggles over the running of the new party. Keir Hardie's *Labour Leader*, launched in March 1894, acted, in practice, as the organ of the ILP's 'establishment' with a Fabian-like attitude to democracy. His opponents saw themselves as democratisers. Blatchford's *Clarion* was their main focus. The question of 'socialist unity' – whether or not there should be a 'fusion' of the ILP and the SDF – became part of this conflict. The failure of the *Clarion* to win any of these debates was to discredit the ultra-democratic, anti-bureaucratic stance of its supporters, to the advantage of 'realists' and of the 'Labour alliance' project.

Democracy and the ILP programme

More than most organisations, the ILP could claim to have grown 'upwards' from local initiatives: of the 115 delegates at the founding conference, 91 represented provisional ILP branches formed in anticipation of the national party.[1] The intention to maintain a high degree of internal democracy was symbolised by the adoption of the title 'National Administrative Council' (NAC) to describe what was more usually called the national executive. Devising the ILP programme was complicated by the fact that local parties had often adopted their own before the foundation conference. Manchester and Salford ILP saw its famous '4th Clause' – which required members to abstain from voting for any candidate 'in any way a nominee of the Liberal, Liberal Unionist or Conservative Party' – as a necessary guarantee of real independence. But it failed to persuade the national party to adopt it.[2]

Democratic goals were prominent in some local programmes. Swinton and Pendlebury ILP, for example, included in theirs adult suffrage, triennial parliaments, 'home rule' for all parts of the Empire, and the referendum. However, when presenting the national programme, Edward Aveling earned 'loud cheers' for demanding 'less political and more social reform'.[3] And, consistently with this sense of priorities, it was proposed to follow the party's 'object' – 'the collective ownership of the means of production, distribution and exchange' – with a list of 'social' demands including the abolition of overtime, piecework and child labour, the legal forty-eight hour week, and 'provision for the sick, disabled, aged and orphans'. True, there was then to follow a 'political programme' – seven items including adult suffrage, the second ballot and the referendum. But Shaw Maxwell, the ILP's first Secretary, and Pete Curran (an organiser for the Gasworkers and much later to be a Labour MP) successfully moved its replacement by the sentence 'The Independent Labour Party is in favour of every proposal for extending electoral rights and democratising the system of government.'

The immediate motive seems to have been to distinguish the new party as clearly as possible from the Radicals. Shaw Maxwell told the conference that adoption of his amendment 'would leave it impossible

---

[1] These figures were given in the *Report from Great Britain and Ireland to the Zurich International Workers' Congress, 1893* presented by the Gas Workers' and General Labourers' Union, the Bloomsbury Socialist Society and the Battersea Labour League (London, 1893).

[2] *Report of the First General Conference of the ILP*, Bradford, 13/14 January 1893.

[3] *ILP Conference Report*, 1893.

for people to charge them with taking planks out of the platform of the ordinary political parties'. The amendment was accepted without dissent – though not before J. L. Mahon, a veteran of the SDF, the Socialist League, the North of England Socialist Federation and the Labour Union, had insisted that he 'did not wish it to be allowed to pass that the idea of these political reforms come from the Radical Party. They came from the Chartist and Workers' party.'[4]

What was the significance of this downgrading of 'politics' in the ILP programme? By refusing to specify particular demands, it left an ambiguous area. Whenever any specific proposal was advanced, it could be argued either that it was already subsumed in the general statement or, conversely, that it was not really what was required to 'democratise the system of government'. Individual judgements were bound to vary. Thus Keir Hardie could support, and Ramsay MacDonald oppose, the second ballot.

Secondly, it left the ILP in a position of passive support; it was merely 'in favour' of, as distinct from committed to campaign for, democratic change. It implied that the latter was the business of others, who could, however, count on the ILP's benevolent support. Just how weak being 'in favour' could be, was seen later in 1893, when the SDF with some trade union support organised, in response to the recent decisions of the Socialist International at Zurich, a Universal Suffrage Demonstration in Trafalgar Square on Sunday 22 October. *Justice* reported that 'Hardie declined to speak . . . and regretted "to find the SDF placing itself in line with mere Radicalism", and talked of our advertising our "desertion of the cause of Socialism".' Inter-party point-scoring, of course; but it is significant that Hardie chose this particular issue to goad the SDF. It was not forgotten. Years later, Hardie became closely identified with the cause of 'limited' women's suffrage – a proposal for 'extending electoral rights' that many socialists opposed as *not* involving 'democratising the system of government'. *Justice* reminded its readers that 'the SDF set on foot agitation for Universal Suffrage when some of those who now regard the question as of supreme moment – notably Mr Keir Hardie – refused to have anything to do with it on the ground that a mere political question of that kind was of no importance whatever.'[5]

Yet 'in favour' could mean smuggling back into the programme the very list of specific 'political' demands the ILP statement was supposed to avoid. Thus, the ILP's London District's version read:

---

4 ILP Conference Report, 1893. *Workman's Times*, 21 January 1893.
5 *Justice*, 21 October 1893; 19 February 1907.

The Bradford Conference declared that:
'The Independent Labour Party is in favour of every proposal for extending electoral rights and democratising the system of Government.'
The London District mention as coming within the scope of such proposals the following
1) Adult Suffrage.
2) Second Ballot.
3) Payment of Election Expenses out of the Rates.
4) Payment of Members on all Representative Bodies.
5) Triennial Parliaments.
6) Abolition of the Monarchy and the House of Lords.[6]

Apart from the substitution of triennial for 'shorter' parliaments and the much more significant omission of the referendum, this was the original programme proposed by the preparatory commission at the founding conference.

Keir Hardie's own position was implacably hostile to the 'merely political'. Commenting on the 1895 ILP conference he wrote in *Labour Leader*:

Nothing gave me greater satisfaction than the absence of any attempt to incorporate any political reforms in the programme . . . As long as we keep clear of political issues we are safe.[7]

This was to remain his view. In 1909 he was to note with satisfaction in *My Confession of Faith in the Labour Alliance* that 'From the first day of its inception the ILP rigidly barred all merely political questions'.[8]

Hardie's reaction to the 1895 conference is significant. What some would regard as a political reform *had* been added to the programme. Prompted by an amendment from the Women's Labour Party of Glasgow, the NAC – of which Hardie was so influential a member – led the conference into adding to the brief reference to 'electoral rights' the words 'to both men and women'. It is clear that for Hardie the women's franchise issue was *social* rather than political: a point we shall return to at a later stage.

To the extent that the party shared Hardie's view, the ILP – like the Fabians – was accepting, in effect, the legitimacy and the adequacy of the existing system of government. The state was neither to be smashed nor transformed: rather it was to be captured in order to institute the social and economic changes which together constituted socialism. Take H. Russell Smart. He was later to be an outspoken critic of Hardie and

---

[6] ILP London District Leaflet, January 1894.
[7] *Labour Leader*, 27 April 1895.
[8] J. Keir Hardie, *My Confession of Faith in the Labour Alliance* (London, 1909), p. 6.

the ILP leadership. But at this point he was described as a 'Fabian'. 'Political freedom', as he proclaimed in one of the earliest ILP pamphlets was already

attained, the democratisation of our institutions is, if not complete, so nearly so, that we have lost faith in the millennium it should have brought and we find that instead of being at the end of our journey we are only at the beginning. The franchise is but the key with which to unlock the gate that bars us from the wealth we have created.[9]

The ILP presidency and the position of Keir Hardie: *Labour Leader* versus the *Clarion*

Initially the *Clarion* gave almost uncritical support to the ILP, with Blatchford describing it in October 1893 as 'the most democratic political organisation ever seen in this country'. But conflict was already emerging over the 'Manchester Fourth Clause'. Participating in a *Clarion* debate on the issue within three weeks of the ILP's formation, Hardie had floated the alternative of pre-election conferences to advise how members and supporters might cast their votes 'as a matter of good policy and sound tactics for candidates of one of the historic parties'.

Blatchford's objections went beyond aversion to the Liberals and Conservatives, or even fears for the continued independence of the ILP. For him it signalled acceptance of 'the Parliamentary method' and of 'Parnellite' tactics. To succeed, this would mean subordinating the party to a leader. Blatchford's notion was quite different.

The socialist aim should be 'to get the general feeling in advance of Parliament'; to strive to exercise a 'moral influence' as the TUC already did, however unsatisfactorily. Only after this hegemony had been achieved would parliamentary politics take any sort of precedence. A 'great . . . Fourth Clause Labour Party' would morally challenge the legitimacy of Parliament and gradually win working-class support. The Liberals – 'shut out from power' by the loss of working-class votes – would split, with their 'capitalist portion' going over to the Conservatives and the remainder to the Labour Party. And '*then* the Labour men could sweep down on the old Parliament and use it for the only purpose for which it is fitted – the embodiment in statutes of the Will of the People'.[10]

This breathtaking scenario implied the maintenance of the highest possible standards of internal democracy in the ILP to secure the

---

[9] H. Russell Smart, *The Independent Labour Party: Its Programme and Policy* (Manchester, 1893), p. 4.
[10] *Clarion*, 4, 11 February 1893.

necessary 'moral influence' and to prefigure the democratic socialist society in its own practice. The *Clarion* took on the rôle of guardian of democratic standards within the party. We have seen how the Halifax councillors John Lister and James Beever were denounced for 'insubordination' in November 1894. When *Clarion* readers asked Blatchford how the ILP should be run, he stressed the unfairness – and danger – of leaving any branch's work to a committee and gave his view that such posts as president and vice-president had no place in a democratic organisation.[11]

Blatchford was not the first to make this criticism of the ILP. As early as May 1894 *Justice*'s columnist 'Sandy MacFarlane' had cited the designation of its officers 'as hon. secs., hon. treasurers and such like' as evidence that ILPers 'conform to the usages and practices of the middle-class politicians'. He also complained that the ILP was infected with 'hero worship' – something which, as we have already seen, the SDF and the Socialist League had both been very suspicious of from the earliest days.[12]

Blatchford's comments triggered off what Hardie later described as 'a sort of craze' for dispensing with presidents and similar officers.[13] Within weeks, Blatchford's friend Leonard Hall had offered his resignation as President of the Manchester and Salford ILP, although its Executive Committee refused to accept it and recorded its opposition to 'the agitation in favour of abolishing presidents and vice presidents'. Blatchford seems to have been surprised and somewhat disturbed by the results of his own influence, at least in this particular case, but he dismissed the argument of the Manchester Executive that instead of pursuing such distractions the party would be better served by concentrating on preparing for the general election:

I think the party cannot be better employed than it would be by establishing itself firmly upon a true democratic basis, and that until it has done that any dealings with general elections will be futile . . . [14]

Unlike the Manchester ILP, some branches acted on Blatchford's advice. For example, in *Labour Leader* it was reported that 'last Thursday Mr Leese tendered his formal resignation as president of the Stoke ILP, and it was then decided to run the branch on truly democratic lines, and in future to have no president or "leader" '.[15]

Inevitably the *national* presidency became the key target for the

[11] *Clarion*, 10 November 1894.
[12] *Justice*, 26 May 1894.   [13] *Labour Leader*, 10 April 1897.
[14] *Clarion*, 1, 8 December 1894.   [15] *Labour Leader*, 24 August 1895.

would-be democratisers who shared the attitudes of Blatchford and the *Clarion*. The presidency survived the 1895 ILP conference, had its name changed to chairmanship in 1896 and, the next year, comfortably survived what Hardie wearily called 'the annual motion for [its] abolition'.[16]

It is difficult to disentangle principled opposition on this issue from the feeling that Hardie's apparent unlimited tenure was helping to build what a later age would call a 'cult of personality'. In fact, Hardie remained as president/chairman till 1900. Pressure persisted, and after the 1899 conference he found it necessary to issue a statement saying that 'if he were thinking of himself . . . he would . . . retire at once.' He wished, he said, to be replaced the following year.[17] He was, though perhaps not so willingly as he pretended.[18] The campaign for the 'abolition of the chairman' – as *Labour Leader* referred to it on one occasion in 1901 – continued after his retirement from the office.

Labour Leader was important in bolstering Hardie's position in the ILP generally and allowing him to make clear his position in this and the other controversies – most of which involved issues of democratic procedure – that raged in the 1890s. In all of them the *Clarion* was the mouthpiece for the 'opposition'. Given Hardie's position in the party, it was inevitable that – as Hardie himself complained as early as November 1894 – *Labour Leader* should be seen as the 'official organ of the ILP'. Both contemporaries and historians have tended to see it in this light.

True, even Hardie occasionally bent with the *Clarion* wind. On one occasion, he suggested a three-year limit on all unpaid office-holders, including members of the NAC though still excepting the national Secretary.[19] But more typically, and particularly in the run-up to the annual ILP conference, *Labour Leader* would mock those who thought the 'abolition of the Presidency an important matter'. It appealed to branches to allow their delegates 'a tolerably free hand at the Conference'. If delegates were mandated on everything, 'a post-card would serve the same purpose and be much cheaper'.[20] And Hardie's hostility to *Clarion*-style notions of democracy became more overt as time went on. On the eve of the 1897 conference he regretted what he saw as the 'monopoly of attention' given to 'constitution-tinkering' and noted:

---

[16] *Labour Leader*, 20 April 1895; 22 February, 11 April 1896; 10, 24 April 1897.
[17] *Labour Leader*, 8 April 1899.
[18] See Bruce Glasier's diary entry, quoted in Laurence Thompson, *The Enthusiasts: A Biography of John and Katherine Bruce Glasier* (London, 1971), p. 116.
[19] *Labour Leader*, 27 April 1895.
[20] *Labour Leader*, 13 April 1895, 14 March 1896.

There is a spurious form of democracy, popular with a certain class of mind, the keynote of which is distrust. If business is conducted in a slipshod fashion in a dirty room it is democratic; if order is preferred to confusion it is autocratic, and the movement is in danger![21]

The ILP conference of the following year, 1898, proved more sympathetic to him. What he called the 'tinkering constitutional amendments' had been swept away: 'More significant still was the strong, healthy criticism of the National Administrative Council for not giving the Conference a definite lead.'[22] Hardie now felt secure enough to inform correspondents complaining of the way the constitutional amendments had been removed from the agenda – or, like George Chew of Rochdale, arguing that ILP policy should be made by referendum – that 'letters which display a lack of knowledge . . . or which tend to mislead, will in future find a resting place in the W.P.B.'.[23]

But in the late 1890s the most uncompromising *Labour Leader* assault on *Clarion* attitudes came not from Hardie himself but from George A. H. Samuel's regular column – written, oddly enough, as 'Marxian'. Marxian had no inhibitions about the desirability of leadership. Early in 1897 he was awaiting the arrival of 'a man strong in the pride of birth or in the conquest of fortune, a man destined to play the great card in the grand style; and the people will follow him to Social Democracy as they have never followed one of their own class'.[24] Not surprisingly, Marxian had no time for the referendum.[25] Provocative Marxian may have been, but Hardie was a wary editor and therefore presumably sympathetic. Nor can we dismiss Samuel as an obscure figure. His potted 'life' was included in a collection of 'Some Interesting Biographies' in *The Labour Annual* for 1896 and his portrait – 'George A. H. Samuel – "Marxian" of *The Labour Leader*' – shared a page with Karl Marx in the same publication![26]

Nothing could have been further from the ideas and attitudes fostered by the *Clarion* than Marxian's view of socialism as 'essentially an aristocratic creed'. And could there be a better example of what Blatchford had called 'Tory distrust of the people' than Marxian's reaction to the crowd watching the return of the 1st Grenadiers?

[21] *Labour Leader*, 10 April 1897.
[22] *Labour Leader*, 23 April 1898. See also the comments on the 1898 ILP conference in Stanley Pierson, *Marxism and the Origins of British Socialism: the Struggle for a New Consciousness* (Ithaca and London, 1973), p. 260.
[23] *Labour Leader*, 30 April, 14 May 1898.   [24] *Labour Leader*, 14 February 1897.
[25] *Labour Leader*, 13 April, 20 August 1898.
[26] *The Labour Annual: A Year Book of Social Economic and Political Reform, 1896* (rpt. Brighton, 1971), pp. 219, 185.

Just . . . . study, the clod-pated bundles of nerves and appetites that constitute the human product of the Capitalist system; and then picture the sort of 'Democrat' who seeks definite and helpful advice from such a mob.[27]

'Socialist unity' and the *Clarion* Referendum

The *Clarion* began to advocate the merger of the ILP and SDF at the time of the 'Real Democracy' debate in the summer of 1894. Both as aim and as strategy, the two issues were taken together. Blatchford encouraged readers to join both organisations, as he had done himself, so as to work for unity. But many remained resolutely 'unattached'. The two parties' rivalry was frequently cited as explanation for the reluctance of the 'unattached' to commit themselves to either. Most would be willing, it was urged, to join a united socialist grouping.

By 1897, pressure from sections of the memberships led to the setting up of an informal committee of prominent SDFers and ILPers which recommended 'fusion' – a complete merger – rather than a looser federation. When this was put to a vote of the members of both organisations only 6,044 participated but, of these, only 886 opposed 'fusion'. The SDF regarded this result as binding. The ILP leadership did not.

In his usual pre-conference appeal to *Labour Leader* readers in April 1898, Hardie attributed the apparently overwhelming support of ILP members to their impression that the NAC favoured 'fusion'. It did not. But delegates insisted on referring the question back to the branches with the proviso that a majority of three-quarters of the 'financial members' would be required for any proposal 'involving the dissolution of the ILP'.[28]

These provisions and the disapproval of the national leadership effectively killed off all prospects of 'socialist unity' for the time being. In the ILP poll, 'fusion' was supported by only 1,695 compared with 2,397 in favour of the NAC's proposal for 'federation'. Incensed at what it saw as the duplicity of Hardie and the ILP leaders, the SDF insisted on standing by the results of the earlier vote and rejected a federal link.[29]

As a result, relations between the supporters of 'fusion' – SDF and *Clarion* – and Hardie's *Labour Leader* became openly hostile from the middle of 1898. Estrangement was accentuated by the two parties'

---

[27] *Labour Leader*, 1, 15 October 1898.
[28] *Labour Leader*, 2, 16 April 1898.
[29] Judith Fincher, 'The Clarion Movement: A Study of a Socialist Attempt to Implement the Co-operative Commonwealth in England, 1891–1914', MA thesis, University of Manchester, 1971, p. 243. For the SDF view, see *Justice*, 15 October 1898.

espousal of totally different electoral strategies. In large part Hardie's dislike of 'fusion' arose from fear that it would damage his 'Labour Alliance' strategy of working with the trade unions where the 'Lib-Lab' element was still strong. Unions might find it difficult to come to terms with a socialist party in which the ex-SDF element forced the adoption of a more uncompromising stance and a more assertively socialist tone.

Meanwhile in *Justice*, Quelch was proposing that Social-Democrats should vote 'steadily Tory' so as to deny the Liberals office and so hasten their disintegration. This policy was later rejected by the SDF annual conference, but an essential strategic element was to detach the 'Extreme Left of the Radicals' with whom socialists could work for social and political reform, from the Liberals. 'Extreme Radical Left' candidates would be supported, unlike other Liberals, and Quelch looked forward to eventual co-operation with 'a reorganised Radical-Democratic, or Socialist-Radical Party'. He was responding to a *Reynolds's News* article the previous week which had described the SDF as 'the only body of genuine, sane and honest Socialists in the Kingdom'. *Reynolds's* editor, W. M. Thompson, was the epitome of an 'extreme left' Radical and democrat. He had chaired the Chartist Jubilee in July 1898, a meeting described by *Justice* as 'undoubtedly the greatest gathering of Socialists ever brought together'. At the Jubilee meeting, a motion was unanimously carried, calling for a 'combined and organised effort . . . by all Democrats and Socialists to realise the outstanding planks of the Chartist platform'.

The resolution went on to suggest a delegate conference of the Radicals, the SDF and the ILP to promote this end.[30] Given the SDF's view of itself as at very least *an* heir – even *the* heir – of Chartism, and its robust commitment to demands for democratic reform, it is not surprising that it should take such a position and be prepared, in principle, to work with non-socialist democrats.

With the two parties working their way into tight strategic corners, political disagreements had long become personal. When *Justice* and the *Clarion* attacked Hardie's friend Frank Smith, Hardie called them liars. He was in turn attacked by Blatchford as 'an obstacle to the progress of the Labour movement . . . universally disliked outside the ranks of his own party'. Hardie, wrote Blatchford, made reckless assertions, sinned 'against good taste' and persistently played to the gallery. The ILP should adopt the initiative and referendum and 'make it a law' that no office should be held for more than a year. He finished by endorsing Alex

[30] *Justice*, 25 June (Quelch's response to Reynolds's), 30 July (the Chartist Jubilee) and 6 August (SDF conference) 1898.

Thompson's recent suggestion that 'a plain manifesto of the aims of British Socialism' should be drawn up and submitted to the vote of all socialist organisations.[31]

This was the rather unpropitious origin of the 'Clarion Referendum'. The idea was taken up by a well-known Salford activist Harry Reade who, in September 1898, suggested a postal referendum on the desirability of a 'United Socialist Party'. Possible 'planks' for its programme could be listed in the *Clarion* for potential members to vote on. Subsequently, a conference could be convened 'and the party ultimately launched'. Thompson responded by precipitately publishing a coupon along the lines suggested in the following week's edition. This was criticised for lack of clarity and a revised version then appeared. Votes already received were cancelled.[32]

As Thompson saw it, the purpose of the referendum was to promote unity among socialists and clarify their views on electoral strategy and on the purpose of electoral politics:

Furthermore, I want to arouse the people from their state of apathy, and to establish definitely in Socialist politics, the principle of direct democratic control. Delegation of authority is always dangerous . . . [33]

Thompson probably underestimated the degree of hostility and the influence of his opponents. Sidney Webb was in Australia, but his private secretary wrote in to reiterate his employer's opposition to 'direct democratic control'. This may have carried weight with others besides the *Clarion* enthusiast Larner Sugden, who also reminded *Clarion* readers that 'the Fabian Society which includes the *élite* of Socialist thought, and which I allow to do most of my political thinking for me . . . ' opposed the referendum and initiative – one of the suggested 'planks' on the *Clarion* coupon.[34]

The *Labour Leader* charged the *Clarion* with trying to lead socialists towards the Liberals; its manager, David Lowe, attacked the rival paper's malign influence:

At a time when the Independent Labour Party was brimful of energy, hundreds of young men were diverted from working through legitimate channels into becoming . . . advertising agents for those who now complain; at a time when all thirsted for good propaganda, branches were diddled into wrangling over the presidency and official positions . . . at a time when there was a semblance of

---

[31] *Clarion*, 30 July 1898. The row over Frank Smith's candidature for the LCC which was the occasion of these public attacks can be followed, starting in the *Clarion*, 30 April 1898, in issues of the *Clarion*, *Justice*, and *Labour Leader* throughout May and June.
[32] *Clarion*, 17, 24 September; 8 October 1898.
[33] *Clarion*, 1 October 1898.   [34] *Clarion*, 1, 15 October 1898.

confidence in each other, members were served up weekly with sneers at 'elected persons'; at a time when introspection was infrequent and progress rapid, disbelief in leaders was preached in season and out of season by those who now bewail the result of their gospel of suspicion and mistrust.[35]

Soon Thompson ('Dangle' to regular *Clarion* readers) was finding in the letters received from *Clarion* readers

a constant repetition of this sort of thing.
Dear Dangle,
  I am sorry to inform you that very few of our members are going to fill up your coupon. Many of them think your idea is to form a new party: while others think you are inclined to work with the Liberal Party.[36]

That the *Clarion* Referendum garnered 8,835 votes is impressive, given its casual inception, the false start, the cancelling of early votes, the accusations of Liberalism and general contemptuous hostility from Hardie and the *Labour Leader* – hardly balanced by the very lukewarm support from *Justice* (which was prepared to go no further than to say that 'it cannot do any harm, and it *may* do some good').[37] This was more than twice the 4,092 who had participated in the ILP's 'fusion/federation' poll, and significantly more than the 6,044 in the earlier joint SDF/ILP 'fusion' vote.

Of the respondents, 5,937 were 'unattached' to any socialist organisation, which demonstrated that the *Clarion*'s 'unattached socialists' did exist in significant numbers. A. M. Thompson interpreted the results as showing an overwhelming majority in favour of 'fusion or federation', large majorities for running socialist candidates at the next general election and against the 'Fourth Clause'. Instead of the latter, the majority was 'in favour of strategically supporting either party *en bloc* – with a slight bias in favour of the Liberals – at the Socialist Executive's discretion'.[38]

Though very disappointed with the numbers participating – he had hoped for 20,000 – Thompson could draw comfort from the fact that the Referendum and Initiative easily topped the list of measures to be included in a 'practical' Parliamentary programme. With 5,965 votes, it was ahead of Old Age Pensions (5,115) and Work for the Unemployed (4,913).[39]

Thompson explained how, had the *Clarion* response been anything like what he had anticipated, he had 'intended to appeal for funds in order to

[35] *Labour Leader*, 15 October 1898.   [36] *Clarion*, 5 November 1898.
[37] *Justice*, 22 October 1898.   [38] *Clarion*, 10 December 1898.
[39] *Clarion*, 5 November 1898; *Labour Leader* and *Justice*: 10 December 1898.

promote the chosen programme in Parliament. My appeals for help for the locked-out engineers brought in a sum of £2,000 in six months – surely, it would have been easy to obtain at least five, perhaps ten thousand pounds for Socialist Parliamentary purposes before the General Election.'[40] This was not now possible.

The efforts of the *Clarion* to promote its version of 'real democracy' in the socialist movement in the 1890s were sufficiently well-supported to at least alarm its opponents. However, the *Clarion* and its sympathisers had committed errors of strategy and tactics. Partly as a result, there was insufficient support for its conception of socialist democracy. In particular, Blatchford and Thompson turned out to be somewhat fickle 'guides' once the time came to move beyond first principles. The story was very soon to be rather similar in the case of the 'Clarion' trades federation.

[40] A. M. Thompson, 'A Socialist Referendum', in Joseph Edwards (ed.), *Labour Annual 1899. The Year Book for Social and Political Reformers* (rpt. Brighton, 1971), p. 41.

5   The pressure to federate: the industrial struggle in the late 1890s

The *Clarion*'s association with campaigns for direct democracy and against 'leaders' was surely one reason why P. J. King offered the paper his scheme for trades federation. But what swiftly became known as the '*Clarion* scheme' would not have come so close to success without the turmoil that the trade union movement found itself in by the later 1890s.

Compared with the 1880s, the movement of the 1890s was characterised not only by wider numbers but also by widening insecurity. This is a key feature. The economic downswing of the early 1890s had seen, in many sectors, an employers' counter-attack. This had left much of the New Unionism either gutted or dependent on stand-down agreements, explicit or otherwise, with particular employers or groups of employers.[1]

Older unions likewise found their gains coming under pressure. If the ensuing years saw – according to most economic historians – a slow recovery in average real wages, they also saw a number of set-piece conflicts: the mining lock-out, the Lancashire cotton-spinners' struggle and the Hull dock strike during 1893; the engineering struggle on Clydeside and in Belfast (1895–6); South Wales mines (1898); Scottish Furniture Trades (1898–9) and above all the London – but soon almost national – struggle in the engineering industry (July 1897–January 1898).

Faced with such threats, the New Unions must have seemed somewhat contingent to their members – in their survival as in their beginnings. This was predictable where job-definition was tricky or impossible, and where many unskilled workers were liable to move between industries, often seasonally. Rivalry for membership was therefore no less inevitable than absurd. It cut across efforts to recover the gains of 1889–90.

---

[1] E. J. Hobsbawm, 'General Labour Unions in Industrial Britain, 1889–1914', in Hobsbawm, *Labouring Men* (London, 1964), pp. 226–67. But see also H. A. Clegg, A. Fox, A. F. Thompson, *A History of British Trade Unions since 1889*, Vol. 1, 1889–1914 (Oxford, 1964), pp. 87–96.

Rumblings

The greater the fear of the employer, the greater the worry at the movement's lack of cohesion. During the 1890s, while people of the 'New' spirit increasingly demanded more from the TUC, it remained organisationally flimsy. Sam Woods's refusal, as secretary of its Parliamentary Committee, to do anything special about the engineers until the last months, might well seem fatally routinist to those who believed the survival of trade unionism to be in question. Yet the maintenance of routine was something of an achievement when Woods himself was less than full-time, lacked adequate secretarial help and was occasionally reduced to sending begging letters to affiliated organis- ations. Members of the PC knew they lacked 'sufficient to meet their own requirements between now and the next Congress'.[2]

Only by taking into account feelings of extreme vulnerability can we begin to understand how Sidebotham, secretary of a 4,000-strong skilled union, could frame a scheme for trade union federation with direct representation only for organisations with more than 10,000 members. Vulnerability was the factor he himself named: he had 'no doubt' his own members 'would have every confidence in placing themselves in the hands of our great unions or federations of unions', since it was 'not in the interest of any great or small unions to stand idly by and see another union crushed out of existence'.[3]

Anti-leadership

Even before the shock of the engineering struggle, other factors, in addition to disorganisation, routinism and vulnerability – tended to increase the animus of some trade unionists against their leaders. One was simply the growth of bureaucracy. As Price well says, union structures were still 'a miscellaneous and confusing collection of committees, personnel and institutions whose spheres of authority and relationships with those above and below them were seldom clearly delineated or precisely defined':[4] an excellent recipe for tensions and lurchings within particular organisations. Associated with this was the growing similarity between 'Old' and 'New' Unionist behaviour and

---

[2] Report of the TUC Federation Committee, as enclosed with the ASRS General Secretary's *Quarterly Report* to the Executive Committee, 3 September 1897, p. 10.

[3] Friendly Society of Ironfounders (FSI) *Monthly Report*, December 1897, p. 5.

[4] R. Price, *Masters, Unions and Men* (London, 1980), p. 227.

ideals.[5] The price of the various stand-down agreements of the early 1890s was, from the union side, the moderation of one's members. Members' resentments might simmer or rebound on the head of almost any union leader.

Thus even so conspicuous a New Unionist – and socialist – as Will Thorne[6] 'came in for a lot of abuse' from a 'minority' of 'wild and furious' builders' labourers – members of the Gasworkers' Union in Birmingham – after he had advised them not to strike. His report – which reveals that a rival 'Federated Builders' Union' had tried to swallow a whole branchful of his disgruntled members, starting with the secretary – suggests he saw nothing unusual about such problems.[7] At the other end of the industrial and political spectrum, Robert Knight of the Boilermakers suffered, as we will see, a more reverberating revolt at the hands of a large section of his London members which both highlights the confusion of strategies and rivalries during the engineering crisis and helps us to understand why 'it was in this period that the notion of "rank and file" came to be regularly counterposed to that of the "officials"'.[8]

Another factor that may have contributed to 'anti-leadership' was generational: 'New' unionism matured and aged, but unevenly. Indeed, as late as 1898, the founding ILPer, Joseph Burgess, could describe the main divisions within the TUC as being between 'the old 'uns and the young 'uns, the men of fixed, not to say fossilised, ideas, and those of fluid, not to say effervescent, aspiration. These latter yearn to translate the poetry of thought into the prose of actuality.' Likewise, Ben Pickard ironised during his 1898 presidential oration to the MFGB: 'I am one of those who are said to be old fossils, who do not believe in the new Unionism, and who do not know how to think for themselves.'[9]

But the behaviour of a unionist as 'New' as Thorne underlines how polemical such characterisations might be. On the PC he seems to have been nearly always 'responsible' – over federation, rather rigidly so, as we

---

[5] For one contemporary account of the 'gradual interpenetration of the two ideals', see the *Railway Review* editorial, 29 December 1899, p. 8.

[6] National Union of Gasworkers' and General Labourers' *Report* for quarter ending 31 March 1898.

[7] For apparent poaching of the Gasworkers – at Elswick on Tyne – see National Amalgamated Union of Labour minute book, 5, 22, 25 February 1898, 4, 11, 18 March 1898, pp. 98, 276.

[8] As Richard Hyman has re-emphasised in 'Mass Organisation and Militancy in Britain: Contrast and Continuities', in W. J. Mommsen and H. G. Husung (eds.), *The Development of Trade Unionism in Great Britain, France and Germany, 1880–1914* (London, 1985).

[9] *Manchester Weekly Times*, 9 September 1898. Similarly, back in 1896 a 'Social-Democrat' Plasterer, T. Patrick, of London no. 10 Branch, in National Association of Operative Plasterers' (NAOP) *Monthly Report*, p. 13.

shall see. This *can* be attributed to the relatively negative rôle reserved for the industrial arena within his SDF socialism, but it does not have to be.[10] Be that as it may, his success in topping the ballot for the fraternal delegation to the USA at the 1898 TUC was said to have been generally 'regarded as a good omen that class [i.e. sectional] feeling is dying out among trade unionists.'[11] In general the divisions over federation did not conform to any 'New versus Old' distinction – much as more ambitious federationists might see themselves as keeping alive the spirit of 1889.

The engineering struggle gave added punch to anti-leadership rhetoric – in which, of course, the 'rank and file' was always the injured party. Sometimes the leaders were seen as simply bad at the job. Late in 1898, a candidate for an ASE district post in Glasgow jeered that 'it would take a powerful microscope to discover the superior knowledge and discretion of our EC officers'.[12]

Sometimes, though, criticism of leaders was more substantive. Hostility to the growing separation of leaders from the membership informed the proposals of the Wharton Hall Lodge, whose 320 members were to have two representatives at the Federal Labour Parliament (FLP) which was to found the '*Clarion*' federation (or National and International General Federation of Trades and Labour Unions – NIGFTLU) a few months later:

Seeing that the [Lancashire and Cheshire Miners'] Federation has decided to hold a Demonstration at Blackpool, we propose that the Officials walk in front of the procession and that no carriages be engaged.

We propose that the FOs [Federation Officers] pay for all their own refreshments.

That no conveyances or lunch be provided out of Federation funds. That no Platforms shall be erected at the Demonstration, but that two Lurries [*sic*] be engaged.

That the Federation do not engage any Capitalist speaker for the Demonstration.[13]

At the TUC, complained a candidate for the ASE's 1897 delegation, 'much time' was 'wasted in picnics'. If elected, he declared, he would

---

[10] There was a range of attitudes to trade unionism in the SDF ranging from virtually hostile to guardedly positive. In general, Social-Democrats were sceptical about the viability of industrial action. See Victor Rabinovitch, 'British Marxist Socialism and Trade Unionism: The Attitudes, Experience and Activities of the Social-Democratic Federation, 1884–1900', DPhil thesis, University of Sussex, 1978.

[11] NAOP, Monthly Report, September 1898, p. 26; Report of TUC delegation.

[12] M. Johnston of Glasgow. Election for no. 1 District. Bound with ASE *Monthly Report* for 1898, p. 5; similarly 'Mr Handyside, Glasgow'. Scottish TUC Minutes, 1898, p. 40.

[13] Motion discussed by EC of Lancashire and Cheshire Miners' Federation on 2 April 1898. Present at the FLP (FLP Delegates' list). The Branch was pro-*Clarion*.

'oppose any motion to adjourn for junketing purposes, and force an amendment against hobnobbing with the Lord Mayor, Lord Tom Noddy, or the Marquis of Slushborough.'[14] Although fun, this was negative. But sometimes alternatives to the separation between leaders and led were hinted at. Some stressed the importance of a large lay presence on union executives. Thus the Sutton Heath miners 'strongly protested against any person serving on the EC . . . who does not work in or about a mine'.[15] Horrocks – author of a minor scheme for federation – criticised the 'management principles' in the TUC's scheme as 'simply the creation of more offices, of which we have enough already. It is marvellous how many persons are desirous of controlling the affairs we ought to control ourselves.'[16]

It was argued, perhaps echoing Blatchford, that 'leaders' – even when, presumably, reduced to a handful – 'certainly ought not to be leaders but advisers'. Take Thomas R. Steels of the Amalgamated Society of Railway Servants. He was making himself famous, at least with historians, for his advocacy of Labour Representation. At this time, he was sneering at 'our trade union servants (who generally call themselves leaders)'. Inevitably, some leaders defended themselves against such criticisms by claiming to be already servants of the membership.[17]

At other times the critique of leaders was recognised as a general, even political one. To 'a Socialist' in the *Weekly Times and Echo*, leaders had

proved themselves as incapable as they are conservative . . . What efforts did they make during the ASE lockout? They simply stood in the way, decorated with red tape, while the men, their wives and children suffered on.

I have spent some time taking stock of these 'leaders' in the House of Commons and it makes me sick. They lick the boots of those they should defy . . . They are Liberals first and trade unionists a long way after.[18]

The TUC 'coup'

A further 1890s development which sapped trust in the TUC leadership was the use which some leaders of the 'Old' regime – based on the predominance of the skilled and of 'coal and cotton' – made of their familiarity with procedure in order to weaken the representation of their rivals. In 1895 they reorganised the basis of representation,

14 A. H. Carwood of London 8th Branch, ASE. *Monthly Report*, 1897 Election addresses.
15 Lancashire and Cheshire Miners' Federation; agenda for conference of 4 February 1899.
16 ASE *Monthly Report*, December 1898, p. 12.
17 *Railway Review*, 10 February 1899, p. 7; 3 March 1899. Clynes in Oldham and District Trades and Labour Council *Report*, October 1898, p. 13.
18 Quoted in the *Clarion*, 27 April 1898.

introducing the block vote and, even more controversially, excluding the representatives of the local trades councils which were seen as wide open to socialists. The use of the proposed new procedures themselves to summon delegates to approve these changes in the TUC's standing orders was widely seen by its victims as a 'coup' – whatever arguments might be made for the substance of the changes.

Under the impact of this, fourteen trades councils sent delegates to a meeting which – significantly for the later attempts to set the *Clarion* federation going – called itself a 'Labour Parliament'. There were even suggestions that a new TUC, more responsive to the New unionism, be formed. It is hard to believe that such suggestions would ever have led to much, but a majority of trades councils which answered a circular from the London Trades Council (LTC) were favourable, in principle, to forming a Congress of Trades Councils. This may be significant in itself. It is certainly significant for the LTC's later rôle in convening an ambitious national conference to aid the Engineers during 1898, after the TUC had shown itself wanting.[19]

The 1895 'coup' seems to have been particularly resented in Scotland and Ireland. This was because the presence of trades council representatives was seen as countering English bias within the TUC. It was certainly a major factor in the convening by Aberdeen Trades Council of a Scottish trades council conference which eventually led to the formation of the Scottish TUC. It was also mentioned as a major factor in creating the Irish TUC.[20] The two bodies were self-consciously fraternal. The Irish liked to view the Scots as having followed their example. Moves similar to the 'coup' had already helped trigger the first Irish congress in 1894. Not surprisingly, both bodies, while on the whole resisting any temptation to extract themselves from under the British umbrella, were open to schemes of federation independent of the TUC – whether their own schemes or, on the other hand, proposals such as the *Clarion*'s which included elaborate provisions for the 'four nationalities' to be proportionally represented on the Federation's EC.[21]

---

[19] See W. H. Fraser, 'Trades Councils in England and Scotland, 1858–1897', DPhil thesis, University of Sussex, 1967, pp. 556f. J. Craigen, 'The Scottish TUC, 1897–1973', MLitt thesis, Herriot Watt University, 1974.

[20] K. D. Buckley, *Trade Unionism in Aberdeen, 1878–1900* (Edinburgh and London, 1955), pp. 48f. Chair's address to the 1895 Irish TUC (National Library of Ireland and International Institute of Social History, Amsterdam).

[21] An *Irish Worker* article reproduced as an introduction to the Irish TUC's 1894 Minutes, implied that Irish and British workers' interests were antagonistic, and compared the British TUC to the 'Imperial Parliament' at Westminster. However, non-antagonism to the British TUC became somewhat of a cliché at the Irish TUC. See for example 1897 and 1898 presidential addresses.

At the 1895 Irish TUC, after the Parliamentary Committee's action which had 'robbed Ireland of her seat' had been attacked from the Chair, delegates supported the call from P. J. Tevenan, the 'Irish Secretary' of the ASRS, for the Irish Congress's own PC 'to consider and report on the practicality' of 'a national federation of trades and labour unions'. (There was to be no minuted word of this at the 1896 Irish Congress, though Tevenan had been 'unanimously elected' to the chair).[22] If some events to be recounted in the next chapter amounted to a revolt against anything, this revolt was against the British TUC, and enjoyed the Scottish and Irish bodies' sympathy.

Insecurity and the engineering crisis

But the major contribution to institutional and attitudinal destabilisation was made by the engineering lockout which throughout the trade union movement amplified earlier rumblings into a full-scale storm. Directly and indirectly, all activists were drawn in and conflicts arose between them and trade union establishments. Robert Knight, the moderate dictator of the skilled, 40,000-strong and very wealthy Boilermakers' Society,[23] recalled how one evening in October 1897 'What was called a Disputes Committee, who crowded the platform, took complete possession of the meeting' and 'in defiance of a request from this office [a significantly bureaucratic phrase for "me"], namely, that the vote should be by ballot . . . demanded a show of hands.'[24]

The meeting in the town hall, Canning Town, was said to have been attended by 1,400 London ship repairers' Boilermakers. They resolved to give notice to come out for the eight hours. Their decision was thought likely to affect up to 2,000 men. A week later it was 'unanimously' upheld – against official forecasts – at another mass meeting. In addition to their own unofficial structure – the 'Disputes Committee' mentioned by

---

[22] Tevenan's motion, seconded by Canty of the Dublin Coast and Grain Labourers' Union is in the 1895 Minutes, p. 32. There is a photo and biography of Tevenan in the 1896 Minutes. By the late 1900s he was living in Stockport and representing the Municipal Employees' Association at British TUCs. Though born in County Galway, he had moved to Liverpool as a child, and had been prominent in the 1890 Hull goodsworkers' strike and the 1892 Hull dock strike. At the 1895 Irish TUC he also proposed a motion for Labour Representation (Minutes, p. 36).

[23] For Knight's bureaucratic dictatorship and for the groundswell against it during the 1890s, see J. E. Mortimer, pp. 9, 116–29. See also Price, *Masters*, pp. 198f., 201, 203, 222ff., 229ff. For a defence of Knight, see Alastair J. Reid, 'Old Unionism reconsidered: the radicalism of Robert Knight, 1870–1900', in Eugenio F. Biagini and Alastair J. Reid (eds.), *Currents of Radicalism and Party Politics in Britain, 1850–1914* (Cambridge, 1991).

[24] Boilermakers' *Monthly Report*, November 1897, pp. 24–7.

Knight and/or 'the men's joint committee' – the rebels seem to have been supported by their District Committee. As Knight himself admitted, the rebels included a majority of the London members, though representing only half the branches. Though he had faced revolts on a District scale before, he declared the London one to be unprecedented 'for the present generation'.[25]

He replied by suspending the District Officials, and his fury spilt into the normally stately prose of his tightly controlled *Monthly Report*. For 'such disloyalty', the London rebels' places were 'being filled today, and after they have had sufficient walking about and are ready for work again, there will be none for them. All the shops in London are now open to our members who want employment.' Apparently 'on pain of expulsion', the rebels had to resume work a fortnight later, 'after much demurring'. Nationally, 25,433 Boilermakers balloted to abstain from the eight-hours movement with only 3,043 against.[26]

Faced with a toughness from employers sufficient to panic many union members and leaders, the movement's institutions seemed all too bent on hindering each other. This increased receptiveness for proposals to alter institutions and perhaps strategies. The Amalgamated Society of Engineers was one of the most prestigious in the British labour movement, and during the early months of their lock-out, Barnes, the Society's recently elected general secretary – and himself an ILPer – was still boasting that the employers' 'mad enterprise' had 'done what it wot not of' (*sic*).[27]

But, as the months wore on, this confidence collapsed. The Clydeside struggle had already signalled success for employers' federation, and trade unionists themselves were noting it: 'It took less than three days for the North East Clyde [employers] to federate', a delegate emphasised during the Dockers' 1896 Annual Meeting. Federated employers demonstrated their effectiveness in further ways during the national struggle.[28]

[25] *Manchester Evening News*, 13, 14, 28 October 1897. Clegg, Fox and Thompson, *British Trade Unions*, p. 150.

[26] *Report by the Chief Labour Correspondent* [of the Board of Trade] *on the Strikes and Lockouts of 1897*, p. lvii. *Monthly Report*, November 1897, pp. 24–7. In 1903, Knight's successor D. C. Cummings – an ILPer, ironically or not – repeated his version almost entirely. *Historical Souvenir of the Boilermakers and Iron and Steel Ship Builders Society, 1834–1904* (1905), pp. 148f. W. Mosses, *History of the UPMA, 1872–1922* (London, 1922), p. 138.

[27] To NAOP in its *Monthly Report*, September 1897, p. 27.

[28] Leason of Hull. Dock, Wharf, Riverside and General Labourers' Union, Minutes of ADM, 18–25 May 1896, p. 18.

Employers' federation: threat and example

The Employers' Federation of Engineering Associations (EFEA) managed to throw the ASE back after, in most London firms, the Society had already won the eight-hour day – which, officially, was the issue at stake. It was the employers who raised these stakes: when the ASE and its nine ally-unions struck in three London firms, the Employers' Federation reverted to a tactic it had taken over and used in the 1896 Clyde dispute and which it had already threatened to use nationally in early 1897.[29] Faced with the dispute in London, employers nationally locked out 25 per cent of those employees who were in the ten unions. In addition, they put up notices that they would 'dispense with' further 25 per cent batches 'on each of the succeeding days'. This tactic, together with sympathetic walkouts by other employees – including significant numbers of non-unionists[30] – meant that fresh groups of workers were repeatedly sucked into the fight. This can seldom have increased confidence amongst neighbouring groups.

Then, after four months, when the Board of Trade finally brought the two sides together, the Employers' Federation brought up the underlying issue. This was not the eight hours, but the 'machine question': 'control over the work process' or, as the employers saw it, 'interference with management'. Earlier in the year, replying to an EFEA 'letter of complaint' over interferences that had occurred in most major engineering centres, the ASE had suggested 'local joint committees in each district . . . with an independent referee, to settle the rates of wages to be paid for the working of machines in dispute'. The employers' position, in summary, was that this would 'have the effect of superseding [their] Federation by Committees with outside referees, who would practically control the management of the employers' works. Their objections to this change were so vital that they declined to make counter-proposals.'[31]

---

[29] The engineering employers of North East England seem to have pioneered it during 1890. J. Zeitlin, 'The Labour Strategies of British Engineering Employers, 1890–1922', in H. Gospel *et al.* (eds.), *Managerial Strategies and Industrial Relations* (London, 1983).

[30] *Report of Labour Correspondent . . . 1897*, p. 155. For the 25 per cent lockout device being used *before* the EFEA's formation, see J. F. Clarke, 'Engineering Workers on Tyneside', in N. McCord (ed.), *Essays in Tyneside Labour History* (London, 1977), p. 120. Two examples of the involvement of non-unionists would be in the Huddersfield and Halifax District of the ASE. Manuscript minutes in Huddersfield District ASE offices and Halifax Borough Library.

[31] *Report of Labour Correspondent . . . 1897*, pp. liiif. Yet in shipbuilding, a similar mechanism was adopted during the same years which, from the employers' – and Knight's – standpoint, worked well: J. F. Clarke, 'Workers in Tyneside Shipyards', in McCord (ed.), *Essays*, p. 120.

But now, after months of lockout, the employers proposed that implementation should be subject to arrangements with individual employees. This proposal was interpreted as undermining the whole purpose of trade unionism. It explains why, in mid-December, and despite having been out for up to six months, ASE members balloted by 99 per cent – and the members of the allied unions as a whole by 68,966 votes to 752 – to reject the employers' terms. It also explains why, with their 'grenadier guards' about to go down fighting, growing numbers of trade unionists believed they discerned a pattern. In branch meeting, national conference or executive committee there grew up a conviction that the unions faced annihilation, or at least reduction to a mere sick-and-benefit rôle.

Thus, on 20 October 1897, when Woods had sufficiently mastered his sense of weakness as Secretary of the TUC Parliamentary Committee to be able to circularise affiliated organisations to help the Engineers with funds, he noted, as facts, not only that the employers had refused government mediation and had thrown many workers not directly involved onto the streets, but also that they wanted to crush trade unionism as such.[32]

The struggle, claimed ASE representatives to a conference in their support called by the London Trades Council in January 1898, 'had developed into a question . . . of completely wiping out trade unions altogether'. On the day of this conference,[33] and possibly from it, a manifesto from 'forty-three of the largest trade unions of the country unconnected with the engineering trade' discerned the employers' object as 'to compel each workman to bargain individually', and therefore as 'an attack upon . . . the fundamental principles of trade unionism': thus, 'if it succeeds, it puts every trade union in danger'. The EFEA, warned John Batchelor as general secretary of the Operative Bricklayers' Society (OBS), was 'the greatest combination of Capital against Labour which we have yet seen in this country'.[34]

Sometimes long memories shaped this feeling of unfamiliarity. The OBS, urging its members during September 1897 to levy themselves for the engineers, noted not only the unprecedented nature of the threat, but also that the ASE had been 'very liberal' with levies for other unions as far back as the 1859 London building struggle.[35]

---

[32] As noted in ASE's *The Lockout 1897–8*, Appendix, or in, e.g. 1897 *Monthly Reports*, Associated Iron Moulders of Scotland (AIMS), inside front and back covers. See also John Hodge's warning to the British Steel Smelters Amalgamated Association (BSSAA), EC Minutes of 23 July 1897.

[33] OBS Documents (Modern Records Centre); *Railway Review*, 7 January 1898, p. 5.

[34] *Annual Report* for 1897.   [35] OBS Documents for 1897.

The employers' apparent victory over the engineers redoubled the pessimism – and also spread the paranoia to other industries. 'The organised workers', observed the ASRS's *Railway Review*, 'are taking to heart the portentious [*sic*] lessons which the engineers' lockout has taught them, and on every hand is heard the tumult and clamour of the rude awakening.' The workers would have to adopt new expedients, warned one ironmoulder, 'if they don't want to be driven back into a state approaching slavery'.[36]

As if to underscore how the clock was apparently being put back, the underlying precedents were spoken of as mediaeval: to a prominent Midlands Boilermaker, 'the policy of union smashing', if successful, would place the workers 'as completely under the thumb of the employers as in the Middle Ages, when to ask for an increase of wages was regarded as an act of conspiracy punishable at law.'[37]

To lose trade unionism was to 'become vassals for the rest of their days.'[38] As if to encourage such telescopings, there was the North Wales Quarrymen's eleven-month resistance to the domineering anti-unionism of Lord Penrhyn – the 'despotic plutocrat' with, in the eyes of one union branch, 'an evidently consuming desire to reduce this section of the workers to the order of serfdom'.[39] Month after month the trades councils arranged levies and appeals, and in many places for the Penrhyn children's choir to be invited. The significance of a struggle that covered almost every aspect of people's lives seemed all too chilling to some.[40]

Even those who did not imagine a tyrant's dungeon, feared that unions stood to become 'mere sick and out of work benefit societies' and that the contest would soon become an elemental one between 'serfdom' and 'manliness'.[41] Fears were fed from nearer home. The Associated Ironmoulders of Scotland (AIMS) grimly reproduced a report that the

---

[36] *Railway Review*, 18 March 1898, p. 8. AIMS *Monthly Report*, February 1898.

[37] W. Sharrocks, a district delegate of the Boilermakers, during a presentation to him at Birmingham, reported in the Boilermakers' *Monthly Report*, January 1898.

[38] Steam Engine Makers Society's General Secretary's address, 15 March 1898, p. 9 (AUEW Peckham).

[39] Aberdeen United Pattern Makers Association (UPMA), *Minute Book*, 23 March 1897 (King's College Library, Aberdeen – as all quoted, from Aberdeen).

[40] Branches: for example, Aberdeen no. 1 (or 2? – indistinct) Branch Amalgamated Society of Woodworkers (ASW), *Minute Book*, 9 February 1897. Nationally even the Boilermakers, *Monthly Report*, February 1897, pp. 11ff.; United Operative Masons and Granite Cutters Union, Aberdeen building branch, *Minute Book*, 1 June 1897. For the North Wales quarry people's struggles and wider British solidarity, see R. Merfyn Jones, *The North Wales Quarrymen, 1874–1922* (Cardiff, 1981).

[41] Derby and District Trades Council, *Annual Report*, 1898. FSI *Monthly Report*, November 1897, p. 6. David Lindsay, of 8 Pickup Street, Heywood, supporter of the *Clarion* scheme. ASE *Monthly Report*, April 1898, pp. 25f. J. Gurning of Peckham.

iron and steel masters were federating on the engineering model.[42] The prolonged Furniture lockout in Scotland was seen as 'a battle for the very existence of trade unionism'. The Manchester Unity of Operative Bricklayers Society (MUOBS) was warned in mid-1898 of 'a combination of employers . . . in the whole of the building trades'. From March to June 1899, this was to prove correct. Though the National Amalgamated Operative Plasterers were the main victims of a three-months' lockout, their opponents the Master Builders' Association blatantly threatened all unions. During March, 'in the most impertinent and arrogant letter . . . [they had] ever penned', they threatened to use the tactics pioneered by the EFEA. And within two months, Yorkshire building workers were indeed subjected to a 25 per cent lockout. Railwaymen on the London and North Eastern were aware that their interest in federation – mainly, as we shall see, in the *Clarion* scheme – had been hastened by provocative behaviour from their employers.[43]

Fears were focussed all the more by reports (first, apparently, in the *Railway Review*, confirmed in the Radical *Daily Chronicle*) that 'the aggressive policy of employers who desire to crush trade unions' was to be given a regular organisation. The *Review* tried to unmask the recently formed Employers' Parliamentary Council as 'only a blind' for an expanded and unrepentantly hostile EFEA, in which 'that old fossil', Lord Wemyss, and his Free Labour Protection Association, were supposedly 'prime movers'.[44]

This information was less than wildly wrong, judging from one researcher who describes the EPC's first meeting on 15 November 1898 as 'attended by a veritable Who's Who of British industry' with 'representatives from the textile, iron and steel, shipbuilding, engineering, building and baking industries'.[45] True, the *Railway Review*'s editorial gave 'abundant' detail of some employers' – at least public – misgivings over going militant. But other details did appear to amount to 'proof' of 'a secret conspiracy at work' for 'crushing the power of trade unionism'. The conspirators' list of aims, which the *Review* believed it had scooped,

---

[42] *Glasgow Herald*, 30 June 1898, quoted in AIMS *Monthly Report*, August 1898.
[43] Aberdeen no. 10 Branch of the United Operative Cabinet and Chairmakers of Scotland, *Minute Book*, 20 October 1898. Manchester Unity Operative Bricklayers Society (MUOBS), *Quarterly Report*, June 1898. See also Postgate, pp. 377f. W. S. Hilton, *Foes to Tyranny* (1963), pp. 179f. Also J. R. Newman, *The NAOP Heritage* (London, 1960). For a modern account see Price, *Masters*, particularly pp. 154, 184–7.
[44] *Railway Review*, 13 January 1899. *Daily Chronicle*, 13 January 1899. *Railway Review*, 7 January 1898.
[45] N. Soldon, 'Laissez Faire as Dogma: The Liberty and Property Defence League, 1882–1914', in K. D. Brown (ed.), *Essays in Anti-Labour History. Responses to the Rise of Labour in Britain* (1974), particularly pp. 223–8.

included 'absolute freedom of contract', the guarantee of its year's profits to any firm embroiled with its workers, and the instant expulsion of any firm settling with them.

As the *Chronicle* implied, these last two provisions had been partially realised during the engineering struggle. So, perhaps the most sinister of all the *Review*'s revelations was that not only the EFEA 'but also the Shipbuilding Federation, Master Boilermakers and indeed all those industries where the trade union element is a powerful and respected factor' were committed to the new initiative or about to be. As Bagwell reminds us, during the engineering lockout, some voices in the railway world had urged policies similar to those of Colonel Dyer – the main activist in the EFEA.[46] The *Chronicle* gave credence to these 'rumours' though it noted that, at least for the time being, 'the field of action . . . [had] been transferred to the law courts'. Apparently, though, the January 1898 settlement had been too mushy for militant employers.

The *Review* drew strength from the *Chronicle* even though the latter was shortly to print an EFEA disclaimer without comment.[47] It remained quick to report indications of militancy from employers – at particular length on a Manchester dinner where the local 'Association of Engineers' pledged themselves to follow the policies of the now late Colonel Dyer by being 'absolute masters' and by treating trade unionism – which, ironically, they too compared, this time for its monopoly of labour, to feudalism – as 'their absolute enemy'.

Despite such alarums and excursions – with each side casting the other as gothic tyrants – trade unionists still sometimes saw their enemy as merely the old one grown larger and fiercer: as 'the gigantic combinations of capital with which we are at present confronted', in the words of one speaker urging federation at the Dockers' Annual Meeting in 1896.[48]

However, as early as the beginning of the 1890s, some trade unionist scouts, such as Leonard Hall, with half an eye on the trust-plagued USA, had described a new enemy species, heaving its deadly way across the industrial landscape. The significance of the 'great combinations', about which one Midlands ASE dinner was speechified to, was that they 'stood instead of private firms, who in the past took an active and positive interest in their employees'.[49] The more imminent a new form of

[46] Bagwell, pp. 185, 197, quoting *Railway News*, 9 October 1897.
[47] For example *Railway Review*, 23 January 1899, p. 6; 24 February 1899. For alarmed concurrence at the top of other unions see, for example, the editorial in the ASE *Monthly Report*, April 1899, p. 5.
[48] Dockworkers ADM, May 1896, p. 17. Similarly the resulting circular, p. 37.
[49] Councillor Jephcott's speech from the chair to ASE Handsworth dinner, reported in ASE *Monthly Report*, May 1899, p. 76.

exploitation seemed, the more nostalgically did a certain trade-unionist rhetoric treat the more familiar face-to-face paternalism. 'Is not the individuality of the employer being lost in the company, and the company in the ring, the trusts and the syndicates which will form the great monoplies?' asked a vice-president of Sheffield Trades Council during a 'frequently applauded' speech to Wrexham Ironfounders. This was not always incorrect, but the sight of the faster-moving USA could encourage telescopings and overgeneralisations.[50]

The USA in fact, served both as a warning and as a competitor enforcing emulation. Dyer of the EFEA might sincerely deny, to the *Times*, 'any desire ever to dictate to or to "smash" the men's union . . . only asking for similar consideration' from the union side. But by an unhappy symbolism, Dyer was himself American, and the leader of the London employers, Alexander Siemens, had obvious German links.[51]

Historians have long disputed the class nature of the Old Unions, the nature or existence of a 'labour aristocracy' and of any 'class bargain' reached with the employing classes during the mid-Victorian years. But union sources in the months during and after the engineering crisis resound with fears that employers were wrecking some vaguely defined underlying arrangement. These fears emphasise once more the depth of uncertainty felt by so many members about their unions. 'It is almost solely trade union action intelligently directed that has raised the British workman to the tolerably independent and self-respecting position he now occupies,' commented Bolton Trades Council – probably from the pen of the semi-Labour Councillor, Robert Toothill – during the engineering struggle, and 'any attempt to take [this away] raises in him a sense of indignant revolt'.[52]

Not surprisingly, the TUC Parliamentary Committee described the employers as 'attacking the rights of the working classes under the beneficient Combination Laws of the country'.[53] Nor need we be surprised that one enthusiastic General Secretary saw federation as 'equal to a new Charter to trade unionism'.[54]

---

[50] John Davidson at an FSI presentation, reported in the FSI *Monthly Report*, July 1898, p. 10. Albert E. Roxby, as candidate for Assistant Secretary, January 1900. ASE *Annual Report*, p. 2,309.
[51] On Siemens, information from Herr Bien of Siemens Museum, Munich, 7 April 1993.
[52] Bolton Trades Council, *Annual Report*, 1897, pp. 8f.
[53] ASE *The Lockout* . . . , p. 111.
[54] Dobson of the National Amalgamated Society of Enginemen, Cranemen, Boilermen and Firemen, *Annual Report*, 30 June 1898, p. 1.

By the late 1890s, many union members at all levels were talking as if their position was being threatened, if not already subverted. Whether the pessimism had political correlations is hard to say. Possibly, it came disproportionately from the 'centre' and 'left'. Within the Boilermakers' – the ASE's jealous rival – the leaders of the Yorkshire district, who were the most explicitly socialist, were also among those readiest to bury the inter-union hatchet in order to square up to 'this new attack of organised Capital', led by 'the union-smashing [Employers'] Federation'.[55]

Confusion and conflict in the unions

The very moderation of many trade unionists showed signs of being pushed into uncongenial territory. Their responses could sometimes read schizophrenically: 'If we are to die', quoted Ben Pickard, MP, during his presidential oration to the 1898 MFGB Annual Conference, 'We will die in a heap.' He went on:

The whole country will be laid idle together, so that if capitalists can live without workers and workers without capitalists, if everyone of us who are poor have to go to the workhouse and colliery owners to the Penitentiaries, all I can say is let the thing be done gloriously, because they say it's murder to kill one man, but all Bishops agree it's glorious to kill numbers. Now I wish to say the trade of the country being so good and prosperous we ought to make a spurt to get every man into the Union.

Pickard had sounded a Zulu War bugle: let British miners close ranks and bleed 'in a heap' at Isandhlwana. But a Nonconformist fart at bishops instantly condensed this rhetoric plop into the limpid common sense of a sliding-scale routine where no capitalist or Lib-Lab worker could conceivably 'live without' the other.

True, like any good peroration, its significance had been underlined beforehand. Pickard had just done two things. He had rebutted employers' accusations that the now desperately hard-pressed ASE wanted 'to manage the whole of the industrial workshops of the country' – or were demanding anything more than a list of 'fair' things. And he had grimly warned Colonel Dyer that 'the people of this country would not stand . . . [for importing] the Pinkerton System from America to watch and beset trade unionism'. But if so stolid a Lib-Lab mind as Pickard's could oscillate like this, what other minds might not?

The engineering crisis exposed other cracks in the union structure, which, to local activists, would have seemed more threatening. The

---

[55] Boilermakers' *Monthly Report*, September 1897, p. 32.

'machine question' impinged differently on different groups of workers, hence on different unions and sometimes contradictorily within the same union. Centrally, while Robert Knight of the Boilermakers led those forces within the Federation of Engineering and Shipbuilding Trades (FEST) that were against joining the eight-hours campaign, he found himself bitterly opposed within his own union by minorities whose size seems to have shaken him – as we saw at Canning Town.

Knight's instructions to his London members soon after the start of the struggle were clearly to withdraw from the eight-hours committee and, thereby, to accept an actual lengthening of their official working day. He seems to have been unanimously upheld by the leaders of the FEST unions, who were dominated by the Boilermakers, to much the same extent that the Allied Trades were by the ASE, and, at a ratio of 7½ to 1, by a subsequent vote of his own membership.[56] But the London reaction exploded at the Canning Town meeting in October. Here, Knight was trying to defend his agreement with the employers – an agreement which embodied and symbolised the Boilermakers' withdrawal. .

From its side, the ASE affected to be mystified since the Boilermakers' London 'District Representatives [had been] in entire harmony with the proceedings of the Joint Committee . . . The other members of the Joint Committee were therefore under the impression that the Boilermakers were with them.' Ominously, though, the Patternmakers had already withdrawn. With this in mind, an ASE writer snarled rather impotently at the 'small sectional unions with which the Engineering Trade [was] pestered'.[57]

In his turn, Mosses, the Patternmakers' leader and historian could 'not . . . too strongly emphasise and reiterate, that the abstention [from April 1897] of our London members from the eight-hours movement was the result of their deliberate choice.' His Executive felt able to describe the results of a London ballot in May on whether to rejoin the movement as 'beneath contempt' and later to 'refuse to be rushed', when 'many . . . members', chiefly from London and Manchester, were – with lockout newly upon them – 'seized with panic'.

In a national ballot, 57 per cent of members – 'under the circumstances', he thought, 'an extraordinarily large proportion' – came down against rejoining the struggle. Histories written from head office – and Mosses could hardly be a more extreme specimen – are hardly likely to exaggerate opposition from less exalted spheres. But this boast that

[56] Boilermakers' *Monthly Report*, August, September, 1897.
[57] ASE *The Lockout . . .* , p. 4. *Monthly Report*, editorial for April 1898, p. 2.

societies such as his were 'small, compact . . . and easily manoeuvred' was precisely one of the ASE's objections to them.[58] With even 'kindred' trades in such unkithlike disarray, and with Knight on the TUC's Parliamentary Committee, Wood's slowness, as its secretary, to initiate exceptional expedients for the engineers becomes all the more understandable. But worse, his own refusal may itself have been tinged with sectionalism. Under attack at the TUC, he pointed out that 'when 300,000 miners were on strike Congress scarcely moved a vote of sympathy':[59] Woods was, of course, a miners' leader.

The 'Trade Union Sedan': the defeat of the engineers

By late 1897 the engineers' position was grave. The financial response from trade unionists was uneven, though immense. This is clear from most trades council and union records and from the ASE's subsequent account. From socialists – a much smaller base – a similar story emerges. Even many trade unionists opposed to the ASE's strategy subscribed their share.[60]

A growing number of unions and trades councils demanded that the TUC convene an emergency conference to aid the engineers. Some also demanded that it 'suggest some scheme for future guidance' – not necessarily for federation but for responding to similar treatment from employers in other industries. As we have seen, such contingencies were expected to arise soon. The Parliamentary Committee's routinism brought the inevitable crop of condemnations.[61]

Emergency gatherings had to be organised from elsewhere. Two national conferences were organised from and held in London: one by the Society of Compositors, the other by the Trades Council. In the first case, a public meeting was held in Exeter Hall on 25 October.

[58] Mosses, *History*, pp. 137, 131.
[59] NAOP *Monthly Report*, September 1898, p. 26. Delegates' report.
[60] From the ASE's figures (in *The Lockout* . . . , p. 13) the *Clarion*'s subscriptions – £2,101 – amounted to about 45 per cent of all those from newspaper readers. The *Daily Chronicle* came second with £1,748 and the *Star* a poor third. *Labour Leader* was a poor sixth, but ILP branches – unlike those of the SDF – contributed a respectable £455. For contrasts between the *Clarion*, ILP and SDF efforts and attitudes, see L. J. W. Barrow, 'The Socialism of Robert Blatchford and the *Clarion* Newspaper, 1889–1914', DPhil, University of London, 1975, pp. 337ff. An example of opponents of the ASE strategy subscribing is the Aberdeen branch of the UPMA *Minute Book*, 24 August, 7 September 1897.
[61] OBS EC 13 December 1897. Prominent among the critics were Sexton of the National Union of Dock Labourers, and Curran of the Gasworkers. Sexton protested at the LTC conference – though 'previous question'-ed. Report by Thorne to the Gasworkers' *Quarterly Report*, 31 December 1897, pp. 22–5.

Subsequently, the Society was to note merely that the meeting was well attended despite short notice, that it showed 'throughout . . . great enthusiasm' and – three months later – that little financial help had come from other London union branches.[62]

Much less shadowy, but in its results more controversial, was the London Trades Council (LTC) conference on 1 January 1898 in the Memorial Hall, Farringdon. Said to represent 'considerably over one million' members from 112 trade unions and trades councils, the participants unanimously agreed to recommend a levy of 3d per member per week for the duration of the struggle, to be remitted via the TUC Parliamentary Committee.[63]

The *Railway Review* believed the conference 'an unqualified success', comprising 'fully two hundred delegates . . . representing one and a quarter million workers'.[64] But the disagreements began with the implementation of this decision. The ASE reported that 'the meeting was one of great enthusiasm, and much was expected from it; but . . . instead of increased support there was a decided falling off in voluntary subscriptions.' One instance would be the Associated Iron Moulders of Scotland. Its EC presumed, correctly, on the members' wish to be represented at the Memorial Hall, at a time when it seems to have believed a settlement to be likely. But after the conference – to which it had wished well – it pleaded that it had already done enough for the engineers.[65]

In any case, the ASE gave the disappointment as its final reason for calling the struggle off. Many outsiders saw this as a 'sudden collapse' and some continued to believe that 'a few more weeks would have proved a success for the ASE.' 'This disaster', recalled the secretary of the Derby Trades Council some months later,[66] 'frightened thousands of timid members out of the ranks . . . a blow on [*sic*] trade unionism from which it will not recover for a long time.' Many ASE members felt that outsiders to this decision included themselves. Towards the end of the year, for

---

62 These efforts, together with later meetings on national federation, complicate claims such as G. Stedman Jones's – in *Journal of Social History* (NY, no. 4, 1974), that London unionism had by now lost its national pre-eminence. Similarly the LTC's national efforts for the Danish workers later on: OBS *Monthly Report*. Reported to the EC of 15 October. London Society of Compositors (LSC), *Quarterly Report*, 3 November 1897, pp. 16f.; 2 February 1898, p. 5.

63 OBS delegation's report to EC, 3 January 1898. ASE *The Lockout . . .* , p. 13. BSSAA EC, 21 January 1898. General Secretary's report of the conference.

64 *Railway Review*, 7 January 1898, p. 1.

65 ASE *The Lockout . . .* , p. 13. AIMS, *Monthly Report*, January 1898, pp. 181f.

66 A Midlands FSI DC in the FSI *Monthly Report*, February 1898, p. 11. Derby and District Trades Council *Annual Report* for 1898.

example, one candidate for a District Delegacy crudely hinted at treachery on the EC. In the context of the Society's recently much-democratised structure, he saw the Executive as unconstitutional in terminating the dispute without again consulting the members.[67] Whatever the variations in blame, many trade unionists must have viewed the future as threatening even larger confrontations. A few imagined that the next depression would bring the EFEA's collapse,[68] but more would have agreed with one railwayman that a depression would rather allow the employers to give trade unionism 'a severe and relentless thrashing'.[69] So we must note at once that these predictions were not to come true.

Of course, the situation varied from industry to industry, but generally the early and middle 1900s were to prove noticeably quiet, so far as strike figures can indicate. Not that the employers' offensive – such as it had been – simply dissolved. But rather it occurred in different arenas, notably the courts. Judgements such as Taff Vale were certainly to threaten union power as much as, say, any late-1890s lockout. Yet, as is well-known, its most visible aftermath was not industrial but political – in strengthening support for Labour Representation. Richard Price has indeed argued that employers – in both industrial and legal confrontations – aimed consciously at strengthening the official union procedures at the expense of the unofficial.[70]

The more this is so, the more strikingly it relates to the developments on which this book focusses. Most ironically of all, the more trade unionists girded themselves to face frontal attack, the more they could and did underestimate the subtlety of the threat they faced. In any case, even had few employers the sophistication which Price imputes to them, there were more mundane reasons for them to have recourse to the courts so soon after the end of the engineering struggle. Legal action against picketing and other union methods was one of the few matters on which a wide range of employers agreed. Beyond this, the Employers' Parliamentary Committee (EPC) like some of its related organisations was too much a 'loose federation of threatened interests', in one historian's words,[71] each with differing priorities. Further, Wemyss was too militant for many of his fellow-employers. Though some had previously been ready to smile on 'responsible' unionism,

[67] Michael Johnston, election address for Organising District Delegacy of no. 1 District, ASE circular, November 1898, p. 5.
[68] Steam Engine Makers' Society, Annual Report, for 1897, p. 17.
[69] Ted Good, Railway Review, 20 January 1899.
[70] Price, Masters, p. 196.
[71] Soldon, 'Laissez Faire', p. 227. For disunity see generally pp. 225–8.

their hardening had been less extreme than his, though no less important. Around 1900, the economic situation did not force employers into militancy so crudely as many unionists seem to have believed. The dark hints of the *Railway Review* at EFEA and EPC 'private confabulations with Cabinet Ministers'[72] were not to prove of obvious relevance for very long. Even conciliation was in the air, with a Conservative President of the Board of Trade proposing 'a National Conciliation Board of employers and workmen, acting as an appeal court'.[73] To judge from entries in union minute books it was well-noticed, though not always seen as very important. And as Soldon, the historian we have just quoted points out, it was the employers who rejected this.[74]

While the industrial recovery smoothed employers' avoidance of strategic confrontation, it also soothed many members' fears and localised their activism. Thus, though Mosses, the Patternmakers' leader, was to remember, 'the numbing effect of the engineers' hours dispute' as having been 'felt for some months after January' 1898, 'the general condition of the trade throughout the year was good'.[75] Generally, in engineering, the trend in most areas seems to have been one of recovery. 'Nearly all trace of the lockout has disappeared,' Barnes was able to announce in mid-1898.[76]

Subsequently, even in Lancashire, one of the Society's oldest members felt he could contrast the 'stampede' back to work after the 1852 lockout with the 'grim determination and almost complete confidence in each other and in their leaders' displayed, he alleged, after the 1897–8 one.[77] That 'confidence' may also have had something to do with the economic situation. Knight, during March 1898, could hear 'a busy hum from all quarters' and could 'scarcely believe it possible that in so short a time the dense darkness should have given place to sunshine and prosperity'.[78]

For the ASE itself, recovery certainly took place. By the end of 1898 it had been able to repay 'the whole of [its] loans incurred during the late dispute and to start the New Year free of debts'.[79]

Plainly, not all areas or sectors or unions recovered simultaneously. But the overall impression was of a recovery which contrasts glaringly

---

[72] *Railway Review*, 27 January 1899, p. 1.   [73] *Daily Chronicle*, 13 January 1899.
[74] Soldon, 'Laissez Faire', p. 227.
[75] Mosses, *History*, pp. 143–7.
[76] ASE *Quarterly Report*, June 1898, p. 2, 'General Secretary's Statement'.
[77] Isaac Nelson, who had joined aged 22 in 1853.
[78] Knight in Boilermakers' *Monthly Report*, March 1898, p. 23; May 1898, p. 17. Similarly, five pages later, the reporter for 'Scotch shipbuilding'.
[79] OBS *Monthly Report*, January 1899. Similarly, ASE *Jubilee Souvenir*, 1901, p. 109. Formal date of repayment to the OBS – 30 December 1898.

with the years following other defeats or retreats such as the early 1870s, the early 1890s or the early 1920s. For whatever an economic overview is worth, the indices assembled by, for example, Cole[80] suggest that economic downswings were not assertive until 1902–3. Given this context, Barnes would be able to remember the impact of the 1897–8 engineering struggle in terms of personal rather than institutional collapse:

of fourteen members of the Employers' executive, more than half of them were dead in a few months, including Colonel Dyer, their resourceful and indefatigable President, and two of my immediate colleagues died soon after from the strain. I had perforce to go away for some weeks. I had my first trip abroad.[81]

1899 inaugurated the trend with 'the lowest total yet recorded' of days lost through industrial disputes.[82]

Admittedly, the ASE's long-fought defeat weakened some unionists' belief in the power of industrial action. But the manner of its end allowed others, not least Blatchford drawing a pro-federation moral from 'The Trade-Union Sedan',[83] to believe in it all the more – on their stipulation that organisation be speedily placed on a firmer footing and 'leaders' cut down to size. Particularly while employers seemed a major threat, interest in federating unions was likely to grow. As one ASEer concluded, 'Federation gave victory to the employers, and want of it gave defeat to the men'.[84]

---

[80] G. D. H. Cole, *A Short History of the British Working Class Movement, 1787–1947* (London, 1952), pp. 27ff.
[81] J. N. Barnes, *From Workshop to War Cabinet* (London, 1924).
[82] *Report of Labour Correspondent . . . 1897*, p. iii.
[83] *Clarion*, 29 January 1898.
[84] 'Paw Chuck', ASE *Monthly Report*, April 1898, pp. 28f.

6 The rise and fall of the *Clarion* federation

It was one thing to conclude that federation by employers could and should be countered by trade union federation; quite another to say how this might be accomplished. And much harder still to turn it into reality. This chapter will look at the only major attempt ever made. This in itself would be more than reason enough for it being our most detailed; here, the anti-bureaucratic impulses which fill much of this book were to power an attempted reorganisation and, some activists hoped, revolutionising of their whole movement. Another reason is that, without proper discussion of that attempt, all existing versions of British working people's history remain more or less distortive.

The late 1890s were characterised by a cacophony of schemes for changing the interrelation of trade unions. Debates on them often developed into a war of each against all. Apart from the ups and downs within the Amalgamated Society of Railway Servants, the main surface-events consist of various inter-union conferences.

Some of these were extraordinary, such as the 'Federal Labour Parliament' (FLP) in July 1898 which founded NIGFTLU, or the spectacular event which aborted discussion on federation at the September 1898 TUC. This allowed the TUC's Parliamentary Committee to postpone matters to a special Congress in January 1899. During the intervening months, the PC moved to undermine NIGFTLU. Some members and leading supporters of the PC resorted to bureaucratic manoeuvrings. Others encouraged inertia. Many more encouraged a fear that the adoption of any scheme but the TUC's – particularly the *Clarion* scheme – would split the whole movement, or certainly disorganise it.

The war of the schemes

This fear was easily spread, for it spoke to trade unionists of any politics. Indeed, many socialists were likely to be more than usually sensitive to such fears. For, particularly during these very months, many ILP trade

109

unionists were trying to bring about a 'Labour Alliance' between the ILP
and the unions, in which union funds would pay for the sending of
independent working class MPs to Parliament.

One can also note that:

1. the 1898 FLP had a representation claimed for it of between 350,000
   and 750,000 – the higher figure (a highly unlikely one) being
   equivalent to roughly half the TUC's own affiliated membership

but that

2. the special January 1899 TUC adopted the TUC's own scheme with
   an initial representation of 340,000.

Finally,

3. the NIGFTLU's executive *seems never to have met.*

By September–October 1899, King and the members of his EC were
roundly blaming each other for this non-event. The EC's accusations
escalated from indecisiveness – in King's fixing of the venue – into hints
of embezzlement; his, into charges that some EC members were doing
everything to undermine his whole scheme from within. He was surely
correct about some, but it is very hard to say how early or energetically
this undermining began.

The 'Clarion' scheme

The alliance of P. J. King with the *Clarion* 'gave the boom' to the movement for federation.[1] At the least, it prepared the ground. That King's
scheme was usually known as the *Clarion* scheme was sometimes said to
have cost him much support, as we shall see. Yet, however unpopular the
Clarion platform in many quarters, it was a national one. From early in
1896[2] as 'an unpaid Agitator' – apparently a compositor's mistake for
'unattached agitator' which was soon dropped – King expounded his
scheme through the year with long intermissions. Throughout 1897, he
expounded it almost weekly.

During these two years, when he might have remained in obscurity as
one of a number of ex-secretaries of recently-defunct unions, he gained
prominence by writing a pamphlet jointly with Blatchford, recently
famous as the author of *Merrie England* – to this day the most successful
socialist book in the English language. In the *Clarion*, Blatchford not only
praised King, but paid him the very *Clarion*, because ironic, compliment
of serialising most of two weeks' worth of King's writing over

[1] Joseph Burgess in the *Manchester Weekly News*, 3 February 1899.
[2] *Clarion*, 8 February 1896.

Blatchford's own pen-name of "Nunquam".[3] Later, when many were to agree that this alliance had brought the question of a national federation to the fore, even one author of a rival scheme admitted that 'a vast majority of trade unionists' had seen 'the table by which Mr King illustrates his lectures' – surely an exaggeration, but an indicative one.[4]

Moves in the *Clarion*'s favour seem to have begun before the 1897 TUC. To take an instance where these were contained more or less from the start, representatives of the London Society of Compositors (LSC) were at a fairly well attended meeting where 'after the *Clarion* scheme had been fully explained and certain of its details criticised, a Committee was appointed to devise the best means of giving effect to [it], with instructions to report to the various trades at an early date.' It is unclear whether this occasion was a London-wide one or wider. But the LSC's *Quarterly Review* saw it as anyway superseded by the engineers' emergency. While this had 'undoubtedly emphasised the need of some sound and far-reaching scheme of federation', it might 'also have diverted attention . . . from the "Clarion" and similar schemes.'[5] In any case, this Society went ahead with its own version, while recommending a locally structured kindred trades' federation as a start.

But during the autumn of 1897, with the engineering struggle, King's impact accelerated. One typical course of development was epitomised on Edinburgh Trades Council, where the proposer of a motion, at the end of November, for a committee to be set up to examine the *Clarion* scheme, had himself, four weeks earlier, persuaded the Council to call on the TUC's Parliamentary Committee to organise a conference 'to take into consideration the . . . means of defending the right of combination', which he saw as under threat.[6] The Trades Council passed both proposals, and the report of the resultant committee marked the start of its seven months' commitment to the *Clarion* scheme.

In the short term, the *Clarion* scheme enjoyed two advantages. Within the late-1890s federation boom, it was the first. More important, it seemed fresh. 'For thirty years, this question has been before trade unionists and I believe', declared one ASE activist, 'that at no time has such a scheme been submitted.'[7] Did the freshness lie more in the scheme's content or in its packaging? There was King and Blatchford's

---

[3] *Clarion*, 16, 23 January. See also 15 February 1896.
[4] Thomas Horrocks in ASE *Monthly Report*, June 1898, p. 12.
[5] London Society of Compositors, *Quarterly Report*, 3 November 1897, p. 21.
[6] Edinburgh and District Trades and Labour Council, *Minute Book*, 2; 30 November 1897.
[7] George Wilson of Swindon. Bound with ASE *Monthly Report*. Selections for Organising District Delegacies, p. 14, no. 8 Division.

emphasis on extreme democracy. There was Blatchford's famously persuasive style. There were what one might call King's 'three equalities' – equality of contributions, of benefits, of representation.

For King, writing just a few weeks before the founding conference of NIGFTLU, the federation was to be much more than a mutual strike fund. It was to be a major part of a qualitatively different kind of trade union movement:

> Our mode of procedure will differ from that of the Trades Congress quite as much as the mode of government of the United States differs from that of Russia . . .
> The Trade Unions of this country must no longer be manipulated and controlled by a bureaucracy . . . The initiative and referendum will do much to check the abuses of irresponsible persons. We shall no longer see a few well-paid and well-groomed officials thwarting the wishes of the overwhelming majority of the men who give them their salaries and look after their interests.[8]

There would be only two full-time officials – president and secretary – assisted by a lay executive. The decisions of the annual delegate meeting, the Federal Labour Parliament, were to be 'submitted to the general body for confirmation'.[9]

But did the scheme amount to such a substantive innovation? Both as advocated and as adopted, it writ many of the contradictions of the time large.[10] Thus, aside from its 'four-nation' structure – which guaranteed at least one Executive member for England, Ireland, Scotland and Wales – its greatest innovation was its referendum provisions which gave members the power to ratify all the proceedings of the Federal Labour Parliament and, between EC meetings, to decide whether to aid member organisations. These provisions were obviously cumbersome, particularly during a struggle. For example, the majority of a union's executive applying for aid had to sign a long list of details about their predicament. This unwieldiness would have probably increased the rôle of the Federation's secretary during crises. The secretary was to be elected at the FLP as were the members of the executive. They, however, were to control the appointing of other national officers. In affiliated unions the rôle of national officials was supposedly safeguarded: there was a

---

8 *Clarion*, 25 June 1898.
9 *Clarion*, 12 March 1898.
10 P. J. King and R. Blatchford, *Trade Union Federation*, 1897. P. J. King, *Good and Bad Federation: The 'Clarion' Scheme more fully Developed and Explained, Alternative Schemes Examined, Criticisms of the 'Clarion' Scheme Answered*, 1898 (*Clarion* Pamphlets). Minutes of Federal Labour Parliament, 1898. P. J. King, *Federation in a Nutshell (With the Rules of the National and International General Federation of Trade and Labour Unions, as adopted at the Federal Labour Parliament at Manchester 18–20 July 1898)* 1898.

provision that 'business . . . be transacted through [each union's] Executive'.

Conflicting interpretations were soon read into the rules on finance, and would probably have asserted themselves had the Federation ever got seriously off the ground. One example would be the pool or 'guarantee fund', which Horrocks (for whom see later) was to pounce on. As amended at the Parliament,[11] there was a low minimum and a high maximum rate of contribution. The low minimum was explicitly designed to attract 'financially weak' organisations – 'the longer they took to contribute to the pool, the longer they would remain out of benefit'.[12] But King then sweetened this lack of benefit by envisaging, in his hopeful way, the weak ones 'coming to arrangements with other federated unions' to receive benefits after all.

And yet, another rule adopted the same day, stipulated that 'the minimum amount [of payment to the guarantee fund] must not be accepted unless it enables the Federation to pay all members engaged in a strike or lockout a weekly sum sufficient to enable them to live in the same degree of comfort as they were accustomed to when in full work.'[13] The most charitable comment is that young organisations seldom take root in tight logical corners – particularly when given such tall growing-orders as the NIGFTLU. As King himself remarked against a rival scheme: 'Federations that depend solely on the enthusiasm of those connected with them must fail.'[14]

Questions of practicality apart, it is easy to see why King's scheme was unwelcome in conservatively-minded quarters. Since membership of the federation was to be open to union branches – and even, as originally conceived, to individual members – it represented a by-passing of the existing trade union structure in at least three different ways. The basis of membership would mean that branches could by-pass their own unions' delegate meetings; the use of the referendum would limit the power of the federation's own delegate meeting; and the whole scheme was being foisted on the trade unions from 'outside', via a socialist newspaper.

The major rival: the 'official scheme'

The *Clarion*'s was not the only scheme attracting interest. Its main rival was the TUC's. The debate at the 1897 Trades Union Congress had

---

[11] Minutes of Federal Labour Parliament 1898, pp. 27, 30, 21.
[12] John Hodges of the Steel Smelters. Minutes of Federal Labour Parliament 1898, p. 21.
[13] Minutes of Federal Labour Parliament 1898, pp. 20–1.   [14] *Clarion*, 3 April 1897.

been in many senses a foretaste. Interest in federation had evidently been rekindled: five unions had submitted motions. After Clarke of the GRWU had moved a composite motion – seconded by Dipper, the socialist and docker – Isaac Mitchell of the ASE had drawn cheers for declaring that federation would already have won the eight hours struggle. Mitchell claimed to have 'instructions' from the engineers of Scotland 'to do his utmost to bring about a scheme of federation'.

For the long term, however, this debate was less significant for enthusiasm than for tensions. First, Mitchell himself managed a passing blow at the Engineering and Shipbuilding Federation (FEST). Secondly, all the miners' representatives abstained: thus the mere one vote, at the end, against the resolution was deceptive. Thirdly, when it passed, J. Havelock Wilson, the now very conservative leader of the seamen, at once demanded that no less than £400 be collected to pay the expenses of the newly constituted TUC Federation Committee before it could so much as meet. True, he was brushed aside from the Chair.

But, fourthly, the chairman himself triggered the most demoralising episode of all. He tried to remove three New Unionists from this committee, on the grounds that they all represented building workers. Had not Congress just resolved – 'without discussion', according to the minutes – to elect no more than one delegate from each trade to the committee? And did not each of the three – John Ward of the Navvies, McCarthy of the Dockers and Clynes of the Gasworkers – have some building workers amongst their members? This pedantry brought on 'a very disorderly scene, which lasted for more than ten minutes'. In the end, the trio were replaced by a Blacksmith, a Tailor and by W. H. Drew of the Textile Workers. Drew had been a pioneer of the Bradford ILP. Coincidentally or not, he was at once removed on similar grounds and replaced by Hornidge of the Boot and Shoe Operatives.[15]

Whether for tactical reasons or from clumsiness, the nearly ten-year-old animosities between 'Old' and 'New' unionists had been revived. By contrast, the Minutes of the Parliamentary Committee after the 1897 TUC resound with harmony. In October Thorne found himself in a minority of two with Chandler of the ASC&J in moving that the first meeting of the new Federation Committee be convened merely to 'be notified that unless sufficient [more?; indistinct] money comes in for the purpose no further meetings of that Committee be held'.

His being outvoted suggests that the rest of the PC, at least by

---

[15] 1897 TUC Minutes, p. 47. The chairman was J. V. Stevens, a Liberal who was President of the Amalgamated Tinplate Workers. The *Dictionary of Labour Biography* claims that he 'conducted business with admirable competence'.

October, had appreciated that direct obstruction *à la* Havelock Wilson had become untactical. In February 1898 the same duo, Thorne and Chandler, were to move a grant – all of £5, or just one-eightieth of the sum we have seen Wilson, obstructively, proposing – to the Federation Committee. The most cynical construction one can put on their switch is that the engineering crisis had made *formal* implementation of Congress resolutions the wisest policy.[16] One can certainly infer that the crisis-month of December found the Committee relatively hard at work.[17]

The results of its labours were meeker than King's. King's plans for what he called a 'Fighting type of federation made a show of tackling many contingencies – *too much arithmetic in it for him!!* as King scornfully italicised one leading trade unionist.[18] The TUC's often left these unposed. It therefore made a less ambiguous impression in the long run. As King and Professor Phelps-Brown have both observed, a few weeks of sizeable industrial solidarity would have bankrupted it. Compared with the *Clarion* scheme it was, in King's phrase 'penny wise and pound foolish' – by a factor as high as twelve.[19]

Constitutionally, what became the General Federation of Trade Unions contrasted with King's potentially disruptive democratism by clearly vesting almost everything in the executives of the member unions. These appointed its 'Management Committee', subject to a vaguely empowered annual 'General Council'.[20] As Pelling remarks, 'it was not a Federation, but simply a committee controlling a fund, and it never became general'.[21] Its Management Committee controlled the granting of benefit – to be decided within seven days of application. While stipulating that 'all business must be conducted through the Executives of the respective Societies', it did provide 'for the votes of members to be taken should a larger contribution [be] required for any special purposes'.[22] As for local involvement, it had no pretensions to the NIGFTLU's four-nation structure, though it did provide for District Committees, with 'two Delegates from each Society located in the District'.[23]

[16] TUC PC Minutes, 12 October 1897; 8 February 1898.
[17] See account on p. 179 of the 1898 *Labour Annual*, which clearly went to press before the struggle was over.
[18] *Clarion*, 18 June 1898.
[19] E. H. Phelps-Brown, *The Growth of British Industrial Relations* (London, 1965) pp. 284ff. King, *Good and Bad Federation*, pp. 18–21.
[20] Report of the January 1899 TUC, pp. 18, 26; Clause V6.
[21] Pelling, p. 113. B. C. M. Weekes, 'The ASE, 1880–1914: A Study of Trade Union Development and Industrial Policy', PhD thesis, University of Warwick, 1970, p. 149.
[22] Report of the January 1899 TUC, p. 26: Rule III 1, Rule V6, Rule VII.
[23] For King's criticisms on all aspects, see P. J. King, *Trades Federation, the Official Scheme. A Crushing Criticism*. 1899 (*Clarion* Pamphlet).

For this and other reasons the TUC's scheme was to be the winner – and, as the GFTU, still is. But this increases the irony that it was initially greeted with uproarious contempt, and this during the peaking of labour movement interest in federation during the early and middle part of 1898[24] – around the time the seemingly doomed scheme came out. It appeared not merely to have 'signally failed among the majority of trade unionists',[25] but actually to be plumbing the depths of unpopularity. Its main weaknesses were financial. Here, for once, King seems to have had most trade unionists agreeing with him. It was a 'milk and water scheme', said the chairman of the ASC&J's General Council during June, concurring with his members' rejection of it. A criticism along these lines came even from the GFTU's future general secretary, Isaac Mitchell.[26] And his sentiments were voiced up and down the movement: 'unworthy of serious consideration' (a Woodworkers' branch secretary and president in Aberdeen), 'mere playing at federation' (a delegate at the Scottish TUC), 'totally inadequate' (Darlington Trades Council), 'cumbersome' (the ASE's *Journal*), and indeed 'a millstone round our necks' (a Gateshead engineer).[27]

Some critics of the TUC scheme even persuaded themselves that it had died of this scorn. At a conference on federation called by the London Society of Compositors (LSC) during the spring of 1898, many were to warm to King's announcement that even Sam Woods himself 'had thrown over the Parliamentary Committee scheme, and expressed himself that it would not be accepted'.[28] King was not alone in his optimism; from nearer the anti-*Clarion* end of the union spectrum, one Belfast Pattern-Maker believed it 'quite evident . . . that the official scheme had been shelved'. Similarly the next month, during a discussion within the Carpenters and Joiners, one motion already assumed that the

---

24 Thus sixty-five branch resolutions had reached the OBS's executive by early June – with, admittedly, a 'considerable' number 'opposed to the [whole] question of federation'; the triennial General Council of the smaller ASC&J attracted thirteen resolutions for the *Clarion* scheme, almost twice the total for any of the others. Operative Bricklayers' Society, *Monthly Report*, November 1898, p. 18.
25 Liverpool and Vicinity United Trades and Labour Council, *Annual Report* for 1897–8, p. 7.
26 ASC&J, General Council Minutes, June 1898, p. 4. ASE *Monthly Report*, April 1897, pp. 17ff.
27 ASW, Aberdeen no. 2 Branch *Minute Book*, 24 April 1898. Scottish TUC Minutes, 1898; ASE *Monthly Report*, May 1898, p. 15 and November 1898, p. 18; ASRS General Secretary's Report till 12 September 1898; similarly a year later (i.e. even after the GFTU had been born) the EC of the BSSAA 'after considerable discussion' decided it was 'useless . . . to take a vote of the membership' on the TUC scheme which would 'never' be sound actuarially. EC Minutes of 21 April 1899.
28 *Daily Chronicle*, 25 April 1898.

coming TUC would reject the scheme, irrespective of the Parliamentary Committee's advice. And again, two months later, and still before the 1898 TUC, the LSC itself seems to have been inviting unions to another meeting 'assuming that the [TUC's] resolution . . . re federation be lost'. Bowerman, the London Compositors' venerable secretary who sent the invitations, was himself on the PC.[29]

The Amalgamated Society of Railway Servants' (ASRS) *Railway Review* was most scornful of all, and, given its weekly circulation of nearly 40,000,[30] the most quoted. Its temporary editor tore into the scheme as a 'miserable failure', a 'chargeless blunderbus that nobody will handle' and spoke of the 'hilarity and undisguised amusement with which the general body of workers regard it': they had 'nothing but pity for the unfortunate existence to which it is fated until such time as the next TUC mercifully strangles it'. When Woods, so bombarded, merely quibbled in reply that the Parliamentary Committee was not the same body as the Federation Committee, the *Review* – like King – read him as disowning the scheme – 'and this, if nothing else, should seal the fate of the Committee's proposals'. Its own journalistic onslaught, it claimed, had 'drawn forth a chorus of unanimous approval and grateful acknowledgement from branches all over the kingdom'.[31]

In the light of all this, it will be no surprise that one reason the London Compositors' May circular gave for organising its own federation conference was that the TUC scheme had 'already been rejected by many societies'. Of course, there were exceptions, though at this stage only one – the Associated Iron and Steel Workers of Great Britain – seems to have rejected the TUC scheme as too ambitious.[32] But, as we shall see, once the scheme became the General Federation of Trade Unions, quite a number did. Even less surprising will seem the claim, in August, by Thomas Horrocks the author of another scheme, that at the following month's Congress the 'official scheme' would have to 'give way against the overwhelming weight of adverse criticism that has arisen'. 'It did not matter so much which scheme was adopted, so long as it was a workable one', Margaret Bondfield proclaimed to cheers at a large meeting on federation.[33]

---

[29] FEST AM Minutes, May 1898, p. 14. Collins, who regretted the *Clarion* scheme's popularity. AS of Litho Printers, EC *Minute Book*, 30 June 1898. ASC&J, GC Minutes, 4 August 1898, p. 108.
[30] ASRS General Secretary's Quarterly Report till 13 June 1898.
[31] *Railway Review*, 18 March 1898, p. 8; 25 March 1898, p. 1.
[32] *Ironworkers' Journal*, December 1898, p. 4.
[33] ASE *Monthly Report*, August 1898, p. 15; *Daily Chronicle*, 25 April 1898.

The other schemes

Her ruthless pragmatism was widely shared because sorely needed. How sorely, is something one can appreciate by examining these other schemes. Whether or not they were all strikingly inferior to the *Clarion*'s and/or the TUC's, their very proliferation condemned nearly all to an early death and, even more important, explains the growing urge to make a start on almost *any* scheme so long as it did not distract or even disrupt trade unionism further. In the end, this urge was to help win the day for the TUC against the *Clarion*. And it may well have been expressed already by Bondfield and her audience.

Numerous other schemes were proposed. The London Trades Council had heard King on his scheme at its November 1897 meeting and had appointed a small committee 'to assist following it up'.[34] It seems to have been little circulated, though by mid-January 1899 it was still being discussed in Huddersfield and rejected by Aberdeen Trades Council's Executive on the comprehensive grounds 'that it would necessitate levies, [was] not democratic enough in its management . . . financially weak, and would be unable to undertake its liability'.[35] The scheme probably only achieved a very partial circulation.[36]

A number of other schemes attracted even smaller amounts of support. That of John Eyre, a prominent member of the General Union of Associated Power Loom Overlookers, was ambiguously supported from the top of the Friendly Society of Ironfounders, mainly as a counter to the *Clarion*'s. For the same reason, it was supported by Keir Hardie's *Labour Leader*, though, very wisely, that paper never became so completely identified with Eyre's scheme as the *Clarion* did with King's. The Ironfounders' *Monthly Review* excused itself as 'not at liberty' to publish the *Clarion* or Eyre schemes, but published the latter four months later, after reprinting Sidebotham's scheme which it preferred to either of the others. East London Ironfounders subsequently recommended Eyre's scheme as, for their Society, the most feasible.[37]

Possibly this was because it comprised 'seven classes of benefits and contributions', according to an Engineer who felt this 'a thing sufficient in itself to condemn it'. The same writer also saw it as 'mostly a rehash

---

[34] LSC *Annual Report* for 1896, p. 28. The LSC's delegate thought this scheme to be 'on the surface a good one'. LSC *Annual Report* for 1898, p. 27.

[35] Huddersfield Trades and Labour Council, *Minute Book*, 15 February 1899 (Huddersfield Central Library) Aberdeen Trades Council, *Minute Book*, 15 February 1899.

[36] Though this included 200 copies being bought by Glasgow Trades Council for 8s 4d, *Annual Report* for 1898–9, p. 20.

[37] FSI, *Monthly Report*, December 1897; March 1898; May 1898, p. 11.

of the *Clarion* scheme with all its defects' – a point, minus the last four words, with which King frequently and heartily concurred.[38] Eyre's scheme, claimed Sidebotham while introducing his own, was 'more in consonance with trade union principles' but 'require[d] time for development' – unlike, of course, Sidebotham's.

Sidebotham's own scheme was, he conceded, 'rough and ready', though its author countered that the *Clarion*'s, despite its greater age, was still 'very complicated and admittedly incomplete'.[39] But his seems to have been open to more serious criticism. One critic, possibly a *Clarion* supporter, complained that it had 'no guarantee [fund] whatever' and without such a mechanism a union might conceivably milk the federation without itself contributing more than an entry fee.[40] Also, as noted earlier, Sidebotham's provisions for representation disenfranchised the smaller unions, such as his own. His scheme was generally less flexible – but therefore, some would have said, less tricky – than the *Clarion*'s. It even provided for a permanent daily committee.

At least within his own ASE – though in addition someone somewhere got out a 'circular on Mr Horrocks' scheme'[41] – Thomas Horrocks of Bury no. 1 Branch was among the most vocal of those authoring schemes of minor significance. But apart from a Bury Federation Committee, it is hard to discover who else he persuaded. Having had his own pamphlet published – though, judging from one complaint, inefficiently distributed[42] – he was able to spend most of four very long letters in the ASE's *Monthly Report* between May and August attacking the *Clarion*'s. Judging from Horrocks's criticisms of the TUC, *Clarion* and Eyre schemes, he saw his own as ensuring simultaneously equal and high benefits, plus fairness to small societies. So its arithmetic may have been hair-raising.

Also within the ASE was the Woolwich Federation Committee, which met more than twenty times to distil the available schemes into its own which attracted a 'meeting of representatives, duly appointed, from the London, Belvedere, Erith, Dartford and Enfield Lock branches', possibly again in mid-November or early December. There also seems

---

38 Similarly Horrocks, ASE *Monthly Report*, August 1898, p. 15, 'R.W., Coventry', ASE *Monthly Report*, November 1898, p. 17. Also Edinburgh and District Trades and Labour Council's Federation Committee, 'is but an attempt to . . . [indistinct] . . . and improve the *Clarion* scheme, but lamentably fails': *Minute Book*, 5 April 1898. King: 'a spoilt and useless piracy'. *Clarion*, 23, 30 April 1898.

39 Sidebotham's scheme is detailed in the FSI *Monthly Report*, December 1897, pp. 5–8.

40 FSI *Monthly Report*, January 1898, pp. 4f.

41 Scottish Typographical Association, Aberdeen Branch, *Minute Book*, 28 May 1898.

42 Tom Proctor in ASE *Monthly Report*, September 1898, p. 15.

to have been a 'voluntary London Committee' at some stage which submitted amendments to the 'Official Scheme'.[43]

One or two other schemes may have achieved a smaller circulation still.[44] There was also a Rochdale and District Trades Federation which a pro-*Clarion* member of the ASE saw as a mere anti-*Clarion* diversion. But since a small Rochdale Trades Federation was listed as represented at the first Federal Labour Parliament, we can imagine that it had been brought round or taken over by *Clarion* supporters in the meantime.[45]

Sometimes, in this 'war of schemes' as the *Railway Review* dubbed it on 21 January 1899, various rivals merely cancelled each other out. For example, the London Society of Compositors (LSC) convened a conference in the Memorial Hall, Farringdon 'to consider the question of federation between trade unions'. The conference adopted the LSC's motion for calling 'a National Congress of Trade unionists pledged to formulate a scheme of National Federation, to be submitted for the approval of their respective constituents'.[46] This cautious procedure contrasts with King's, but seems to have achieved even less.

This conference, as has been noted, seems to have heard King sympathetically. The LSC's invitations to it went out on or about 24 May,[47] but again hesitantly: 'the date and place of the conference to be fixed after a sufficient number of replies have been received'. By this time, the TUC had issued its own scheme, and the LSC's own *Quarterly Report*, in May, contained solemn warnings against the presumption of trying to duplicate such august exercises. The ASRS and the ASE decided against accepting – given that the coming TUC was to discuss federation. So did most of the other organisations that had replied to the Compositors by the beginning of August. That month, the LSC's *Quarterly Report* also named the recent FLP as a probable factor. In other words, an initiative as gingerly promoted as the LSC's stood, by now, little chance of joining the *Clarion* v TUC 'first division'.

The spring of 1898 saw further ambiguous decisions from the Scottish

---

[43] ASE *Monthly Report*, May 1898, p. 2 editorial. ASE General Office Report, p. 52. But there also seems to have been at some stage a 'voluntary London Committee' which 'submitted a series of amendments of [*sic*] the Trades Congress Scheme.'

[44] *Souvenir* of the 1881–1930 gatherings of the Yorkshire Typographical Association. Typographical Association, NEC *Minute Book*, particularly 5 March; 11, 25 June; 23 July; 6 August; 22 December 1898; 25 March; 15 July; 17, 22 August 1899.

[45] *Railway Review*, 11 March 1898, p. 10. Minutes of Federal Labour Parliament 1898, List of Delegates.

[46] *Daily Chronicle*, 25 May 1898.

[47] Report to quarterly delegate meeting of 3 August 1898, p. 25. AIMS EC 29 June 1898. ASRS Documents; General Secretary's Report till 12 September 1898. TUC PC Minutes, 7 June 1898.

and Irish TUCs. Though the 1897 Scottish TUC had 'subjected the *Clarion* scheme to a running fire of eulogy', according to Katherine Bruce Glasier in the obviously biased *Clarion*, its Parliamentary Committee a year later had refused King's request – typically on a mere fortnight's notice – to be allowed to address the full Congress.[48] But Congress overruled the PC by 68 votes to 14. The day after King's speech, the speakers were 'almost unanimous' for the *Clarion* scheme, in preference to the Scottish TUC's own. However, they rejected by 44 votes to 27 a proposal from Robert Smillie to set up a committee to implement it.[49] They thus kept their support vague – whatever King himself might believe. All the same, in July, Smillie was to be one of the three delegates representing the Scottish TUC's 120,000 affiliated members at the Federal Labour Parliament, which he chaired and where he topped the poll for the Provisional Committee.[50]

Probably, King should have evaluated the support of the Irish TUC at least as ambiguously as he should have the Scottish. Meeting in Belfast during May–June, the Congress heard its president deduce from the engineering struggle the need for a 'powerful federation' and, soon after, a motion on the *Clarion* scheme was proposed by a local Councillor and seconded by P. J. Tevenan, who mentioned his ASRS's support. An amendment for 'local and national federation of kindred trades' was fairly narrowly defeated, after King had spoken at length. Other speeches had been both for and against.[51] Subsequently, King was to claim the vote was unanimous, but in fact he was confusing this vote with the preceding one for a vague motion for federation in general.

The crunch: the NIGFTLU versus the GFTU

Through the spring of 1898, King radiated chaos. The founding FLP had been rumoured to be due some time in May in Manchester, and to be for the purpose of 'explaining and considering' his scheme.[52] But others believed it to be taking place in Carlisle in June.[53] It was also supposed by some to be convened in London – 'to launch the scheme' according to one member of Edinburgh Trades Council.[54] Again, it

---

48 *Clarion*, 3 April 1897. Scottish TUC PC Minutes, 19 March 1898.
49 This can be found in the TUC Minutes of the 1898 Congress, pp. 39f., or in AIMS *Monthly Report*, March 1898, inside cover. Also *Clarion*, 7 May 1898.
50 FLP Minutes, pp. 12, 35.
51 Irish TUC Minutes, 1898. Also summarised fairly extensively in NAOP *Monthly Report*, July 1898.
52 BSSAA EC Minutes, 25 March 1898.
53 For example TUC PC *Minute Book*, 7 May 1898.
54 Edinburgh and District Trades and Labour Council, *Minute Book*, 5 May 1898.

was sometimes supposed to be taking place at the end of June – which was rumoured to be the appointed time until two weeks before.[55] Yet, in the event, the Scottish TUC's Parliamentary Committee had to reconvene 'hastily' on a Tuesday in order to deliberate on King's invitation to a meeting at Carlisle that Saturday, for preparing the FLP – now scheduled for 18 July – which is when it actually took place.[56]

Naturally, many organisations felt unable to commit themselves at such short notice.[57] King was also asking Trades Councils to distribute his invitations to the FLP themselves – which even some vaguely sympathetic councils took as an impertinence.[58] (A month after the FLP he was even asking one organisation which had never attended, for contributions towards the expenses!)[59] Admittedly, King could be forgiven if he believed himself to be riding on the crest of a wave. For example, between 2 and 20 May 1898, he was to address twenty-three lodges of the North Yorkshire and Cleveland Miners' and Quarrymen's Association alone[60] – not that these can have been a particularly strategic group of workers. His scheme remained under discussion in the branches of various other unions.[61]

Support was particularly visible in the Railway Servants. The ASRS' AGM of October 1897 had carried 'with cheers' and by 39 votes to 8, a motion supporting King's scheme. The EC was left with the task of interpreting this – as when it replied to the TUC's scheme – as definitely committing them 'to the *Clarion*'. Early in 1898, ten ASRS branches had reported discussions on federation – mainly in favour of the *Clarion*. Wigan Branch also formed an ASRS Central Clarion Trades Federation Committee, and was to have two delegates at the Federal Labour Parliament in July. During March, this Committee advocated supporting

55 Agenda, but not Minutes, of the Conference of the Lancashire and Cheshire Miners' Association, 30 May 1898. ASRS General Secretary's *Quarterly Report*, to 13 June 1898, quoting Benshaw Branch.
56 Scottish TUC Minutes, 22 June 1898.
57 For example Nottingham and District Trades Council, *Minute Book*, 29 June 1898. Nottingham and District Hosiery and Finishers' Association, *Minute Book*, April 1898.
58 For example Liverpool Trades and Labour Council, *Minute Book*, 29 June 1898, by 24 votes to 7: only three weeks previously it had once again endorsed his scheme against the TUC's, but most uneasily – by 13 votes to 10 with 14 'remaining neutral'.
59 Nottingham and District Hosiery and Finishers' Association, *Minute Book*, 21 September 1898.
60 North Yorkshire and Cleveland Miners' and Quarrymen's Association, *Minute Book*, 14 April 1898.
61 OBS *Monthly Report*, 25 April 1898. North Yorkshire and Cleveland Miners' and Quarrymen's Association, *Minute Book*, 20 May 1898. CIAS EC *Minute Book*, 7 May 1898. AIMS *Minute Book*, June 1898.

only pro-*Clarion* candidates for the Society's October AGM.[62] At the FLP, in addition to the presence of the Society's General Secretary, Richard Bell, who was elected to the Provisional Committee third in the poll, the ASRS had the highest number of branches directly represented – fifteen branches by sixteen delegates. One of these, Harry Orchard, 'secretary of the Manchester Exchange Branch, and also secretary of the London and North Western Railway Passenger Staff Movement', claimed to have been 'selected by a committee representing fourteen branches of this society'.[63]

But, perhaps inevitably, King's very seizing of the time frightened off some of the timid. An example would be Edinburgh Trades Council, whose support for the *Clarion* scheme had been considerably strengthened after it had compared the latter with three rival schemes – those of the Scottish and British TUCs and Eyre's. Its next minuted discussion was triggered by King's invitation to the FLP. By only one vote – a big drop after the previous discussion – it was decided merely to distribute his circular to affiliated societies.[64]

King and his supporters were already labelled as men in a hurry. Back in the London Trades Council's *Annual Report* for 1897, James Macdonald, its secretary and an SDF member, had warned against 'rushing into new schemes of organisation or trade federation'.[65] As we will see, there may have been deeper reasons beyond King's control, which allowed such comments to do damage.

Worse, in the ASRS itself and precisely during these months, opinion was rallying against King. A full two months elapsed following the October 1897 AGM before its EC decided to proceed by circularising other union leaderships. Into the spring and early summer of 1898, the *Railway Review* continued to encourage branches to push the *Clarion* scheme around their local labour movement. But at the EC's June meeting, the General Secretary was complaining that, of 1,530 organisations, including trades councils, which he himself had circularised, only 42 had replied and of these only 2 had agreed then and there to adopt the *Clarion* scheme, while 27 'were promising to give it consideration'.[66]

Thereupon, the Executive resolved to 'regret that the feeling is so

---

[62] *Railway Review*, 15 October 1897; 15 April 1898. Similarly Stafford Branch, 29 April 1898.

[63] Minutes of Federal Labour Parliament 1898, pp. 35, 9.

[64] Edinburgh and District Trades and Labour Council, *Minute Book*, 5 April, 5 July 1898.

[65] London Trades Council, *Annual Report* for 1897, p. 6. The LTC had been no friend of the TUC over the engineers and federation issues, and the – Cigarmaker – president of the conference it had organised was to move a criticism of the PC at the 1898 TUC.

[66] *Railway Review*, 29 April 1898, p. 1.

apathetic towards the proposals known as the *Clarion* scheme as not to justify us in [pursuing] the matter as initiators.' Further, it 'unanimously resolved' that their General Secretary's attendance at the FLP would be conditional on their avoiding the commitment 'to all details of the scheme' which, along with other trade unionists including King himself, they had read the invitation to the Parliament as involving.[67]

Worse again, at branch and district levels, even before June, some members began to worry about finance. In April, A. Moss of New Cross branch attacked the *Clarion* scheme for its 'serious financial liabilities'. At first, to judge from branch reports, this line did not have a shattering impact. But after the FLP, it did. Moss saw his opponents based 'chiefly in the Northern districts.' Yet even in the North West, members in at least Ashton and on the Manchester District Committee grew worried that their Society might find itself isolated from other unions if it pushed for the *Clarion* too hard.[68]

The NIGFTLU launched: the Federal Labour Parliament

So, the July 1898 Federal Labour Parliament, which formally founded the National and International General Federation of Trade and Labour Unions, convened in an uncertain context. Superficially, it was to prove a resounding success for King and the *Clarion*, symbolised on the first day by the unanimous vote of thanks and by the telegram to the same effect to the *Clarion* editorial board signed by Smillie, Toyn, Turner and T. Wilson as president, vice president, treasurer and secretary of the Parliament. The same could be said for the proceedings as a whole. It unanimously resolved 'to adopt the fundamental principles of the *Clarion* Scheme of National and International Federation' on the motion of John Hodge, representing 4,300 members of the Steel Smelters' Association, Manchester.

Towards the end of the first day, delegates defeated an amendment from C. Harrap (Liverpool Branch, Litho Artists) and A. C. Verity (representing Barnsley Trades Council, but also an ASRS executive member) and thus reaffirmed King's intention that they, and delegates at future FLPs, could be overruled by detailed returns of branch votes on all the issues under discussion. Harrap, and W. George of the Liverpool ASRS who had been elected to chair the Standing Orders Committee, then bent with the same wind and clarified a rule in such a way as to make

---

[67] ASRS General Secretary's *Quarterly Report*, to 13 June 1898. ASRS EC Minutes, 13 June 1898, paragraphs 28–32, pp. 59f.
[68] ASRS EC Minutes, 8 April, 13 May, 19 August 1898.

all the FLP decisions subject to ratification by the majority of members of affiliated unions. The passage which they got deleted would have reverted to treating these unions as blocks in their own right: 'where the majority of the members' unions [i.e. *not* 'branches' *nor* 'of the members'] favour the motion, that motion will be considered carried, and the Labour Parliament will be unable to interfere with it'. Plebiscitary democracy was riding high.

The second day began with 'some hours' on finance. 'During the three days' sittings, no rule . . . aroused keener interest.' This was hardly surprising: irrespective of wider aims, finance was the first purpose of any federation. In the upshot, the level of contributions was not lowered – the voting was 36 to 54 – but the speed at which they could be paid was made flexible, subject to the proviso that no union could derive funds directly from the federation until it had paid its full proportion into the 'Guarantee Fund'.

On the officeholders, Harrap and Turner's suggestion was unanimously accepted that instead of these being all elected by the FLP, only the secretary should be, while the rest should be selected from and by the thirteen Executive Committee members elected by the Parliament. All elections, apparently, were to be annual.

In contrast to the rhythm of the second day, delegates began the third by adopting with little discussion a large number of constitutional rules to do with the Executive and officeholders, plus a very *Clarion* rule which, for certain periods, allowed a virtual referendum of all members of affiliated unions over whether to support a particular struggle. Other provisions to do with arrangements during disputes, with membership and, again, with finance, also followed with seemingly little discussion and only minor amendment. Rules to do with the Federation's 'Objects' and with the finer details of FLPs and elections to the Executive, were disposed of with equal dispatch.[69]

For King himself, *the* federation – his – was now 'already formed'. 'It only remains,' he trumpeted in late August, 'for the TUC to fall into line.'[70] But, more accurately for the future, the *Railway Review*'s report on the FLP on 29 July, seems to have been penned by some virtuoso in equivocation – *despite* starting with the proclamation that 'the Federation of Trade Unions became an accomplished fact in Manchester last week', and despite mentioning that Bell had himself been elected treasurer.

And in the labour movement generally, one ASE member – 'An Ignoramus', of Openshaw 3rd Branch – who was clearly no friend to the

69 Report of Federal Labour Parliament 1898, pp. 14, 17, 18, 19, 21, 27–32.
70 *Clarion*, 20 August 1898.

TUC Parliamentary Committee or to 'leaders' – could claim that 'with one exception only, namely the Amalgamated Carpenters and Joiners, no association or organisation was pledged to a definite policy or scheme'.[71] This may have been an exaggeration (he omitted the ASRS here) but it underlines how expectantly people were waiting till the September 1898 Congress of the TUC in Bristol.

The 1898 TUC and the January 1899 Special Congress

Many had no doubt that federation was to be the 'most important matter to come before Congress',[72] – and even 'the only question of supreme importance'. But fate intervened: the Colston Hall, where the TUC was meeting, burnt down the night before the federation discussion was due to take place. Thereby, 'the life was knocked out of the Congress'.[73] The organ, which groaned while burning, should have had King's name on it.

The morning after, the Parliamentary Committee can still be observed amid the ruins, smiling at the camera for, as it then chanced, their annual photograph. The President informed delegates that they 'must take the minutes as read, as they were burnt'[74] – which must have been incorrect, since they were later printed – along with belongings of many delegates. The Congress resolved to postpone discussion on federation – though not on other matters – to a special New Year Congress. The postponement proved overwhelmingly to the PC's advantage. Near the nadir of the 'official scheme's' popularity, a fluke (we must assume) had spared it from a vote, and had postponed discussion of alternative schemes.

By luck or design, proponents of the TUC scheme managed to convert postponement into, from the NIGFTLU point of view, a cancellation. The postponement resolution talked of 'the formation of a federation of trades, having as its basis the Federation Committee's Report, as now submitted, with amendments, and that full opportunity be given for discussing any amendments', if submitted four weeks before the Congress.[75] These terms were to remain ambiguous to some. But not to others.

Thus, while Robert Knight, as President of the TUC Federation Committee, spoke on the morning after the fire with some restraint, he

---

[71] ASE *Monthly Report*, October 1898.
[72] AIMS *Monthly Report*, retrospectively, November 1898.
[73] BSSAA General Secretary's report on the Congress to EC, 21 October 1898.
[74] NAOP *Monthly Report*, Delegate's report, September 1898, p. 28.
[75] Scottish TUC Report, pp. 64f.

seems to have enjoyed himself later at a 'meeting of all those delegates whose societies had sent in resolutions on the subject'. His sneers at the *Clarion* scheme drew 'disapproval from some delegates and cheers from others' as he insisted that 'if they were going to have a workable scheme it must . . . not be one that took twenty or thirty articles and numerous letters in the newspaper to explain it'.[76]

Even worse, during the same month and the next, the *Clarion* scheme suffered its greatest single defeat so far. In September, Bell of the ASRS reported to his Executive on the Federal Labour Parliament of two months previously, and emphasised that the Parliament had called for fees of ten shillings per member. This sum was to be treated as part of the Guarantee Fund which, among other things, was to be forfeit if the union left the Federation. The Executive, none the less, accepted this demand with only two dissentients. Whether or not some of the majority voted with misgivings, their decision triggered a backlash.

For, at the following month's AGM, the NIGFTLU supporters lost overwhelmingly. And this, it seems, was largely because of financial worries. Even some of those who had supported the *Clarion* during the previous, 1897, AGM now claimed to have done so in ignorance of its financial aspects. Meanwhile, the Standing Orders Committee had refused King's request to be allowed to address the meeting. This was to prove a mild foretaste, for him, of the January 1899 TUC. The AGM Chairman warned, and explicitly hoped, that this would mean the end of ASRS support for the NIGFTLU 'at least for the present' – although as we shall see, support persisted spottily through at least 1899.

It seems that most unions viewed the January 1899 Special TUC as simply a continuation of September 1898 and signified this by picking the same delegates.[77] This assumption confirmed the belief that the January Congress would be open to discussion of all schemes. In this belief, some branches continued writing to their national leaders against the TUC scheme and in favour of the *Clarion*'s. Others objected to what they saw as the Parliamentary Committee's 'attempt to foist on us' its own scheme. The Leeds branch of the Amalgamated Union of Cabinet-makers did this in December,[78] and were endorsed by a national vote – admittedly of only one tenth of the membership – during the ensuing

[76] BSSAA Report of the TUC in August *Monthly Report*, p. 218.
[77] FSI *Monthly Report*, December 1897, p. 1. Also for example AIMS *Monthly Report*, November 1898; LSC *Quarterly Report*, 2 November 1898, p. 20; ASRS EC Minutes, 12; 17 September 1898; Amalgamated Society of Lithoprinters' *Minute Book*, 30 October 1898.
[78] Amalgamated Union of Cabinetmakers, *Monthly Report*, December 1898.

month. Other pro-*Clarion* union branches curtly denounced the forth-coming special TUC as 'a farce'.[79]

However, for most, in the aftermath of the FLP, the prospect of discussing all schemes promised to be daunting. Only an optimistic minority believed that this was what a special meeting of the TUC should be for.[80] Most elaborately, Tom Proctor of the ASE – an ILPer, and also President of Plymouth Trades Council – wanted his own version of a Special TUC to meet as far ahead as the spring of 1899, so that it could be prepared for by local meetings organised by trades councils.[81] Chance was to grant his wishes for a special Congress. But it only worsened the confusion. At one extreme, Mawdsley – 'Sage of Ancoats' or otherwise the Conservative leader of the Cotton Spinners – was heard to remark that the question of federation was shelved 'for an indefinite period'. Other leaders were rumoured to have uttered similarly. At the other extreme, many continued to believe, with James Sexton of the NUDL, that the official scheme 'had been rejected'.[82] This would only have boosted any false confidence among King's supporters.

With clearer sight, many others – sympathisers or not – suspected, with Horrocks, that the January Congress would 'simply meet to launch the Parliamentary Committee scheme'.[83] By the end of October, King claimed to have got wind that some of his own Executive Committee were speaking for the TUC scheme,[84] and that at least one union Executive had heard from the PC that the official scheme alone was to be discussed in January. In King's punctuation: 'no amendments [were to] be allowed except those dealing with the official scheme!!!' Within another three weeks, members of the PC were explaining this officially.[85]

'I should not be surprised', agreed one framer of a rival scheme during the next month, 'with all the condemnation of the official scheme, that [*sic*] when the curtain is let down at the end of the special congress . . . if there is much alteration other than what has already been agreed on.'[86] And yet, his same letter announced that his own committee had recently

79 Wharton Hall Lodge of the Lancashire and Cheshire Miners' Federation in the agenda to the LEMF conference of 10 December 1898 (NUM Bolton).
80 For example Amalgamated Union of Cabinetmakers, Minutes of Delegate Meeting 25–30 July 1898 – one week after the FLP.
81 ASE *Monthly Report*, September 1898, p. 14.
82 ASE *Monthly Report*, October 1898, p. 20. NAUL *Minute Book*, 14 October 1898.
83 ASE *Monthly Report*, October 1898, p. 22.
84 *Clarion*, 22 October 1898.
85 Repeated in P. J. King, *Federation in a Nutshell* (1898), p. 11: Mr Robinson, General Secretary of the Amalgamated Society of Beamers, Twisters and Drawers to his Society's conference in Blackburn. *Clarion*, 12 November 1898.
86 The secretary of the Woolwich committee. ASE *Monthly Report*, November 1898, p. 19.

been instructed, by a meeting of delegates from the London area, to cut the confusion and 'to amend the [TUC] scheme by incorporating' . . . portions of his scheme.

Here lay a major confusion. Given that the PC was openly counting on the TUC scheme remaining the basis for discussion, should the aim be to defeat this at the start of the proposed Congress, or to amend it with something as different from the original as one might wish? Those who felt pessimistic about doing either, comforted themselves instead with hopes that the Federation would be easier to amend after it had been set up. Such hopes were widespread, and they probably assisted those union executives that sought to simplify everything by, however regretfully, supporting the PC.

Thus the EC of the AIMS stipulated that if the ordinary members voted to be represented at the January Congress, 'this declaration', would 'be taken as a mandate . . . favourable to the principle of federation'.[87] More fully, though the BSSAA's members had 'voted in favour of the *Clarion* scheme' and had, as their general secretary reminded his Executive on receipt of the TUC's circular detailing arrangements for January, done so 'in the belief that it was a better scheme than what was known as the Official Scheme', the likelihood still was that

the Special Congress that was to be held would no doubt improve that scheme. It might be that some of the principles of the *Clarion* scheme might be embodied in it. At any rate, what everyone wanted was to get the best scheme, and the more the question was discussed, the more likely were we to strengthen weak points.

Accordingly, the Executive invited branches to send their amendments only to the Official Scheme.[88]

To such ambiguities, January proved a hard end. The agenda placed an amendment by two of King's supporters – for opening the discussion to any scheme and not merely the TUC's – in splendid quarantine for the opening moments. The chair, after unsuccessfully appealing to them to withdraw it, announced that their motion involved the suspension of standing orders. This was rejected by 665,000 votes to 177,000 – most of these, interestingly, from the ASRS. Meanwhile, King found himself 'wander[ing] the purlieus . . . an ostracised man'. According to Joseph Burgess, whose phrase this is, 'the officials of the FLP' had been 'currying favour with the old gang by making a scapegoat out of Mr King'.[89]

[87] AIMS *Monthly Report*, November 1898.
[88] BSSAA EC Minutes of 31 October 1898, pp. 257f.
[89] *Manchester Weekly News*, 3 February 1899.

It is true that the defeated amendment would have vastly increased the travails of the Congress. It specified:

that the merits of each [scheme] be considered in the following order, viz., the first and last alternatively until the list is exhausted.
The Official Scheme
Mr Dipper's Scheme
Mr Eyre's Scheme
The Woolwich Scheme
The Clarion Scheme
Mr Horrocks' Scheme
The London Trades Council Scheme
And furthermore, if this Congress decides on adopting any scheme, that any delegate be at Liberty to hand in Amendments within six hours of the adoption of whichever scheme the Congress has approved of.

Faced with this, it seems all too likely that freshly-arrived delegates anticipated that not merely the list would end up 'exhausted', and preferred 'to get Federation by whatever means they could'.[90] One can glean an unusually vivid, because naïve-sounding, impression of what was occurring within the hall from an ordinary branch member of the Cabinetmakers. As his union had passed its representation to the local, Manchester, branch, he found himself blown into the Congress by what he called a 'sidewind'. He was understandably breathless at where he had landed. By the end of the Congress, however, he had recovered sufficiently 'to get the views of the most prominent leaders of the Labour World [including his fellow-socialist O'Grady and other Furniture leaders] some of whom are very advanced in ideas, and, without exception, they expressed themselves as having done very well and were for trying the Federation Committee's Scheme as amended.' And he continued:

Nowhere did I come across any ardent lover of the *Clarion* scheme, the one which, according to the letters which have circulated through our union from different branches, I was bound to give the preference wherever possible. Never, except where grouped among the six other schemes, and where they were all voted out of Court, . . . did the *Clarion* scheme get the shadow of a hearing. I felt this all the more from the fact that, not only was my mandate clear, but having been a *Clarion* reader from the first number [1891], and having followed the scheme from the time it first was advanced in its columns I was naturally inclined to give it a hearing.[91]

[90] Gregory, of the Manchester United Carters' Association, January 1899, TUC Minutes, p. 15.
[91] Amalgamated Union of Cabinetmakers, *Monthly Report*, February 1899.

The NIGFTLU fades away

The two main schemes had now become rival federations. The slow start of the GFTU is now a matter of record: the quick fade of NIGFTLU is still not, even in its bare bones. One can note Blatchford's 1901 declaration – made in passing, during an argument with Ben Tillett – that he did 'not believe it was shelved because it did not suit the case; I believe it was shelved because many of the union leaders did not like Mr King. I believe in Mr King's scheme, and I did not believe that the scheme or the man had fair play.' One can also note that the NIGFTLU survived into at least 1905,[92] when a probably 'bored' *Clarion* gave a few details – placed, curiously, on its clubs-page, alongside socialist cyclings and scoutings – of a NIGFTLU 'Federal Labour Parliament'. The only NIGFTLU personality mentioned was 'Mr Bancroft'. Conceivably, this was the 'A. Bancroft' of the one-thousand-strong Bolton Operative Spindle and Flyer Makers' Friendly Society, who was present at the 1898 FLP and was elected to the Committee. But even in the *Clarion*, NIGFTLU seems to have become an uncommented relic. And King, at least, went unmentioned.

To gauge exactly when the NIGFTLU ceased to be a meaningful organisation is difficult. True, towards the end of 1899, its second FLP not only re-elected King as secretary, but also appointed no less than seven regional organisers.[93] Whether or not these were merely part-time is unclear. But even if they were, it testifies to unflagging determination among at least some adherents. However, an awareness must have been widespread, through 1899, that the race between the two federations to secure affiliations would be won by the one that retained the greatest momentum. If so, these seven appointments may have been one big last gamble, rather than a coherent strategy for growth.

In any case, for the GFTU side, Mawdsley – of all people, in the light of his negative attitude during the previous year – was during March circularising an invitation to a 'private conference on Trades Federation' to be held on 20 April.[94] This may have been the meeting of sixteen unions on whether or not to join the GFTU, mentioned within the

---

[92] *Clarion*, 12 October 1901; 17 November 1905.
[93] *Clarion*, 4 November 1899; probably in Birmingham on 30 October. Leeds Trades and Labour Council *Minute Book*, 22 October; Huddersfield Trades and Labour Council *Minute Book*, 25 October; invitations circulating early – for once – by 9 August (Aberdeen UTC), but for '2nd Annual Conference' in Carlisle, not Birmingham. Invitations for Birmingham were being discussed as late as 21 October (CIAS *Minute Book*).
[94] For example, *Minute Book* of Council of the Amalgamated Society of Operative Lacemakers and Auxiliary Workers, 8 June 1899 (Nottingham Central Library).

London Society of Compositors early in May as having taken place 'during the past month'. Yet the response to the GFTU seems to have remained disappointing for, in June, a Parliamentary Committee circular was announcing an extension of the period for joining the Federation.[95] Clearly, affiliations were coming in slower than many had expected. 'Conspicuous' absentees. Thorne alleged, included 'unions whose leaders used to prate . . . loudly' for federation.[96]

In the event, his own Executive was within eighteen months to ballot his members on whether to walk out. At first, the Gasworkers had been among the keenest unions in the GFTU – at least officially: its officials were urging its merits on the membership verbally and in print throughout 1899, and Curran was on its Management Committee. At the 1899 GFTU Committee meeting, Curran chaired and Thorne, all too symbolically, was doorkeeper.[97] The union's GFTU 'entrance fees', noted in its July *Report*, amounted to £163 and by the end of April 1901 'the total amount paid to the Federation had topped no less than £7,771½. By the end of 1900, though, Thorne was fuming at the Federation's 'red tape' which was making it merely 'an institution for piling up money'. The main bone of contention seems to have been the refusal by the Federation's Management Committee to grant funds for some of his members.

This, to Thorne, was 'taking advantage' of Curran's absence in the USA on a TUC delegation. The Federation's rules, said Thorne, needed revising so as to 'make it a powerful machine for fighting in the cause of Labour'. As it turns out, the membership and a special congress of the Union seem to have accepted Clynes's advice to improve the GFTU from within; but the Union now affiliated on a lower scale of payments and benefits.[98] Thorne could have taken more note of statements such as that of Isaac Mitchell of the ASE, elected as the Federation's General Secretary, rejoicing that there was already 'a little more negotiating and less striking' which allowed the GFTU to 'confine expenditure entirely to management'.[99]

Overall, the GFTU claimed 340,000 members affiliated via forty-four societies in July 1899 and, a year later, 409,000 via seventy-two – clearly on average small – societies.[100] On the NIGFTLU side, the going was obviously tougher. True, there were one or two paper triumphs in store.

[95] LSC *Minute Book*, 3 May, 10 June 1899.
[96] Report to GW&LU till 1 July 1899.
[97] Report to GW&LU till 30 September 1899.
[98] Report to GW&LU till 29 December 1900. Same till 29 March 1901.
[99] Mitchell in ASE *Annual Report* for 1900, pp. iif.
[100] Curran's opening speech to the GFTU's 1901 Annual GC Meeting (TUC).

Thus, at the end of 1898, King felt bound to warn, in the *Clarion*, that some rogue had been asking for £2,000 in one-shilling shares for the 'Federal Labour Parliament' – an enterprise seeking to lighten the pockets of either an unexpectedly large number of rich enthusiasts or, more likely, as many as 40,000 trade unionist suckers.[101] More seriously, during early 1899, when King reissued his *Crushing Criticism* – or 'Krushing Kriticism', as the *Clarion* insisted – of the TUC scheme, the *Bradford Labour Echo* found it 'difficult to see how the official scheme can survive the publication of this pamphlet'.[102] Unfortunately, this amounted either to spitting into the wind or whistling in the dark – as can also be seen within particular unions.

Thus, in the ASRS, a number of branches stayed faithful even after the October 1898 AGM had rejected the scheme. Examples are: Cudworth[103] – where the speaker mentioned was W. Mellor, presumably the delegate listed as present at the 1898 FLP from 'Stairfoot, Wombell and Royston Branch';[104] Patricroft, where 'a branch of the *Clarion* scheme was formed which members of this or any other branch may join';[105] possibly Stoke on Trent, where 'the balance sheet from the local committee of the *Clarion* scheme was read'; and certainly Preston, where a 'large attendance' at the half-yearly meeting decided to 'still adhere to the *Clarion* scheme of federation'.[106] Printed argument among members continued for almost a year. And, more collectively, the Northern District Committee,[107] and the branches at Gateshead (of roughly 569 members), Bensham, St Helens Central, Ormskirk, Newcastle Central and Southport[108] all continued to agitate for the *Clarion* scheme – only to be overwhelmed again at the 1899 AGM.

In other unions, the Edinburgh branch of the Sheet Metal Workers and Coppersmiths heard of a 'communication' from the 'Secretary of the Clarion scheme' early in May,[109] though what about is not recorded. Probably also during May or early June, King had addressed an audience of 300 in Glasgow which, the Ordinary Delegate Meeting of the Scottish

[101] *Clarion*, 24 December 1898.
[102] *Bradford Labour Echo*, 15 May. Report to GW&LU.
[103] *Railway Review*, 4 November 1898.
[104] Minutes of Federal Labour Parliament 1898, p. 9.
[105] *Railway Review*, 18 November 1898. The contact was 'A. Decimus' of 14 Pauline Street, Weaste.
[106] *Railway Review*, 18 November 1898. The words are those of the reporter, but 'a resolution was passed thereon.'
[107] ASRS Documents. Bell's report till 12 June 1899, p. 7.
[108] *Annual Report* for 1899. Supplementary agenda for AGM, 3–6 October 1899.
[109] Sheet Metal Workers, Coppersmiths, Edinburgh Branch, *Minute Book*, 5 May 1899.

Typographical Association was informed, was disappointingly small, given that all local printworkers had been invited.[110] Allegedly King himself, by the end of October 1899, had still not managed to convene an EC meeting 'nor placed any financial settlement before the contributors'[111] – an omission which this source also blamed for NIGFTLU's imminent doom. Allegedly again, 'a movement was on foot to convene a meeting of the EC', where King would have had to explain himself. Whatever became of this 'movement', any knowledge King may have had of it can hardly have tended to lessen the shrillness of his denunciations of intrigue in all directions. However, in December, he was inviting the Edinburgh Bookbinders – presumably amongst others – to 'a meeting' somewhere on 'January 6th' 1900, where 'Trades Federation' was to be 'fully explained'. The NIGFTLU 'Organiser for Scotland' was also issuing circulars.[112]

In general, much of the NIGFTLU support must have evaporated. Thus Aberdeen no. 1 Branch of the Woodworkers, which had collected actively for the Bethesda quarrymen and later for the Engineers, had been led by its secretary – who was also its Trades Council delegate – in unanimous support of the Federation till at least October 1898. But fourteen months later, after some lengthy discussion on federation – and possibly also some building-trade regrouping – the branch was rejecting 'a communication' from King.[113] From a NIGFTLU viewpoint, the Central Ironmoulders' Association of Scotland (CIAS) showed a particularly depressing evolution. Their executive branch – Falkirk – accepted a self-invitation from Isaac Mitchell as leader of a deputation for explaining the rules of the GFTU. The visit seems to have been successful – Mitchell granting the *Clarion* the now hollow consolation of equal honours with the engineers' struggle in forwarding the cause of federation. Even more significantly, the CIAS's meeting had already resolved to print the GFTU rules and to refuse King's tardy invitation to the 1899 (Birmingham) FLP.[114] The most significant aspect of this refusal may be that it was moved by the same member, J. Logan, who, a year previously, had moved for emergency strike-money to be diverted for paying King's expenses to a meeting on federation, a meeting which

[110] Scottish Typographical Society, Ordinary Delegate Meeting Minutes, 12, 17 June 1899.
[111] BSSAA EC Minutes, 28 October 1899.
[112] Edinburgh Bookbinders, *Minute Book*, 19 December 1899. Aberdeen Trades Council, *Minute Book*, EC of 22 November 1899.
[113] Woodworkers, Aberdeen no. 1 Branch, *Minute Book*, 11 October 1898; 10 May, 26 December 1899.
[114] CIAS EC *Minute Book*, 18 November, 9 December, 21 October 1899.

the CIAS had already tried hard to publicise among other trades in the Falkirk area.[115]

By the second half of 1898, one can also imagine some fall-off of interest in the entire federation issue. 'The whole question went so flat one would be inclined to think that our members had buried it', one leading member of the Woolwich ASE complained in November.[116] Whatever the timing and whatever the unevenness, such an apparently bubble-like collapse would be particularly damaging to anyone seeking to make headway against the main current.

Though some of its supporters were still vocally on deck, the National and International General Federation of Trade and Labour Unions was sinking.

---

[115] CIAS EC *Minute Book*, 10 September, 15, 21 October, 12, 19 November, 3, 10, 17 December 1898.
[116] ASE *Monthly Report*, November 1898, p. 19.

Part 3

7 The early 1900s: a hinge period

There is always more than one way of telling a story. Let us summarise a simple one. In the first twenty years of the modern socialist movement in Britain two distinct tendencies gradually solidified. One was idealistic or even utopian, and committed to strong radical notions of democracy to be pursued unwaveringly first within the movement and then, using that movement, to transform the state utterly. The second was more realistic and accepted the democratic possibilities of the 'British constitution' with only a few reservations.

The failures of the 1890s, above all the ultimate fiasco of NIGFTLU, effectively saw off the first tendency for all but the incurably romantic and permanently immature. The second tendency, guided by the statesmanship of Keir Hardie and Ramsay MacDonald, became flesh as the Labour Representation Committee (or Labour Party as it was already unofficially called).

The story can certainly be told in that way. But it is mistaken in regarding the British socialist movement at the beginning of this century solely in terms of the evolution of the Labour Party. The bodies of opinion represented by *Justice* and the *Clarion*, which were highly critical of and sometimes hostile to the emerging party, remained active in every debate and conflict.

Only the ILP – and then only what its critics called its 'official section' – was fully committed to Labour. The SDF withdrew from the Labour Representation Committee in 1901, while the leading Fabians busied themselves with, arguably, their most successful piece of 'permeation' in promoting the Conservatives' 1902 Education Act. This isolated them from other socialists, who saw the abolition of the school boards as part of a process of 'rolling back' democratic and working-class advance. It also diverged from the policy of the LRC.

Meanwhile, the South African war overshadowed domestic politics. By dividing opinion on pro- and anti-war grounds, it blurred the distinction between socialists and democratic Radicals and opened the way for an attempt to launch a working-class-oriented National

139

Democratic League with a neo-Chartist programme. Soon afterwards, the revival in a militant form of the women's suffrage movement also posed questions of democratic principle. These three issues were important preoccupations in the earliest years of the century, but other unresolved arguments continued.

1902 saw something of a repetition of the *Clarion* campaign of 1898. There was a forthright attack on Hardie by Blatchford, criticism of the lack of democracy in the ILP, advocacy of the referendum and a new agitation for 'socialist unity'. The latter was detonated by the dramatic withdrawal from the Dewsbury by-election of the ILP candidate, Edward Hartley, who criticised the machinations of the 'official ILP' in attempting to run him against Harry Quelch, the SDF candidate already in the field. The initiative of the Kelmscott Club's 'Sub-Committee on Socialist Unity' was rejected by *Labour Leader* as a 'wretched little conspiracy' by SDFers to 'nobble' the ILP.

The rift between radical and conservative interpretations of democracy was to be underlined by the exceptionally clear statement of the Fabian Executive in November 1908. (See below, pp. 165–6.) The terrain of the 1890s had favoured radical democrats in as much as success, relatively, had been in 'making socialists'. If conversion on the scale Blatchford hoped for failed to occur, at least socialist ideas and values had been widely disseminated. In such a propaganda phase, the distinctive and uncompromising nature of the radical version of socialist democracy with its full-blooded demands for 'popular government' could be advantageous. In the 1890s the 'practical' alternatives seemed abstract, whether Fabian 'permeation' or, after the debacle of the 1895 Election, the electoralism of the ILP.

In the 1900s the 'realists' had more working in their favour. The various projects of the ultra-democratic *Clarion* had failed, while the new LRC did at least have the air of what Alex Thompson called 'business meant'. If Labour could achieve some modest parliamentary success with the promise of greater things to come, the ideas of those most identified with this – Keir Hardie, Ramsay MacDonald – were bound to be taken more seriously. Meanwhile, Blatchford's following was thrown into disarray by his support for the Boer War and was offered little but a simplistic view of self-serving 'leaders' and repetition of argument from first principles with little in the way of practical suggestion.

None the less, three issues of the early 1900s – The National Democratic League, the 1902 Education Act, Women's Suffrage – showed in their different ways that divisions of issues of democracy along lines which this book has made familiar were not a thing of the past. Nor was the LRC the only game in town.

The National Democratic League: 'belated and mutilated Chartism'

The National Democratic League (NDL) was founded, largely by W. M. Thompson of *Reynolds' News* in October 1900 – just a few months after the LRC. It was a conscious revival of Chartism, as the title of its founding conference, the Democratic Convention, suggests. Although none of the nationally-organised socialist bodies supported the venture, local branches and individual socialists did participate. The most notable was Tom Mann who became the NDL's Organising Secretary and wrote a pamphlet, *Why I Joined the National Democratic League*, which appeared in April 1901.

The enormous Tory majority owed something, he conceded, to relative prosperity and to 'Khaki fever'. But he saw it as, more than anything else, reflecting the lack of unity among the 'many thousands of Socialists, tens of thousands of Labour men, and hundreds of thousands allied to no party, but with essentially strong Democratic tendencies'. The NDL as an 'umbrella' organisation could 'weld together the Democracy' leaving each affiliated body 'to prosecute their ideals' while uniting to support the basic seven-point programme of political reform: (1) Adult Suffrage, (2) Automatic Registration with a three months' qualification, (3) One Man One Vote (i.e. no plural voting), (4) Official Expenses of Elections to be defrayed from State funds, (5) Second Ballot, (6) Payment of Members, (7) Extinction of the Hereditary Principle in the Legislature.[1]

Only in supporting the Second Ballot did the NDL really go beyond the initial platform of the 1881 Democratic Federation – and it stopped short of demanding the triennial Parliaments, Irish Home Rule and land nationalisation that had figured in the DF programme. Nevertheless, twelve SDF and twenty ILP branches were represented at the Convention.[2]

Nationally the socialists greeted the NDL with varied degrees of dismissiveness. In the *Labour Leader*, 'Marxian' described the programme as 'a trifle old-fashioned'. Were it secured, 'what will prevent the slaves from voting for their masters?' he asked characteristically. Enough working-class power already existed, if the class had the will to use it. If Liberals asked people to 'vote about votes' the Conservatives would always win. Radicalism was 'hopelessly fossilised'. This view was

---

[1] Tom Mann, *Why I Joined the National Democratic League*, April 1901, pp. 6–7.
[2] Richard Price, *An Imperial War and the British Working Class: Working Class Attitudes and Reactions to the Boer War 1899–1902* (London, 1972), appendix II, p. 247.

reinforced by Hardie in the same issue of the *Labour Leader*: the NDL was a retreat even from Chartism.[3]

For once, Alex Thompson agreed. He considered the NDL in his referendum pamphlet *The Only Way to Democracy*: 'The trouble does not *begin* to be touched by the remedy of the London Democratic Convention' (original emphasis).[4] *Some* NDL supporters shared Thompson's enthusiasm for direct democracy, if not the absolute priority he gave it. Tom Chambers, the first secretary of the Workers' Union, was suspicious of 'only ways'. Had not the *Clarion* said that trades federation was the 'only way'? Chambers was, he said, an 'ardent believer' in the referendum and initiative. His own Transport Workers' Federation had 'adopted the referendum as against the delegate meeting' and it had worked well for the last two years. But parliamentary reform was a precondition of obtaining the referendum in the state.

Thompson's reply in the same issue of the *Clarion* argued that the referendum was easier to obtain than reforms, like the abolition of the Lords, which could be accomplished only by a 'bloody revolution': 'the demand for the Referendum is not a frontal attack . . . [but] a flank movement . . . No statesman dare directly oppose it, if insistently demanded, in these days of pretended Democracy.' It had, after all, been 'blessed and sanctified' by Salisbury, 'the leading anti-democratic politician of our time'.[5] Thompson restated this position in reply to a letter from Tom Mann who had written: 'I agree with 98 per cent of your pamphlet. The only part I differ from is the relative times to realise the objects of the League and the Referendum, and I do not share your fears as to professional politicians.'[6] Though the NDL had not adopted direct legislation, Mann looked forward to the attainment of 'popular government' in his pamphlet promoting the NDL:

Neither an hereditary nor elected Second Chamber is wanted; indeed, it would be far better to do away with the House of Commons and the People govern themselves by means of the Initiative and Referendum, than to have a House of Lords. Great headway is being made in Switzerland in the use of the Referendum and also in New Zealand, whilst some of the Trade Unions are resorting to this plan instead of holding so many delegate meetings.

But the time was not ripe, he went on, for promoting direct legislation in British government. The more modest reforms supported by the League would have to come first.[7]

---

[3] *Labour Leader*, 3 November 1900.
[4] A. M. Thompson, *The Only Way to Democracy*, Clarion Pamphlet no. 35 (London, 1900), p. 9.
[5] *Clarion*, 1 December 1900.
[6] *Clarion*, 8 December 1900.   [7] Mann, *Why I Joined*, p. 12.

For its part, *Justice* also stood aside; 'Where are the Democrats outside the Social-Democratic movement?' Like Thompson it was scathing about the NDL's omission of direct legislation and like Hardie it criticised its timidity. 'It was with considerable difficulty that the proposition to make so elementary a democratic principle as adult suffrage part of the programme was carried', and the result of the Convention justified the SDF Executive's decision not to take part.[8] A little later, replying to readers who favoured participation in the NDL, 'Tattler' criticised the omission of shorter parliaments, proportional representation, and the referendum and initiative, but added that nothing was to be gained by 'our bothering about mere political reforms just now'.[9]

Meanwhile Hyndman was putting much greater emphasis on the limitations and dangers of democracy than he had ever done previously. In a *Justice* leader on 'Democratic Form and Socialist Substance', though he claimed that the SDF had always worked consistently for 'a complete reconstruction of political institutions', he insisted that 'Democratic forms are merely the means to an end'. Unless democracy delivered 'good social conditions for all within a reasonable period', it would be no better, judged by its results, than 'our present happy-go-lucky admixture of monarchy and aristocracy, brewery and pilfery'. It was a blunder to advocate democratic forms by themselves. 'That is why we see with regret men who might achieve much in their day going off on a wrong scent after a belated and mutilated Chartism.'[10]

Hyndman's article on 'Democracy' in *The Social-Democrat* presented an even less optimistic view.

The democratisation of our political constitution . . . might easily be worse than a despotism unless accompanied by thorough social education . . . Democracy without education is a reactionary force in modern times. If the enfranchisement of a mass of deteriorated, uneducated voters will tend to throw back this essential education, then I am not in favour of such enfranchisement of such 'democracy', however convinced I may be of the truth that the whole adult population will take an active part in the administration of Socialism, when Social-Democracy itself is constituted.

If anyone could show that 'education' would improve under 'a capable Caesar', then Hyndman would be 'a Caesarist for the time being'. The

---

[8] *Justice*, 22 September, 3 November 1900.
[9] *Justice*, 15 December 1900.
[10] *Justice*, 3 November 1900. Compare Herbert Burrows's reference, in *Justice*, 9 January 1901 to 'that feeble and weak-kneed parody of Chartism, *Reynolds's* Democratic League'.

'cheap press' had 'introduced into all modern democracies, educated or uneducated, many of the characteristics of a mob.'[11] Ironically, Hyndman was now echoing the Fabians' warnings to the 1896 International – and even their much-denounced 'Caesarism'. He was taken to task by the Social-Democrat veteran Frederick Lessner; 'Tattler', in a notice of Mann's NDL pamphlet, reiterated that the SDF was in favour 'of adult suffrage and payment of members and all the other reforms the League champions'.[12]

How can we explain this striking change? It was after all only two years previously that the SDF, and Quelch in particular, had been much criticised by Hardie's *Labour Leader* for supporting co-operation with the same 'Extreme Left' Radicals who had now initiated the National Democratic League. Clearly, the climate engendered by the war, with its manifestations of popular imperialism, and the Conservative 'khaki election' triumph, is a large part of the explanation. We can also detect the influence of contemporary fears about the 'deterioration' of the nation.

The way events could undermine faith in democracy is also clear in this comment on the NDL campaign which appeared in *Justice* in September 1901: 'in our opinion, the majority of those *Reynolds's* and the NDL wish to enfranchise are precisely the people who have supported the imperialist policy here at home and are most susceptible to outbursts of jingo feeling, as well as bribery'. Or, as 'Tattler' had put it some weeks earlier, 'As a matter of abstract justice every man and woman should have the vote; but I am by no means eager to enfranchise all the men and women who are unenfranchised until they have sense enough to use the vote more intelligently than the majority did at the last election.'[13]

If apparently widespread jingoism among the working class was a major cause of, temporary, disillusionment with democracy, another was the way the war revealed the weakness of non-socialist Radicalism. Richard Price has shown that the SDF played a disproportionate rôle in the organised opposition to the South African War, with the formation of Stop-the-War Committees in the provinces dependent on the local strength of SDF branches.[14] This revelation of the Radicals' weakness helps to explain why cooperation with them raised so much less enthusiasm than in 1898.

[11] H. M. Hyndman, 'Democracy', *The Social-Democrat*, 5, 2, February 1901, 38–41.
[12] *Justice*, 9 March, 20 April 1901.
[13] *Justice*, 7 September, 22 June 1901.
[14] Price, *An Imperial War*, p. 24. The national chair of the STWC was the prominent Nonconformist, Dr J. Clifford. The movement had been inspired by W. T. Stead's 'Crusade for Peace'.

But there is also the question of the internal struggles in the SDF. The Social-Democrats' desire to avoid a 'split' and keep the De Leonist 'Impossibilists' in the organisation was a major reason for the SDF's withdrawal from the Labour Representation Committee. In Scotland, 'Impossibilists' had forced the Federation to leave the parallel Scottish Workers' Parliamentary Committee.[15] In 1901 the 'Impossibilist' leader, Leonard Cotton – who was to be expelled from the SDF in 1903 and to go on to become a founder member of the Socialist Labour Party and its secretary from 1910 onwards – was a member of the Executive. To him and his comrades, any consorting with the ILP, the trade unions and the Fabians to achieve Labour representation was unworthy of socialists. How much more so would be co-operation via the NDL with Radicals and Liberals in a campaign for electoral reforms?[16]

SDF support would have probably made no substantial difference, but in any event the NDL came to little. Its list of 'names' on its General Council was impressive enough, and by April 1901 Mann was able to list thirty-two London and forty provincial branches. Yet the following month he resigned from the secretaryship.

In 1903 an amendment intended to allow the affiliation of the League was defeated at the LRC conference by 118 votes to 48. The amendment would have allowed organisations other than trade unions, socialist and co-operative societies 'prepared to adhere to the objects of the [Labour Representation] Committee' to join. The mover was the veteran trade unionist John Ward. He was acting in the name of his Navvies' Union, but he was at the time also the chairman of the NDL. His seconder, W. E. Clery, made it plain that the specific issue in question was the affiliation of the League. Pete Curran of the Gasworkers and James Sexton for the Dock Labourers opposed. Sexton said that 'If they passed this amendment, Liberal Associations, Tory Associations, and the 9d Goose Clubs could affiliate.' This rejection by the LRC ended any prospect of cooperation from that quarter.[17]

[15] Frank Bealey and Henry Pelling, *Labour and Politics 1900–1906. A History of the Labour Representation Committee* (London, 1958), p. 164; Victor Rabinovitch, 'British Marxist Socialism and Trade Unionism: The Attitudes, Experience and Activities of the Social-Democratic Federation, 1884–1900', DPhil thesis, University of Sussex, 1978, pp. 221–4; Chushichi Tsuzuki, *Henry Hyndman and British Socialism* (London, 1961), p. 138.

[16] For the 'Impossibilist' split and the subsequent history of the two 'splinters' it produced, see Walter Kendall, *The Revolutionary Movement in Britain* (London, 1969); Raymond Challinor, *The Origins of British Bolshevism* (London, 1977); Robert Barltrop, *The Monument: The Story of the Socialist Party of Great Britain* (London, 1975); and Thomas Bell, *Pioneering Days* (London, 1941).

[17] *The Labour Party Foundation Conference and Annual Conference Reports, 1900–1905*, 1967, pp. 103–4.

The League was still represented at the 'National Labour Conference' on adult suffrage organised by the SDF in July 1908.[18] But *Justice*, which had prematurely announced the NDL's collapse as early as 2 August 1902, produced its obituary notice on the League a year later. Here the SDF again underlined its determination to maintain an exclusive claim to the mantle of the Chartists. Friendly relations with W. M. Thompson and *Reynolds's Newspaper* had, said *Justice*, always been maintained, but the NDL, lacking 'a definite economic base' and with a heterogeneous membership, had been doomed to failure from the start. The League had taken 'upon itself enormous credit for Crooks' return at Woolwich'. (Crooks had been elected as a Labour MP in a straight fight with the Conservatives in a by-election at the beginning of the year.)

Yet Crooks is a member of the capitalist Cobden Club. Imagine Ernest Jones, or George Julian Harney, or Bronterre O'Brien, or Stevens, or Ball, or Sadler or Oastler, as a member of [that] plutocratic coterie. Yet these were the great leaders of the English people of whom we call Social-Democrats – Bronterre O'Brien first used the term 'Social-Democrats' in 1839 – are the legitimate heirs and successors.[19]

School Boards or county councils? Socialists and the 1902 Education Act

The Education Bill controversy was unusual – for the period we are discussing – in that socialists found themselves ranged *against* change, instead of demanding it. They opposed, that is, the Conservatives' kind of change. That what was widely perceived as an important democratic issue could be approached by defending the status quo, helps to explain why there was an unusually wide measure of agreement.

The reactions of the socialist movement to the Education Bill have been analysed in Brian Simon's *Education and the Labour Movement*. Our account focuses on those aspects which concerned democratic form and democratic 'machinery'. Was the objective of maximising popular control best met by bodies elected locally solely to administer education – the School Boards set up under the 1870 Education Act – or via committees of the all-purpose local authorities? Subsidiary issues were the electoral system used, the effects on women's political rights, and the legitimacy or otherwise of the practice of co-option.

The central issue – the question of the 'directness' of control of the organs of local administration – was to arise again in the debate on the proposals of the Royal Commission on the Poor Laws some years

[18] *Justice*, 1 August 1908.   [19] *Justice*, 1 August 1903.

later. It had surfaced already at the time of the abortive 1896 Education Bill which had foreshadowed the 1902 Act.[20] At that time *Justice* had opposed the abolition of school boards on democratic grounds, while in the *Labour Leader* Fred Brocklehurst had argued in favour of transferring their functions to the omnibus local authorities.[21]

When the battle was joined, the SDF proved to be the most unwavering supporter of the School Boards among the socialist groupings. In this respect, it was in tune with the position of the LRC and the TUC. Rodney Barker tells us that 'For three years the TUC organized opposition to parliamentary candidates not pledged to alter the 1902 Act'.[22] Yet the near-unanimity of the trade unions had much to do with the Liberal objections to putting Church schools 'on the rates'. By contrast, Social-Democrats were concerned to distance themselves from Nonconformist opposition.[23] For them the issue was one of democratic control.

As for the other socialist organisations, the ILP and the *Labour Leader* were, on the whole, supportive of the School Board principle, the *Clarion* relatively uninterested in the issue, while the Fabian Society, with some very strong dissent particularly from Stewart Headlam, not only backed the 1902 Education Bill but also played an important part in promoting it.[24]

The 1902 Act arose out of the attack on the London School Board's provision of evening classes and of 'higher grade' schools – which provided education beyond the age-group catered for by compulsory elementary education. This attack culminated in the famous Cockerton Judgement of 1900. Meanwhile the Fabian Society was preparing a tract, drafted by Sidney Webb, *The Education Muddle and the Way Out*. Its support for transferring School Board functions to the omnibus local authorities caused controversy in the Society, and this considerably delayed publication. A Members' Meeting discussed the project in May 1899 but the pamphlet was not published until January 1901.

It placed great emphasis on the need for administrative coherence and, against the School Boards, it alleged a 'decay of public interest' with voting turnouts often as low as 20 per cent. At the same time the Boards

---

[20] Brian Simon, *Education and the Labour Movement, 1870–1920* (London, 1965), pp. 159–61.

[21] *Justice*, 4 April, 9 May, 20 June 1896. *Labour Leader*, 11, 18 April 1896.

[22] Rodney Barker, *Education and Politics 1900–1951: A Study of the Labour Party* (London, 1972), p. 20. See also Simon, *Education and the Labour Movement*, p. 228.

[23] See for example E. E. Hunter, 'The Non-Conformist Conscience and Education', *Justice*, 1 November 1902.

[24] A. M. McBriar, *Fabian Socialism and English Politics 1884–1918* (London, 1962), pp. 212–16.

were 'fiercely hated by large sections of the people'. Other Fabian objections applied equally to the Boards and to proposals for new Education Councils with wider functions since, the Tract argued, 'public bodies directly elected to manage schools will be elected largely on theological grounds'.[25]

Nothing could be in greater contrast to the Social-Democrats' position. *Justice*'s defence of the Boards had already begun with the claim that the system used to elect them was 'the most democratic that exists in this country', since it

approaches most nearly to the only democratic method of elections, proportional representation, and is the only system which in any way secures any share or representation to minorities, while safeguarding the rule of the majority. In Belgium, and even in Switzerland, with the initiative and referendum, our comrades are agitating for proportional representation. Yet it is now that our so-called Progressives bring forward so reactionary a proposal as the elimination of that system where it to some extent exists.[26]

School Board elections were conducted according to a cumulative vote system whereby each elector had as many votes as there were candidates to be elected. This allowed 'plumping', i.e. giving all one's votes to a particular candidate, and thus greatly facilitated the representation of minorities, including in some places Social-Democrats.[27] As the SDF saw it, the Education Bill was intended to remove the control of education from growing socialist influence facilitated by this form of 'proportional representation': instead control was 'to be relegated to the County Councils where the reactionists are all-powerful'.[28]

Stewart Headlam was an Anglo-Catholic and Christian Socialist cleric. He was also a Fabian. He had been elected to the London School Board, the major target of the Conservative 'reform' plan, as an 'Independent Progressive' and now chaired its Evening Class Committee. He was, therefore, very directly involved in the controversy.[29] In June 1901 he took the rather unusual step – for a Fabian – of writing a long letter on the subject to *Justice*:

It is sometimes too glibly said that 'the democracy never goes back'. If the Government's Education Bill is carried this will be no longer true . . . one of the most important rights which the people have won for themselves will be

---

25 *The Education Muddle and the Way Out. A Criticism of English Educational Machinery*, Fabian Tract no. 106, January 1901.
26 *Justice*, 15 December 1900.
27 See Simon, *Education and the Labour Movement*, p. 147 for a description of 'plumping'.
28 *Justice*, 18 May 1901.
29 F. G. Bettany, *Stewart Headlam: A Biography* (London, 1926), ch. 14.

taken away. The right, I mean, of the people to manage [education], by means of their own elected representatives, and . . . of a rate limited only by the people's will . . .

This 'stolen right' was to be transferred, not even to the County Councils themselves, but to 'an authority half of which, minus one, is to consist of persons nominated by certain "interests", while the councillors forming the majority would not be elected for specific educational purposes':

Now this is one of the most serious blows which has ever been aimed at popular government. It is engineered largely by Fabians and Tories who despise the people. It will result in the whole of education being managed by highly-paid officials; the only thing the people will have to do with the matter is to pay for it. . . .

But on this . . . all Democratic Socialists should be united and should be in earnest.[30]

This raised the question of who exactly were 'Democratic Socialists' in Headlam's sense. Certainly, the SDF was 'in earnest'. Social-Democrats were far from satisfied with the existing system, but they liked Tory and Fabian ideas for change a good deal less. Dora Montefiore described the notion of the 'scholarship ladder' as 'in reality the survival of the fittest from a frightful competitive system'.[31]

But the central Social-Democrat objection was to the increased remoteness of control. The arguments were rehearsed, repeated and elaborated over a long period:[32]

The School Boards have been a reflex of public opinion, and the remedy for their defects is not to transfer the control of education to . . . anti-educationalists absolutely free from public responsibility but to educate public opinion up to the higher ideals in the matter of education.[33]

Justice anticipated how this remoteness of control would manifest itself in practice under the new system:

if you, as members of an SDF branch, believe John Brown would be a good man to help manage a local school in your name, you first have to chance his being elected to the council; you have then to chance that council appointing him to its education committee; you then have to chance that this Committee will appoint him to be a manager and you then have to chance that the permanent clerical majority of managers will listen to him.[34]

[30] *Justice*, 8 June 1901.
[31] *Justice*, 29 March 1902. *Justice*, 1 June 1901 (Dora Montefiore).
[32] See for example *Justice*, 24 May; 11, 25 october 1902; 11 April 1903; 8 December 1906.
[33] *Justice*, 24 May 1902.   [34] *Justice*, 11 October 1902.

The similarities between Balfour's Education Bill and the changes advocated in the Fabians' tract were not lost on other socialists.[35] This helped to confirm for the SDF the identification of the Fabian Society as a bunch of would-be bureaucrats seeking to nip democracy in the bud. When the London School Board supported the principle of directly elected educational authorities, some members voted against, including Graham Wallas. *Justice* commented:

> Mr Wallas is a Fabian, and as a Fabian, does not believe in democracy, or democratic control, but pins his faith on the bureaucrat and the 'expert'. We have previously shown the Fabian influence in the anti-democratic Education Bill of the Government.[36]

When the new LCC Education Committee passed over as possible co-optees 'well-known friends of education and the interests of children like Stewart Headlam and Mrs Bridges-Adams', *Justice* was not surprised that a section of the Committee were reportedly in favour of excluding the Press:

> The object of those responsible for recent educational legislation has been to remove education as far as possible from direct popular control . . .
> But that is precisely what Progressive Fabian friends of the London Education Act, like Mr Sidney Webb, desire.[37]

Justice continued to give the issue considerable attention much longer than the other socialist papers. In May 1906 it found itself in the unusual position of applauding the statement made by A. W. Jephson of the Progressive Party on his resignation as LCC councillor for Walworth. His judgement that the new system had replaced sympathetic school management by mechanical official control found a ready response from *Justice* which also claimed that, by excluding the public from its Education Committee meetings, the Council had 'done its best to destroy what public interest there was in education'.[38]

Justice was far clearer than other socialist organs. True, the *Labour Leader* had started with a sturdy defence of the School Boards. In July 1901, it declared them under 'insidious attack'.[39] But this was not to endure. More surprisingly, the *Clarion*, despite its fervour for 'popular

---

[35] Frank Colebrook in *Justice* commented that the 'likeness is amazing', while the *Reformers' Year Book* for 1902 noted that the '*Education Muddle*' tract had 'attracted much attention during the spring of 1901, because much of the policy it advocated was embodied in the Bill brought forward by the Government'. *Justice*, 6 September 1902. *The Reformers' Year Book 1902*, ed. Joseph Edwards (Brighton, 1972), p. 40.

[36] *Justice*, 13 December 1902; similarly 18 April 1903.

[37] *Justice*, 26 March, 2 April 1902.

[38] *Justice*, 26 May, 8 December 1906.   [39] *Labour Leader*, 20 July 1901.

government', seemed surprised by the controversy. It had given little attention to it. Anti-School Board opinions had been expressed by Brocklehurst and by Hartley, with only Margaret McMillan defending the Boards and their Higher Grade Schools.[40] Then the 1902 ILP conference condemned the Education Bill on the grounds that it would withdraw education from popular control and subsidise denominationalism. Yet, even so late, R. B. Suthers's reaction was to ask 'what there is undemocratic about the new arrangements?'[41] The following week the paper gave a platform to Shaw to pour scorn on the SDF and ILP alike; neither organisation was, he asserted, socialist. Both were comprised of 'sound Radical Individualists of the old school' who had 'rallied to the old Liberal standard against the Education Bill'. For him, with his Fabian insistence on the modernity of 'representative government', 'the mere fact that the representatives at these conferences insist on their being called "delegates" show[ed] that their democracy belong[ed] to the nineteenth and not the beginning of the twentieth century'.[42]

On the other side of the argument, Montagu Blatchford contributed two mildly pro-School Board pieces and Headlam a lengthy article. Rehearsing the arguments for direct control and against co-option he concluded:

> The Bill is a straight, direct blow against Democracy and Municipal Socialism. The people are plainly told that they are not fit to manage their own educational affairs; that there are superfine people who will not offer themselves for election, but are too good to be lost. Demos is 'off'; the young gentleman at the Bureau is to take his place . . .
> The Bill . . . will be carried by an unholy alliance between the bureaucrats and certain ecclesiastics – between Mr Webb of the Fabian Society . . . and the Dean of St Paul's . . . [43]

At the 1902 LRC conference the real debate took place on a Fabian amendment to delete all reference to supporting ad hoc authorities from an ILP motion. Surprisingly perhaps, Philip Snowden seconded the amendment, arguing that, in view of the 'keen division of opinion' Labour should not commit itself to 'particular details' on the form of educational authorities. Perhaps even more surprisingly, MacDonald denied that the question was one of 'mere details' and claimed that control by elected representatives would be nominal if County Councils replaced School Boards. Several union speakers opposed the Fabian

[40] *Clarion*, 9 February (Brocklehurst) 1901; 21 March (Hartley), 20 July (Macmillan) 1902.
[41] *Clarion*, 4 April 1902.
[42] *Clarion*, 11 April 1902.   [43] *Clarion*, 23 May 1902.

amendment. J. Baker pointed out that women were ineligible for election to County Councils. He announced 'he would oppose any proposal which limited the opportunities of women engaging in public work'. The amendment secured a derisory 15 votes and the ILP motion was carried overwhelmingly.[44]

The main discussion of the School Board issue in the *Labour Leader* followed, rather than preceded, the ILP annual conference that April. It was initiated by an anonymous 'Board School Teacher' who claimed that the NUT's support for the School Boards reflected the desire of elementary schoolteachers to become secondary school teachers, which might happen if the Boards became the single education authority. The School Board system, she or he claimed, encouraged 'faddists' and 'in the majority of cases Higher Grade Schools have been created to "dish" Grammar or Science Schools.' In response, Snowden described the Bill as 'a class attack on democratic education'.[45]

Then at the end of May 1902 the *Labour Leader* carried an article by Shaw entitled 'Socialism in a Bad Way' in which he elaborated his earlier *Clarion* attack on the opponents of the Bill. He claimed full credit for the Fabian Society as the intellectual author of the measure:

The Education Bill is obviously founded on our tract 'The Education Muddle and the Way Out'; so we naturally do not join in the Radical outcry against it. The other professed Socialists do, being, as I've explained, always soundly Radical when it comes to practical legislation.

This could, he claimed, be seen in the proceedings of the recent SDF conference:

the abandonment of the old catastrophic revolutionary balderdash and the pious platitudes about socialisation of the means of production and exchange and so forth has left nothing behind but old-fashioned Chartist Radicalism. They call for the Enfranchisement of Women and for Taxation of Land Values (now a Radical commonplace). They denounce the Education Bill . . . because it has the immense merit of attempting to abolish that insufferable nuisance, *ad hoc*, the School Board, and put the schools into the hands of a committee of the County Council, with the power to co-opt a minority of selected members – an admirable expedient which has worked well in London. This they call 'undemocratic' just as any very old-fashioned Trade Unionist would.[46]

It is noticeable, and significant, that Keir Hardie had taken no real part in the debate up to this point. Even now, Shaw's diatribe drew from him only a half-hearted defence of the School Board cause.[47] In sum, whereas

---

[44] *LRC Conference Report, 1902*, p. 74.   [45] *Labour Leader*, 12, 19 April 1902.
[46] *Labour Leader*, 31 May 1902.   [47] *Labour Leader*, 7 June 1902.

Justice had defended the School Boards – and indeed was to return to the issue periodically for more than four years – the ILP's lukewarmness grew into hostility. A few months after Hardie's half-heartedness, his *Labour Leader* anti-democrat 'Marxian' belatedly unmasked the Bill as

not an education Bill at all. It is a School Management Bill, and the outcry against . . . rate-aid to the denominational schools is sheer jabberknowled balderdash.
. . .
From the Socialist point of view, the 'Education' Bill may be allowed to go through without shouting. Make no fuss.[48]

'Adult suffrage' or 'women's suffrage'?

The 'militant' women's suffrage campaign forced socialists to take a stand, not only on the general principle of the political equality of women – to which with very, very few exceptions they all subscribed, at least theoretically – but on the degree of priority to be given to it among other desirable goals. Perhaps the most difficult question of all, was whether to support 'women's suffrage' (meaning votes for women on the basis of the existing male qualifications) or to continue to call – very fitfully up to this point – for full adult suffrage.

In the 1890s when the 'limited' suffrage was the demand of what were later to be called the 'constitutional' women's suffrage organisations, both *Justice* and the *Labour Leader* had supported adult suffrage. That some SDFers – apart from Belfort Bax whose anti-feminism was notorious within the Federation – tended to interpret adult suffrage as manhood suffrage, is suggested by a letter from Annie Hicks in 1887 insisting that the term included women.[49] But to say that this equation of 'adult' with 'man' was the standard Social-Democrat response is quite clearly wrong. Karen Hunt, in her study of the SDF and the 'Woman Question', rightly detects ambivalence in the Federation's failure to accord any sort of priority to the demand for adult suffrage, while acquitting it of trying to advance male suffrage under camouflage – 'It was not deliberately conceived as a smokescreen for a manhood suffrage campaign, for none followed.'[50]

In 1902 when Dora Montefiore argued that there was an inconsistency between the second article of the SDF programme (which insisted that

---

[48] *Labour Leader*, 8 November 1902.
[49] *Justice*, 24 September 1887.
[50] Karen Hunt, 'Equivocal Feminists. The Social-Democratic Federation and the Woman Question, 1894–1911'. PhD thesis, University of Manchester, 1988, p. 324.

'no project of law should become binding till accepted by the majority of the people') and *Justice*'s support of protective legislation for women workers 'who have no means of making their wishes known or of enforcing those wishes', 'Tattler' replied:

I am all for universal suffrage, by which I mean every adult, man or woman, having an equal vote. And if women, then, choose to vote away the barriers which have been erected to protect them from savage, unrestricted competition – why let them. But that would be a retrogressive, not a progressive, step, and it does not seem to me to accord with Socialist theory or principle to advocate it.[51]

The ILP, it will be remembered, added a specific reference to the enfranchisement of women to its 'political programme' in 1895; and the *Labour Leader* gave more space to articles on this question in the 1890s than either *Justice* or the *Clarion*. *Clarion* coverage was sparse before 1904. What all rejected, with seeming unanimity at this stage, was what *Justice* labelled from 1892 onwards the 'Fine Lady Suffrage'. When, in 1897, Ferdinand Faithful Begg, a Conservative MP, made one of his several attempts to promote a – 'limited' – women's suffrage bill, *Justice* dismissed the Begg Bill as 'illogical' and stated the position it was to maintain throughout:

As Social-democrats we stand for universal suffrage. Every man and woman who is called upon to obey the law should have an equal voice in the making of the law. That is what we understand by democracy . . . Right or wrong . . . democracy is the only sound principle.[52]

As though not to be outdone, *Labour Leader* called Begg's effort the 'Countess Drawing Room Suffrage Bill' while its resident anti-democrat confirmed that 'for all merely political reforms Marxian confesses an unbounded contempt'.[53]

The nucleus of the 'militant' suffrage campaign, centred on the Pankhursts, was closely associated with the ILP and concentrated initially upon work with women workers in the North. Like her mother and late father, Christabel Pankhurst was, at this time, an ILP member. Emmeline Pankhurst had been an NAC member in 1898–9. At the 1902 ILP conference she moved a motion which was seconded by Fred Jowett. It read:

That in order to improve the economic and social condition of women it is necessary to take immediate steps to secure the granting of the suffrage to women on the same terms on which it is, or may be, granted to men.

---

[51] *Justice*, 11, 18 October 1902.
[52] *Justice*, 13 February 1897.   [53] *Labour Leader*, 27, 13 February 1897.

This stimulated a counter-proposal in favour of 'adult suffrage'. The similar start of the second motion shows its reactive nature and thus highlights the major weakness of the adult suffrage campaign in the 1900s. On the other hand, tactical detailedness suggests a greater degree of political 'know-how', although to judge from its minutes the NAC failed to carry out this resolution. The second motion read:

That in order to improve the economic and social condition of the people of England it is necessary to take immediate steps to secure to every responsible adult the right to elect and serve on all public bodies. This Conference requests the NAC to draft a Bill that would secure such rights, submit it to the branches, and if approved, to ask Keir Hardie to introduce it into the House of Commons at the earliest possible date.[54]

Both motions were passed. In retrospect, this marks the beginning of a 'split', not only in the ILP but more generally in the socialist and suffrage movements. In *One Hand Tied Behind Us*, Jill Liddington and Jill Norris sum it up: 'The bigger wrangling between adult suffragists . . . and women suffragists . . . was extremely complex, and persistently dogged events for over a decade.'[55] From about this time, material on women's suffrage began to appear more frequently in the *Labour Leader*. During 1902 and 1903, correspondents included Isabella Ford, a member of the ILP's NAC, Christabel Pankhurst and Esther Roper, the Secretary of the North of England Society for Women's Suffrage. Andrew Rosen is not entirely correct to say that the foundation of the Women's Social and Political Union (WSPU) in October 1903 went unmentioned in the *Labour Leader*. A letter announcing the foundation of the new organisation did appear at the end of that month.[56]

Speedy success in exploiting ILP and wider Labour support seemed to have been achieved when the 1904 LRC Conference unanimously instructed its MPs to introduce a 'women's suffrage' bill. Moved by Wilkinson for the Burnley Weavers and seconded by Isabella Ford, the motion read:

That this Conference agrees with the principle of the Franchise being extended to women on the same basis as that allowed to them for parochial purposes; and that the Members of Parliament connected with the Labour Representation Committee introduce a Bill in the House of Commons dealing with this subject.[57]

[54] *Report of ILP Conference, 1902. Labour Leader*, 5 April 1902.
[55] Jill Liddington and Jill Norris, *One Hand Tied Behind Us: The Rise of the Women's Suffrage Movement* (London: Virago, 1978), p. 180.
[56] Andrew Rosen, *Rise Up Women! The Militant Campaign of the Women's Social and Political Union* (London, 1974), p. 32. *Labour Leader*, 31 October 1903.
[57] *Labour Representation Committee Conference Report*, 1904, p. 73.

The 'Countess Drawing Room' jibe seemed to have been forgotten. Only after that year's ILP conference, which reaffirmed support for 'women's suffrage', did major signs of disagreement emerge. A Bradford reader, 'Neal', complained that, if the 'energetic women' promoting the franchise question were allowed their way, the issue would dominate the ILP which would 'be turned from other pressing questions towards realising the vote for women'.[58] Soon after this, Snowden agreed that 'a suddenly-developed and all-absorbing interest in the cause of women's enfranchisement does not entitle to condemn wholesale and bitterly all who refuse to abandon all other political work for a limited women's franchise'. He pointed out that the Conference had again supported both 'women's' and 'adult' suffrage. 'If the ILP is determined to concentrate its efforts upon a legislative attempt to extend the franchise, it must make up its mind what it wants. It cannot be promoting an Adult Suffrage Bill and a Women's Representation Bill at the same time.'

Snowden went on to estimate that votes on the existing basis would enfranchise only about 500,000 of the 12 million adult women. The arguments for enfranchising the remaining $11\frac{1}{2}$ million, he urged, applied equally to the 4 million unenfranchised men. He concluded that the ILP should not *agitate* for the 'limited' suffrage, but should accept 'any measure however meagre' conceded by Parliament.[59]

From this point, the lines between 'women's' and 'adult' suffrage supporters became ever more sharply drawn. The former argued that the most pressing need was to 'advertise' the specific grievance of women as women and that, though leaving many women unenfranchised, the 'limited' measure would, in Christabel Pankhurst's words, 'strike the death-blow to the aristocracy of sex'.[60]

On the other side, 'adult suffrage' supporters soon added to their argument that 'women's suffrage' was undemocratic, their prediction that its implementation would, as Gertrude Tuckwell put it 'increase class disabilities under the guise of attempting to remove a sex disability'. The 'limited' franchise would strengthen Conservatism and might well actually prevent adult suffrage.[61]

Ada Nield Chew of Rochdale and H. Jennie Baker of Stockton-on-Tees criticised 'women's suffrage' supporters whom they saw as middle-class people trying to exploit working-class support for their own ends. Baker drew a parallel with 1832: 'The nearest precedent to the immediate position is, I think, when the middle-class men of England made use of the workers' agitation to secure the vote for them-

[58] *Labour Leader*, 2 April 1904.   [59] *Labour Leader*, 16 April 1904.
[60] *Labour Leader*, 23 April 1904.   [61] *Labour Leader*, 19 August 1904.

selves . . . '[62] By the autumn of that year 1904, there was news of the formation of an Adult Suffrage League whose members included Margaret Bondfield, H. Jennie Baker and Ada Nield Chew. The latter described it, in a letter to *Labour Leader*, as an organisation composed of 'Socialist women who are disgusted with the ILP's betrayal of working women's interests' i.e. by its support for women's suffrage'.[63] This initiative was immediately denounced in the *Labour Leader*, notably by Teresa Billington and Ramsay MacDonald, as a devious Liberal manoeuvre to lure unsuspecting Labour women into opposition to the ILP, and by the end of the year the adult suffragists, alienated by the ILP paper, began, as so many other dissident ILPers had done previously and would do in the future, to turn to the *Clarion*. In a letter to Blatchford's paper, Ada Nield Chew alleged that *Labour Leader* had on two occasions 'religiously excluded' one of her main arguments on 'women's suffrage'. She must have been taken aback – and her suspicions confirmed – when the following week there was a denial that her letters had been excluded, not from the *Labour Leader* editor, who might be presumed to take the decisions about which correspondence to print, but in a letter from Rachel Scott, the Secretary of the WSPU![64] How could she make such an authoritative statement – unless she was, in effect, overseeing the paper's letter columns?

On this issue the key person on the *Clarion* was not Blatchford or Thompson, but Julia Dawson who presided over the paper's 'women's page'. 'Julia Dawson' was Mrs D. J. Myddleton-Worral (d. 1947) who, among many other projects, was credited with starting the '*Clarion* vans'. She had supported 'women's suffrage' but had now come round to the adult suffrage position.

Anxious to refute the damaging charges that the 'limited' measure would strengthen middle-class Conservatism, the ILP's NAC resolved, in January 1905, to ask all its branches to ascertain the proportion of 'working women' on the municipal electoral lists.[65] The results appeared to show that 82 per cent of those enfranchised by the 'limited' suffrage would be working women. This conclusion was challenged by Jennie Baker who pointed to the ambiguity of the term 'working women' and claimed that some branches were including shopkeepers and others not normally regarded as working class. Andrew Rosen has described the survey as 'worthless'. In addition to the question of the definition of

---

[62] *Labour Leader*, 7 October 1904. For Ada Nield Chew (1870–1945), see, *Ada Nield Chew: The Life and Writings of a Working Woman*, presented by Doris Nield Chew (London, 1982).
[63] *Labour Leader*, 11 November 1904.
[64] *Clarion*, 16, 23 December 1904.   [65] *Minutes of the ILP NAC*, 28 January 1905.

'working women', only 50 out of 300 ILP branches returned the questionnaire. The constituencies that had these active ILP branches were not likely to be typical. And some categories of potential women voters were excluded.[66] However, the WSPU and other suffragist organisations were throughout this period to cite these survey results as positive proof that the vast majority enfranchised by a 'limited' bill would be working class.

Meanwhile the adult suffragists had scored a major success when the 1905 LRC Conference carried an amendment from the London Trades Council, a stronghold of the SDF, describing full adult suffrage as 'the only Franchise Reform which merits any support from Labour Members of Parliament'. This replaced the original motion endorsing the 'limited' Women's Enfranchisement Bill then before Parliament, despite a strong plea by Emmeline Pankhurst. Moving the amendment, Quelch argued that the motion 'placed sex first, but it was not the place of the LTC to place sex first; they had to put Labour first in every case'.[67]

The socialist movement was now split on familiar lines. The SDF, with veteran adult suffrage activist Herbert Burrows taking the lead, identified itself closely with the new Adult Suffrage Society and was lined up with Julia Dawson of the *Clarion* against the *Labour Leader* and the ILP. There were some differences from earlier episodes, however. The Fabian Society was not taking any prominent part in the debate. In the *Clarion*, adult suffrage was very much Julia Dawson's campaign. Indeed as late as 1908 Blatchford exasperated his colleagues by declaring 'I am in favour of adult suffrage, of course. But I am not opposed to the Limited Bill.'[68] Essentially, though, the division followed the usual pattern. This pattern was by now tending to impose itself on any new issue, particularly one concerning democracy. It was crystallised at the Easter conferences of 1905 of the two socialist parties. The SDF carried unanimously a motion 'strenuously to oppose' the Women's Enfranchisement Bill – a 'limited', 'women's suffrage' affair – and continue to support adult suffrage as 'the only Socialist and democratic franchise measure'.[69] In contrast, an amendment on similar lines was rejected by the ILP, 126 votes to 29, thus reaffirming support for 'Adult Suffrage with full political rights and privileges for women, and the immediate extension of the Franchise to women on the same terms as men'.

---

[66] *Labour Leader*, 14, 28 April 1905. Rosen, *Rise Up Women!*, p. 35.
[67] *LRC Conference Report*, 1905, pp. 235–7. The conversion of ILP Chairman Philip Snowden to the 'limited' suffrage cause was attributed by many at the time to the influence of Ethel Annakin, who was to marry him a few weeks after the Conference. This view is endorsed in Colin Cross, *Philip Snowden* (London, 1966). See pp. 63–4.
[68] *Clarion*, 10, 17 July 1908.   [69] *Justice*, 29 April 1905.

'At the heart of the disagreement between adultists and suffragists', Sandra Stanley Holton has argued, 'was the question of whether economic–class or sex–class subjection was more fundamental in the construction of social inequality'. Similarly, Karen Hunt has written: 'Crudely what was at issue was the primacy of sex or class.' And as Les Garner emphasises, 'for the socialist feminist the dilemma was agonisingly acute. She was torn between loyalty to her class and loyalty to her sex.'[70] This is certainly true, and the unanswerable nature of that question has much to do with the problems that many socialists, women and men, had in arriving at a satisfactory position.

But there is another, related, dimension. For the convinced proponents of 'women's suffrage' the crucial principle was, indeed, the equality of the sexes. As Hardie put it at the end of 1904, the aim was 'an immediate equalisation of the sexes'.[71] Enfranchisement 'on the same basis as men' symbolised women's claim to social equality. From this standpoint how 'limited' that enfranchisement would be in practice was irrelevant.

It clearly did matter for those concerned about what they saw as the political interests of the working class. But even many who might have supported a symbolic advance of sexual equality in another area were uneasy because the symbolic demand was for voting rights: this necessarily brought into play another principle, that of democracy. And here, votes for women had to be seen in the context of other democratic demands. Thus, when the demand for an immediate move towards sex equality appeared to conflict with what these proponents understood as democratic principles, there was a real dilemma which many resolved by deciding that democracy must override equality. Thus *Justice* was able to bracket together support for the 'limited' franchise and opposition to the second ballot as being both 'Against Democracy':

It is curious how anti-democratic sentiments and theories grow with people who once abandon sound Socialist principles.

. . . we have the chiefs of the ILP at Liverpool supporting a measure for a limited suffrage for women . . . which tells directly against the democratic

---

[70] Sandra Stanley Holton, *Feminism and Democracy. Women's Suffrage and Reform Politics in Britain 1900–1918*, 1986, pp. 57–8. Karen Hunt, 'Equivocal Feminists', p. 303. Les Garner, 'Suffragism and Socialism: Sylvia Pankhurst 1903–1914' in Ian Bullock and Richard Pankhurst (eds.), *Sylvia Pankhurst. From Artist to Anti-Fascist* (London, 1992), p. 61. For the complexities of the 'women's suffrage' versus 'adult suffrage' dilemma, see also Les Garner, *Stepping Stones to Women's Liberty – Feminist ideas in the Women's Suffrage Movement, 1900–1918* (London, 1984).

[71] *Labour Leader*, 9 December 1904.

principle of equal political rights for all . . . Now we have Mr Ramsay MacDonald writing against another democratic principle – the second ballot . . . With a second ballot everybody would be free to choose and it is not easy to see how anyone claiming to be a Socialist could bring himself to vote against it.[72]

Having made their judgement about the relative importance of the priorities involved, some socialists saw no reason to question their decision, but others were so uneasy that they either changed their minds, or attempted to bridge both positions via the 'womanhood suffrage' pressed for by the Women's Co-operative Guild. Changes of position by Charlotte Despard, Dora Montefiore, and Sylvia Pankhurst exemplify this unease. The subsequent career of Ada Nield Chew (whom we have seen so vehemently attacking the 'limited' version, yet who later became an organiser for the – 'limited' suffragist – National Union of Women's Suffrage Societies) suggests the difficulties that many working-class and socialist women in particular must have experienced in deciding exactly where they stood.[73] By 1911 she was writing to *Common Cause* explaining that she had previously been unable to

see that anything less than Adult Suffrage would be of any use to the working woman, and therefore opposed the limited measure as being reactionary. Now, after many months of anxious thinking, I have come to the conclusion that we cannot get on at all whilst women have no means of even presenting their point of view . . . and that to be determined to wait until all women can vote is as reactionary and as impracticable as to oppose all reform because it does not go as far on our way as we wish it . . . [74]

The suffrage was the most intractable of the democratic issues which divided socialists in the early years of the century. But, like the other two conflicts we have examined in this chapter, an extra edge was given to the disagreements by the sense that not only a chronological corner had been turned in 1900. The 'practical' was beginning to seem more deliverable. It was one thing, said some, for the 'very old-fashioned Trade Unionists' and believers in 'Chartist Radicalism' who mistook themselves for socialists, to get themselves caught up in 'merely political' demands, but the danger – though never very great – that the National Democratic League might become a rival to the LRC increased the urgency of 'rubbishing' such behaviour. It was one thing for the Fabian Society to have a theoretically narrow and restrictive notion of democracy and to reject scathingly the referendum and initiative. It was a different matter

---

[72] *Justice*, 11 February 1905.
[73] Chew, *Life and Writings*, pp. 42–55.
[74] *The Common Cause*, 16 February 1911. Quoted in Holton, *Feminism and Democracy*, pp. 59–60.

when, as with the Education Act of 1902, Fabians seemed to have successfully 'permeated' the government. Opinions differed, and were hotly debated, as to which was really easier to achieve: 'limited' women's suffrage or full universal suffrage. But underlying the vehemence of the arguments was a sense of urgency, founded upon the belief that *something* was possible in the area of franchise reform.

In this situation, temptations to be 'practical' were much more alluring than ever before. One response, that of the SDF, was to recognise the dangers and hold sternly aloof from them, fearful that the least compromise could lead inexorably to abandoning everything:

No one goes entirely wrong all at once, but a little step out of the straight path means so little, and there are so many temptations to take it. It leads to a short cut to the end in view . . . But it is the first step that costs, and the others are easier still . . . [75]

Yet there was never any chance that this line could be generally held, once Labour moved from the stage of propaganda to full political engagement. The question was increasingly, not whether there would be adaptation and compromise, but their nature. What would be the terms of engagement in the political system? Crucial to this was how socialists saw, or could be persuaded to see, the state.

[75] *Justice*, 11 February 1905.

8 Socialists and the state

The 'gulf' reaffirmed

Should Social-Democrats accept the label 'state socialists'? Considering this question in 1905, Hyndman concluded that they should not for two reasons. There was an 'ever-present danger of fostering Caesarism and crystallising bureaucracy'. Also, state control could leave intact 'competition, wage-earning and the whole of the forms of wage slavery.' This was the antithesis of Social-Democracy which aimed at 'a complete social revolution, which shall abolish the present State and establish a Society' in its place. The state, as opposed to the community, he went on, had always been based on class privilege and property. Once private property 'in the powers of producing and distributing wealth' had been abrogated, the state, as a force dominating the people and 'holding the balance' between conflicting interests would be replaced by 'a co-operative Social-Democracy'. Although it would be necessary to 'use the State against both landlords and capitalists' during the 'transition period', this would be done with the express intention of bringing about 'an end to the State'.[1]

The 'state socialism' from which Hyndman wished to distance 'Social-Democracy' was well represented during the same year by Ramsay MacDonald's *Socialism and Society*. When the book appeared, *Labour Leader*'s reviewer, 'G' (Glasier?), called it the ILP's 'most important contribution . . . to . . . international Socialist Literature' and, in particular, as a 'tremendous assault' on Marxism. His treatment of the state was singled out for praise.[2] What MacDonald himself called the 'positive view of the State' was predicated upon a biological analogy:

The Socialist refuses to regard the State as a mere collection of individuals, the majority of whom coerce the minority; he regards it as the means of expressing a will which belongs to the minority as well as the majority, because the minority

[1] *Justice*, 15 July 1905.   [2] *Labour Leader*, 4 August 1905.

is organically connected with the community for which the State is acting . . . [and] because . . . the communal life is as real to him as the life of an organism built up of many living cells.[3]

The biological analogy could take many forms. One was to interpret society in terms of the most familiar of all organisms, the human body. An extreme example was presented to *Labour Leader* readers in 1912 by T. D. Benson, the ILP Treasurer. Benson realised that his article, 'Socialism and Syndicalism; a Biological Study', had implications 'not altogether agreeable to the present idea of Socialists'. He predicted that 'There will be a governing or organising class, corresponding to the brain, but an organising class whose only motive for existence is service to the community – a class which, also, may be hereditary under Socialism, perhaps must be so.'[4] Of course, it would be unreasonable to hold MacDonald responsible for Benson's socialist eugenics. 'Social Darwinism' of one variety or another was commonplace in the early years of the century and it was hardly likely to by-pass socialists entirely. The notion that socialism would be the work of the 'superman' or of a 'samurai' élite was familiar to readers of Shaw and H. G. Wells. Another example is in Keir Hardie's *My Confession of Faith in the Labour Alliance.*

The same instinct which leads a herd of buffaloes or a pack of wolves to follow the older and stronger member of the herd or pack, operates in like fashion in a great democratic movement. It is the truest and purest form of democracy.

When, following the book's publication by the ILP, Leonard Hall protested against this statement, the unrepentant Hardie defended it as one that 'should commend itself to every ultra-democrat'.[5]

MacDonald remained the major exponent in Britain of an 'evolutionary' socialism drawing authority from Darwinian analogies. It is often forgotten today just how prolific a writer he was during the last pre-war decade. *Socialism and Society* (1905) was followed by *Labour and the Empire* (1907), *Socialism* (1907), the two volumes of *Socialism and Government* (1909), *The Socialist Movement* (1911), *Syndicalism: A Critical Examination* (1912), and *The Social Unrest: Its Cause* (1913). Some of these at least, like *Socialism and Society*, which reached its sixth

---

[3] James Ramsay MacDonald, *Socialism and Society*, 1905, p. 133. This was the second volume of 'The Socialist Library', published by the ILP, of which MacDonald was editor. He had initiated the series. The NAC had agreed to take full financial responsibility for the venture. See *Independent Labour Party, NAC Minutes*, 3 April 1905, p. 21.

[4] *Labour Leader*, 7 June 1912.

[5] J. Keir Hardie, *My Confession of Faith in the Labour Alliance*, 1909, p. 13. *Labour Leader*, 28 May, 4 June 1909.

edition in 1908, were quite widely read. And that year the *Labour Leader* noted approvingly that MacDonald's organic view of society 'kills two fallacies with one weapon – the fallacies of Individualism and Marxism'.[6]

MacDonald's key position in the movement ensured widespread attention and lent his views an 'official' aura. His 'scientific' theory seemed based on science more up-to-date and all-embracing than Marxism's political economy. To a large extent MacDonald was dressing up the 'common sense' of many Labour supporters in the trappings of theory. As Bernard Barker puts it in his introduction to *Ramsay MacDonald's Political Writings*, 'The instincts of Keir Hardie were made rational in the self-taught erudition of MacDonald.'[7]

Like us, the *Labour Leader* reviewer of *Socialism and Government* (1909) singled out MacDonald's treatment of political organisation:

It is here that the author strikes across the current democratic opinion, condemns certain ideas which are growing in popular favour, as in principle opposed to the scientific conception of the State, and in practice detrimental to state efficiency.

The 'condemned' ideas were proportional representation and the referendum. MacDonald's opposition to them would, the reviewer went on, 'cause a little commotion in many minds'. The reviewer's summing up of MacDonald's position was perceptive:

MacDonald emphasises the necessity of regarding the State as a collective entity with organs and functions, with inherited tendencies, and in the course of development.
. . . where the political democrat insists on popular rights, MacDonald insists on the citizen's duties . . . where the one insists on equality the latter insists on qualifications. In a word, in politics, the advocate of Social-Democracy (using the word in its broadest sense) lays stress on 'Democracy' the author of *Socialism and Government* lays stress on 'Social'.[8]

In July 1914 the *Labour Leader* quoted Professor Gilbert Salter's judgement that MacDonald was 'on the working of the Constitution the very strictest of Conservatives'.[9] We can venture further: MacDonald, with his appeals for 'reverence and deference' for Parliament's 'dignity and authority'[10] drifted on wings of evolutionist analogy towards the airspace of Edmund Burke. For MacDonald, indeed, most of the essential elements of democracy already existed: 'The modern State in most civilised countries is democratic, and in spite of remaining

[6] *Labour Leader*, 20 November 1908.
[7] Bernard Barker (ed.), *Ramsay MacDonald's Political Writings* (London, 1972), p. 2.
[8] *Labour Leader*, 26 November 1909.   [9] *Labour Leader*, 9 July 1914.
[10] William English Walling, *Socialism As It Is: A Survey of the World-Wide Revolutionary Movement* (London, 1912), pp. 149–50.

anomalies and imperfections if the masses of ordinary people are agreed on any policy, neither rich electors, privileged peers, nor reigning houses could stand in their way.'[11] Against this, the American socialist W. E. Walling quoted comments from the Radical, J. A. Hobson:

'Under a professed and real enthusiasm for a representative system', as opposed to direct government, Mr Hobson finds that there is concealed 'a deep distrust for democracy' . . . he protests that 'the false pretence that democracy exists' in Great Britain has proved 'the subtlest defence of privilege'.

Behind MacDonald were, as we have seen, the Fabians. Walling was right to see them, and especially Webb and Shaw, as 'idealising the State' and directing British socialism 'from the first almost exclusively against the abstraction "individualism", and not against the concrete thing, the capitalist class'.[12]

As we saw earlier, the *Report on Fabian Policy* of 1896 had explicitly rejected all notions of 'direct democracy' or 'popular government'. More recently, the Fabian Executive Committee in November 1906 had been even more explicit than ten years previously on the question of democracy.

Democracy is a word with a double meaning. To the bulk of Trade Unionists and labourers it means an intense jealousy and mistrust of all authority, and a resolute reduction of both representatives and officials to the position of mere delegates and agents of the majority. From this point of view, democracy would find its consummation in a House of Commons where, without any discussion, divisions were taken by counting postcards received from the entire population on questions submitted to the people by referendum and initiative.

Because the Fabians have given no countenance to this attitude they have been freely denounced as undemocratic and even Tory. Fabian democracy is in fact sharply opposed to it and certain to come into conflict with it at almost every step in the practical development of Socialism. We have always accepted government by a representative deliberative body controlling an expert bureaucracy as the appropriate public organisation for Socialism. When asked where government by the people comes in, we reply that government has to be carried out by division of labour and specialization as much as railway management has; and what Democracy really means is government by the consent of the people.
. . .
Between these two conceptions of the elected person . . . there is a gulf which will sooner or later become a party boundary; and this gulf unfortunately cuts the Labour movement right down the middle.[13]

---

[11] MacDonald, *Socialism and Society*, p. 132.11.
[12] Walling, *Socialism As It Is*, pp. 50, 54.
[13] *Report of the Special Committee appointed in February 1906, to consider measures for increasing the scope, influence, income and activities of the Society. Together with the Executive Committee's Report and Resolutions thereon.* Fabian Society, November 1906, pp. 38–9.

As we will see, this prediction was to be particularly plausible during periods of social unrest.

'Popular government' in early twentieth-century Britain

On the 'popular government' side of the divide too, there were many who actively deepened the 'gulf'. In 1900, for example, A. A. Watts produced a series of articles for *Justice* entitled 'The SDF Programme Amplified'. The first three dealt with the election of 'all organisers', with 'legislation by the people', proportional representation and the 'Citizen Army'. Watts constantly stressed how much existing practices 'fell short of democracy:

> It is a mockery as I will show. Firstly, more than half the population (the female portion) are absolutely shut out from any part in choosing the delegates; secondly, only a portion of the remainder have any participation in the business; thirdly, those elected do not administer on behalf of the people, the few who really carry on the business being chosen and appointed by one person only (he sometimes not even being among the elected delegates), who in his turn received his mandate from the hereditary *non-elective* monarch! . . . the process of exhaustion could go no further.[14] (original emphasis)

In these conditions, Watts argued, the law-making process involved so little consultation that most people were 'quite ignorant of what legislation was passed'. By contrast,

> we assert most emphatically that no legislation, no laws, can be binding upon the people unless the majority express their acceptance of them.
> Thus . . . Social Democrats are asking for that without which no people can be free.

Only rarely, Watts continued, when the issues that divided Liberals and Conservatives were questions of major importance, did electors have even a slight influence 'and then it is in the heat of a General Election, and with only the merest knowledge of what the Bill under discussion really contains'. In these circumstances, self-government was an illusion:

> As steps to realise and hasten this we advocate the payment . . . of members of Parliament and all local bodies, and also the official expenses of elections, adult suffrage, triennial Parliaments, proportional representation, and the second ballot. These reforms together with the institution of the initiative and referendum . . . will go a long way towards obtaining complete freedom from class domination.[15]

[14] *Justice*, 11 August 1900.   [15] *Justice*, 25 August 1900.

Watts's third article explained that proportional representation meant that 'minorities should be considered and if possible represented', while 'The referendum provides that all laws passed by the national assembly or Parliament shall, on requisition of a certain number of electors, be referred to the whole of the electors to vote upon', and that the initiative extended the principle to include the right of the electorate to put forward their own legislative proposals.[16]

In these respects the SDF was in line with the decisions of the Socialist International which, also in 1900, concluded that it was 'the duty of the Socialist Party everywhere to agitate for universal suffrage and proportional representation' and to seek to 'acquire and maintain everywhere the referendum and initiative as the prerogative of popular sovereignty'.[17]

In those European countries with massive conscript armies controlled by privileged officer corps which played an actually or potentially decisive rôle in the state, democratising the army had to be an important priority for a broad spectrum of socialist and democratic opinion. In Britain the Citizen Army was, as a *Labour Leader* critic later called it, 'one of the pet prodigies of the Social-Democrats'.[18] It had little or no appeal outside SDF ranks, and in the long run proved divisive there too, after it had become inextricably linked for many with the campaign to introduce conscription as in the National Service League, with the 'German Menace' warnings of Hyndman, the less measured ones of Blatchford, and jingoism and militarism generally.[19] But, for its supporters, the Citizen Army was 'the only form of military organisation compatible with democracy – with popular institutions and national liberty'.[20] Harry Quelch produced a pamphlet advocating the 'Armed Nation' in 1900 and Will Thorne, who remained as much a Social-Democrat as some other Labour MPs remained Liberals, introduced a private member's bill for a citizen army in 1908.

When, on this latter occasion, some objected that the Labour Party did not support the idea of the citizen army, *Justice* retorted that neither did the party support 'limited' women's suffrage but this had not deterred Hardie, Snowden and others.[21]

The issue has to be seen in the context of the SDF's frustrated efforts

---

[16] *Justice*, 8 September 1900.   [17] *Justice*, 6 October 1900.
[18] *Labour Leader*, 4 September 1908.
[19] See Walter Kendall, *The Revolutionary Movement in Britain 1900–1921. The Origins of British Communism* (London, 1969), ch. 3.
[20] *Justice*, 5 September 1908.
[21] *Justice*, 12 September 1908.

to get Labour to adopt a programme – *any* programme – to which its MPs would be committed. There was also the SDF's outrage at the activities of 'limited' suffrage supporters in the Parliamentary group. Probably, Thorne's bill was to some extent intended to force the issue of a definite programme or at least as a frustrated 'two-can-play-at-that-game' move. The question of the Labour programme and the relationship of the group to the party will be examined in the next chapter.

Viewed as a democratic device, there were two crucial aspects to the citizen army. The larger one was supposedly to remove the coercive power of the state by generalising it throughout the –male – population. The citizen army was to be quite different from forces like the Volunteers or the new Territorial Army, which

arms, and trains, only those who are perfectly willing, for sheer love of fighting, or any other reason, to be the tools of our masters. As against the voluntary system we should prefer conscription. But we are far from advocating conscription or compulsory military service . . . What we advocate is . . . compulsory and universal military training . . .

Conscription involves the withdrawal of men from civil life, keeping them herded together in barracks, establishing them as a caste, as 'soldiers' as distinct from civilians or citizens. Conscription, or any form of military service means a standing army of men, decivilised . . . in antagonism to the great body of the people, the citizens. The compulsory military training we advocate carries with it the avoidance of these evils. It means that every citizen shall be trained to act as a soldier at need, but no one shall become merely a soldier or cease to be a citizen.[22]

The second aspect, integral to the larger intention, was the internal democracy of the citizen army itself. Thorne's bill provided for a Central Administrative Board elected by ballot by members of the force and for the election of officers, subject to their meeting the criteria laid down by the Board, by the men in the unit. Members would retain full civil rights and it was specified that the citizen force was only to be available for national defence and never to be used in civil disturbances.[23]

Many socialist opponents were not against the citizen army in principle. Their case is well summed up in 1908 at the time of Thorne's Bill by the *Labour Leader*'s comment that 'every soul outside a lunatic asylum perfectly well knows . . . [that no] capitalist Parliament or Government between now and the downfall of capitalism would ever dream of' such a measure. Five years later Alf Barton denounced the idea

---

[22] Harry Quelch, *Social-Democracy and the Armed Nation* (London, 1900), p. 6.
[23] *Justice*, 29 August 1908.

as playing 'into the hands of the National Service humbugs'. *Justice* naturally argued the opposite: that it was the failure to offer any democratic alternative for the real problem of national defence which played into such hands.[24]

As an idea, the citizen army must be seen in the context of the conception of 'popular government' peculiar, in Britain, to the SDF. This extended beyond the familiar aim of democratising legislative power by radical parliamentary reform and 'direct legislation' to seeking the most direct forms of control and accountability for every executive or administrative function of the state. Hence the commitment to the School Boards – or to their replacement by some equally 'direct' Education Councils.

Hence also the similar position taken on the question of the abolition of the Boards of Guardians at the time of the Reports of the Royal Commission on the Poor Laws in 1909. At that year's SDP Conference – the SDF had become the Social-Democratic Party in 1907 – Fred Knee read a paper 'on the dangers arising from the multitude of non-representative and nominated bodies which are rapidly tending to deprive the people of control of their affairs'. A motion, successfully moved by Hyndman and Burrows, drew attention to 'the serious danger arising from unelected bureaucratic authority in every department, which is filching away the liberties of the people without their being aware of it'.[25]

When the Poor Law Commission's Minority Report appeared in pamphlet form, *Justice* conceded that its proposals were better than those of the Majority but expressed 'considerable misgivings' about the proposal, common to both Reports, to abolish the Boards of Guardians:

There is a tendency, very prevalent nowadays, in the direction of removing all administration from the control of directly elected bodies to that of close committees of experts and bureaucrats. This tendency is distinctly anti-democratic and mischievous.[26]

Hyndman urged that 'The same pernicious influence which is creating the New Bureaucracy deliberately destroyed the School Boards of England' and substituted an arrangement whereby, to local councils, 'the education of children has become of less importance than the question of tramway fares'. Similarly, Social-Democrats were for Labour Exchanges 'under the control of the working people, not for wage-reducing bureaux

---

[24] *Labour Leader*, 4 September 1908. *Justice*, 15 November 1913. *Justice*, 25 July 1908.
[25] *Justice*, 17 April 1909.
[26] *Justice*, 31 July 1910.

kept up at public expense under the exclusive control of such a crew of corrupt factionists as have been appointed by the present government'. The Poor Law proposals were 'another insidious attempt to strengthen the forces of bureaucracy and I very much regret that George Lansbury should have been party to such dangerous recommendations'.[27]

During the winter of 1910–11 *Justice* carried a series of more than a dozen articles by George C. Swanson detailing the Minority Report's findings and Social-Democratic objections to them. Swanson preceded the series with a denunciation of Sidney Webb as the inspirer of the Report and as an arch-mistruster of democracy. The Report's proposals for compulsory retraining and detention colonies for the recalcitrant were 'too reactionary even for Balfour and Asquith'.[28]

Later in the same series, Swanson discerned more broadly a subtle but relentless undermining of democratic ideas and practices:

When the School Boards were abolished a few years ago, few people realised what the change really meant both as regards the education of their children and the consequent centralisation of government. There is evidence that the monarchist idea, accompanied with a tendency to restrict the government function is growing in this country . . .

He went on to blame the failure of the socialist movement as a whole to resist this anti-democratic tendency on the malign influence of Fabianism:

Too long have we regarded this bureaucratic fancy of the Fabians as something to be smiled at, and now they have gone so far as to include this vicious suggestion in the recommendations of a Royal Commission, and have managed to persuade the Independent Labour Party, in their blindness, to endorse it, besides sending some of their propagandists running around the British Isles to promulgate the doctrine; it is time for us to expose and oppose them.[29]

The SDF was indeed much more isolated on this issue than they had been at the time of the School Board controversy. The 1910 Labour Party Conference supported a motion moved by Lansbury endorsing the Minority Report and the ILP election manifesto gave a prominent place to the Report's proposals.[30]

Even more clearly than the Education Bill this issue showed up the difference between the Social-Democrat and *Clarion* conceptions of 'popular government'. In the *Clarion*, Suthers described the Minority Report as being 'based on a thoroughly sound democratic and socialist

[27] *Justice*, 27 August 1910.
[28] *Justice*, 22 October 1910, reprinted from the *Letchworth Citizen*.
[29] *Justice*, 11 February 1911.   [30] *Labour Leader*, 18 February, 25 November 1910.

foundation', and the paper favourably reviewed the pamphlet version. For the *Clarion*, 'popular government' was almost exclusively a matter of 'direct legislation'.[31] 'Direct legislation' or the initiative and referendum had become the hallmark of *Clarion* democracy in the 1890s as we saw in an earlier chapter. Here, during the 1900s there was a marked American slant in the paper. This is hardly surprising when one considers that, every other year from 1898 to 1906 and every year except three from 1907 to 1918, at least one US state adopted the referendum and initiative (or, in a few cases, the referendum only).[32] Articles by Professor Frank Parsons of Boston Law School, and Eltweed Pomeroy, the President of the Direct Legislation League, were given front-page prominence. The League had been formed in the early 1890s and Pomeroy, like several of its leading propagandists, had come to 'direct legislation' via the single-tax movement.[33]

Pomeroy's argument was thus inextricably economic as well as political. 'Business combinations' – 'grinding monopolies . . . vast, powerful and subtle despotisms really governing the people without their consent, really taxing them without representation'[34] – were bad enough in private hands. And their threat would increase: 'as well as controlling the necessities of life,]they] are . . . getting control of our Government'. Yet state ownership had even greater dangers:

If the time ever arrives when the Government owns and operates the means of production, distribution and exchange, and the Government is owned by the few, for the benefit of the few, we will then have a slavery beside which medieval serfdom was small and weak, beside which chattel slavery was insignificant.

To avoid the danger, it was necessary to establish truly democratic control over the state *before* the state was brought to take over the industrial and commercial monopolies.

The first monopoly which the people must own, control and operate is the monopoly of Government. The people must actually own and operate their own Government, and I know of no other way of doing this than by Direct Legislation; the Initiative and Referendum. The Government is supreme in the land, and the corporations are only supreme because they control the Government. Let the people actually control the Government by Direct Legislation and they will have supreme power. The powers that now control the Government, and through it the people, will then fight, lie, bamboozle, cringe, and fawn for the

---

[31] *Clarion*, 13 February, 18 June 1909.
[32] Thomas E. Cronin, *Direct Democracy. The Politics of the Initiative, Referendum, and Recall* (London, 1989), p.51. See table 3.1.
[33] Cronin, *Direct Democracy*, p. 50.
[34] *Clarion*, 9 February 1901.

existence in exploiting the people. They will be partially successful in these operations at first. But as the people get the knowledge and power of experience, the fighting, fooling and fawning will become less and less effective. Direct legislation is the only means by which they can get the absolutely requisite knowledge and experience. When the people actually control the Government, which they can only do by Direct Legislation, then they will not fear any advance towards Socialism, because if they find it is a mistake they can retrace their steps. At present we are advancing rapidly towards a false and bastard Socialism; advancing without our volition, without any power to check or guide or retrace . . . [35]

This anticipated much of Belloc's warning of the dangers of the approaching 'Servile State', a notion whose impact on British socialists we will discuss in a later chapter. At the time of the Pomeroy *Clarion* articles their author was visiting Britain and offering to lecture on 'Democracy, Direct Legislation, American Politics, Methods of Socialism, and Christian Socialism.[36] He quickly became as convinced of the class basis of British opposition to direct legislation as, on the opposition side of the fence, the Fabians were that its supporters were 'Trade Unionists and labourers'. In Britain, Pomeroy argued, the actual governing of the country was the province of the upper-middle class. 'They are bureaucrats and not democrats at heart. They believe in machinery . . . This is why some leaders of the Fabian Society have opposed Direct Legislation. This belief in machinery will in the future be the cause of their downfall.' He had found a 'profound ignorance' among the middle classes about the 'masses'.

For instance I was so repeatedly told that Direct Legislation was unpopular in England that I believed it, until I began to speak. Among the English workmen Direct Legislation is not unpopular; it is unknown. I believe there was not a single working men's audience that I spoke to on Direct Legislation but I had three quarters of them with me before I closed.[37]

The referendum as 'practical politics': 1910–11

The irreconcilable positions on direct legislation we have seen established among British socialists during the 1890s and reinforced in the early 1900s held firm on the single occasion when, fleetingly, the referendum became an issue of parliamentary politics.

During the 'constitutional crisis' between the two elections of 1910, the Conservatives came to see it as a way of combatting the Liberals from a less obviously reactionary stance than the defence of the hereditary

---

[35] *Clarion*, 16 February 1901.
[36] *Clarion*, 9 February 1901.   [37] *Clarion*, 4 May 1901.

principle in the House of Lords.[38] The 'Lansdowne resolution' which was debated in the Lords in November 1910 included the demand that in future 'a matter of great gravity which has not been adequately submitted to the judgement of the people', should, if the two Houses could not agree on it, be settled by referendum.[39] The question of a referendum became a key issue in the election campaign. The Liberals decided to make as much as possible out of the Conservative intention to use it to block Liberal measures such as Home Rule and the 'People's Budget'. They challenged their Tory opponents to pledge themselves to put their own major policy, Tariff Reform, to the same test. Egged on by most of the Unionist press, led by the *Observer*, Balfour took up the challenge: on 29 November he publicly committed himself to putting Tariff Reform to a referendum.

Both *Justice* and the *Clarion* urged that socialists should not abandon the referendum merely because it seemed to put them in the same camp as the Tories. *Justice*, which had already congratulated Balfour for his stand on the referendum in an 'Open Letter' published the previous week, noted with disgust the fickleness and partisanship of many erstwhile supporters of direct democracy:

Hitherto all democrats and Radicals, as well as many Liberals, have professed to be in favour of the Referendum . . . but no sooner does Balfour suggest that . . . the referendum might be used . . . than hey presto! all is changed, and Liberals, Radicals and Labourists fall to denouncing the Referendum as . . . a device of the evil one.[40]

Meanwhile, in the *Clarion*, J. Cartmel – otherwise J. Cartmel-Robinson, the Christian Socialist vicar of Hoxton – appealed to that paper 'to open up the question of the referendum' and to socialists generally to be put off neither by Tory support nor Liberal opposition.[41] The *Clarion* needed little prompting, and for some weeks the '*Clarion* debate on the referendum' once more occupied a prominent place in the paper.

During the debate a significant difference emerged between two democratisers, Walter Crane, who like the Social-Democrats stressed the *particular* need for foreign policy and defence issues to be settled by referendum, and Alex Thompson who wanted such matters entrusted to 'permanent officials unaffected by the fluctuations of party' because he believed that such questions were beyond the competence of the electorate. 'When the voice of the majority rules in matters which

---

[38] See Neal Blewett, *The Peers, The Parties, and The People: The General Elections of 1910* (London, 1972), especially pp. 174–5.
[39] Blewett, *Peers, Parties, People*, p. 172.
[40] *Justice*, 14, 24 December 1910.   [41] *Clarion*, 9 December 1910.

the majority are clearly incompetent to understand, the voice of the majority is painfully like the cackle of geese, and geese do not always save the Capitol.' The referendum, Thompson concluded, should only be used 'in regard to matters directly appertaining to the people's lives and needs'.[42]

Most contributors favoured the referendum and some were particularly pleased by what Thompson called 'the Tory attempt to dish the Whigs', though only one correspondent, Charles L. Marson, went so far as to raise a cheer for the 'Good old semi-Socialist Tories! They are often the true revolutionists – witness the factory acts and much else.'[43]

Disillusionment was swift. Before Christmas, Thompson was castigating the Tories for their 'insolent declaration' that the offer of a Referendum had been a one-off commitment during the General Election campaign and had now been withdrawn.[44]

The *Labour Leader* took an equivocal position when Balfour's pledge made the referendum an issue, recommending perusal of Hobson's *Crisis of Liberalism* and Jane T. Stoddart's *Against the Referendum* for the cases for and against the device.[45] It became definitely hostile on the news that a referendum in Australia had rejected some proposals by the ruling Labour Party. It added that Swiss history showed 'that in that country the representatives of the people are more advanced than the people themselves, and that the referendum, in consequence, acts as a drag on organic change.'[46]

By contrast, though *some* Social-Democrats dissented on the referendum question – Belfort Bax argued that democracy in the sense of majority rule could only have significance 'after, and not before, the establishment of a Socialist Commonwealth'[47] – the general commitment was made clear editorially: 'to us democracy is a principle fundamental to our Socialism . . . and the reference to the people of any project of law is essential to democracy.'[48] *Justice*'s stance on the referendum was recognised by at least one Conservative MP.[49] The Fabian response to the whole episode was very different. They republished Clifford Sharp's *The Case Against the Referendum*. Sharp took much the same view as MacDonald, whose *Socialism and Government* he quoted with approval.

---

[42] *Clarion*, 16, 23 December 1910.   [43] *Clarion*, 16 December 1910.
[44] *Clarion*, 23 December 1910.
[45] *Labour Leader*, 16 December 1910.
[46] *Labour Leader*, 5 May 1911. The *Leader*'s interpretation of the significance of the Australian referendum was challenged the following week in a letter from G. B. Clark.
[47] *Justice*, 18 February 1911.
[48] *Justice*, 1 July 1911.   [49] *Hansard*, 26 April 1911.

Electors were more susceptible to the influence of the press, Sharp argued, than any reasonably honest public-spirited representative assembly. Minorities would suffer both because they had more difficulty putting their case to the whole people than to a representative assembly and because voters would only consider their personal opinions, whereas a representative had 'the semi-judicial function of . . . deciding how far it might be right that the wishes of this or that minority should receive consideration'. The central issue was whether to pursue the ideal of 'majority rule' or that of 'government by consent'. Should legislation be decided 'by the mere counting of heads or by methods which allow of a more or less accurate estimation, both quantitative and qualitative, of all the forces and currents of opinion at work in the community'?

True, Sharp did make some concessions to the supporters of direct legislation. He dismissed 'the widely prevalent notion that the Referendum has a conservative effect upon legislation' and conceded that 'it remains undeniable that a series of popular votings on important questions would be calculated to have some extremely valuable educational results'. All that could be said against this argument was that 'even education may be bought too dearly'.[50]

But, Sharp insisted, the argument that opponents of the referendum were élitist was wrong. Elected representatives were not superior to their constituents; it was simply that they had greater access to evidence relevant for making legislative decisions: 'A representative body is "superior" to the electors for the purpose of legislation in precisely the same sense as a jury is superior to the public for the purposes of giving a just verdict.'[51] In a long review in *Justice*, Edward Hartley gave Sharp credit for having recognised 'its educative value as the strongest argument in favour of the referendum'. But Hartley dismissed Sharp's argument concerning the power of the press even more airily than the latter had rejected the educational argument:

I am prepared to admit that it is very probable that the democracy, not having learned to democ, would for a while make foolish mistakes. But what is life but an education built upon the foundations marked all through by mistakes?

Sharp's central argument in favour of 'Government by Consent' Hartley simply dismissed as 'laughable':

So far from being an argument against direct government, I should use it exactly the other way round. The supposed argument against majority rule is really an

---

[50] Clifford D. Sharp, *The Case Against the Referendum*, Fabian Tract no. 155 (London, 1911), pp. 7–10, 19.
[51] Sharp, *Case Against Referendum*, p. 17.

argument in favour of minority rule, but it seems to me that if majority rule would be a tyranny, minority rule would be much more so.[52]

Reviewing Sharp in the *Clarion*, Victor Grayson commended his 'excellent and useful' facts on the history and current use of the referendum. But he thought the 'argumentative part' bore 'the unmistakable Fabian impress. That incurable British bourgeois vice of "running the lower orders" for their own good . . . '[53] The fears which underlay this 'vice' had already been epitomised during the '*Clarion* debate on the Referendum' initiated by Cartmel-Robinson. Some historians see Shaw's rôle as a critic of democracy reaching its fruition in the 'Revolutionist's Handbook' in *Man and Superman*.[54] But in the following letter to the *Clarion* he surely surpassed himself.

I think Cartmel must be mad. Under Government by Referendum, I should expect the first year's legislation to include the following measures, carried by overwhelming majorities of the People:
1. Ten years penal servitude for all avowed socialists.
2. Imprisonment for life for all avowed Atheists.
3. Establishment of a Triumvirate with complete Dictatorial powers, consisting of the King, Lord Roberts, and Sir Herbert Beerbohm Tree.
4. Abolition of all Rates and Taxes.
5. Execution of Robert Blatchford for blasphemy and his appointment as Commander-in-Chief of the army (under the impression that he is two different persons).
6. Abolition of sanitary inspection.
7. Reduction of the age of part-timers to six years, except in special cases reducable by magisterial order to two and a half years.
8. Burning alive of Bernard Shaw.
9. Exclusion of all foreigners from the British Islands and exclusion of all foreign goods except tobacco.
10. Disfranchisement of all low common people without carriages and servants.
11. War on Germany.
12. War on America.
13. Martial Law in Ireland.
14. War on Japan.
15. Reduction of the fleet and substitution of the personal prowess of Lord Charles Beresford for costly armaments.
16. — England will have ceased to exist before they get to No. 16.[55]

---

[52] *Justice*, 22 April 1911.
[53] *Clarion*, 12 May 1911.
[54] E.g. A. M. McBriar, *Fabian Socialism and English Politics 1884–1918* (London, 1962), p. 85.
[55] *Clarion*, 16 December 1910.

Among the inevitable barrage of criticism and repudiation that this Shavian *tour de force* triggered, the *Clarion* was happy to quote the *Manchester Guardian*'s comment that Shaw had only to 'push that doctrine far enough to cease to believe in Parliamentary institutions or elections at all'.[56]

[56] *Clarion*, 30 December 1910.

9 Parliamentary socialism? Labour in Parliament

While other socialist strategies of the 1890s foundered, Keir Hardie's 'Labour Alliance' of trade unions and socialist organisations was launched as the Labour Representation Committee in February 1900. Its parliamentary toehold was to become a wedge of thirty MPs with the 1906 election largely as a consequence of an unacknowledged, but already fiercely criticised, 'understanding' with the Liberals. The decision of the Miners to affiliate, increased the Parliamentary Group to forty-two after the elections of 1910. Was Labour to be truly independent or to relapse into becoming a semi-detached annexe of the Liberal Party with little to distinguish it from that older working class group, the 'Lib-Labs'?

Before 1906, socialists dissatisfied with the performance of Labour MPs could still hope for a radical improvement when a larger contingent containing more avowed socialists was elected. Those remaining, or becoming, dissatisfied after 1906 found such optimism harder. Critics continually pushed for change.

From the start, Labour faced three interconnected questions. What should be its programme? How far should MPs be bound by this programme and by the decisions of party conferences? What strategy and tactics should the Parliamentary Group pursue? These questions implied even deeper ones: was Labour to assimilate itself to the model of the 'historic parties' and to become in effect a parliamentary faction with a supporting electoral machine, rather than a social and political movement with a parliamentary extension? Would Labour in Parliament set out to transform, or at least modify, the governmental system or would it simply work towards the capture of the supposed levers of power?

In the Commons, Labour MPs found themselves members of a prestigious national assembly with its own established practices and 'time-hallowed' attitudes which did not necessarily square with those of the socialist and Labour movements. At one extreme, had Labour entered as a majority or even a much larger minority holding the balance of power, it might have felt freer to try reshaping parliamentary institutions. At the other, in the days when independent Labour representation had been confined to a tiny handful, a socialist MP could adopt an attitude of personal defiance and mount 'demonstrations' as Hardie had done in 1892–5. But the middling size of the 1906 intake tended to work against both these alternatives and to edge Labour towards accommodating itself to the established order in the, not unreasonable, hope of extracting concessions. The lack of a definite programme of any kind could only accentuate this tendency.

A programme for Labour? 1900–1906

A programme could have been adopted prior to 1906, but successive LRC conferences refused to do so. Policy motions were passed which could be seen as an *ad hoc* programme of sorts, yet the status of conference resolutions was unclear.

The 1901 conference declared unanimously in favour of adult suffrage, the 'abolition of all political monopolies', and the payment of elected representatives and election expenses. It opposed imperialism, and 'respectfully invited' the government to settle the South African War by arbitration under the Hague Convention.[1] The 1902 conference condemned the Taff Vale decision and passed an ILP motion supporting 'specially elected' education authorities, an elementary-school-to-university system and other education reforms.[2] Two years later Free Trade was endorsed and 'Chinese slavery' in South Africa condemned.

These resolutions were nearly always couched in terms of expressions of opinion; the extent to which they constituted party policy was unclear. More specific was the successful motion with the wording 'this conference instructs the Labour Party in the House of Commons to draft and bring in a Bill to pension all men and women after the age of sixty years'.[3] Similarly in 1905, all LRC representatives were *instructed* to 'bring prominently forward the municipalisation of the drink trade'.[4] In passing these resolutions, the Conference was taking for granted its authority over Labour MPs.

But it was easier to instruct, than to enforce. Even before 1906 there had been many instances of Labour MPs and candidates behaving in a manner which outraged socialists. Even in the absence of definite programmatic requirements, they still managed to offend by failing to maintain that independence from the Liberals that should have

[1] *LRC Conference Report*, 1901, pp. 19–20.
[2] *LRC Conference Report*, 1902, pp. 24–5.
[3] *LRC Conference Report*, 1904, p. 52.   [4] *LRC Conference Report*, 1905, p. 55.

constituted their distinction from the 'Lib-Labs'. Richard Bell, general secretary of the ASRS since 1897, was the major offender. He spoke for the Liberal candidate at Newport in 1901, attended the inaugural meeting of the London Liberal Federation in 1902, and supported Liberal by-election candidates at Newmarket and Liverpool.[5] This led directly to a resolution at the 1903 conference, making more explicit the independence from other parties to be expected of LRC candidates and MPs.[6] But the only sanction was a report by the LRC Executive to the appropriate affiliated organisations. Rather than restraining Bell, this precipitated him into a more overtly 'Lib-Lab' alignment and led to his complete break with the LRC.[7] The successful by-election recruits of 1902/3 – Shackleton, Crooks and Henderson – were also far from exemplifying any LRC independence.[8]

Bell received some qualified support from an unlikely quarter when 'Tattler' pointed out, in *Justice*, that the much-criticised MP had never pretended to be other than a Liberal. It was, he said, the fault of the LRC. It had failed to adopt the SDF motion for placing the movement on 'a definite basis'. Therefore it was illogical to complain about Bell.[9] The foundation conference had indeed not only rebuffed the SDF's attempt to commit the LRC to the 'class war' and to socialisation as an 'ultimate object', but had also rejected another proposal which would have entailed the drawing up of a 'Labour platform' of 'four or five planks'. Though accepted as an amendment by 59 votes to 35, this had then been withdrawn in favour of a further amendment, moved by Keir Hardie, with no reference to any sort of programme other than leaving it to the 'Labour group' in the Commons 'to agree upon their policy' and 'cooperate with any party which for the time being may be engaged in promoting legislation in the direct interest of labour' while 'opposing measures having the opposite tendency'.[10]

At the 1901 conference, SDF delegate Dan Irving questioned the adequacy of this 'independent Labour' formula: 'He did not think that the purposes of this movement would be fulfilled by merely returning working men to the House of Commons. He wanted to know what were the political opinions of candidates'.[11] The ILP, which had been accused by the SDF of betraying socialist principles when it failed to support the latter's 'ultimate object' motion in 1900, tried its own version in 1901.

---

[5] Frank Bealey and Henry Pelling, *Labour and Politics 1900–1906. A History of the Labour Representation Committee* (London, 1958), p. 139.
[6] *LRC Conference Report*, 1903, pp. 27–9.
[7] Bealey and Pelling, *Labour and Politics*, pp. 193–7.
[8] *Ibid.*, pp. 205–8.   [9] *Justice*, 2 April 1904.
[10] *LRC Conference Report*, 1900, pp. 11–12.   [11] *LRC Conference Report*, 1901, p. 15.

The conference was invited to declare in favour of the transfer of private monopolies to public control 'as steps towards the creation of an industrial Commonwealth founded upon the common ownership and control of land and capital'. Bruce Glasier stressed that 'it was not intended as a test resolution in respect to candidates' but rather as an invitation to 'declare the political ideal of the movement'. This distinction was too subtle. John Ward was convinced that it would be regarded as such a 'test', Curran thought that it ought to be, and Quelch moved an amendment which would have made it so. A successful moving of 'previous question' consigned motion and amendment alike to oblivion.[12]

A programme of more immediate demands was discussed in 1903. A composited motion, moved by West Ham Trades Council, sought to instruct the Executive to draw up such a document and submit it, together with any proposed amendments from affiliates, to the next year's conference. But D. C. Cummings of the Boilermakers stressed the difficulty of satisfying all the different unions and socialist societies. He argued that a 'hard and fast programme' would 'lead to dissension'. He was supported by Ben Turner who thought that 'programmes wrecked parties' and by Keir Hardie who suggested that there was 'no occasion for programmes at the present time'.[13] Hardie declared that 'this new party must be a Labour Party, knowing neither Socialist, nor Tory, nor Liberal' and insisting that the only 'ism' should be 'Labourism'.[14]

The difficulty, of course, was that, whereas socialism might be a real 'ism', Labourism was programmatically void unless it was understood to mean whatever policies were adopted by the LRC conference – in which case it *did* mean having a programme of sorts. Alternatively it could mean whatever policies Labour MPs cared to pursue. This interpretation would hardly commend itself to the wider movement. But apart from that consideration, since four out of the five Labour MPs at the time were scarcely distinguishable from the 'Lib-Labs' and interpreted their rôle in narrow terms of promoting the interests of their particular trade union sponsor, there was difficulty in achieving even minimal unity.[15] Not everybody shared Hardie's faith in the 'Labour alliance' *tout court*, which was what 'Labourism' amounted to.

Commenting upon Hardie's statement at the Conference, a *Clarion* editorial asked:

---

[12] *LRC Conference Report*, 1901, pp. 20–1.   [13] *LRC Conference Report*, 1902, p. 36.
[14] *Labour Leader*, 28 February 1903.
[15] Bealey and Pelling, *Labour and Politics*, ch. 8, especially pp. 201–6.

If avowed Socialists are going to water down their principles and programmes for the sake of the fleshpots of Independent Labourism, what will be the difference between such conduct and that of the Liberal-Labour man who waters down his Labourism in order to gain the sops thrown by the Liberal Party?[16]

Analogously, for Belfort Bax, the LRC stance was symptomatic of the ascendancy of 'Revisionism' with its appeal to 'practical politics'. He noted that 'the object for which the party exists, or is supposed to exist, matters not; the chief thing is to score a success for the party organisation as such.'[17]

Attempts to commit the LRC to a programme of some sort continued. At the 1904 Conference a West Ham Trades Council motion, this time omitting adult suffrage, failed once again.[18] But the 1905 Conference passed, without discussion, an SDF-inspired resolution declaring the LRC's 'ultimate object' to be 'the overthrow of the present Competitive System of Capitalism, and the institution of a System of Common Ownership of all the means of Production, Distribution, and Exchange'. Yet it then went on immediately to refuse to commit itself to 'enforce the hearty adoption' by LRC candidates of all legislative proposals emanating from the even more moderate TUC. Clearly, pious resolutions were one thing; but the adoption of a definite pledge to infinitely more modest goals was too close to real life.

An exchange, included in the official conference report, brings out neatly what really was at issue.

A. Gould (Hull Trades Council) opposed the motion and argued that the formation of a programme should be left to their Members of Parliament.
H. Quelch (London Trades Council) considered that it was the duty of the Party as a whole to formulate a programme. It was *ultra vires* for their representatives in Parliament to take this work in hand. What they wanted was a programme they could offer to their Members and their candidates . . . to accept or stand down.[19]

Thus, the LRC went into the 1906 election, after rejecting *all* attempts to establish a uniform programme for candidates via the annual conference, or to establish the principle of the responsibility of MPs to the organisation outside Parliament. Following the election, the LRC Conference once more rejected both a London Trades Council bid to instruct the EC to formulate a programme and an amendment to adopt the legislative proposals of the TUC. Charles Duncan, who had just been

---

[16] *Clarion*, 6 March 1903.   [17] *Justice*, 30 May 1903.
[18] *LRC Conference Report*, 1904, p. 48.   [19] *LRC Conference Report*, 1905, pp. 20–1.

elected MP for Barrow-in-Furness, commented that 'They had enough programmes to go on with for the next hundred years.'[20] This outcome settled the question. Labour's first sizeable and potentially effective parliamentary group would begin, at least, uncommitted to any programme and free from control by the Conference. In this respect, therefore, Labour had opted to conform to the pattern of the established parties.

A leader for Labour?

Would the new party also adopt established practice by appointing a recognised parliamentary leader? This was a simpler, more 'visible' issue than the control of policy, and one where considerable opposition from within the movement could be expected if Labour were simply to accept the norms of its new environment. There was a wide spectrum of opinion which would regard the very notion of a 'leader of the Labour Party' with extreme distaste.

Immediately following the general election, the *Clarion* journalist Harry Beswick interviewed J. R. Clynes, fresh from his electoral triumph in Manchester. Even at this time Clynes was scarcely a voice of radicalism, so his reactions when asked 'Who will lead the new Party?' may be taken as an indication of what was then a conventional position:

Clynes looked diplomatic. 'I have my own opinion as to who should lead', he observed. . . . 'we are no longer a few scattered individuals. We are at least a Party. My own view is favourable to the appointment of a sessional chairman, instead of a permanent leader.'

I told Clynes that I thought this plan would be wiser than giving a man autocratic power . . .

Clynes did not fear any danger of this sort. The men, he pointed out, were not so characterless as the ordinary Party-made MPs, who are prepared to vote *just as their leaders tell 'em to.* 'Our Party', he claimed, 'is made up of a number of leaders.'[21] (original emphasis)

Fred Jowett who, as the next chapter will show, was highly critical of parliamentary procedure, was much more forthright than Clynes. Turning aside from a report on the 1906 Conference, he put his own position on the leadership issue to *Clarion* readers:

. . . the Labour Party has not and cannot have any leader in the same sense that the ordinary Parties have leaders.
. . .

---

[20] *Labour Leader*, 23 February 1906.   [21] *Clarion*, 26 January 1906.

> It cannot be too clearly understood . . . that in the Labour Group the members all have equal rights when they meet together to decide on all matters affecting their work in Parliament.

By this time Hardie had been elected as the Group's chairman. Jowett conceded that in an emergency he might have to exercise his own discretion.[22]

A curious episode at the 1906 ILP Conference suggests that those who thought like Jowett were right to make their position clear from the start. The *Labour Leader* reported that

> Somewhat unexpectedly the delegates rejected the Council's suggestion for the abolition of the office of chairmanship of the party – though demands in that direction had been made by a considerable number of branches at every previous conference.

The *Labour Leader*'s comment was disingenuous. The circumstances of 1906 differed from previous years in one important respect. To have abolished the ILP chairmanship, leaving only an NAC chairman chosen by the Council itself, would *at this point* have inevitably tended to enlarge Hardie's standing as a focus and figurehead in his rôle as chairman of the Parliamentary Group. The leadership of the ILP – and in those days when ILP membership was the normal form of *individual* membership of the Labour Party as a whole, effectively of the Labour Party as such – would have been transferred into Parliament under the control of Labour MPs.[23]

The attempt to abolish the ILP chairmanship was renewed in 1909. As Victor Grayson interpreted it, the intention was to strengthen the hold of 'The familiar quartette, viz: Keir Hardie, J. Ramsay MacDonald, Philip Snowden and Bruce Glasier'. From their point of view, he argued, the continuance of the one important office elected by the ILP Conference 'left open all sorts of terrible possibilities'.[24]

'Roads to ruin': the programme and the question of accountability after 1906

By 1906 the Social-Democrats were beginning to cite the failure of the Labour Party to adopt a programme and the lack of accountability of Labour MPs as the main justification for the SDF's withdrawal. Its annual conference of that year rejected rejoining the Labour Party by 52 votes to 29, but agreed, by 52 to 18, to seek reaffiliation 'as soon as its

22 *Clarion*, 23 February 1906.
23 *Labour Leader*, 20 April 1906.   24 *Clarion*, 9 April 1909.

constituents and delegates publicly accept a definite programme in harmony with the principles of socialism'.[25]

This was something of a *post facto* rationalisation. The SDF had contributed to bringing about the state of affairs it was criticising by failing to stay in the party where it could have pressed its case. That Social-Democrats continued to promote via trade union bodies such as the London Trades Council the idea of a definite programme may have been the worst of all worlds since it enabled opponents to complain of their inconsistency and their exploitation of trade union bodies. As *Justice* itself reported, one of the tactics used by opponents at the 1907 LRC conference to deter support for a Paper Stainers' motion to commit the Parliamentary Group to work for the socialist 'ultimate object' was to protest, as Pete Curran did, against the SDF 'endeavouring by a sidewind to get its policies adopted by the Conference'.[26]

At the end of 1906 *Justice* explained more fully the SDF's position:

> No one suggests that this programme should be one of details, or that the Parliamentary Group . . . should be 'cribbed, cabined and confined' in all matters of tactics or policy. But we do maintain that the objects aimed at, and the broad principles upon which the Party is based, should be formulated in a programme for the guidance of the Parliamentary Group. We maintain, further, that such a programme should be formulated by the Party Executive, and not by the Parliamentary representatives, and based on the resolutions of the Party Conference.[27]

Events were soon to show that these were no abstract arguments, but definite practical choices which would be made, consciously or by default, in the near future. An immediate issue was 'women's suffrage'. And it proved a striking one.

At the end of 1906 Hardie had informed *Labour Leader* readers that 'the Labour Party, as a party, has agreed to place a Bill for the political enfranchisement of women in the front rank of its programme for the next session'.[28] What authority had Hardie to make such a pronouncement when the policy of successive LRC conferences had been to support 'adult' rather than 'women's' suffrage? The 1906 conference had even decided that the latter was 'a retrograde step and should be opposed'.[29] Such objections were immediately heard.[30]

Only when the terms of an amendment to the Labour Party

[25] *Justice*, 14 April 1906.
[26] *Justice*, 2 February 1907.
[27] *Justice*, 15 December 1906. See also *Justice*, 5 January 1907 for the endorsement of this position by Will Thorne, the only SDF member among the Labour MPs.
[28] *Labour Leader*, 21 December 1906.
[29] *Justice*, 24 February 1906.   [30] As from F. H. Rose, *Clarion*, 11 January 1907.

Conference's standing orders to be proposed by the National Executive became known, did the broader significance of Hardie's statement become clear. Had the Executive had its way, the following would have been adopted as a Standing Order:

That resolutions instructing the Parliamentary party as to their action in the House of Commons be so amended by the Standing Orders Committee as to register the opinions of the Conference without prejudice to any future action that may be considered by the party in Parliament.[31]

Predictably, protest was loud and prolonged. In the *Clarion*, Edward Hartley confessed that he had always been at issue with the 'leading men' on this question:

The rank and file should decide the policy and the leaders carry the flag.
They have always insisted not only on carrying the flag but on deciding what motto the flag should bear.
This is undemocratic, and the members should stop it once and for ever.[32]

The argument against the National Executive proposals was rehearsed at great length in *Justice*. They were, said 'Tattler', 'preposterous'. It had been argued, he wrote, that for Labour MPs to accept instructions from the party conference would reduce them to the rôle of delegates:

It is quite true that Members of Parliament are representatives, not delegates.
. . .
That I readily grant, but fail to see what it has to do with the right of the Conference to formulate the broad lines of policy which the Parliamentary Group should follow.
. . .
In opposition to any suggestion that the Conference should exercise its authority, it is argued that the Parliamentary Members are answerable to their constituents and not to the party. When it is pointed out that it is the party and not the constituents which has to formulate the policy and programme which the constituents are supposed to have endorsed, we are told that Members are not delegates but representatives, which . . . has, in this connection, no application.

Hardie's objection was, 'Tattler' concluded, an example of the doctrine that any control over MPs was to be prevented if possible, and that non-MPs 'are to pay the piper but . . . may not call the tune'. In the same issue of *Justice*, Fred Knee predicted that major conflicts would take place at the Labour Party conference on these issues. But he believed the battle already largely lost. To an outsider, the proposed Standing Order might 'smack of audacity', but in reality it merely made 'Statute law, so to speak, of the law the Group in Parliament have

[31] *Justice*, 19 January 1907.   [32] *Clarion*, 18 January 1907.

become unto themselves'. Not only had the 'Thou shalt' of previous conferences been 'contemptuously ignored' but their 'thou shalt nots' had been treated even more contemptuously, as the 'women's suffrage' issue showed.

The same tug-of-war over policy between Parliamentary Group and party, Knee recalled, had occurred in other countries and it seemed that it was 'inevitable for men in a national assembly to lose touch with the live facts outside unless the organised Party keeps them up to scratch'. Should the Executive's proposal be accepted, he concluded, 'the Conference should . . . cease to waste time and money by holding its annual meetings, and let the members of Parliament play ducks and drakes as they like'.[33]

When Theodore Rothstein, a former member of the SDF Executive and much later a central figure in the creation of the British Communist Party, took up the cudgels the following week he wielded them with rather more aggression against 'the shining lights' of the Labour Party and their equivalents elsewhere:

these gentlemen regard it as an intolerable tyranny that their hands should be tied by general guiding principles laid down by party conferences . . . The result is invariably the same – alliances with the Liberal and Radical parties, betrayal of the interests of the working class, and for some perhaps, a seat in the Ministry or a snug administrative post.

There is . . . apart from personal ambition, usually something else in this clamour for Parliamentary independence – it is the other opportunist trait, [the] exaggeration of the importance of Parliamentary work.[34]

In the event, the results of the 1907 Conference were mixed. On balance they represented a victory for the 'shining lights', though at the cost of a more ambiguous position on the status of conference decisions than the Executive had intended, and of a rebuff on the question, so close to Hardie's heart, of 'women's suffrage'.

The Executive revised its proposed Standing Order to read:

That resolutions instructing the Parliamentary Party as to their actions in the House of Commons are to be taken as the opinions of the Conference, on the understanding that the time and method of giving effect to these instructions be left to the Party in the House in conjunction with the National Executive.

The change was made, according to *Justice*, in order 'to avoid a crushing defeat'.[35] In practice, it left the Parliamentary Group with almost as free a hand as in the original version. But the ambiguities of the

---

[33] *Justice*, 19 January 1907.
[34] *Justice*, 26 January 1907.   [35] *Justice*, 2 February 1907.

formula adopted with the inclusion of the magic word 'instructions' proved sufficient to contain the critics. The revised version was approved, despite determined opposition from Quelch and Ben Tillett.

Keir Hardie argued that, with seventeen motions seeking to give definite instructions to the Parliamentary party on the agenda, there was a great danger that at the next conference it would be alleged that 'they had shown favouritism in selecting some of these' as against others. Therefore MPs must be given the explicit right to decide priorities for the parliamentary session.[36]

There were, indeed, several attempts at the 1907 Conference to commit the Party and its MPs to a definite programme. One motion, seeking to anchor the parliamentarians to the socialist 'ultimate object', and another moved by Quelch for the London Trades Council, to make TUC resolutions the basis for the Labour Party programme, were both defeated. The latter proposal, warned Shackleton, 'was not so innocent as it looked' since TUC policy included the raising of the school leaving age to sixteen. 'It would be impossible for him to support such a proposal, for to do so would involve the loss of his seat in the House of Commons.'[37]

A third motion, moved by Tillett (and paralleled by one from Thorne) sought to institute a procedure for consulting the affiliated membership on the question of a programme and its status *vis-à-vis* the MPs. A questionnaire would be circulated to members asking them whether Labour MPs should accept socialism as a principle, and be pledged to support the legislative proposals of the TUC and . . . the General Federation of Trade Unions. The questionnaire would also ask whether Labour's Executive should be instructed to submit a proposed Parliamentary programme to the next Labour Party Conference, and finally whether these proposals should be submitted six months prior to the conference and be subject to amendments from affiliated organisations. This motion was joined by another proposal to 'secure united and consistent action' by MPs by making the Executive the sole authority 'on the matter of supporting any Parliamentary measures'. All these proposals were lost, as was an attempt to limit the number of MPs on the Executive.[38]

Bruce Glasier, in *Labour Leader*, headlined the attempt to commit the Parliamentary Group to the 'ultimate object' as 'Bringing Socialism into Dishonour'. He sneered at Tillett's and Quelch's 'curious assertion that

[36] *Labour Leader*, 1 February 1907.   [37] *Justice*, 2 February 1907.
[38] *Labour Leader*, 1 February 1907. *Justice*, 2 February 1907.

every socialist ought to be a Trade Unionist'.[39] But the most dramatic event of the 1907 conference was Keir Hardie's statement at its conclusion. To understand the background to this we must look back to the run-up to the recent Cockermouth by-election. There, the WSPU had run a separate anti-Liberal campaign, taking an impartial stance between the Conservative candidate and Labour's Smillie, who came bottom of the poll.

Criticism within the ILP focussed on the activities in Cockermouth of Christabel Pankhurst and Teresa Billington. Both were ILP members and the latter had indeed been appointed an ILP organiser in 1905.[40] In a letter to the *Labour Leader*, Smillie himself alleged that Christabel Pankhurst had written to the local ILP secretary asking for arrangements to be made on her behalf and had stayed at the home of an ILPer, with the implication that such assistance had been obtained under false pretences. He also said that Mary Gawthorpe, who arrived to assist Labour in the by-election hot-foot from a 'votes-for-women' campaign in Leeds had been refused permission to speak from the WSPU platform because she had already spoken for Smillie.[41]

The Manchester and Salford ILP held a special meeting to discuss the incident. This called, by 90 votes to 3, for the expulsion of the two members by their own branch. Neither Pankhurst nor Billington had taken up the invitation to attend this meeting. Their own branch, the Manchester Central ILP passed a resolution, by 19 to 8, saying that it did not approve of the position taken by Manchester and Salford 'inasmuch as the two members have simply endeavoured to carry out the immediate extension of the franchise to women, which is included in the official programme as one of its objects'.[42]

One local ILPer, George Thompson, alleged in a letter to the *Labour Leader*, that the Manchester Central committee had been 'packed' on behalf of the suffragettes.[43] Even the ILP's NAC was stirred into regretting the treatment of Smillie, an ILPer pledged to support a Women's Enfranchisement Bill. Though it also appealed for calm, it did point out that 'loyalty to the constitution and the policy of the Party' was essential.[44]

The outrage in those parts of the Labour Party less sympathetic to the WSPU can readily be imagined. Here, as critics saw it, was a clear case of biting the hand that feeds. The WSPU had been founded with vital

---

[39] *Labour Leader*, 1 February 1907.   [40] *Labour Leader*, 26 May 1905.
[41] *Labour Leader*, 24 August 1906.
[42] *Labour Leader*, 31 August, 7 September 1906.
[43] *Labour Leader*, 14 September 1906.   [44] *ILP NAC Minutes*, 26/27 October 1906.

assistance from ILP branches and members. The ILP had supported the suffragette demand for the 'limited' women's suffrage, even though this had caused internal dissension and had led to accusations from other socialist organisations that it had thereby shown itself undemocratic, anti-working class and anti-socialist. Yet the WSPU had continued to exploit this ILP goodwill and its resources while stabbing it in the back.

At the 1907 Labour Party Conference, 'women's suffrage' was once more rejected in favour of 'adult suffrage'. Without any doubt, this result was made more certain by the events just described.

No less galling for Hardie, when the same conference debated the Executive's proposal for the Standing Order governing the conduct of the parliamentary party, he had come under bitter attack. One opponent (Robert Morley) alleged that 'the resolution [had been] deliberately framed to excuse Mr Hardie's action' on women's suffrage. Worse, Morley asserted that Hardie – whose friendship with the Pankhurst family was well known – had 'come under the influence of women's petticoats'.

Right at the end of the Conference, Hardie was due to move the customary vote of thanks to the hosts, the Belfast Trades Council, and to the Press. Doubtlessly, expecting the routine platitudes, delegates were stunned to hear him say:

> The intimation I wish to make to the Conference is that, if the motion they carried this morning [i.e. the one rejecting 'women's' in favour of adult suffrage] was intended to limit the action of the party in the House of Commons, I shall have to seriously consider whether I shall remain a member of the Parliamentary Party.
>
> I say this with great respect and feeling. The party is largely my own child.[45]

If Hardie intended to use this resignation threat to rally support, it was a serious misjudgement, all too reminiscent of his earlier premature announcement of the 'Labour Party's' decision to promote a 'women's suffrage' bill. Unqualified approval of the statement came only from committed 'limited' suffrage supporters like Isabella Ford.[46] Even the *Labour Leader* was embarrassed. Its editorial described Hardie as 'unique . . . and chief among working class . . . leaders of our day', but added:

> we must respect no less the feeling of many Socialists who, alarmed at the recent attempts to subordinate the whole purpose of the Labour and Socialist movement to the one question of votes for women, have declared that they also cannot prove false to their principles.[47]

---

[45] *Labour Leader*, 1 February 1907.
[46] *Labour Leader*, 8 February 1907.   [47] *Labour Leader*, 1 February 1907.

Both Tillett and Morley quickly protested against what they saw as the *Leader*'s misrepresentation of their conference contributions, the latter adding with reference to Hardie, 'I hope we have not got a Saints' Calendar yet, or come to the founding of a cult of the infallible'.[48]

Justice's comments were surprisingly restrained. It went so far as to support Hardie for the leadership of the Parliamentary Group, while criticising his action. The suffragettes, said *Justice*, had tried 'to make a catspaw of the Labour Party. It . . . greatly . . . regretted that the Parliamentary Group should, in defiance of the mandate of the Party, have identified themselves with this movement'.[49]

If, *Justice* concluded, support for 'women's suffrage' was continued, it would again demonstrate 'the futility of the Conference and the unconstitutional supremacy of the Parliamentary Group, a supremacy which the Executive endeavoured to make constitutional by a direct vote of the Conference'.[50]

In the *Clarion*, Hartley saw the incident as confirming the views he had expressed before the Conference. Hardie had made a 'sharp sudden challenge to democracy' which could not be ignored: 'To take up something contrary to the opinion of a large section of the members, then when defeated on a vote to threaten to resign is the opposite of democracy. The question now is shall Hardie rule the Party? Or shall the Party rule Hardie?'[51] Hardie's immediate reaction was to persevere with a 'women's suffrage' bill. Arthur Henderson, on the other hand, clearly wished to avoid confrontation. The week after the Belfast Conference he wrote:

As a Party, I consider we are bound to accept the instructions of the Conference, at any rate to the extent that we cannot ballot for the limited Bill. [However] . . . every [Labour MP] is committed very definitely to the enfranchisement of women. [So] . . . should the question be decided upon the lines of the limited proposal, most of the [MPs] would feel honour bound to vote for it. [Though] I have the strongest desire to respect the feelings of the Conference, . . . I must . . . have some regard to those I directly represent in Parliament. This is an aspect of our position not sufficiently kept in mind during our great national conference.[52]

We can now see how those who had supported the adoption of a definite programme could reasonably argue that it would have included, in the light of earlier conference decisions, a commitment to adult suffrage and that since Labour MPs would have been elected on that

---

[48] *Labour Leader*, 8 February 1907.
[49] *Justice*, 2 February 1907.   [50] *Justice*, 9 February 1907.
[51] *Clarion*, 1 February 1907.   [52] *Labour Leader*, 8 February 1907.

basis, no conflict between the views of the party and pledges to constituents could have arisen.

If Henderson was conciliatory, Hardie was the reverse. He described
the laying down of a programme as 'the road to ruin', and argued that to
be successful the parliamentary party needed to be free to select the best
way forward, something which could be decided 'only [by] those on the
spot, whose fingers are on the pulse of Parliament'. Moreover, while
Henderson believed the clear decision of the conference debarred the
Parliamentary Group from promoting 'limited' suffrage legislation,
Hardie announced that 'If the opportunity occurs I shall raise the
Women's Suffrage question' as an amendment to the Address.[53] Hardie
had been reduced to this tactic by recent decisions of the Group:
private members' bills balloted for by Labour MPs had to be those
selected at the Group's meetings, and a 'women's suffrage' bill was not
to be one of them.[54]

The 1907 Conference established the position that was to remain
substantially the same for the rest of the period. Those who believed, as
MacDonald put it soon after, that 'an adaptation of Socialism to
Parliamentary methods . . . is essential' were in the ascendant. Significantly, in the same article, he rejected as a waste of time 'All propositions
for what is called "direct democracy"' including, naturally, the
referendum, while at the same time advocating 'women's suffrage' – to
be followed 'as speedily as possible' by 'adult suffrage' – shorter
Parliaments and the payment of MPs.[55]

One corollary of the MacDonaldite view of Labour's rôle was
flexibility – seen by opponents as opportunism – over alliances or understandings with the Liberals. This in turn entailed, necessarily, both the
avoidance of too precise a party programme and also the same independence for Labour MPs as enjoyed by Conservatives and Liberals, from
control by extra-parliamentary sponsors. This went easily with a general
acceptance of existing norms of parliamentary procedure and behaviour.

That such attitudes would have less appeal to activists other than MPs
is evident. For most of them, parliamentary activities, though important,
were still only part of the party's work and the behaviour of the
Parliamentary Group ought to cohere with, and be supportive of,
the general strategy and approach of the wider movement. From this, it
was a short step to insist that the party as a whole should have the final
say on policy and should enjoy some control over its MPs.

An exchange in the *Labour Leader* in 1907 between MacDonald and

[53] *Labour Leader*, 15 February 1907.
[54] *Clarion*, 15 February 1907.   [55] *Labour Leader*, 1 March 1907.

Russell Smart illustrates the divergent approaches very well. Smart summarised MacDonald's position and then criticised it from his own perspective:

> The road to Socialism . . . is to be made easy by moulding the measures of the party in power, by criticising their details and improving them where possible by collectivist amendments. [MacDonald's] view of Parliamentary work is largely limited to its effect upon the House. He fails to see that while the Labour Party may conciliate or even awe the Government, and win the admiration of [MPs] for its sensible and orderly conduct, it may yet fail to impress the public mind or raise any enthusiasm outside.[56]

MacDonald replied that 'In essence Smart's view is this: Parliament is only a propaganda platform, and I dissent from that'.[57]

What Robert McKenzie, in his study of *British Political Parties*, has called the '1907 formula' fell some way short of complete victory for those on Hardie's and MacDonald's side of the fence. The adoption of the NEC's original proposals would have established, as McKenzie emphasises, 'almost exactly the same relationship between the party in Parliament and its mass organisation outside as that which had always existed in the Conservative Party'.[58]

By contrast, for the critics, Labour had already gone too far in that direction.[59] Indeed the party continued, during its formative years, to refuse to copy the established parliamentary parties by subordinating itself to a 'leader'. The relatively modest status and rôle of the Chairman of the parliamentary party – together with the short periods for which the office was held by Keir Hardie (1906–8), Henderson (1908–10), Barnes (1910–11) and thereafter MacDonald – reflects the general suspicion of personal leadership in the movement.

Even those MPs most anxious to claim a large degree of autonomy for themselves as a Group were unwilling to follow Liberals and Conservatives in this respect. Some trade union MPs feared that they might be pulled along further and faster than they wished. And, as Pelling suggests, the very closeness of the first election for the chairman-ship helped to prevent the emergence of a 'leader'.[60] But no doubt McKenzie and Pelling are right in believing that even at this early stage, MacDonald was out to develop the chairmanship in the direction of permanent leadership. Certainly the *Clarion* thought so. In 1911 it

---

[56] *Labour Leader*, 17 May 1907.
[57] *Labour Leader*, 24 May 1907.
[58] R. T. McKenzie, *British Political Parties: The Distribution of Power within the Conservative and Labour Parties*, 2nd edn (London, 1963), p. 397.
[59] See for example the report by Fred Knee and the editorial in *Justice*, 3 February 1912.
[60] Henry Pelling, *A Short History of the Labour Party*, 2nd edn (London, 1965), p. 20.

contrasted Clynes's 1906 statement rejecting the need for a permanent leader with a recent report suggesting that moves were afoot to make the Chairmanship of the Parliamentary Group permanent.[61]

The irreducible suspicion on the part of the *Clarion* and its supporters was well reflected in 1910 in a review of the autobiography of John Wilson, MP. As if to trigger a Pavlovian reaction, Wilson had entitled his book *Memoirs of a Labour Leader*. The *Clarion* reviewer began twitching:

> Not to have been a Labour Leader and not to have written the story of your life, or have it written for you, argues a very commonplace character in these early twentieth century times. In the days of our youth the rewards for good conduct at Sunday School took the form of literature of the 'Log Cabin to the White House' class. Today the budding youth of the greatest Empire feeds its aspirations on 'From Workshop to Westminster', 'From Butcher's Bench to Parliamentary bar', 'From Cab Rank to Cabinet Rank', or some other impossible jumping of place to fame and glory.[62]

Already by 1907 Labour's performance in Parliament was subject to indignant and disillusioned criticism from many socialists. No one could reasonably expect thirty MPs to somehow produce socialist legislation, but ILPers like E. F. Garratt wanted ' . . . the House of Commons, and through it the country, to get the full benefit of having in its midst whole-hearted Socialists, whose message will not halt at the niceties of procedure and the dignities of debate, nor be strangled by an over-careful policy'.[63] There must have been many who agreed with Herbert Dean's criticisms of the Parliamentary Group in another letter to *Labour Leader*:

When, as a result of the antiquated legislative machinery of the House, session after session passes, and the questions upon which the enthusiasm and self-sacrifice of the rank and file are founded are shelved, it becomes time to choose a critical moment to defy tradition, to throw respectability to the winds, and to insist that these matters be dealt with immediately in spite of all the precedent to the contrary.[64]

Within weeks of this letter, the triumph of Victor Grayson in the Colne Valley by-election (July 1907) provided both a symbol of the discontent of socialists with the Labour Party and an experiment in the 'propaganda' approach. A member of the ILP, Grayson had run without Labour endorsement and contrary to the wishes of the ILP 'leadership'. Sadly, Grayson had little to contribute except ardour for the cause. But the very fact that an inexperienced and virtually unknown man in his

---

[61] *Clarion*, 10 February 1911.   [62] *Clarion*, 8 July 1910.
[63] *Labour Leader*, 7 June 1907.   [64] *Labour Leader*, 28 June 1907.

mid-twenties could become a hero overnight – and to some socialists a legend for generations – merely on the basis of less than three years as an MP, should have given pause to those who were soon, under the influence of Syndicalism, to dismiss the importance of electoral politics altogether.

With the propagandistic view of parliamentary activity, there often went the expectation, or at least the hope, that Labour MPs would challenge a system perceived as falling short of 'representative government' let alone of 'real democracy'. This partly explains why Grayson was able to strike such a chord merely by displaying a defiant attitude and making 'scenes' in the Commons. To those for whom, on the contrary, democracy could be equated with the existing system, Grayson's approach was at best unseemly and counter-productive. But to those who regarded that system as not even minimally democratic, such rebellion and obstructive behaviour could seem like a blow – by proxy – by the powerless against a repressive incubus.[65]

---

[65] On Grayson and Colne Valley, see Reg Groves, *The Strange Case of Victor Grayson* (1975); David Clarke, *Colne Valley: Radicalism to Socialism* (London, 1981); and *Victor Grayson, Labour's Lost Leader* (1985).

10 Parliamentary democracy? 'Fred's obsession' and the path to the Bradford Resolution

A critique of Cabinet government

Even before the 1906 election, a species of socialist criticism had emerged which was to become of crucial importance in the immediate pre-1914 years. Its focus was what Hyndman, especially, had always called 'the unconstitutional Cabinet', as contrasted with the committee system in local government. The latter seemed to many a model of democracy.

The wide appeal of such a view sprang in part from the fact that socialist and Labour politics were locally well-established before they acquired a national foothold. The 1906 election meant, for some new Labour MPs, a transfer from the local state to the centre. Compared with local government, many features of the House of Commons were bound to seem undemocratic and baroque. F. W. Jowett, with his considerable experience on Bradford City Council, fits this pattern. Even more important was the large body of activists with similar local government backgrounds whose interest in Parliament was greatly increased by their hopes and expectations concerning the performance of 'their' MP.

That Labour should contest 'the tremendous power vested in that close oligarchy known as the Cabinet' was an argument that first H. Russell Smart and later Jowett had put, before 1906. As early as 1901 Smart wrote:

> Parliament has deprived the Government of its regal head, but has left the authority of ministers not only undiminished, but actually increased by voluntarily allowing them to assume all the powers formerly exercised by the monarch. It is true ministers are dependent on the will of the majority, but unfortunately the members of that majority are themselves dependent on the Government.
>
> A Parliamentary seat is a valuable privilege which members are loth to lose. A hostile vote means a dissolution, and a possible return to obscurity on the part of the defaulters. Further, ambitious members have to look to Government for patronage, titles, office and consequently there is every inducement for members to maintain their party in power.

The result was that the parliament/government relationship was reversed; instead of being the controlling power, Parliament had 'become a voting machine to register the decrees of Government and to maintain ministers in office'. Smart contrasted this situation with the committee system of local government. The latter's extension to national level would ensure, he claimed, 'efficient and progressive legislation'. In the end, he said, Parliament should become 'a single-chambered legislative council without a government, or itself the government and capable of administering the national business'.[1]

Before his election as MP for West Bradford in 1906, Jowett also had begun the attacks on Parliamentary practice which foreshadowed what his fellow MPs came to regard as 'Fred's obsession'.[2] By 1905 Jowett was contributing a regular 'ILP letter' to the *Clarion*. In March of that year he turned his attention to the question of cabinet government, reaching similar conclusions to Smart:

the theory of Cabinet responsibility to the House of Commons and to the people for all its actions, in general and in detail, is one of the most mischievous delusions that constant repetition has ever succeeded in foisting upon the public.
. . .

As a matter of fact, the executive business of the State is not brought under the review of the people's representatives, except so far as it is revealed in the accounts, or as the Minister concerned chooses to give information, either in answer to enquiries or otherwise.
. . .

The party man in Parliament, whether Tory or Liberal, has no more control over the actual business transacted in the people's name than the partisan spectator at a football match has over the game in progress.

It would be the business of the Labour Party in Parliament to take the earliest opportunity to break down the system of Cabinet responsibility, Jowett concluded.[3]

Following the general election, the *Clarion* asked Labour MPs their initial reactions to Parliament. They were not very impressed. References to 'stupid forms of procedure' (Barnes), 'fossilised traditions' (T. Fred Richards) abounded. James O'Grady wrote that 'it would take the columns of a whole *Clarion* to express in picturesque and full-flavoured language, what I feel about the procedure alone of the Mother of Parliaments.' Barnes, Hodges and Richards mentioned the need for

---

[1] *Labour Leader*, 20 July 1901. See also Smart's article in the previous week's edition and his pamphlet *The Right to Live*, The Worker Series, no. 2 (Huddersfield, n.d.), pp. 4–5.
[2] A. Fenner Brockway, *Socialism over Sixty Years, The Life of Jowett of Bradford (1864–1944)* (London, 1946), p. 232.
[3] *Clarion*, 3 March 1905.

more committees. Even MacDonald wanted 'a little reform of its machinery'.

Jowett's comments were very much in line with those of his colleagues. He complained that the 'star artists chew the cud too much', and that the Commons had little control over the Executive. 'The forms and procedure . . . give an immense advantage to those members who belong to the legal profession, which they use mischievously against the public interest.'[4]

The *Clarion* invited Jowett to contribute weekly 'Notes on Parliament'. Jowett's *Clarion* articles combined informed commentary on the latest Parliamentary activities with criticism of the structures and procedures involved. More often than not, he used a recent event to illustrate the general working of the system. Where the issues involved were important to socialists, Jowett sought to show that the defects of the current set-up were damaging in the short term as well as in the long. He was ideally placed, as an MP, to do this. But he had to prove resistant to the process of gradually becoming reconciled to the existing state of affairs through habit and familiarity. Jowett's great merit as a critic of the system was that he was able to do this.

In March 1906 he reiterated the case for the committee system as a replacement for the Cabinet. He did not expect this to be achieved in the foreseeable future, but:

There is no reason in the world why the whole of the nation's executive business should not be under the control of committees, nor is there any reason why the legislative business should not first be thrashed out in Committees, the Committees in each case to be composed of members of all Parties. When this is done there will be an end to bureaucracy in national affairs. Incidentally, there will also be an end to Party Government as it exists today, for it will then be possible to obtain a conscientious vote on every separate question, whereas at present no vote can be taken on any issue which the Government declares to be a question of confidence without endangering the Government itself and along with it every principle and measure for which it stands.[5]

The following week he illustrated the lack of parliamentary control of accounts and lashed out at examples of time-wasting formalities in Parliament.[6] In May he turned his attention to sinecures and the rôle of the Privy Council.

An order in Council has all the force of law without a suspicion of democratic support, as not even all the members of the Council itself need to be called upon to confirm it. It is the most outrageously irregular and irresponsible body in the

---

[4] *Clarion*, 3, 10 August 1906.
[5] *Clarion*, 23 March 1906.   [6] *Clarion*, 30 March 1906.

world, civilised or uncivilised. The President of this precious institution – fit only for Bedlam – has no real duties whatever unless he happens to hold some administrative office along with it.[7]

There were few undemocratic aspects of the system that Jowett neglected to bring to the attention of *Clarion* readers. He attacked the long-winded voting procedure in the Commons and emphasised the need for control over the bureaucracy in the light of the de facto power of permanent officials.[8] Jowett was educating his readers about the detailed working of the parliamentary and governmental system at the same time as agitating for its reform. It seems unlikely, for example, that many readers had even heard of 'legislation by reference' or considered the implications of the rôle of Government draughtsmen before 1908 when Jowett drew their attention to these issues.[9]

He used the example of the inadequacy of parliamentary control over the GPO to rehearse his case for a Committee System, concluding that as things stood, 'The Post Office is a working example of Socialism without democracy', which might be better than capitalism but was not what socialists wanted.[10] How many electors were aware, he asked, 'that by the common consent of both Parties in the State the only power the House of Commons possesses over the huge national departments rests on an entirely fictitious supposition that it can refuse to pay the annual bills?'[11]

In the area of foreign policy, Jowett was concerned that Edward VII was 'being encouraged to meddle with affairs for which he cannot be called to account', particularly with the formation of the 'Triple Entente' of 1907.[12] He attributed the growing tensions between the European powers to 'secret diplomacy and the overpowering influence which experts and permanent officials exercise over successive ministers in turn': another example of the need for real parliamentary control through the committee system.[13]

His early experience of the Commons served only to confirm the conclusion he had already reached and shared with *Clarion* readers, in 1905, about the nature of the British system of government. In the summer of 1906 he had written: 'It is not Democracy, it is not even representative government – it is something very different from either.'[14]

[7] *Clarion*, 4 May 1906; reader's counter-attack and Jowett's reply, 18 and 25 May.
[8] *Clarion*, 11 May, 17 August, 16 November 1906.
[9] *Clarion*, 1 May 1908.
[10] *Clarion*, 24 May 1908.
[11] *Clarion*, 1 May 1908 (Special May Day Supplement).
[12] *Clarion*, 17 July 1908.
[13] *Clarion*, 7 August 1908.   [14] *Clarion*, 3 August 1906.

Decades later, Fenner Brockway testified to the 'sensational effects' of Jowett's articles at this time: 'There was a general conviction among Socialists that the procedure of Parliament was obsolete, but before Jowett's exposure the practices of Parliament were not understood.'[15]

In 1909 Jowett laid out his arguments at greater length in a *Clarion* pamphlet, *What is the Use of Parliament?* He shared Thompson's belief that the referendum should replace the Lords as the ultimate check on the House of Commons,[16] but for him the *first* priority was to get rid of the Cabinet:

Cabinet responsibility is to the present system of Parliamentary government what the keystone is to the arch of a bridge. It maintains the two-party system, and so long as it remains in its place the people through their representatives can never control the Executive.[17]

According to Jowett, the replacement of Cabinet government by a committee system on the local authority model would kill two birds with one stone. Not only would committees be less open than ministers to manipulation by permanent officials, and parliamentary scrutiny of the administration be made more searching and effective, but the discipline-maintaining threat to resign if defeated upon an issue of 'confidence' would be removed.

If State departments were placed under committee control, not only would the system of single Ministerial control go, but the two-Party system would go with it. If the decisions of a Committee consisting of members of every political party are reversed by the full body to which it reports, nothing in the nature of a political crisis follows.[18]

The powers of ministers should, therefore, be transferred to committees, though existing ministers might be brought in as chairmen. It was the duty of every socialist or democrat, Jowett maintained, to make 'unceasing protest' against a system which placed 'the management of public business out of the reach of public control'. Socialism was literally impossible as things stood, for 'until some change of the kind takes place, every transference from private to public ownership will mock at us'.[19]

Returning to his theme that representative government – let alone democracy – had still to be achieved in Britain, Jowett continued: 'The

[15] Brockway, *Socialism*, p. 71.
[16] See, for example, *Clarion*, 2 November 1906; 4 December 1908.
[17] F. W. Jowett, *What is the Use of Parliament?*, Pass on Pamphlet no. 11 (London, 1909), p. 18.
[18] *Ibid.*, p. 28.
[19] *Ibid.*, pp. 28–9.

present system cannot be defended . . . It is unworthy of the nation which pretends to live under representative Government'.[20]

Blatchford, who summarised Jowett as concluding that Parliament needed 'to be taken to pieces and rebuilt on wholly different lines',[21] gave him editorial support, and the *Clarion* canvassed Labour MPs for their reactions. Most were favourable to Jowett's ideas. But there was an ominous lack of enthusiasm, though only W. T. Wilson seemed to find Jowett's writings 'too long and laboured to be effective'. Curran, Taylor and Parker, among the Labour MPs, and Grayson, the 'Independent Socialist', gave general support to the criticisms. Barnes singled out the democratisation of the administrative departments as the most urgent reform, but added a – significant – warning against 'belittling' Parliament. Crooks said that he had long supported the committee system and Snowden hoped that the pamphlet would make the reform of Parliament a 'burning question'.[22] Clynes expressed support for Jowett's views but believed that the system would have to be reformed by a succession of small and gradual changes.[23]

Two things are clear. On the one hand neither Jowett's diagnosis nor his prognosis were viewed as being particularly startling – as they would certainly be if an MP were to put them forward in the 1990s. But on the other hand, those who expressed their support showed little of his single-minded sense of outrage. The feeling seemed to be that he was right in principle, but it was 'Fred's obsession' rather than a major priority.

Jowett could do little as an individual MP. He submitted evidence to a Commission on Procedure which reported, finally, in 1914 without noticeable effect.[24] As a propaganda move during 1908, he put down an 'early day motion' calling for a committee to be set up on Commons procedure. It was to include no member who had sat in a previous Parliament. His object was 'to bring home to people the point that old members are so familiar with the unbusinesslike procedure here that they are unable to see that it is wrong'.[25] Individual activity of this kind might help to draw attention to the issue, but only deliberate co-ordinated action by the Parliamentary Group would have had any real chance of producing change.

Moreover, it followed from Jowett's own argument that, the longer the matter was left, the more Labour MPs would become habituated to

[20] *Ibid.*, p. 32. See also his article on 'The Reform of Parliamentary Procedure' in *The Reformers' Year Book 1909*, ed. Clifford D. Sharp (rpt. Brighton, 1972).
[21] *Clarion*, 26 February 1909.
[22] *Clarion*, 12 February 1909.   [23] *Clarion*, 5 March 1909.
[24] Brockway, *Socialism*, p. 233.   [25] *Clarion*, 10 July 1908.

the existing system and blind to its defects. A good example of this process can be found in Clynes's *Memoirs* published in the late 1930s:

> During the first days in the House nearly all the new Labour Members of the 1906 Parliament were inclined to resent the cumbrous formalities imposed by the ceremonies of the place.
> . . .
> Since that distant day we have learned a lesson that has been acquired by each succeeding generation of Members. Behind the cumbrous formalities of Parliament lies the wisdom of long experience. Flaunting procedure in the Commons has never brought a cause nearer attainment or a Member nearer fame.[26]

It was already clear, even at 'that distant day', that, if the Parliamentary Group was going to act in the manner Jowett wished, pressure would have to be mounted on it through the Labour Party Conference. For Smart, Jowett and other supporters of change, the route lay through the ILP. But their problem was that those who formed the major obstacle to the adoption of Jowett's strategy, or any kind of venturesome policy, were also the leadership of that organisation. As a result the battle took place largely in the ILP.

'Some foul reptile . . . dropping poison'. The attack on the ILP's own 'Cabinet'

In May 1908 Russell Smart argued that 'The NAC . . . is like the Cabinet; it has an inner circle. Four men – Hardie, MacDonald, Snowden and Glasier – have assumed control of the whole organisation including the newspaper.' Much like parliament in relation to the Cabinet, the ILP had become 'a mere machine' for registering their decrees: 'all wires are in their hands, the newspaper is theirs, one of them always occupies the chair at annual Conference, and the power that they have acquired enables them to impose their will upon the Conference and the Party even when the general sentiment is opposed to them.'

This dominance was possible because 'the NAC is a well-organised body knowing what it wants and how to get it, while the Conference is an amorphous mass of well-intentioned, inexperienced men with no common understanding and no opportunity of consultation previous to the Conference'. The ILP's evolution was parallel to that of the political system and had resulted within the party in the 'formation of an inner ring or Cabinet which has no constitutional authority' and to whom the annual conference was 'merely an interlude in which a number of

---

[26] The Rt Hon. J. R. Clynes, PC, MP, DCL, *Memoirs, 1869–1924* (Hutchinson, 1937), p. 116.

delegates met together to enjoy an annual holiday, discuss a vast number of unimportant matters and go through the unnecessary formality of re-electing them to office year after year'.

The *Labour Leader* rejected Smart's criticisms as 'a deliberate attack on the older members of the Council'. It accused him of being part of an 'organised effort to nobble the next Conference of the Party in the interests of a clique of dissentients who have wholly failed to show any justification for their insidious criticisms'. Glasier, the editor of the *Leader*, claimed that an article by Smart submitted before the ILP Conference had been refused because it constituted 'touting for votes' by inviting members to support the election of new NAC members, including Smart himself. Smart's article – 'The ILP in Danger' – was subsequently published in the *Huddersfield Worker*. According to the *Labour Leader*, the 'organised effort' emanated from the Huddersfield and Colne Valley branches.[27]

That area remained a centre of discontent in the ILP for some time. In December 1908 a letter from the Huddersfield ILP branch secretary, O. Smith appeared, significantly, in *Justice*. After hearing Smart speak on 'The Disorganisation of the ILP and a Remedy' the branch had resolved to call for 'a more effective and democratic control . . . over the ILP members of Parliament, the NAC, the *Labour Leader*, and Election Policy'. They also decided to seek the cooperation of other branches to promote the necessary amendments to the ILP constitution.[28]

By this time a 'split' in the ILP, with the dissidents leaving to try to form a new united socialist party with the SDP and other socialist organisations, was already a real possibility. But arguments for continuing the fight within the organisation were still carrying the day with most of the critics. In January 1909 Leonard Hall made a strong plea in a letter to the *Clarion*: 'Secession at this juncture would be sheer waste of an existing and exceedingly hopeful machine, which it seems to me absurd to hand over without an effort to a really tiny minority who resent all criticism as blasphemy and regard Elected Persons as sacrosanct'.[29] If Hardie's reaction was anything to go by, the 'Elected Persons' were beginning to feel anything but sacrosanct. Prior to the 1909 ILP conference, he commented on the would-be democratising motions which had appeared on the agenda:

> It almost looks as though some foul reptile had crept through parts of the movement dropping poison as it went, which has sprung into agenda resolutions. I know that the Conference will brush all this contemptuously aside . . .

[27] *Labour Leader*, 8, 15, 22 May 1908.
[28] *Justice*, 19 December 1908.   [29] *Clarion*, 29 January 1909.

There is bitterness in the thought that few of these resolutions are the spontaneous outcome of the branches. Some malign influence of a personal kind has clearly been at work, and it shows a sad want of responsibility on the part of these branches that they allow this kind of thing to influence their decisions.

Even for Hardie, with his taste for animal imagery, this was strong stuff. He concluded: 'It is clearly evident that many branches have not yet learned to distinguish between a political party and a propaganda organisation. The Labour Party in the House of Commons is the one, and the ILP is the other.'[30] From his, very different, standpoint, Smart was clear about the importance of what was at issue:

This contest . . . raises the whole question of democracy. Hitherto our conception of popular government has been to give as many people as possible the opportunity of electing their rulers. It is now asked, Why have rulers? The people should rule. The leaders should obey. It is a revolution that is proposed – nothing less.

Those who allowed their thinking to be done for them soon lost the power of independent thought. This, Smart maintained, was the danger in the ILP. He traced the way the present problems had arisen:

The General Election gave us a number of members of Parliament before we were quite ready for them, before we had established a proper conception of the function of a member of Parliament and his relationship to the Party.
. . .
. . . our MPs very naturally assumed that they were to be as other MPs and the most prominent of them were to be as the chiefs of other Parties and form a Cabinet. They considered it their right and duty to direct the public policy of the movement.
. . .
What is our position on the question of the House of Lords on which the Liberal Party will endeavour to run the next election? We shall never know until we read a speech one morning from Mr J. R. MacDonald or see that Mr Philip Snowden has been appearing on the 'neutral' platform of 'The Society for the Abolition of the Veto of Hereditary Legislators'. Then all that will be left for us to do will be to follow their lead with that deep discontent that paralyses effective action.

It was necessary that the ILP should have a 'mouthpiece', independent of MPs. Hence, said Smart, the 'numerous resolutions to exclude MPs from the NAC'. When an important question divided opinions, a referendum of ILP members should be held.

[30] *Labour Leader*, 19 March 1909.

And so we should bring our MPs under our control, which would be good for us. We should break up that insidious Cabinet system which is death to independence of thought and character. We should establish that democracy in our organisation which we hope to extend some day into all national affairs.[31]

A special ILP conference to deal with constitutional changes was to be held on the Saturday immediately preceding the regular 1909 ILP annual conference. Victor Grayson, for one, was suspicious of the motives of the conference managers and predicted that it would be 'hot'.[32] In fact, the Special Conference rejected most of the proposed changes and resolved by 203 votes to 163 to allow constitutional amendments only every third year. Significantly for what followed, the conference appeared to face both ways on the question of whether the ILP should finance any members who, elected as MPs, refused to join the Labour Parliamentary Group. That such a position should be taken immediately was firmly rejected by 282 to 98. But even more decisively, delegates voted by 322 to 64 to operate in such a fashion only after the lifetime of the current Parliament.[33]

This odd position reflected a large degree of sympathy for Grayson, which was to become clearer in the conference proper, on the issue of the cancellation of his lecture engagements. Following much bad feeling, Grayson – and Hyndman – had refused to appear on the same platform as Hardie at a meeting at Holborn town hall the previous November. According to the NAC report, 'this in conjunction with other matters caused us to decide that it was useless to try and arrange from Head Office meetings for Mr Grayson and on 19 November he was written to with that effect'. This move, with its timing, was bound to appear spiteful given that it penalised Grayson financially too.[34] Grayson and his supporters succeeded in 'referring back' those paragraphs of the NAC Report dealing with his lecture engagements.

When the election for the NAC took place, Hardie, Snowden and MacDonald were successful on the first ballot, but the strength of critics in the party became clear when Smart managed to tie with Glasier, though in the second round the latter came through by 239 to 181. Then Jowett beat Anderson, the 'official' candidate, in the election for Chairman. Soon after this Hardie made the surprise announcement that he wished to 'respectfully decline' the position to which he had been re-elected, though when pressed he agreed to reconsider the matter.

But on the final day, not just Hardie but the rest of the 'quartette' –

---

[31] *Clarion*, 19 March 1909.   [32] *Clarion*, 9 April 1909.
[33] *Clarion*, 16 April 1909.
[34] *ILP Conference Report, 1909*, p. 15. *Justice*, 17 April 1909.

MacDonald, Snowden and Glasier – suddenly tendered their resignations. Neither a motion of support, moved by Ensor and carried with only about ten dissenters, nor even the reversal of the earlier decision on the Grayson paragraphs could persuade them to withdraw their resignations. Meanwhile in the *Leader*, Glasier was complaining of interference in the ILP's affairs by *Justice*, by the *New Age* (the paper edited by A. R. Orage, one of the founders of Guild Socialism) and – of course – by the *Clarion*.[35]

Here was a crucial test. The 'quartette' were indeed behaving exactly like a Cabinet, sharing a collective responsibility and resigning when they had in their judgement lost the confidence of the conference. In the light of the arguments and the vehemence of members such as Russell Smart, the critics of the 'quartette' should have rejoiced to see the back of them. They should then have ensured that the ILP was run according to very different notions of democracy and that neither any of the 'quartette' nor anyone with similar pretensions was ever again elected to the NAC.

Smart, after all, recognised the widest implications of what, writing in the *Labour Leader* soon afterwards, he called the 'Crisis in the ILP':

> It is a revolt which, when successful in our own organisation, will be carried into the Labour Party and will ultimately affect our system of national government. It is directed against the cabinet or caucus system which enables a few clever men to have complete control of the coach and drive the passengers where the leaders please.
>
> What is the ILP conception of democracy? Is it that of the average Liberal or Tory? Is it to surrender all thought and initiative to a few clever men, merely changing them if we are dissatisfied for another set of rulers who may do slightly better or slightly worse?

From this viewpoint, the 'quartette's' resignation might well, then, be the 'crunch' for the future of not just the ILP but the whole movement. The ultimate feebleness of Smart's position was revealed when he ended the same article by urging ILP branches to refuse to accept the resignation of 'the deserters' or to nominate candidates for their replacement.[36] A week later, W. C. Anderson considered what he aptly called Smart's 'Damp Squib'. What conclusions, he asked, followed from the analysis Smart had presented? 'Apparently these four men who he [says] . . . have tricked and dishonoured the movement should be compelled to remain in command. Verily an amazing solution.'[37] Indeed it was.

---

[35] *Labour Leader*, 16 April 1909. Original voting to refer back the Glasier paragraphs was 217 to 194 votes. Later voting to reinstate was 249 to 110.
[36] *Labour Leader*, 23 April 1909.
[37] *Labour Leader*, 30 April 1909.

The 'Bradford' policy and the 'Green Manifesto'

In contrast to Smart, Leonard Hall displayed a better sense of tactics on this occasion. Proclaiming that 'no individual is indispensable in this world', he scorned the lengths the ILP Conference had gone to in, as he put it, 'eating humble pie'.[38] There had been no fewer than 83 candidates for the NAC places vacated by the 'quartette' and 44,537 ILPers voted in the members' ballot. How much the critics still had to do in the ILP was shown when Anderson, closely identified with the 'deserters', topped the first ballot with 5,253 votes and was eventually elected together with Mary MacArthur, Clynes and Lansbury.[39]

In the meantime, Smart had already displayed more tactical incompetence. The *Labour Leader* announced:

We have received from Mr Russell Smart a communication which he entitles 'A Challenge'. In it he offers to allow himself to be nominated for the NAC, on condition that some other member of what he calls the 'Junta', except Mr Keir Hardie, will agree to put himself in competition against him. He goes on to anumerate [sic] the special items of policy for which he will stand – several of these items being, we may remark, in direct opposition to the decisions of the annual Conference.

We must decline Mr Smart's invitation to make our columns the medium of introducing sporting galas into the business of the ILP. We must decline also to countenance any attempts to rush the offices of the Party.[40]

An experienced *frondeur* like Glasier, the *Labour Leader*'s editor, had no difficulty in turning the democratic tables on someone like Smart. The latter, meanwhile, was busy explaining in the columns of the *Clarion* that 'regard and reverence' would prevent him from standing against Hardie, but that he wished to stand against any other 'Junta' member to attempt to reverse 'the centralising policy of the last few years which has produced such discord in the Party and disaster at the polls'.

He would stand, he went on, for the following principles: 'The control of the Parliamentary policy and public appearances of ILP members of Parliament by the Party or a committee elected by the Party', decentralisation of executive power and devolution to regional bodies in the ILP, and the restoration of branch autonomy in election policy. This last would have meant that a branch could run an ILP candidate in a Parliamentary election without Labour Party endorsement. The proposal, given its edge by the Grayson affair, had been rejected by the recent ILP conference.[41]

---

[38] *Labour Leader*, 23 April 1909.   [39] *Labour Leader*, 9 July 1909.
[40] *Labour Leader*, 30 April 1909.   [41] *Clarion*, 30 April 1909.

As usual, ILP dissension was both reflected and fed by *Clarion/Labour Leader* hostility. Blatchford rejected the charges of interference in ILP affairs.

> The ILP has availed itself of our help and service and has officially treated us as enemies.
> . . .
> While Bruce Glasier remains editor of the official organ of the ILP we shall treat that organ as we have treated it for years – with silent disregard.[42]

Blatchford did not have long to wait. Glasier resigned as editor at the beginning of May. In his resignation statement he claimed that during his four years in the post, the print order for the paper had risen from 13,000 to 43,000, falling back in the summer and autumn of 1908 to 37,000 as a result of 'vexatious policy dissension' but then recovering to 38,000.[43]

Jowett's position was very different from that of Smart and the other vociferous critics in the ILP. He accepted the 'Labour Alliance' unequivocally and rejected the idea that Labour MPs should simply use Parliament as a dramatic stage from which to appeal to public opinion.

> I do *not* agree that the House of Commons is the place for propaganda – that it is a debating assembly where rival politicians should discourse at length about their differences fancied and real. That view has been the curse of Parliament, as I have tried over and over again to explain. If the democracy has any use for Parliament it is to make it work and not talk.[44]

Jowett believed that the immediate priority was to make a reality of representative government rather than to try to replace it at once by 'democracy'. As Grayson and the *Clarion* moved relentlessly towards a definite break with the 'Labour alliance', Jowett maintained his distance without moving any closer to MacDonald and his allies. Explaining that he was quite out of sympathy with the *Clarion*'s view he resigned as a regular *Clarion* contributor in March 1910. But the parting seems to have been amicable. Despite the announcement the following week that his articles would now appear in the *Labour Leader*, there were no personal attacks or accusations of bad faith from either side.[45]

In the meantime, the indecisive first election of 1910 had posed the problem of Labour's relationship to the Liberal government most urgently. This in turn provided an opportunity for Jowett's radical policy of undermining Cabinet government. According to H. N. Brailsford, the press assumed there would be a Liberal-Labour coalition. He believed

---

42 *Clarion*, 23 April 1909.   43 *Labour Leader*, 7 May 1909.
44 *Clarion*, 6 December 1907.
45 *Clarion*, 4 March 1910. *Labour Leader*, 11 March 1910.

that nothing beyond 'a loose combination, based on the merits of each measure', could be tolerated. Joseph Burgess thought that one-third of the ILP were 'critical' but that one-third would 'support the Parliamentary leaders . . . in any policy they may approve'. The critical balance was held, he argued, by people like himself who would be 'immediately swung over into opposition' if the ILP became compromised through the Labour Party. Burgess urged the ILP to disaffiliate from the latter, given recent hints by Snowden and MacDonald that the Parliamentary Group could, without reference to the Labour Party Conference, commit the party to coalition.

Replying the following week, MacDonald maintained that Burgess was 'theorising about an unreal world'. If the government was committed to some major part of Labour's programme the latter could not help but 'give it some measure of general support'. Independence inevitably had to go into the background with the growth of the party:

For myself, I see the Party growing into a dominant power in the State by a series of coalitions. We shall unite with section after section . . .

Socialism is not going to come about by the adherence of individuals but by the surrender of whole schools of thought and wings of armies. Thus I never think of coalitions by which we are absorbed, but of coalitions which 1) are political and temporary and for specific objects, which are incidental to the 2) coalitions which are permanent and organic, and which mark the adhesion of masses of men to us.[46]

MacDonald thought that Labour should keep the Liberals in power, supporting them if necessary on issues where government policy fell short of, or even ran counter to, that of the Labour Party. On their side, the Liberals would pledge future legislation of the kind Labour desired. In practice this meant, for example, guaranteeing support for Lloyd George's Insurance Bill in return for the introduction of state payment for MPs, a move made urgent by the effects on the Labour Party of the Osborne Judgement.[47]

The absence of a definite Labour Party programme and the ambiguity of the '1907 formula', which (as noted) seemed to give the annual conference power to 'instruct' its MPs while leaving 'the time and method' of carrying out the instructions to the Parliamentary Group 'in conjunction with' the National Executive, greatly aided the pursuit of such tactics. Moreover, it was easier for MacDonald, who personally supported so many Liberal proposals including the contributory principle in national insurance, to reconcile himself to giving general

---

[46] *Labour Leader*, 4, 11, 18 February 1910.
[47] Henry Pelling, *A Short History of the Labour Party*, 2nd edn (London, 1965), p. 27.

support to the Government, than it was for those, like Jowett, who were bitterly opposed to the Insurance Bill and to many other Liberal policies.

Only a narrow vote of 190 to 170 – against discussing motions on maintaining independence from the Liberals – prevented a debate at the 1910 ILP Conference. But Jowett was able to use his speech as chairman to outline the arguments for adopting the policy of 'voting on merits'. He predicted that British politics were entering into an era in which governments with small majorities would become the rule, with Labour MPs, consequently, often finding themselves holding the balance of power. A clear decision on Labour's parliamentary strategy was needed:

the question we have to put to ourselves is whether, in these circumstances, we shall vote on the principle under consideration or on other issues for which the government in office is supposed to stand but which at the time are not mentioned.

My predecessor in office last year [i.e. MacDonald] put before you in eloquent language which we all admired some very wise reflections concerning the necessity of maintaining the power and influence of Parliament as the only means of securing social changes likely to endure. I mention this, merely to express if I may, my hearty agreement with that part of the case he then presented. And now, I, in my turn, desire to direct attention to the scarcely less important . . . root question concerning Parliamentary Government which will surely come before us, viz: Shall we, or shall we not, fall in with . . . the regular routine under which a Cabinet postulates . . . a programme as it pleases, we on our part agreeing to support them or otherwise according as to whether or not . . . measures to deal with questions of special interest to us are promised.

I am no believer in wild outbursts deliberately thought out beforehand to bring representative institutions into disrepute. Apart from such institutions the people have, as my predecessor said, no means of expressing their will, except by methods of violence which are generally followed by a long period of reaction. But I do believe that the party which sets itself to establish the authority of the elected representatives of the people as against successive Juntas of which Cabinets are composed will do great service to the country and increase the respect of the public for Parliamentary government.

. . .

It is for us to simplify the tortuous methods of parliamentary government by steadily voting according to our convictions on each question as it comes down to us, leaving others to adjust the machinery to their own convenience as they may.[48]

Jowett did not stand for re-election as ILP Chairman, and he was replaced by Anderson, but he was elected as a 'national member' of the NAC. Of the 'big four' resigners of the previous year, only Glasier, their

---

[48] *ILP Conference Report, 1910*, pp. 34-5.

sole non-MP, stood in 1910. He was re-elected in a run-off ballot against Joseph Burgess.

But it was four other NAC members who provided the *cause célèbre* of the year. They published what became known – from the colour of its cover – as the 'Green Manifesto', a pamphlet entitled *Let Us Reform the Labour Party*. The episode, like Smart's maladroit wager the previous year, is another example of the way that ILP critics so often wrong-footed themselves and played into the hands of their opponents. The issue of substance – the policy and tactics of the Labour Party – were at least partially obscured by a vehemently waged debate on the democratic propriety of the way the pamphlet was issued.

By describing themselves as NAC members on the title page, the 'Manifestists' – Leonard Hall, C. T. Douthwaite, J. H. Belcher and J. M. McLachlan – opened themselves to accusations of 'usurpation of authority' which even their sympathisers had to admit.[49] The debate in the *Labour Leader* continued throughout September and October with the paper reporting many branch resolutions. These were divided on the substantive question of policy, but very largely critical of the way in which the 'Manifestists' had acted. Hall, in particular, should have known better than to appear to take the name of the NAC in vain. Only the year before, he had protested against the official publication by the ILP of Hardie's *Confession of Faith in the Labour Alliance*.[50]

Let Us Reform the Labour Party was, in fact, a plea for the policy put forward so much more skilfully by Jowett in his chairman's speech at the ILP conference. The 'Manifestists' made this quite explicit in a letter replying to criticisms. What they denounced as 'Revisionism' amounted to supporting the Liberal government in return for concessions on matters of special interest. They wanted this abandoned in favour of Jowett's policy of 'voting on the merits of the question . . . regardless of the consequences'. They grandiloquently termed this 'Revolutionist'.[51]

Jowett was the only member of the NAC against censuring the pamphlet's authors (these four not, of course, voting). He had tried to move a milder motion regretting that the four had issued such a state-ment 'without affording their colleagues any opportunity of discussing the matter with them'. When this failed to find a seconder, Jowett voted against the censure motion on the grounds that its terms were 'unjustly severe'. He also suggested, in vain, that attention ought rather to be concentrated on the issue of party policy.

---

[49] *Labour Leader*, 26 August 1910.
[50] *Labour Leader*, 28 May 1909.   [51] *Labour Leader*, 12 August 1910.

He too was soon under attack for inconsistency: he had, on the one hand, accused the Parliamentary Group of bartering its support with the Liberals, and, on the other, asked that his accusation not be printed till after the (second 1910) general election. Since, said the *Labour Leader* at the end of October, he had 'refrained from giving any testimony in support of the charge' the matter could be regarded as settled'.[52] The delayed letter finally appeared in print on 30 December. It was accompanied by a renewed *Labour Leader* attack on him. Why had he asked for the delay in publication if he believed in the Group voting 'regardless of consequences'? Why had his election address 'evaded the House of Lords issue when the policy of the ILP was clear'? Finally, why had he 'watered down his socialism' during the campaign. The evidence given on this last point is revealing about the different views of the relationship between democracy and socialism held by Jowett and his assailants. He had written in his election address:

I am a Socialist, but I hold that it is in the interests of every school of thought to maintain the machinery of government in a position to respond by means of executive and legislative action *to the average opinion of the people. I admit most readily that the attempt to proceed far in advance of public opinion is to court reaction*.[53] (original emphasis)

All through January 1911 accusations and counter-accusations went to and fro in the pages of the *Labour Leader*. And in the *Clarion*, Hall and his co-Manifestists gave their version of what had happened at the October 1910 NAC meeting. According to their account, Jowett had agreed the delay in publishing his accusation, when urged that he would damage Labour's election prospects if he publicly continued the dispute. The *Labour Leader* had, claimed the Manifestists, used Jowett's good natured compliance as a stick to beat him with.[54]

The much-delayed letter had argued that the situation was now very different from that of the 1906–10 period. Then, it had been possible to vote against the government without endangering its majority. Even at that time, though, there had been more than one instance when such considerations were allowed to override the 'merits' of the particular issue. In the new finely balanced Parliament, the Labour Group had deliberately refrained from moving a 'Right to Work' amendment to the King's Speech for fear of bringing down the Liberals. Labour had drifted, said Jowett, into this position, leaving individuals like MacDonald to

---

[52] *Labour Leader*, 19 August, 2 September, 9 September, 7 October, 28 October 1910.
[53] *Labour Leader*, 30 December 1910.
[54] *Clarion*, 20 January 1911. *Labour Leader*, 10 February 1911.

define the party's approach. He went on to link his 'voting on merits' policy to the fundamental question of reducing the autocratic power of the Cabinet:

Fear of defeating the Government, and of a possible general election in consequence, is the whip which drives members to vote against their convictions. The party which defies this whip and breaks down the domineering power of successive Cabinet juntas will establish the authority of the elected representatives of the people, a thing worth doing for its own sake.

In response, MacDonald at first claimed that Jowett had failed to raise the issue before the Parliamentary Group during 1910. Later, conceding that this was not true, he claimed Jowett had done so 'in such a casual and ineffective way that it did not strike me at the time that he meant very much'.[55]

For a short period, admittedly, the Parliamentary Group looked set to take a line close to Jowett's; the new chairman of the Group, Barnes, made statements indicating Labour's refusal simply to support the government's policy on the House of Lords. According to Jowett's biographer, Fenner Brockway, the 'effect was electrical: for the first time Labour gained the initiative in the struggle with the Upper house'.

But the effect was quickly undone by public disclaimers by MacDonald and others.[56] In any case, Barnes was not against bargains as such. 'It is not that we have huckstered', he insisted, 'but that we have occasionally given ourselves away so to speak, without huckstering.'[57] Barnes's attitude did something to encourage greater optimism among critics about the performance of the Parliamentary Group. Even the 'Manifestists', in their letter to the *Clarion* concerning the Jowett affair, singled Barnes out as a heartening exception. For them, though, the rule was subservience to what they insisted upon calling the 'Caucus'.[58]

The scene was now fully set for the debut of the celebrated 'Bradford Resolution'. The major issue at the 1911 Labour Party Conference was the question of adapting to the new circumstances following the Osborne Judgement, which threatened the party's finances by making it more difficult for trade unions to undertake political action. The Bradford policy first appeared as an amendment to a National Executive motion. It was not an auspicious beginning. Moved by Councillor Glyde of Bradford, it sought to instruct the Parliamentary Group to vote 'steadfastly on the merit of every question'. According to Fenner Brockway's

[55] *Labour Leader*, 30 December 1910, 6, 13, 20 January 1911.
[56] Brockway, *Socialism*, p. 105.
[57] *Labour Leader*, 13 January 1911.   [58] *Clarion*, 20 January 1911.

contemporary report in the *Labour Leader*, nobody came forward to continue the debate after the amendment had been moved and seconded, with the result that MacDonald, choosing to exercise his right of reply as mover of the main motion at this stage, delivered a 'masterly speech' which resulted in the amendment being defeated 'without a "division" '.[59]

The Bradford policy was presented better at the ILP Conference two months later. Before the debate, an attempt to 'refer back' the NAC's condemnation of the 'Manifestists' had been defeated by 233 votes to 39, so it was at some considerable psychological disadvantage that Leonard Hall moved the Harborne Branch motion incorporating Jowett's criticisms of 'the overpowering political influence now exercised by Ministers, who treat nearly every important issue as a vote of confidence'. It requested the Parliamentary Group to 'declare their intention to force their own issues and to vote steadfastly on the merits of the questions brought before them'.

Even the *Labour Leader*'s account (by Brockway) shows how serious was the support for Jowett's 'voting on merits' policy. It also shows the resort of the ILP leadership to procedural manoeuvres in order to avoid the motion being carried. Brockway reported that:

Mr F. W. Jowett was greeted with loud applause as the author of the new line in policy. He said that the resolution went to the roots of Parliamentary Government . . . It did not seek to establish anything of the nature of direct legislation but rather would establish as a reality Parliamentary Government. What did the ILP want? They wanted the Executive and Administrative Departments of State run on democratic lines so that the people could control and influence them. The present Parliamentary system barred both these objects. It was Cabinet Government . . . and not Representative Government. The Government of today controlled the time of the House of Commons with the exception of a few hours which were not worth mentioning. The only way of criticising the agenda of the Government was when the reply to the King's Speech was moved in the House. It was absolutely essential if the Labour Party were ever to make itself felt in the House that it should maintain its right to add or subtract from the Government's Agenda.

Was the Labour Party to consider . . . any implied threat on the part of the Government . . . that . . . they would resign? 'I say as a democrat, No' explained Mr Jowett. If it be thought desirable for the sake of the labouring classes that [Labour] should move an amendment in regard to the unemployed, then they should move that amendment be the consequences what they may.

The case was no better with respect to the administrative departments of State. The theory was of single ministerial control, which was at intervals subject to the vote of the House on departmental estimates. Over and over again, on questions

---

[59] *Labour Leader*, 10 February 1911.

of great importance . . . when they moved an amendment to the vote they were told that they were threatening the Government. He was certain that if they went forward boldly on the merits of the question both parties would be forced to change this practice. It has been said that a Budget stood together and could not be broken up. The result of that theory was shown in 1909 when the Labour Party decided to move a reduction in the tea tax, but they were kept out of the lobby at the last moment when it was seen that there was a danger of defeating the Government.

In reply, MacDonald said that though he agreed with much that Jowett had said, the policy he proposed was 'absolutely meaningless'.

Take the tea tax. He was not present on the occasion to which Mr Jowett referred and was therefore in no way responsible. At first, the Party decided to vote against the tea tax but later they found out that this amendment was to be the means of combining on the part of the Tories against the whole budget. When that situation had developed, what was the merit of the tea-tax reduction? . . . The merits of the case were always the whole case in all relationships.

MacDonald's arguments were rejected by George Lansbury in a powerful speech supporting the amendment. If MacDonald's policy was pursued, he argued, they would never be able to reform parliamentary procedures and would come to be more and more under Cabinet control. The House of Lords might be abolished only to leave the Commons 'entrenched behind a bureaucracy more able to stem progress'. Labour would in any case be unable to wrest concessions from the Government if the latter knew that the Parliamentary Group was unwilling to endanger its continuance in office, and with payment for members it would be even more difficult for Labour MPs to take the risk of following an independent line. Turning to MacDonald's contention that Hall's motion was meaningless, Lansbury concluded:

If the intellectuals of the movement complain about the terms of the resolution, let them put down some other words which would make it clear to the men and women of the slums that even in Parliament we are true to what we say outside, namely that Liberals and Tories are the enemies of the people and Socialism is their only hope.

Following Lansbury's speech there were insistent demands that the proposals be put to the vote, which were, however, diverted by a successful motion for adjournment moved by Hardie.[60] Later, when the debate was resumed, the Jowett policy was supported by Mclachlan, Burgess and – reluctantly, he said – by R. C. K. Ensor.

We should note here Ensor's then-recent book, *Modern Socialism*, as set

---

[60] *Labour Leader*, 21 April 1911.

forth by Socialists in their Speeches, Writings and Programmes. Among its findings were that the programmes of the major Continental parties, like that of the SDF/SDP in Britain, aspired to 'popular government' by means of devices such as the referendum and initiative, shorter parliaments elected by proportional representation or the second ballot with strict delegation or the 'imperative mandate', the citizen army, and in some cases the election of the judges and the right of recall for 'elected persons'. In this perspective it was the ILP and the Fabian Society which were out of step; their demands went no further than triennial parliaments and the second ballot. Similarly, as Ensor made clear, only these last two, of all the socialist parties in the survey, supported 'limited' women's suffrage. Elsewhere the demand was always for 'adult suffrage'.[61]

When the debate resumed at the 1911 ILP Conference, Ensor cited Continental examples where Cabinets did not resign when defeated on a vote. He thought that 'It was a fundamentally unsatsifying thing that our electors should return to power, not a Parliament, but a Cabinet and that they could not have a new Cabinet without a new election'. But opposition to the 'merits' policy came from Barnes who feared it would be manipulated by Liberals and Tories, from R. C. Wallhead who argued that the 'man in the street' wanted Lloyd George's Budget safeguarded, and from J. J. Mallon who said that Labour MPs would be 'bewildered' as to the meaning of the 'merits' policy which, if adopted, would simply take away the liberty of the Party'. The debate ended after Hardie, who described MacDonald as 'the greatest intellectual asset in the movement', appealed to the conference not to press it to a definite conclusion. The 'previous question' was then carried, a procedure which Jowett characterised as 'blacking motions'.[62]

This left the ILP without a definite policy, but the debate had shown that Jowett's approach to parliamentary policy had substantial support. In 1914, as we shall see in a later chapter, the ILP Conference would adopt what had become known as the 'Bradford Resolution'. This might well have happened a year or more earlier, with important consequences for the Labour Party, had not so many critics of Labour's performance, like Leonard Hall, despaired of the fight within the ILP and, in September 1911, seceded to follow what turned out to be the mirage of forming a 'new Socialist Party' alongside the SDP and many 'Clarionettes', Meanwhile, Jowett, firmly committed to the 'Labour

---

[61] R. C. K. Ensor, *Modern Socialism, as set forth by Socialists in their Speeches, Writings and Programmes*, 3rd edn (New York, 1910), pp. 319–58.
[62] *Labour Leader*, 21 April 1911.

alliance' dug in for the long haul. Even before the 1911 ILP conference he had resumed his regular 'parliamentary' articles in the *Labour Leader*, putting forward the case against Cabinet government and single ministerial control. He illustrated them with a stream of fresh contemporary examples.

11 Background to syndicalism: the legacy of the NIGFTLU's failure

It is not difficult to understand the appeal of syndicalist ideas (i.e. of revolution via a general strike, led by a federation of single-industry unions) for those whose starting point was the 'real democracy' of the more radical sections of the socialist movement. Both the syndicalist method of 'direct action' and the syndicalist goal of industrial self-management seemed to offer direct ways for workers to exercise power without politicians, officials and other intermediaries. Both method and goal had similarities to those of the referendum and initiative, or of Social-Democrat arguments for keeping the control of Schools and Poor Law Administration as direct as possible. At the same time, syndicalist ideas had a further class appeal: to the militant, or potentially militant, industrial *worker* rather than to the seemingly more abstract and non class-specific *citizen*.

Nor is there much difficulty in understanding the appeal of syndicalist ideas among union activists, irrespective of their exact political allegiances. We have underlined one central reason for syndicalism's resonance: disillusion among many activists with the Labour Party. Historians have suggested further reasons, not least anger and renewed confidence at the end of a deep though relatively brief economic downturn, growing frustration among the organised at the trammels of procedure and officialdom, and among many of the unorganised at their own powerlessness. All these further reasons are plausible, but the problem is that few of them had been absent during, say, the early 1870s, the late 1880s or late 1890s. Nor was there qualitative novelty in syndicalist arguments. Rather, what was new was, firstly their grouping together as one 'ism' and, secondly, their seeming simplicity. These two factors were what gave them wings among friend and foe.

And here, surely, further fuel was injected from what was narrated earlier in this book. Memory of the dangerous confusions and time-wasting complexities involved in the federation-debates of a mere eleven to thirteen years previously was surely present among many activists or their immediate successors. Oral memory is notoriously treacherous. But

218

memory's unreliability does not lessen its power. And if there was one lesson which former militants of the 1890s would have drawn from the shambles of federation – described perhaps over a mug of tea in the signalbox or a glass of 'four ale' in the local Trades and Labour club with perhaps one or more younger activists, wrapt or indifferent, listening too – this lesson was surely a yearning for clarity. Of course, where the confusion among the older militants was underplayed, 'leaders' and perhaps 'leadership' were all the likelier to be scapegoated. This too would have prepared listeners for syndicalism.

'Some dozen years ago', Tom Mann reminded his readers in the opening sentence of his *Industrial Syndicalist* during 1910, 'there were thousands of Unionists and Socialists seriously discussing . . . the possibility of uniting for real fighting purposes, all the Industrial organisations. The best men of that time wished, in essence, all that is now covered by the term "Industrial Unionism".'[1] It is significant that the leading exponent of British syndicalism sensed that the earlier agitation for trades federation remained a positive memory worth appealing to.

The negative aspect of that memory also added to syndicalism's attraction. During the late 1890s, militants had had grievances – against 'leaders' for example – very similar to those which they or their immediate successors were to have around 1911. Their remedies, however, had been more confused. The present chapter examines these confusions.

P. J. King

For the long term, the least resounding of these was P. J. King himself. He was accused of inefficiency, and factionalism. The first is plausible, though hardly unique to him.[2] The second fed and was fed by his increasingly obvious failure. His anti-leadership accelerated the process. Worse, once the TUC scheme had become the GFTU, his refusal to surrender was bound to seem to some 'a despicable "dog in the manger" policy'. He was also alleged 'to run [NIGFTLU] as a one man concern'.[3] Whatever the balance of reasons, even a sympathetic member of King's

[1] *The Industrial Syndicalist*, vol. 1, no. 1, July 1910, Nottingham, p. 51.
[2] E.g. on Sam Wood's behaviour, OBS *Monthly Report*, entries for 22, 28 December 1897; 5, 19 September 1898; 25, 28 December 1899.
[3] Scottish Typographical Association, Ordinary Delegate Meeting, 12–17 June 1899 (National Library of Scotland). Proctor saw the very timing of the FLP as factionally motivated (*MWT*, 17 July 1898); 'Ted Good', *Railway Review*, 13 October 1899.

own committee, J. B. Williams of the Musicians' Union, bemoaned that 'the progress of the Clarion scheme . . . [had] been damned to the greatest extent, if not entirely, by [its] originator himself . . . The Official Scheme [had] been given the start that the Clarion Scheme should have had.'[4]

Institutional inertia

But this was to let King's opponents off too lightly. For, in addition to straight opposition, some union officials used other means to put the NIGFTLU out of court. At local level, King implied that the Manchester and Salford Trades Council, despite a well-attended meeting that voted unanimously for his scheme, had called a public meeting to discuss Eyre's alone.[5] Certainly, the secretary of Edinburgh Typographical Society had to apologise for his 'unintentional oversight' in not printing resolutions in favour of 'general nationalisation and the Clarion federation scheme' – only to bring down on his head 'an acrimonious discussion in the course of which some rather forcible and expressive language was used towards [him].'[6] At the head of the Lancashire and Cheshire Miners, Thomas Ashton seems to have succeeded in mislaying one important resolution.[7]

At national level, probably the most simple ploy was to influence the voting. For example, the Executive of the Friendly Society of Iron-founders (FSI), when distributing ballot-forms on Federation, managed to 'refrain from' comment while simultaneously noting that the ASE had recently come down in favour by a proportion of roughly 6$\frac{1}{2}$ to 1.[8] (As we shall see in a moment, this particular use of the ploy failed.)

Some executives tried hard to edit out the NIGFTLU. 'There is', ASE members were told, 'some misunderstanding re [the 'Vote on Federation'] . . . We want only to record the members voting for and against the Manchester [i.e. the TUC] scheme.'[9] More clearly, the Operative Bricklayers' executive, when confronted by sixty-five branch resolutions on federation, cut the Gordian knot by unilaterally declaring that 'the Clarion scheme is not before our members at present': the need, it proclaimed, was for instructions to the Society's delegates at the

---

[4] *Clarion*, 12 October 1899.
[5] *Clarion*, 23 April 1898.
[6] This may have been his own euphemism: ETS *Minutes of Proceedings*, 23 August 1898 (National Library of Scotland).
[7] *Clarion*, 18 June 1898.
[8] FSI *Monthly Report*, July 1898, p. 6.   [9] ASE *Monthly Report*, April 1899, p. 52.

Manchester TUC. Therefore pro-Clarion branches should class themselves as opposed to the TUC scheme.[10]
But this logic also could be turned. Thus in the FSI, while sixty-one
branches voted on the TUC scheme (and, very narrowly, supported it)
sixty-two did not vote. Whatever the number of apathetics, the Executive
was

> informed that a large number of members refrained from voting on the [TUC]
> scheme, because [they were against it] whilst others were of the opinion that
> if they voted against it that would be taken that they were against 'any' scheme of
> Federation . . .

The EC's retort was long, dusty, and predictable: unlike many
branches it 'considered that one scheme at a time was enough', therefore
the TUC's should be taken 'as a basis'.[11] Similarly, the ASC&J's
executive tried to consult its members exclusively for or against the
TUC's scheme, a tactic which some branches tried to sidestep by
sending resolutions rejecting the TUC's *and* supporting the *Clarion*'s
scheme.[12]
A year later, the ASRS seems to have landed itself in the worst of both
worlds: its members were asked to vote both on the TUC scheme and on
'SOME Federation Scheme'. Little more than one-sixth of the membership responded. These voted by more than two-to-one against the
TUC's and about 60 per cent against 'SOME . . . '. But, in addition to
the one-sixth, there may have been up to 2,750 spoilt papers – something
that Bell, the General Secretary, left totally unclear by including them
within the total number of papers returned. Ninety-two of the spoilers
had written 'In favour of the Clarion scheme only', and one branch,
Gateshead (with 569 members according to the *Annual Report*) had
refused, on the same grounds, to vote at all. Understandably, the ASRS's
Executive 'unanimously resolved' that, 'in view of the diversity of
opinion', they regretted that they were 'unable to deal further with the
question'.[13]
Admittedly, given 'the diversity', it is hard not to sympathise with
these union executives as much as with King. But the point is that few
executives did anything to resolve such complexities in favour of some-

---

[10] Statement on the 'Branch Voting Paper', enclosed in 1898 ASE *Annual Report*,
probably after 9 June 1898.
[11] FSI *Monthly Report*, October 1898, pp. 4f.
[12] *Clarion*, 25 June, 2 July 1898. For a contrast, see BSSAA, *Monthly Report*, August 1898.
[13] ASRS EC of 12–16 June 1899, p. 36. Accidentally or not, Bell in the *Annual Report* for
1899 (p. 4) jumbled the question on 'SOME' and on the TUC's, thus giving the latter
the narrower defeat.

thing so innovatory and uncertain as his scheme. No less important, they possessed certain weapons and advantages which avowed innovators such as the *Clarion*'s supporters lacked. One weapon was apathy, or arguments adducing it. A delegate at the Scottish Typographical Association claimed:

Many members had no idea what federation really meant as they had not considered it. In his own Branch . . . when the subject was under consideration, the question was asked – 'Who knows anything about the official scheme?'. They had never seen it; and when . . . informed that every man had got a copy of it they were astonished.[14]

Another weapon was anxiety. If the result of all the efforts was to be the solidification of two rival federations, the Labour movement would certainly be anything but more united, as the proponents of both had intended, but might well be split more fundamentally than ever. Their rivalry was all the likelier to have a similarly divisive effect on kindred trades federations where these were already operating.[15]

This fear gave an obvious advantage to upholders of existing institutions such as the TUC, once this body could be said to be bestirring itself to fight the current threat to the labour movement. During the crisis of the engineers, the executive of the OBS, refusing or sidestepping the invitation to the London Trade Council's conference, reminded itself that the TUC was 'the most representative body for trade unions in . . . this country' and implied the same in refusing King's invitation to the FLP during June.[16] In this perspective, suddenly-accelerated efforts such as King's were bound to be denounced as attempts to bully the labour movement's 'proper authorities'. Earlier, even one mover of a pro-*Clarion* resolution at the 1897 ASRS AGM had protested that he would not have agreed to it, had he heard earlier of the setting up of the TUC's Federation Committee.[17]

Given the feeling of urgency, plus the confusion and the fear of disruption, one can hardly be surprised at the widespread disposition to give the TUC scheme, with all its faults, a try. As the London Society of Compositors' own Report yawned (even while reproducing the Society's

---

14   1899 FSI Ordinary Delegate meeting, pp. 75f.
15   Risk of general split, Robert Allan at 1898 STUC; of splitting kindred trades noted at the spring 1899 meeting of the FEST quoted in AIMS *Monthly Report*, May 1899, pp. 52f.
16   Minutes of meeting of 13 December 1897 in OBS *Monthly Report*. Same, 22 June 1898. Similarly, *Quarterly Report*, 4 May 1898, pp. 19f.; 3 August 1898, pp. 11ff.; June *Monthly Report*, EC of 20 June 1898. Leeds Trades Council Minutes, 7, 29 December 1897.
17   Report in *Railway Review*, 15 October 1897: Cox of Quakers Yard.

own circular to other unions for a conference on federation), formulating another scheme would be 'going over the same ground again, and indefinitely delaying' the achievement of any federation at all. 'If the rules of the Federation are not as we would like them . . . then our duty is to try and alter them, which can be done better from the inside of the Federation than outside of it', wrote Will Thorne.[18] After all, from the opposite viewpoint, another ASEer whose personal scorn extended to the TUC's scheme as much as to 'leaders' generally, could nevertheless echo his reasoning:

The first step towards federation is not to formulate scheme or schemes, but to get federated. The scheme after all is only a matter of detail, and will assuredly right itself after having been tested, and deficiencies rectified or made good.

Other ASEers expressed similar views.[19]

In this connection, the ASRS is again interesting. 'What are we to do?', asked a *Railway Review* New Year's editorial, dated less than three weeks before the January TUC: 'Are we to fold our arms, shrug our shoulders and do nothing?' By definition, no: 'The great thing is to make a start, even if only in a small way, provided it be on safe lines and in the right direction.' 'The best thing to do at the present juncture', it repeated two weeks later, 'is to get . . . federated on some workable basis at once. The fact is greater than the method.'[20]

Unfortunately, as noted, the membership's vote was soon to force the EC into paralysis on federation for some time – into, in effect, shrugging its shoulders. One reason for this must have been that, during the intervening six months, the Society's delegation to the January 1899 TUC had penned a report that was surprisingly pessimistic, given that the Society had repented of its support for the rival *Clarion* scheme only four months previously.[21] Relevantly, the delegation did include Nathan Rimmer who had been at the first FLP and Thomas R. Steels the strong advocate of Labour Representation; Steels's advocacy still left him, at least, 'favour[ing] the Clarion scheme'.[22] In any case, the delegation stated as their 'firm opinion' that the outcome of the Congress was 'at best . . . a mere skeleton'. They not only regretted that Congress had refused to suspend the standing orders, but they also tried to explain away the ASRS's own abandonment, by its 1898 AGM, of the

---

[18] LSC *Quarterly Report*, till 4 May 1898, pp. 19f. GW&GLU *Quarterly Report* for four months till 1 April 1899.
[19] ASE *Monthly Report*, April 1898, p. 17.
[20] *Railway Review*, 6 January 1899, p. 1; 20 January 1899, p. 1.
[21] In *Quarterly Report* till 6 March 1899.   [22] *Railway Review*, 24 February 1899.

NIGFTLU. And they finished by repeating that 'in Federation [lay] the only hope of the workers', though only, of course, via 'a financially sound and morally just' scheme. Did these banalities conceal one or two powerful men's hankering after the NIGFTLU?

Here, it is important that the main officially-mentioned source of ASRS discomfort was merely that the NIGFTLU was proving abortive. 'So far', the *Railway Review*'s first January statement of 1899 had bemoaned, the 'discussion [on Federation had] been practically a barren one. The Federal Labour Parliament which met in July does not give promise of rallying to its side the unions of this country, and a federation without unions is no federation.' Or, as one pro-Clarion railwayman was to bewail during March, 'it [was] nearly all cackle and no laying'.[23]

Certain other anxieties would have worked against federation of any kind. The engineering crisis would have strengthened these even while underlining, to many people, the need for federation. True, many smaller organisations may have been particularly susceptible to blanket impressions that they, especially, had 'everything to gain and nothing to lose' from national federation. But once these impressions had worn off, their susceptibilities may have turned into fears that national federation might swallow them up. Even members of middling-sized organisations feared, with Horrocks of the ASE, that the GFTU would subordinate at least the small unions to the domination of 'coal and cotton' – as still, he felt, occurred in the TUC itself.[24]

Opinions varied but anxieties remained. The *Clarion* scheme in particular was alleged to favour small organisations against large.[25] On the other hand, Horrocks claimed that it favoured strong against weak. The proposed mechanism which drew these contradictory criticisms was the 'guarantee fund' or 'reserve' which, Horrocks believed, involved 'too large a financial responsibility to [*sic*] small societies', as well as 'an insecurity of benefit to the large', since every society was entitled to draw out in benefits no less than what it had paid in. On the other hand, while King, in order to try to be fair to both small and large, had levelled up the total to be paid to a small society so as to equal that paid to a large one, he had also, recognising that the small would thereby gain too much per head, envisaged that it should pay much of what it was now entitled to, into the Fund. Horrocks taunted King with subordinating small to big

23 *Railway Review*, 6 January, p. 1; similarly 24 January 1899. 'Exam' (*sic*) in *Railway Review*, 3 March 1899.
24 ASE *Monthly Report*, October 1898, p. 22.
25 George Aspinall of Handsworth, election address for no. 3 Organising District Delegacy bound with ASE *Monthly Reports* for 1897.

and with assuming that strikes would be small in size – a fundamental error, he felt, in the light of the experience of the 1890s.[26]

Some other objections were less intricate, and were made also to other schemes, including the GFTU. The Amalgamated Union of Cabinet-makers worried that the GFTU – let alone the NIGFTLU – would reduce unions' autonomy within 'a polyglot committee, upon which the smaller societies can have a possible but not a probable chance of official representation, and which may consist of members having the least possible knowledge of the special requirements of the trade involved.'

There are broader indications that the worry over autonomy was a general one, not least in relation to disputes.[27] Significantly for a recent and very strident convert from the NIGFTLU to the GFTU, Isaac Mitchell admitted to his fellow ASEers that 'a considerable proportion of the trade unionists of the country [were] antagonistic to some of the [GFTU's] provisions . . . particularly in relation to representation and local autonomy'.[28]

Some unions urged the same considerations to argue against even kindred trade, let alone national, federation. The general secretary of the Steam Engine Makers argued that even kindred federations had proved 'spasmodic'. They rose 'into existence during prosperity, and make a wide field for the demagogue for the time being; but when this individual cannot carry out his predictions of future victory . . . the associations [sic] lapse'.[29] Can one wonder, therefore, that the *Clarion* scheme's alleged perfection, complexity or ambitiousness were each sufficient to condemn it for many unionists? For there were further, larger questions: of strategy. These were distilled later by syndicalists into ones of structure.

Strategy and structures

The forces for inertia which we have just examined become even more important when we see how the NIGFTLU raised strategic issues – often incoherently at points where coherence was at a premium. Even worse, it was frequently undermined from various directions by the existence of

26 ASE *Monthly Report*, June 1898, p. 13; similarly May, p. 16. And July, pp. 9ff.
27 AU of Cabinetmakers, July 1899. disputes: e.g. Bolton OCSA, *Annual Report* for 1898, p. 125; LSC *Quarterly Report*, till 3 May 1899, p. 22.
28 Bound with ASE *Monthly Reports* for 1899, election of delegates to (September) 1899 TUC, p. 9.
29 James Swift, General Secretary, Address 'on behalf of the EC' SEMS in *Annual Report* till 15 March 1898, pp. 15f.

different conceptions for the re-structuring of trades unionism – whether 'Nationally', 'Internationally' or plain 'Generally'.

'This Federation', proclaimed the NIGFTLU's 'Objects', which passed unopposed at the founding FLP,

> is established for offensive and defensive purposes: its principal object is to protect the trades unions of this country from annihilation at the hands of any capitalist combination, by placing them on strict terms of equality with any masters' federation that may be hereafter formed.[30]

But what did 'equality' mean and imply?

For many unionists, one, if not the, central dilemma which had necessitated calls for national federation and for other more or less fresh departures, was that the employers were seen as 'taking a leaf out of our book, by finding out what combination can do'.[31] The conclusion was crystal clear: there was no doubt whatever that 'strikes and lockouts will be carried out in a very different manner to what has been the case in the past'.[32]

Yet there were crucial disagreements over what strategic lessons to draw from such observations. Was it adequate to demand, as did Isaac Mitchell when successfully seeking election as an ASE delegate to the 1897 TUC, that 'the federation of employers be . . . met by the federation of the workers'?[33] What type of federation would be best, and what type stood most chance of adoption in late-1890s Britain? Would fully federated workers outflank fully federated capitalists, or be out-flanked? Particularly if the first, would conciliation or escalation ensue and, if the latter, how big were the stakes? Either way, should the workers supplement federation with other expedients such as cooperation or 'political action' (such as Labour Representation)? And if, anyway, the weaker, should workers actually replace industrial action with one or some of these? More or less faced or blurred, such questions were the stuff of debate during and after the engineering struggle. In one way, or probably in many, they form part of the background to the at first slow support for Labour Representation, which historians know so much about.

These questions may also form part of the background to the trend,

---

[30] *Report of FLP*, p. 32.

[31] G. H. Clarke, MUOBS General Secretary, in MUOBS *Quarterly Report*, June 1898. As early as their May 1897 ADM, the Dockers' Union were told that the Clydeside engineering employers had 'copied' federation from the unions 'and used with more success than the workmen'. DWR&GLU ADM 1896, pp. 17f.

[32] Clarke in MUOBS *Quarterly Report*, December 1897; he had made this his refrain since at least September.

[33] ASE, election-addresses for TUC delegacies, 1897, pp. 8f.

more than a decade later, towards industrial revolt and to the complex of responses labelled 'syndicalism'. As early as 1899, one ASRS railwayman could put the phrase 'War of Folded Arms' into inverted commas – as if he knew it to be already a cliché.[34] And, a year earlier, another railwayman, this time the 'Secretary of the Federation Committee' (conceivably the one based in Wigan), had envisaged a strategy which was to be associated more with 1911 than with 1898:

Railwaymen should be the most powerful body of workers in England today . . . For if [they] were only united for offence and defence, they would bring the country to a standstill within seven days. It would not require a long fight, full of sorrow and suffering, but it should be short and sharp.

An escalatory perspective such as this did not necessarily go with federation alone. This particular writer was also associating it as much with amalgamation (for which see the end of this section) as with federation. He assumed the two would reinforce each other. He claimed to 'know for a fact that there are hundreds of members of the Associated and Pointsmen's society ready and willing to federate, if the officials would only move'.[35] But at this time, escalation was linked far more frequently with federation than with amalgamation. 'What', King and Blatchford asked resoundingly, 'would the federation do if half the men in England were out'? 'Bring out the other half!'[36] 'Federation would', Sidebotham believed, 'soon dispose [of] employers' federations.' This raised questions of aim. An ASE district candidate stated more roundly during 1897 that 'full national federation', if properly managed, 'could soon (to quote from our own rules) "assist in altering the competitive system of industry for a cooperative system, in order to secure a full share of the fruits of our labour"'. Many enthusiasts, in other words, saw federation as simply impregnable.[37] For even before a strike became general, it was possible for one socialist ASEer, Albert Roxby, in an exceptionally long-winded manifesto for the National Assistant Secretaryship, to believe that

in case of trouble in the coal trade, or, still more, the stoppage of the railways, the amount of assistance these sections would receive from the Federation would lead the country straight into one of the greatest crises from which it has ever suffered. The government would then be compelled to intervene, and, failing

---

[34] *Railway Review*, 7 April 1899, G. W. Chappell.   [35] Same, 29 April 1898, p. 8.
[36] King and Blatchford, *The Federation of Trade Unions, 1897*, 1899.
[37] *Sidebotham FSI Monthly Report*, December 1897, pp. 5–8. John Sharland of Bristol, for no. 7 division. Bound with ASE 1897 *Monthly Reports*, pp. 7f. Similarly, and merely within one union: G. Lindsay and Mark Batty, in the FSI's *Monthly Report*'s reply, November 1897, p. 6, and September 1898, pp. 4f.

an amicable adjustment, would be compelled to nationalise both mines and railways, thus bringing two of the largest sections under State control at once . . . [38]

But at least as frequently as *Blitzkrieg*, federation could allow trench warfare where the main munition was money. Here too, some saw success as assured.[39] With federation, believed one London cabdriver, the Engineers' 'strike income would have been never ending . . . whilst the income to the employers from their federation would have always been a diminishing quantity, from the natural consequences of loss of trade'.[40]

Some, however, saw finance as an area where even federated unions were doomed to be outflanked. Sometimes, this pessimism was part of a conservative position against all newfangled expedients from federation to socialism. Some saw any escalation as similarly doomed. 'The balance of power would not be altered, and the only result [of Federation]' warned R. D. Welford, a Stanningley Ironfounder, 'would be the extension of the . . . area of any possible dispute.' 'The logical conclusion of trades federation', reasoned one speaker at the 1898 STUC, 'was a general strike.' This, for him, amply refuted all arguments for Federation.[41]

More than *Blitzkrieg*, trench warfare was compatible with what one might call the 'deterrent' version of federation: federation viewed as a

---

[38] Miscellaneous ASE documents 1897–8 (LSE library), pp. 30–5. Predictably, Roxby was against kindred-trade federation and for amalgamation of the smaller societies into the ASE or else for national federation – whose 'moral outlook' would, he believed 'deter any number of Lockouts'; secondly, for 'Political Action', to transfer the class struggle to the floor of the House of Commons; thirdly for the belief that continued employers' militancy placed the labour movement at a decision-point between advance or extinction. His peroration on the historical significance of it all is most significant for its exceptional length. Albert E. Roxby: 28 years old in 1898. Fitter. Seven years in the ASE and already four times president of Portsmouth no. 2 branch. Also sometimes on District Committee and Trades Council. Previously in a Jarrow branch where he experienced a demarcation dispute with Plumbers as resulting from employers' manipulation. For the first Assistant Secretaryship, he had only one branch's nomination. His only opponent was 58 years old, had been in the Society 37 years and had 272 nominations. Nevertheless, Roxby got 5,037 votes (election address bound with 1900 *Annual Report*, p. 29).

[39] AU of Cabinetmakers: Report of the July 1898 Delegate Meeting, p. 41. Bound with 1898 *Monthly Reports*.

[40] W. Sorby in *Cab Trade Record*, May 1898, p. 10. This 'Official Monthly Report of the London Cab Drivers' Trade Union' was necessarily as detailed on court cases as on union questions. In addition, it had recently noted that Field Marshal Lord Roberts of Kandahar had consented to be a vice-president of the Cab-Drivers' Benevolent Association (April 1898, p. 6).

[41] R. D. Welford, FSI *Monthly Report*, August 1898, pp. 13ff.). 1898 STUC *Minutes*, p. 41 (Mr Allan).

weapon which 'rationally' should never, and 'therefore' would never, be used by either side: 'Gigantic Federation on both sides is bound to bear the highest standard of reason in our day and generation. Says Count Moltke "Tis the sword that keeps the sword in its sheath"' said General Secretary Count Thomas Dobson, congratulating his National Amalgamated Society of Enginemen, Cranemen, Boilermen and Firemen on their joining the GFTU late in 1899.[42] The GFTU, in fact, was hailed by the leaders of unions as different as the Gasworkers and the 4,500 strong Amalgamated Society of House Decorators and Painters, as furthering conciliation and lessening strikes.[43] 'Reason', for such as Dobson, meant conciliatoriness, if not formal conciliation.

In this perspective, some viewed federation as merely a means towards arbitration: it was 'with a desire to do away with that devastating affair called a strike', said one Bradford ironfounder (who also supported Labour Representation and collectivism) that he 'supported a scheme of federation; for by federation we hope to gain arbitration' by 'command[ing] the respect of employers'.[44] And the FLP itself, via its 'Objects', hoped that 'By placing the workers in a position of comparative independence, to have as far as possible all disputes between masters and men settled amicably.'[45]

Support for deterrent, conciliatory federation speeded a shift by some people with a leftwing image, such as Barnes, away from militancy. Near the start of 1899, an editorial in his *Monthly Report* treated federation as one aspect of an evolution from 'indulgence by either side of [*sic*] mere "wild cat" tactics'. While still assuming a rank-and-file aggressiveness, he assumed just as frankly that it would be switched on or off. Given this, then 'reason, . . . the dictates of humanity' and 'public opinion' would be on the workers' side. Barnes was soon personally advocating a high-productivity-high-wage economy, which he was shortly to observe as a visitor to the USA – a country more often seen in union circles as a paradise for employers.[46]

---

[42] NAS of ECBF, *Half-Yearly Report* till 31 December 1899, p. 6.

[43] Mark Hutchins as GW&GLU President in *Quarterly Report* till 30 September 1899. E. C. Gibbs as General Secretary to the AS of House Decorators and Painters: *Annual Report* for 1899 (4,548 members).

[44] J. F. Atkinson, FSI *Monthly Report*, October 1898, p. 7. His collectivism: May 1899, pp. 14ff. The whole disputation between him and Welford was merely as to whether Federation would speed arbitration, which both wanted.

[45] Federal Labour Parliament, *Minutes*, p. 32. Similarly, President of Aberdeen Trades Council, at April 1898 Scottish TUC, *Minutes*; *Railway Review*, 28 January 1899, p. 7; Birmingham Trades Council *Monthly Bulletin*, 7 January 1899, ASE *Monthly Report*, September 1899, p. 57; November, p. 62; December, p. 66.

[46] ASE *Monthly Report* February 1899, p. 4. Same, May, pp. 6f.

If such a perspective could be entertained by former militants, it is hardly surprising to find others taking conciliation and arbitration as actually substituting for federation. In 1898 – a few hours, as it chanced, before the TUC fire – the President of the Wellington Trades Council addressed Congress on New Zealand's new scheme of compulsory arbitration.[47] In 1901, the Chairman of the Amalgamated Society of Carpenters and Joiners' (ASC&J) triennial General Council, though wistfully preferring *Clarion* federation as against the GFTU, was to note with relief that 'compulsory arbitration' was 'every year gaining more support . . . and if an Act to this effect is passed, the necessity for Federation on present lines will cease to exist'.[48] If such confidence appears blinkered, other arbitration-enthusiasts were yet more so. One Gorton ironfounder discovered this, after he had warned of the danger of such schemes as long as landowners and capitalists dominated parliament and the state. His leaders replied in no-nonsense fashion that he was 'entirely wrong in assuming that the Government for the time being has anything to do with the administration of the law', which was 'left with those appointed for that purpose.'[49]

However, arbitration was more often recognised as among those expedients which raised questions wider than trade unionism as such. One of these was co-operation. Though frequently considered, it was seldom taken in isolation (or, except for debating purposes, as 'versus' trade unionism). When it was, this was at unusual moments – as in the ASE *Monthly Report*'s first editorial after the 1898 defeat, where 'capital' was bitterly seen as 'all powerful' so that, apparently, withdrawing into cooperative separatism meant 'becoming ourselves the owners of the instruments of production'.[50]

No less strategically, cooperation was sometimes combined with other expedients. It could, for example, be advocated with the *Clarion* scheme. Thus a former delegate to the ASRS's 1897 AGM called for his Society to 'meet the monopolists and capitalists on their own ground and with their own weapon, i.e. capital'. This could 'only be done', he continued, 'by consolidating our forces into one strong federation doubled with cooperation.'[51] Or it could simply be associated with 'federation'. Thus,

---

[47] For one discussion of this see Edinburgh, TLC *Monthly Bulletin*, 4 October 1898.
[48] ASC&J Triennial Council, 1901, *Minutes*, p. 8; W. T. Wilson who also presided in 1898; similarly AIMS *Monthly Report*, May 1899, pp. 52f.
[49] Editorial interpolation in contribution by Mark Batty to FSI *Monthly Report*, September 1898, pp. 4f.
[50] ASE *Monthly Report*, February 1898, pp. 2f.
[51] 'Anti-Sceptic', *Railway Review*, 15 april 1898. (He, though, believed strength would boost reason: a belief still compatible with rejection of 'half-hearted measures'.)

at the 1898 Irish TUC, the mover of a motion for simply this (which was to be passed unanimously) hoped 'to accumulate funds so that, wherever practicable the workers may try cooperative production, rid themselves of the wages system and reap the full reward of their labours'.[52] As Cole and others have pointed out, the decades around 1900 were, quantitively, the climax of producers' cooperation: with some people also, perhaps, in terms of strategic ideas.[53]

During the second half of the nineteenth century, co-operation and 'socialism' were often seen as opposed. Analogously, those trade unionists who were against socialism often saw socialism as against trade unionism. Such differences erupted at all levels of the labour movement, not least at the highest. For example, a long and vicious row took place at the Miners' Federation 1898 Conference on whether the two were opposed. Had not the ILP's Keir Hardie talked of trade unionism as 'played out'? Eighteen months later, Dobson of the NSA of ECBF was still proclaiming, 'I do not agree with those pessimistic people who . . . [declare] that trade unionism is played out'.[54]

Not surprisingly, this led some to suspect that 'but for the fact that the Clarion scheme was submitted by the Clarion, it would . . . have been unanimously adopted by trade unionists'.[55] Some declarations of support for King's scheme were indeed made avowedly despite the Clarion's socialism. At the, from the Clarion viewpoint, seemingly triumphant 1897 AGM of the ASRS, one delegate protested that it was 'ridiculous to boycott a scheme simply and solely because it comes from a Socialistic source', and another 'declared that this Clarion scheme gave their ILP friends a splendid opportunity of airing their views'.[56] But he was oversimplifying. The Clarion might have large, though as we have seen variable, associations with the ILP, but ILPers – just as SDFers – stood at most points of the federation spectrum.

Socialism was not the only political aim discussed in connection with federation. The February 1899 editorial of the ASE's Monthly Report recommended not only deterrence-plus-reconciliation, but also an attack on landlordism by a political alliance of workers and industrialists, led by the workers.[57] King, preparing the Minutes of the founding FLP argued

---

52 Councillor Taylor of the Belfast Linen-Tappers, Irish TUC Minutes, 1898, p. 46.
53 G. D. H. Cole, A Century of Cooperation (London, 1947), p. 206.
54 NAS of ECBF, Annual Report, till 30 June 1898.
55 Mr Bandyside of Glasgow at 1898 Scottish TUC (Minutes, p. 40).
56 'It did not matter whether [it] came from the ILP or the Western Morning News, he should support it because it was true': respectively, Grundy and Holmes, Railway Review, 15 October 1897.
57 ASE Monthly Report, February 1899, pp. 4f.; similarly one member, April 1898, pp. 28f.

for taxation of ground-values: 'instead of acting as buffers between the royalty-footpads and the workers, [the employers] should not only stand aside but assist us in getting at them'.[58] As we have seen, where the politics of Federation-supporters is visible, it ranged from socialism to Lib-Labism; and some supporters from anywhere within this range seem to have been open to land-reform, to cooperation, and to equally 'old' radical ideas. Thus there can be no greater error than to assume that those Federation-supporters who did not see themselves as socialists (presumably a majority) lacked wider aims of their own. And among both socialists and non-socialists many a formulated aim would have been familiar to their grandparents.

None the less, irrespective of long-term broad aims, strategy was easier to agree on. And here, increasingly, discussion centred on Labour Representation. Sometimes, it and national federation were seen as excluding, sometimes as assisting, each other.

Sometimes national federation excluded Labour Representation, sometimes vice versa. Thus, in the ASRS, Nathan Rimmer of Wigan, a former EC member, who represented his branch (as noted) at the 1898 FLP and his union at the January 1899 TUC, argued that Labour Representation should be rejected as the more divisive of the two. One of his co-thinkers believed that if federation could be accompanied by 95 per cent union membership, it would generate sufficient 'moral force' (which he defined in such a way as to include the threatening of physical) to be able to overrule any government without a single Labour Representative in the Commons.[59]

Occasionally, national federation was taken to be merely a stop-gap until Labour Representation arrived. Thus, at the March 1897 Scottish TUC, Bob Smillie, – a miner and ILPer – preferred 'Parliamentary effort in the way of collectivism'; but meanwhile the fact that 'employers in all trades were combining . . . made it necessary that unions should be more firmly federated'.[60]

More frequently, though, federation was seen as actually hastening Labour Representation. The two were to work in harness. Frequently, Federation and Labour Representation were mentioned as equally desirable and the matter was left at this point – as by one leader of the ASC&J,[61] or by Thorne of the Gasworkers. But other statements were a little more concrete. One Scottish Ironmoulder believed that

[58] FLP *Minutes*, pp. 6f.
[59] *Railway Review*, 18 August 1899, p. 6; 7 July 1899, p. 7; 24 January 1899.
[60] STUC *Minutes*, 1897, pp. 26f.
[61] W. T. Wilson, chairman at the 1898, 1901 and 1904 Triennial General Councils of the AS of C&J, spoke for both at the first (*Minutes*, pp. 4f.), gave his casting vote for

if each member of the Federated Trades would pay only a shilling per annum for a fund for labour members, we could soon have such a force at our backs, that all our demands would be granted without recourse to the strike or getting lock out [*sic*] . . . Trade unionism of itself cannot save the workers.[62]

When the GFTU arrived, some hoped it too would speed Labour Representation. Within the ASE, support for both Federation and Labour Representation was particularly in evidence. Thereby, one member believed, 'all great conflicts between Capital and Labour would be fought out on the floor of the House of Commons'[63] – a comforting perspective only three months after the end of the lockout, surely. Tom Proctor – the Devonport ILPer – was wordily demanding both during the next lockout, as weapons in 'the Class War!!':

Our society was in favour of the legal method [i.e. the eight hour day by legislation] but knowing the workers as a whole was [*sic*] not sufficiently intelligent to make a parliament pass an eight hours law, we had to fight for it in the meantime in the old trade union fashion.[64]

Isaac Mitchell wanted the Society to formulate, for the next TUC, schemes for both federation and Labour Representation. Barnes 'wanted federation to gather up and focus the opinion of the working people, and use them through various public bodies'.[65] Numerous candidates for positions within the Society were more or less detailed in their support for both.[66] Sometimes, national and kindred trades federation were treated as mutually exclusive. Occasionally, this was to the latter's disadvantage.[67] In any case, whether seen as supplementary or as alternatives to national federation, a number of schemes for federation of kindred trades were under discussion during this period, for example, in printing, building, and on the railways (which failed, as noted, through

affiliation to the LRC at the second (*Minutes*, p. 46) and spoke for it at the third (*Minutes*, p. 5). GW&GLU General Secretary's *Quarterly Report* till 30 September 1897.

[62] AIMS *Monthly Report*, February 1898, p. 3: 'Yours fraternally, South Side'.

[63] 'Paw Chuck' ASE *Monthly Report*, April 1898, pp. 28f. Similarly Peckham's J. Gunning, pp. 29f.

[64] ASE *Monthly Report*, December 1897, pp. 10ff. and more politely in his election address for the no. 8 division, Organising District Delegacy, p. 4; *Monthly Report*, July 1899, pp. 21f.

[65] March 1898, *Monthly Report*, p. 77. ASE *Monthly Report*, December 1899, p. 66.

[66] Bound with 1899 *Monthly Reports*, Organising District Delegacy for divisions 4, 7 and 8, pp. 5f.; J. E. Scholefield of Oldham; James Steer (also Secretary of Woolwich Trades Council; R. Dening of Swindon).

[67] MUOBS *Quarterly Report*, June 1900; refusal of kindred federation on 5 April 1900.

members' apathy).[68] There were also networks of local federation within particular trades and industries.

Sometimes, the traditional craft or inter-union prejudices were fully mobilised against national federation. At an extreme, the supporters of national federation were occasionally seen as spongers and scroungers; 'societies whose funds are very low and require the use of others'.[69] This remark issued from the building industry, where at least recent local kindred trades federations seem to have generated some experiences of this type.[70] More than once, speakers at the ASRS's 1898 AGM advocated breaking with the NIGFTLU in these terms: a Liverpool branch secretary sneered at people unprepared to 'put their hands into their pockets, instead of someone else's pocket', and the president was cheered for denouncing 'the motion [sic] that had got abroad that [the ASRS] had some money, and there were not a few persons who wished to spend it . . . and many . . . thought . . . they could trade on it'.[71] Often such fears and prejudices needed merely hinting at.

Not surprisingly, existing kindred trade federations were often upheld in preference to anything wider. And some 'union' leaders seemed to have feared wider federation, on the argument that theirs were already 'federations'. As the Lancashire ILPer and Gasworkers District Secretary, J. R. Clynes, wrote, 'Our Society is practically a Federation of Labourers'.[72] Where 'Federation' was actually embodied in the organisation's name and structure, some conservatives behaved as if particularly threatened. Thus Thomas Ashton of the Lancashire and Cheshire Miners' Federation inserted into the agenda of a conference in December 1898 a long and waspish argument, ending with the 'following question for consideration of the Branches: 'Would any of the existing schemes of Trades Federation . . . benefit the miners more than the MFGB? If so how?'[73]

For him, in other words, to support federation with non-miners meant betraying miners. During the few weeks separating this agenda from the

[68] LSC *Quarterly Report* till 3 November 1897, p. 21. MUOBS as above: *Minutes* of ASC&J 1901 GC, pp. 67f. ASRS General Secretary's *Report* till 12 March 1900, p. 6, and till 17 September 1900, p. 28.

[69] Long statements in name of EC in AU of Cabinetmakers *Monthly Report*, July 1899.

[70] As suggested in Postgate, same, pp. 359f.

[71] *Railway Review*, 14 October 1898, p. 8: the Liverpudlian was Alex McLaren, who was probably socialist. For McLaren, see also *Railway Review*, 30 June 1899.

[72] GW&GLU *Quarterly Report* till 30 September 1897; similarly his Sunderland counterpart, H. Lynes, *Quarterly Review* till December 1897.

[73] Bound between agenda for conference of 10 December 1898 and the annual balance-sheet, and clearly a few weeks before the January 1899 TUC.

January 1899 TUC, the MFGB's Annual Conference sat through what can only be called a vicious slanging-match. Pickard, from the chair, reiterated (by retracting) a statement that Toyn of North Yorkshire was a 'traitor' who ought to be 'muzzled', and then threw the same mixture at Smillie of Scotland. Politically, Toyn was a fellow Lib-Lab, whereas Smillie was ILP. But both had offended by representing their members at the FLP. (Allegedly, Pickard had first uttered the phrase to Toyn's face at Bristol during the 1898 TUC there; this earlier insult may reveal something of the state of mind of some union leaders after King's Federal Labour Parliament roughly two months previously and before the Colston Hall had so obligingly burnt down.) The same MFGB conference had earlier heard Woods. He spoke as the Miners' Vice President more than as Secretary to the January TUC which was due to meet in two weeks (and where he, Pickard and Ashton were among the MFGB delegates). Woods rejected national federation 'until the miners themselves were federated' – a reminder, of course, that not all miners were in the MFGB. Ashton himself would have felt schemes such as King's to be horribly similar to the chaotic structure which he had been striving to wean his own union away from, while under attack for his conservatism from a large minority of his membership.[74]

At other times, existing or possible federations of kindred trades were seen as ways *towards* something wider. Even Ashton, in his very same intervention, could argue that 'the first step to perfect Federation is to begin with one trade . . . If societies in one trade cannot agree to federate what hope can there be of establishing a Federation of all Trades?'

It was a relatively tiny step from talking of kindred trades federation as a vehicle towards national, to seeing it as fundamentally determining a national federation's structure. 'For ourselves,' reasoned the EC of the Scottish Ironmoulders, 'we are inclined to the belief that the only Federation we can ultimately have is that of kindred trades, and when these are formed then they can form a Consultative Board from the various Federations'.[75] This was among its reasons for staying out of the new GFTU. And at the GFTU's very founding meeting, immediately following the fateful vote to uphold standing orders and

---

[74] As noted, though, Pickard had rowed no less bitterly at the previous year's MFGB conference, this time with Smillie over socialism. See R. Page Arnot, *History of the Scottish Miners* (1955), pp. 95f., for verbatim; R. C. Challinor, 'Trade Unionism in the Coal Industry until 1900', PhD thesis, University of Lancaster, 1970, particularly pp. 279–84, 293.

[75] AIMS *Monthly Report*, May 1899, p. 52 and inside cover.

against rival schemes, the Liverpool-based NUDL, led by Sexton its ILPer Secretary, was defeated even more quickly in its motion to structure the new national federation as a federation of kindred-trade federations.[76]

It is evident from Sexton's earlier canvassing for this move amongst other unions, that it was supposedly under the auspices of the International Federation of Ship, Dock and Riverside Workers (IF of SD&RW). He was certainly under pressure from this International.[77] Thereby he introduced yet another factor complicating the scene. After all, the 'I' in the NIGFTLU stood for 'International', and while this certainly referred to the 'four nations' of the British Isles whose existence very much conditioned its own structure, many of its more sanguine adherents may have been confident that sooner or later it would square up to the capitalists from wherever they might try to outflank it – from the Continent or further afield. Thus for one ASEer, though federated employers could beat federated workers, the latter would really win because their federation would be international.[78]

None the less, the incidence and prospects for international federation were, not surprisingly, particularly uneven. The IF of SD&RW was, for obvious reasons, the most developed. Mann and Tillett's Dockers' Union credited itself with this body's foundation during the late 1890s, and its proceedings are particularly full of practical internationalism. The need for international federation had also been the main moral that Mann had drawn from the engineering crisis. Yet, by the spring of 1899, he was taking the new GFTU, feeble though he felt it to be, as an excuse for downgrading the International Federation to the role of a correspondence bureau. The union's Delegate Meeting backed the downgrading. In subsequent years, the respective magnitudes of the union's spending on international and national activity were reversed in favour of national. Ironically, at the International Federation's 1898 conference, two London delegates from Mann's own Dockers' Union had proposed to transform the assembled delegates into an 'International Federation of Workers'. (The only speaker to support them had been another British delegate.) And instead, though still ambitiously, delegates had

<hr />

[76] January 1899 TUC *Minutes*.
[77] NAUL EC *MB* 10, 14 October 1898. At its 1898 conference, the Federation had used Sexton's excuse on his withdrawal (that his union saw National federation as a precondition for International) in order, in his absence, to saddle him with a Transport Workers' Federation (*Report of the 2nd Annual Conference of Ship, Dock, and River Workers at the Club and Institute Union, Clerkenwell*, pp. 2, 12) (International Institute of Social History, Amsterdam).
[78] Reply of 'Trunnions' to 'Ichabod', ASE *Monthly Report*, June 1898, p. 15.

unanimously preferred a proposal for an International Transport Workers' Federation.[79]

But outside conference-halls – and apart from solidarity funds, fraternal delegates, and greetings – international federation was at best at the germination stage, except with unions in lands of English language and emigration. In the ASE, one or two candidates demanded international federation and around the autumn of 1899 numerous resolutions reached the EC 'suggesting closer alliance with our co-workers abroad.'

But this was the same month as the Society's members voted quite overwhelmingly to give further funds to their brothers in Denmark. Here, employers had widened a lock-out, which had originated in the building industry, to at least six other trades, including unrelated groups like tailors, merely 'with the purpose of preventing the workmen from contributing support to the locked out builders.'[80] Aid from some British trade unions and trades councils to the Danish struggle was patchily massive. Nationally, most of the 1899 fund-gathering was organised by the London Trades Council with the endorsement of Sam Woods, and with the roving advocacy of a Danish MP named Hansen. Over £3,000 was subscribed.[81] But efforts such as these for Denmark only underline the extent to which international union solidarity was exceptional.

In any case, from a narrowly trade union point of view, to the extent that the employers were thought likely to aid each other internationally, then the same arguments against kindred federation applied on the broader level as much as the national. Firstly, as the NIGFTLU supporters were particularly fond of observing, the larger the proportion of an industry that was involved in a conflict, the less useful a kindred federation or any other workers' organisation confined to that industry.[82] Secondly, to make sectional unity a stepping stone to national unity was

---

[79] Mann at 1899 Delegate Meeting. *Minutes*, p. 7. Dockers' Delegate Meeting, p. 15. 1897–1900 *Annual Reports*. 1898 Conference Report of International Federation of Ship, Dock and Riverside Workers, p. 10.

[80] Board of Trade's *Labour Gazette*, September 1899, p. 267.

[81] LTC *Annual Report* for 1899, pp. 4f., 23–6: the lists underline how national the response was. Incidentally, the SDF's 'Trafalgar Square collection' of £4 10s was more than four times the total given via the *Clarion* newspaper: an internationalist contrast with *Clarion* lavishness during the British engineering struggle?

[82] E.g. P. J. King: an 'unassailable' argument, according to one Scottish printer (STA ODM), pp. 75f.: Grieve of Edinburgh. Similarly, ASE *Monthly Report*, April 1898, editorial; or resumé of discussion in the FSI's Darlington-based no. 7 District (FSI *Monthly Report*, February 1898, p. 11). Outflankability could also be used as an argument against kindred-trade federation without any alternative being proposed, as in the 1900 special GM of the Edinburgh branch of the Bookbinders and Machine Rulers Consolidated Union (*MB*, 6 July 1900 (National Library of Scotland)).

– except in the longest term – to try the method of advancing 'through sectionalism to unity', which, as the *Railway Review* noted, seemed by definition absurd.[83] Just as Mann on the international, so on the national, level, many unions were to see their actual or probable membership of the GFTU cutting across their sympathies for kindred trades federation.[84] Some organisations probably preferred it this way.

Finally, in our long list of expedients which underwent redoubled discussion during the late 1890s, are a ragbag which one can label 'amalgamation'. Terminologically and in practice, this often overlapped with federating kindred trades. For the Operative Bricklayers' Society's (OBS) General Secretary, John Batchelor, federation came second in desirability to the aim of 'only one union in each industry'. One of his members went further: kindred federation was better than national, but tighter unionisation was better than either.[85] Such ideas could admittedly be heard in large societies – as from an ASRS member who, drawing the moral from the victory of 'Dyer and Co', announced that he was also in ASLEF so as to help amalgamate the two Societies.[86]

Possibly, the more skilled the organisation, the greater the variety of positions in favour of amalgamation or tightening of organisation. It is true that kindred federation continued sometimes to be preferred out of skill separatism. This was well symbolised by Frank Smith, for whom the small Amalgamated Union of Cabinetmakers, of which he was General Secretary, was 'second to none as a skilled trade'. For him, 'if kindred trades federation cannot be satisfactorily worked in the first instance, there is no great hope of Federation of all Trades being a success and worked efficiently by representatives of extreme societies':[87] 'extreme' perhaps, in being peripheral to the trade, and not merely in their politics.

It is equally true that, where one's Society was the largest in the trade, amalgamation could harmonise both with the interest of that society, and with socialist principle. Thus Tom Proctor, self-described as critical 'of the Clarion scheme and the holding of what was called the Federal Labour Parliament', praised his ASE's resolution to the 1898 TUC that there should (in his words) 'be a rule for the gradual reduction of the

---

[83] *Railway Review* editorial, 2 June 1899; similarly, FSI *Monthly Report*, November 1897, p. 6 (A. Lindsay of Heywood); February 1898 (District no. 7).

[84] The report of AS of C&J's 1904 Triennial General Council talked of 'numbers of . . . societies' taking this line (*Minutes*, p. 50).

[85] John Batchelor in OBS *Annual Report* for 1897. OBS *Monthly Report*, June 1898, p. 5: L. Watson of Stalybridge branch.

[86] G. W. Chappell, *Railway Review*, 29 April 1898, p. 8.

[87] *Annual Report* for 1898 of the AU of Cabinetmakers. Smith, of course, was 'no relation' to the ex-Salvationist ILPer. *Annual Report* 1899.

number of societies in the same trade'. It would 'if adopted in a national scheme of federation, tend towards a less difficult . . . scheme of management'.[88]

Greeting the GFTU's foundation, one ASE candidate was so hopeful as to demand 'thorough amalgamation' via the TUC itself.[89] In other words, support for any federation-scheme could easily go with support for amalgamation. Particularly among ordinary activists, the two were often blurred – or at least, were seen as allied so closely that the exact terms of the alliance could be left to sort themselves out at some later stage. After all, a key feature of 1897–9 in many unions and areas was the profusion of efforts towards the reform of union structures – this has surely become all too clear by now in this book!

At this stage, all one need say on the late-1890s relations between amalgamation and other trade-union restructurings as compared with relations during the 1910s, is that those of the 1890s were more complex and varied. As well as being more confusing to the historian, they may often, also, have themselves been more confused. For, what remedies did the enemies of 'leadership' propose?

Alternatives to 'leadership'?

Some expedients for ending or limiting leadership were mainly symbolic (for example, Wharton Hall's preference for 'Lurries' over platforms). But many unionists seem to have demanded a more fundamental democratisation. For example, a London member of the National Association of Operative Plasterers (NAOP) demanded 'as a Social Democrat' that branches should be autonomous from the District Committees and that the members should vote directly on all issues. He felt 'our system by voting by delegates' was 'very unjust'.[90] Supporters of the NIGFTLU were disproportionately sympathetic to such views. Thus, two particularly pro-*Clarion* ASRS branches were to move, at the 1897 AGM, that the Society's delegates to the TUC 'be elected by the branches and not by the EC as at present'.[91] And Glasgow and Aberdeen Trades Councils, amongst probably other organisations, demanded even

---

[88] ASE *Monthly Report*, September 1898, pp. 14f.
[89] Alfred Foster of Bradford-cum-Beswick Branch, Organising District Delegacy election for no. 3 Division 1899, *Monthly Report* electoral manifestoes, p. 4.
[90] NAOP *Monthly Report*, September 1896, pp. 25f.: T. Patrick of London no. 10 Branch, who also contributed in May 1896, p. 31 and November 1898, pp. 28f.
[91] Quakers Yard. The other was Denton: ASRS *Supplementary Agenda for AGM*, 5 October 1897, pp. 6f.

that all alterations or additions to Rules of *any* Scheme of Trades Federation should before their adoption be remitted to the various trades federated for a vote of their members *prior* [our emphasis] to their being brought up at any Delegate Meeting of representatives of the Federation.[92]

True, what the Webbs called 'primitive democracy' was wider and usually older than support for King's scheme. None the less, the *Clarion* scheme was the most 'primitive'. It probably depended most on the strength of such a radically democratic approach – and unfortunately on its own conceptual coherence. King certainly viewed his constitution as comprising the referendum-principle, and even a routine FLP's duty was 'simply' in his eyes 'to register the decisions of the [members] obtained by Referendum'.[93] The referendum was also to operate in relation to the decisions of the AGM, to the investment of Federation money, and even – 'between the times of meeting of the General Executive' – to the recognition and support of disputes, at least if time allowed. Had King's scheme ever passed the preliminary stage of founding conferences, British trade unionism might, in the short term at least, have come to a booming, buzzing rank-and-file confusion. The scheme's referendum-like practices would have weakened the internal power of many union executives; all transactions of the annual FLP were to be 'submitted to the vote of the general body' who could refuse their 'confirmation' for anything.[94] This Rule had actually been made more plebiscitary at the founding Federal Labour Parliament.[95] Blatchford, no less than King, was sufficiently untactical to proclaim that 'the present very unsatisfactory and cumbersome plan of delegating the affairs of Labour to small committee of the annual TUC [would] become obsolete.'[96]

As has become abundantly clear, long before and after the NIGFTLU episode the *Clarion* was peculiarly identified with arguments for the initiative and referendum. Some trade unionists supported these as national political devices. Thus, Aberdeen Trades Council demanded them 'in the interests of political purity and democratic legislation'. The 1898 Scottish TUC unanimously called for the twin devices at the British level in order to, if necessary, overrule the Westminster parliament.[97]

Internally, some unions had long had such devices. In others, there were sometimes calls for these. Within the ASE, the advocate by now

---

[92] Aberdeen UTC *MB*, 5 June 1898, our emphasis.
[93] *Federation in a Nutshell*, 1898, p. 12. *Clarion*, 24 December 1898.
[94] *Federation in a Nutshell*, Rules 13, 17, 28, 34 and 35.
[95] FLP *Minutes*, p. 17.
[96] *Clarion*, 31 January 1897, after a diatribe against leaders.
[97] Aberdeen UTC *MB*, 1 March 1899 or later: circular to this effect was noted by AIMS on 20 May (AIMS *MB*). STUC 1898 *Minutes*, p. 50. Repeated 1899.

best known to us would be Tom Proctor who believed that the functions of the Society's Delegate Meetings – 'the making of new rules and the final court of appeal' – 'should be entrusted to the vote of the whole society, and thus . . . give more general satisfaction all round'.[98] Not that such calls were always successful. Thus the Scottish Typographical Association's 1898 Ordinary Delegate Meeting rejected by 48 votes to 8 a motion to replace Delegate Meetings with the referendum.[99] But the overall status of the initiative and referendum amongst unions was untidy precisely because, here, it was not merely abstract but rather routine. For, firstly, many of the smaller craft societies and some others had traditionally enjoyed full referendum, and sometimes – in effect – initiative, rights. And, secondly, many other unions of this and other types enjoyed varying elements of both; 'a vote of the trade' was the most frequent term. Proctor, on the same occasion, could claim 'these points' to be 'working well in other societies'. The ASE – which, in some workplaces, was growing less exclusive towards semi-skilled workers while remaining in bitter rivalry with smaller skilled societies – was in some ways increasing its own rank-and-file control, but via the delegate system more regularly than via the referendum. To the extent that the tactical situation for supporters of the initiative and referendum was complex, it is peculiarly hard for historians to deduce lack of support from lack of extant evidence of agitation.

Similarly with opposition to 'leadership' as such. This could sometimes blossom into a full-blown theory of structurally caused conspiracy. It thus implied a need to restructure trade unionism. One railwayman, himself a member of both ASRS and Enginemen's Society, believed that general secretaries 'secretly' worked against any union unity, particularly federation:

The executive committees or committee had weakly allowed themselves to be led . . . by them. For instance, say, a general secretary may be editor of his society or union organ; he, consequently, admits into the columns letters promoting grade jealousy . . . and all other kinds of selfishness. Why . . . ? Well, simply because federation would mean the abolition of his useless work.[100]

Directly, he seems to be saying no more than that fewer unions would mean fewer general secretaries. But he may conceivably have intended something more.

---

[98] Bound with the ASE 1898 *Monthly Reports* election for EC – man for no. 8 Division, p. 5; similarly 'Mechanikos', ASE *Monthly Report*, November 1897, pp. 10f.
[99] STA ODN (13th) *Report of Proceedings*, 12, 17 June 1899, pp. 32f.
[100] 'Pro Federation', *Railway Review*, 12 May 1899; similarly 'Mr Handyside, Glasgow', Scottish TUC 1898, *Minutes*, p. 40.

Others certainly did, but were fatally unclear on what to do. Thus, within the ASRS (again), probably the main argument which undermined support for the *Clarion* was, as seen, the question of finance. With shattering effect, the EC used it before and during the 1898 AGM and ordinary members did the same through many months before and after. What is significant is the response of federation enthusiasts. True, some merely tried to refute the contention that large sums were at stake, and some simply defended the high contributions as being no higher than those that Society members made already towards particular ad hoc solidarity funds. Some also claimed, predictably, that the AGM had underestimated the rank and file's willingness to pay up.[101] What is far more significant, though, is that only belatedly did any one of them reach print with the argument that the EC's very wording of the spring 1899 ballot was incorrect, because it had 'bracketed together' the question of 'some Federation scheme' with ' "are you prepared to pay the necessary expenses and contributions, in addition to present contributions" '? This writer, a *Clarion* enthusiast, went out of his way to prove the 'bracketting' wrong. And the point, here, is that his argument was that federation would 'be an important epoch in our history and would warrant a reconstruction of contributions and benefits'.[102] In other words, federation would not merely regroup the unions but would revolutionise them. Yet this aim, probably restricted to tiny minorities even of *Clarion* supporters, was usually stated rhetorically and perhaps conceived only vaguely – so far as one can tell.

By contrast, one can be definite about at least King and the *Clarion*'s growing animus against all 'leaders'. As we have seen, the struggle within the ILP had already encouraged the *Clarion*'s main writers to elaborate a set of arguments against 'leadership ' – whether by individuals, committees or delegate conferences. With ease, *Clarion* writers switched targets from socialist, to trade union, infightings. This obviously suited King too.

It is true that anti-leadership was to appear again amongst the sympathisers of syndicalism. In 1910, one delegate at a syndicalist gathering could warn against 'form[ing] another bunch of leaders. Leaders had betrayed them again and again in the past. They would

---

[101] E.g. 'A Lever Puller', *Railway Review*, 20 January 1899, p. 7. Similarly 'one of the rank and file', 10 February 1899.

[102] 'Federation', *Railway Review*, 8 September 1899, p. 7. He went on to repeat the frequent *Clarion* supporters' assertions that the reconstructed contributions would not total more than before, and that, had the EC segregated the financial question in a separate ballot 'or at any rate' into 'separate columns on the voting paper . . . a different result (I feel sure) would have been obtained'.

betray them again. They must see to it that they did not have too much leadership.'[103] But there were to be more sturdy beams in the syndicalist building – unlike in that of King and the *Clarion*, whose opponents recognised its anti-leadership as overstrained.

In almost the last article that King wrote in the *Clarion* and with failure probably staring even him in the face, he extended his case until it snapped, lashing friends and waverers along with foes. He promised 'to show that one paid servant of a trade society possesses actually more power than 40,000 members of the rank and file' and, wider still, 'that the influence of the Secretary of a Trades Council is greater than that of all the other members together'.[104] It is hard not to believe that much of his sympathisers' anti-leadership animus was not also directed at humble union officers when these people opposed them. However understandable this might be, it still laid them wide open to counter-attack. All that the defenders of leadership had to do was to argue its indispensability, implying that the anti-leadership case failed to explain how the functions of 'leadership' would be filled, let alone reorganised. They could also counter with a 'you too':

In the first way, the *Railway Review* sophisticatedly defended

Trade Unions and their leaders [against] those who argue that democracy and leadership are incompatible. Whether that be so or not, the fact remains that unions, like cooperative and kindred bodies, have to pay men to manage their business, and [to] guide them during times of stress . . . Probably no body of men [were] exposed to such a fire of criticism than [*sic*] union leaders.[105]

Secondly, superficial or not, charges of sloth could be shifted from 'leaders' to 'members'. 'We hear at times,' reported Dobson of the NAS of ECBF, 'of general officials not being in too great a hurry . . . Is it not possible that the members themselves, in many instances,' were slothful? (Most heinously, for him, many were slow to send him their branch-accounts.)[106] And as for King's own advocacy, he was particularly wide open to such counter-attacks. Mitchell's reply to him in the *Clarion* during October 1899, was, in the event, virtually to bury him – since Blatchford and his 'Bored' were ceremoniously dumping him during the same week. 'The desire,' Mitchell diagnosed, '(so long harboured) to expose trade union officials has become father to the thought that

---

[103] W. G. Kerr from Brighton Trades Council: minutes of first conference on industrial syndicalism, Manchester, 28 November 1910, p. 24 (*Industrial Syndicalist*, 1974 edn).
[104] *Clarion*, 23 October 1899.
[105] *Railway Review*, editorial, 22 August 1899, p. 8. Similarly, 6 October 1897, an insertion in Newton Heath no. 2 Branch's report; J. R. Clynes in *Annual Report*.
[106] *Report* for half year till 31 December 1899.

they are all fools or knaves.' Such 'officials' ranged 'from the general secretary of the most powerful union down to the doorkeeper of the most humble branch . . . In spite of your denunciation of leaders, you are the narrowest and most intolerant leaders I know.'

In any case, King's hostility to 'leaders' obscured the fact that his support had not been restricted, on any definition, to the 'rank-and-file' alone. This was particularly predictable in the uncertain atmosphere of 1897–8. As J. B. Williams, one of King's own Committee-members pointed out, the Scottish TUC, on the occasion when it had supported the *Clarion* scheme, 'generally comprised among [its] . . . delegates . . . the much . . . abused Labour leaders', These ogres had, in reality, proved unable to terrorise their allegedly cowering rank and file into supporting the NIGFTLU.[107] As for individuals, King could hardly have spoken to so many Cleveland Miners' Lodges without the support of Toyn, their President since 1875. In the early days of his scheme, King had, correctly or not, claimed support from Burns and also from Thomas Burt – that is to say from a famous ex-socialist New Union figurehead and from a veteran Lib-Lab miners' leader. He also claimed support from the secretaries of the National Union of Clerks and the tiny Operative Lath Renderers.[108]

More generally, 'leaders' hardly obstructed the sort of initiatives King might have approved. A number found their initiatives or support for levies of the membership in aid of the Engineers challenged by traditionalists who used auditors and even lawyers to block them. Later on and more ambiguously, there were complaints that 'many' supporters of federation were 'conspicuously absent'[109] from the new GFTU's General Council. True, these laggards undoubtedly included such leaders as Knight who, despite his chairmanship of the TUC's Federation Committee, had always been adamant that his own Boilermakers would not stomach any additional federation other than the FEST. But they may also have included some soured NIGFTLU sympathisers. This is one possible reading of an editorial remark in the *Monthly Report* of the ASE that 'many who had . . . had full opportunity of making their influence felt in the framing of the new scheme at Manchester [i.e. at the January 1899 TUC] . . . had failed to give their members the necessary lead'. In any case, that last phrase underlines the obvious fact that any

---

[107] *Clarion*, 14 October 1899. Williams also accused the *Clarion* of suppressing opposition to its scheme.

[108] *Clarion*, 4 September, 27 March, 24 April 1897.

[109] Virtually the same phrase in, e.g., NS of Drillers and Holecutters *Quarterly Report* till 30 June 1899, p. 6: Joshua Butterworth, General Secretary. And ASE *Monthly Report*, August 1899, p. 2, editorial.

leader risked unpopularity when committing his members to paying increased subscriptions which, for all save the richest societies, seemed inevitable on entry into any federation.

At branch level, leadership could be no less important. The active one-tenth of the Edinburgh Bookbinders who virtually ran the branch, continued to push for the NIGFTLU (as also for Labour Representation at all political levels) for a whole year after having been clearly shaken by other members' lack of response. Some of these activists even proposed to authorise their national officials to send fees to the NIGFTLU without balloting the branch[110] – something that, had it come from the NIGFTLU's opponents would surely have been unmasked as 'ignoring the rank and file'.

The obvious importance of *branch* leadership can be seen in the 'plumping' of many branches 100 per cent for or against in votes on the *Clarion* scheme and other expedients,[111] a procedure open to exactly the same 'democratic' objections as the *Clarion* liked to make against the 'delegate system'. One member of the ASRS, during the year when his Society supported the *Clarion* scheme, actually demanded that branches supporting the rival schemes be punished by the Executive: something he would, we may readily imagine, have denounced on principle in other circumstances.[112] Not just organisationally but conceptually, NIGFTLU hit the buffers. Among some militants the din surely echoed for a decade.

---

[110] In the event, they need not have worried: of the half of the membership who did vote, three-quarters supported the NIGFTLU: Edinburgh Branch of the Bookbinders and Machine Rulers' Consolidated Union, *MB*; prefer *Clarion*: from 30 June 1898; special meeting to be called by handbill: 26 October 1898; the meeting: 22 January 1898; attempt to prevent ballot: 6 October 1899; figures: 27 October 1899.

[111] E.g. BSSAA vote-figures in August 1898, *Monthly Report* already mentioned; NAOP's in its June 1898, pp. 36–41, where Eyre's narrowly beat the *Clarion*'s.

[112] *Railway Review*, 11 March 1898, p. 10.

12 Avoiding the 'Servile State'. The impact of syndicalism and Guild Socialism

There are three major contrasts between the agitation of the late 1890s and the better known ones of the early 1910s. First, the latter period saw far greater self-confidence and size of struggle. Secondly, there was a greater clarity about 'leaders'. Thirdly, this clarity was rooted in a wider one about broader aims and strategies. Not surprisingly, these aspects reinforced each other.

First, although the late 1890s actually saw a slow advance in numbers of trade unionists affiliated to the TUC, we have heard these years resounding to the widespread belief that an embattled retreat was taking place. Sometimes, these sounds swelled to something like panic. They came from people of any politics between the Liberals and the SDF and from any level of the trade union movement. Here, the contrast with the mood and the achievement of the later years speaks for itself. These saw the biggest surge in unionism since the period around 1890. It swept up broader groups than many observers, even then, had thought organisable.

Secondly, whereas such ideologists as there were in the 'New Unionist' movement of around 1890 seem at first, as we saw, to have thought that leaders and even organisations old and new would let themselves be swamped by the surge towards universal organisation, the Federation-agitators of less than a decade later were all too often hamstrung by an anti-leadership rhetoric which combined cliché with an extraordinary instability and confusion. Their syndicalist successors were often no less prolific on the topic of leaders. *The Miners' Next Step*, to take their best-known text, devoted much space to it. But they were more specific with an organisational rather than a moralistic approach. The problem was now more clearly leadership rather than leaders as individuals.

Thirdly, syndicalists' far greater clarity about strategy and tactics went with a far greater clarity about aims. *The Miners' Next Step* offered a precise objective:

to build and carry an organisation that will ultimately take over the mining industry, and carry it on in the interests of the workers . . . The coordination of all industries on a Central Production Board who, with a statistical department to ascertain the needs of the people, will issue demands on the different departments of industry, leaving to the men themselves to determine under what conditions and how [sic] the work should be done. This would be real democracy in real life, making for real manhood and womanhood. Any other form of democracy is a delusion and a snare.[1]

At the level of ideas, the oft-remarked élan of the 'direct actionists' should be understood partly in terms of a widespread sense of relief among British workers that so many old knots and tangles were apparently being sliced through, and so resoundingly. Not least for syndicalist miners, the lines of their new organisation and how to achieve it from within the existing South Wales Miners' Federation were clearly sketched out. Even more striking, they had just been explicitly pre-figured in the method of the pamphlet's very authorship – i.e. in the practice of the 'Unofficial Reform Committee'. The contrast with the way the 1890s' schemes for federation were authored is obvious but enlightening. Whereas the Unofficial Reform Committee document had been discussed back and forth from lodges to committee and back again,[2] we can surely doubt whether any of the 1890s schemes had emerged from any process so democratic – least of all the main rival to King's scheme, that of the TUC. And King's itself was, so far as can be discerned, the fruit of the distilled wisdom of one 'Unpaid Agitator', leader of a now defunct New union, who could rely on blasts of criticism from the massed ranks – of the half-dozen members of the *Clarion* 'Bored'.

The latter consisted of a bunch of individualistic journalists, each busily frying her or his own fish. Admittedly, these personages enjoyed a rich relationship with a – for British socialists – large readership. But the relationship was nevertheless, in its quietly cheery way, demagogic and it involved responsibility to no organisation or persons. And the readership was almost certainly the most disparate and the least working-class of the socialist press.

Obviously, the authorship of *The Miners' Next Step* is an unrepresentative high point: as far as syndicalist publications went, the *Industrial Syndicalist* revolved self-evidently round Tom Mann (with Guy Bowman's financial management). Still, *The Miners' Next Step* – its

---

[1] *The Miners' Next Step* (Tonypandy, 1912; rpt. London, 1972), pp. 30–2.
[2] W. Ness Edwards, *History of the South Wales Miners' Federation*, vol. 1 (London, 1938), p. 70. Holton, *The Miners' Next Step*, pp. 84–5.

authorship as much as its content – was an ideal example, available for at least gesturing towards, of all that Mann was still agitating for.

So far, we have merely been comparing the agitation of 1909–14 with its earlier equivalents. Inevitably, much of this has involved contrasts. Yet a mere ten years and four months separate the January 1899 special congress of the TUC, which marked nightfall for King, from Mann's return to Europe from Australia, an event which is taken as marking the sunrise of British syndicalism – or conventionally was, until 1976 when Bob Holton persuasively showed this to have been a process more than an event and, more usefully to our own argument, to have begun even earlier. Such a short interval must surely have involved some continuity.[3]

We would formulate the position as follows. Those enthusiasts for King's or other federation-schemes who did not completely drop out in discouragement after about 1899 were not necessarily even going to remember much details of their conclusions. One thing, though, which they were all likely to remember was the sheer confusion of so many aspects of the whole federation agitation. The confusions had come with and fed on a defensive situation in which many official leaderships had seemed both necessary and unreliable. Even by itself, such a memory was surely likely to make activists hope that advocates of any further schemes for turning their movement upside-down should at least be clearer on aims and strategy.

This clarity seemed precisely on offer from many syndicalists – and, with the return of prosperity after some years of high unemployment, from a situation which had suddenly become open to militancy again. This time – unlike the last time when high unemployment had suddenly been succeeded by boom during 1888–9 – there would be much less confusion about official leadership. This time – though the rhetorics of each period did overlap with that of the others – leaders were seen not so much as during the late 1890s, in terms of Old as against New, or as 'old 'uns' as against 'young 'uns' (Burgess) or traitors as against friends (King) but simply as hamstrung by the same self-defeating structures of their organisation. These were seen as self-defeating because undemocratic and unresponsive, therefore, to the 'rank-and-file'.

In this minimal sense, the trade union agitation of the late 1890s had not been a waste of time. Minimal but still vital among many militants, it may well have functioned as a negative preparer of the way for syndicalism. Of course, we are not suggesting a happy ending or a stable solution. Syndicalism too had its incoherences. But it was fruitful in stimulating responses – often vehemently hostile – from virtually all

3 Holton, *British Syndicalism 1900–1914: Myths and Realities* (London, 1976).

sections of the socialist and labour movements. The fall of NIGFTLU had implicitly challenged the simplicities of *Clarion* democracy, but syndicalism was the catalyst for a much wider and more explicit debate on the nature of democratic socialism. Our account will concentrate, less on the story of syndicalism itself than on its wider impact on 'orthodox' socialism during the immediately pre-war years of the 'Great Unrest'. Syndicalism was, among many other things, the most radical reaction to Labour's perceived failure. It entailed a complete, and often contemptuous, rejection of Parliament and 'politics'.

By contrast, for those who despaired of 'reforming' the Labour Party but stopped short of syndicalism – in some cases only just short – the villain of the piece seemed to be the subordination of socialism in the alliance with the trade unions; the answer lay in socialist, as distinct from Labour, representation.

The success of Victor Grayson in the Colne Valley by-election of July 1907 without Labour Party endorsement greatly heartened those who subscribed to such views. It triggered a 'socialist revival' and led, via local 'socialist representation committees' and the last of the *Clarion*'s 'socialist unity' campaigns, to the formation of the British Socialist Party (BSP) by a merger of the SDP, dissident ILP branches and individual members, 'unattached' local socialist societies and *Clarion* groupings. Grayson, in close association with the *Clarion* of which he became 'political editor' for some time, played a crucial rôle in launching the BSP at a 'Unity Conference' in 1911.

But it was a disparate organisation. In the *Labour Leader*, Fenner Brockway commented that the ILP had 'never been divided by such vital differences of opinion as were apparent at [BSP] gatherings'.[4] Considering the history of the ILP's internal affairs, this was pretty damning. Indeed, the whole of the socialist movement, including the ILP, was experiencing a period of intense turmoil. Syndicalist-influenced opinion was strong within the BSP; but so was the determination of the former Social-Democrats to resist it and to retain their famous 'palliatives' which had survived the 'splitters' of 1884 and the De Leonist 'Impossibilists' of the early 1900s. Though the 'palliatives' – which included adult suffrage, proportional representation, and the referendum and initiative – were excluded by the Unity Conference, the first regular BSP Conference of May 1912 restored them.[5]

As the NIGFTLU and other episodes demonstrated, the *Clarion* was always better at whipping up enthusiasm for new initiatives than at sustaining them. It began to distance itself from the new socialist party

---

[4] *Labour Leader*, 6 October 1911.   [5] *Justice*, 7 October 1911; 1 June 1912.

even before the Unity Conference took place.[6] One index of the widening gap, less than a year later, was the reappearance in the paper in May 1912 of Jowett's 'Parliamentary Notes' which, it will be remembered, had migrated to *Labour Leader* in March 1910, essentially because of *Clarion* hostility to the 'Labour alliance'.

From 1912, Lansbury's *Daily Herald* provided an alternative umbrella for 'rebels', and before long complaints appeared in *Justice* about BSP members organising *Daily Herald* League meetings featuring Tom Mann expounding the virtues of syndicalism.[7] In spite of all efforts, the BSP was rapidly becoming little more than the SDP under a new banner. Its 1913 Conference was a shambles. In his closing address, Hyndman told delegates that the Executive Committee had been divided into 'two antagonistic factions' and that, elected to the chair against his will, he had found its meetings 'almost intolerable'. *Justice* complained of the poor attendance, the badly arranged agenda, and the inadequacy of the Standing Orders Committee. It also deplored the 'scenes' that had taken place.[8]

Soon after, everything was again in the melting pot when the BSP came under pressure from the International Socialist Bureau to affiliate to the Labour Party. There had been those, notably Hyndman and Dan Irving, who had favoured this course back in the days of the SDF/SDP, and since the Social-Democrats, more than any other group, always saw themselves as a semi-autonomous section of the international movement, the ISB's urgings carried much weight. With the benefit of hindsight, the BSP seems like an aircraft design that looked impressive on the drawing board but whose prototype-trials revealed that some of its engines were too weak to lift the machine while others, insufficiently secured to the structure, would tear themselves loose once run at full power.

Admittedly, issues other than syndicalism, notably militarism and the 'German menace', played their part in BSP discord. But syndicalism – in the broadest sense – was the greatest single factor.

Syndicalism's Social-Democratic critics

The appeal of 'real democracy' together with the general suspicion of the 'parliamentary methods' pursued by Labour and the strong feelings

---

[6] *Clarion*, 14 July 1911.
[7] *Justice*, 19 April 1913. See letter from Albert Ward. For the importance of the *Daily Herald* League in the immediate pre-war years, see Holton, *British Syndicalism*, pp. 185–6.
[8] *Justice*, 17 May 1913.

of solidarity in struggle produced by the unprecedented strike wave of the 'Great Unrest', explains why syndicalism could obtain a sympathetic hearing from so many socialists. Yet the strong antipathy to syndicalism among Social-Democrats, particularly long-standing members of the 'Old Guard', sprang, in part at least, from the same general roots.

This is not as paradoxical as it appears. Sympathisers saw the democratically positive elements in the doctrine, while critics were sensitive to the negative aspects. To the former, a worker taking 'direct action' was asserting his or her full humanity: attempting to gain control of personal destiny and becoming an active force in history rather than a passive order-taker. To the latter, while the ends were most desirable, a large question mark hung over the means. Was not 'direct action' always minoritarian in practice? It might be justified as the protest of the individual against the tyranny of even democratically-reached decisions. Further, in a society where most important decisions were made by powerful minorities, other minorities might have no option but to defend themselves similarly. But syndicalism seemed to be advocating such minority action as the main, indeed the only, method of taking the offensive. Were methods that were appropriate in fighting the autocratic employer equally justifiable in the struggle against a state which was, if not democratic, at least liberal in the sense of permitting more or less unfettered propagation of political ideas? Was not syndicalism, at bottom, simply anarchism in a new guise?

Every new idea of policy begins necessarily as the property of a very small minority. But there was a world of difference between that minority seeking to get its way by converting others, and the short-circuiting of this process by an exercise of economic (or other) power. The commitment to the conversion of the majority was at its most uncompromising with Blatchford, who often expressed the view that 'socialism was the best system for socialists' and saw the movement's main task as 'making socialists'. Social-Democrats, like Harry Quelch for instance, did admittedly talk sometimes of being ready to use any means 'from the ballot to the bullet'. But Quelch only defended the use of force in situations where there was no possibility of carrying out propaganda and electoral politics. In reality, the SDF position, by the 1900s at least, was not so different from that of Blatchford who explicitly rejected 'revolution' on democratic grounds.

Some Social-Democrats came to see, or to sense, a hidden and unintended authoritarianism in syndicalism – another variety of what one regular *Justice* contributor called, referring to the arson campaign of the WSPU, the 'anarchist intimidation of the majority by a minority'.[9] The syndicalist case was, for many Social-Democrats and particularly the older ones, tainted by its advocates' seeming closeness either to anarchism or to the De Leonist 'Impossibilism' which had caused such trouble within the SDF during the early 1900s. Hyndman's complaint, in 1903, that his 'Impossibilist' adversaries 'refuse to accept the ruling of the majority of the organisations they belong to, they vilify everybody who differs from them and they say what they know perfectly well to be untrue about the men with whom they claim to be working', was virtually identical to the charges levelled later at syndicalists and their sympathisers in the BSP.

The idea of bringing down capitalism by a general strike went back to the general unionism of the early nineteenth century, if not to Thomas Spence's 'National Holiday' around 1800. It informed some of the early initiatives towards 'trades federation' which we have examined earlier. But, for the 'Old Guard' of the Social-Democrats, it was – quite explicitly – the badge of anarchism. Even W. M. Thompson and *Reynolds's News* were accused by *Justice* of 'turning anarchist' when they published an article supporting the general strike in 1904.[10]

At first, in 1906, J. B. Askew's regular 'International Notes' in *Justice* presented syndicalism sympathetically as a reaction to the over-stressing of parliamentary politics and relegation of trade union activity to a subordinate role.[11] But less than a year later, at the beginning of 1907 he was hoping 'that the Italian proletariat will see now how impossible it is to allow the Anarcho-Syndicalists, as they are called in Germany, to remain in the party'.[12] Similarly, *Justice* condemned the 'abortive Anarchist policy of direct action' adopted by the Industrial Workers of the World (IWW) in the USA[13] and Hyndman later commented that 'the Industrial Workers of the World are not of this world yet, and are not likely to be unless its advocates change their tactics from top to bottom'.[14]

The problem for Social-Democrats was how to tread a middle path between 'reformist' parliamentarism and 'revolutionary' syndicalism without losing the support of the 'practical' to the former or the 'idealist' to the latter. From the Social-Democrat standpoint, both of these undesirable alternatives mutually reinforced one another. In a report on the French Socialist Congress, *Justice* observed that

too much importance is attached to Parliamentarianism by all our Continental friends just now, and that fact tends to develop the quasi-Anarchism of the 'direct

[9] *Justice*, 19 April 1913.   [10] *Justice*, 29 October 1904.
[11] *Justice*, 19 May 1906.   [12] *Justice*, 19 January 1907.
[13] *Justice*, 3 November 1906.   [14] *Justice*, 23 January 1909.

action' Syndicalists, which would be welcome if it were a corrective to undue Parliamentarianism, but is, unfortunately, much more likely to encourage than to check the tendencies it is promoted to oppose.[15]

A turning point in the development of syndicalism in Britain, marking a transition to something approaching a national movement, was the return of Tom Mann from Australasia, where he had spent the previous eight years, in 1910.[16] At first, *Justice* welcomed his return, and even after he began publication, with Guy Bowman, of the monthly *Industrial Syndicalist* he was still referred to as 'our comrade and friend' and assured of SDP support.[17] The first issue of the new publication received a friendly review in *Justice*.[18]

But things soon changed. By the time of Mann's arrest in March 1912 for publishing the famous 'Don't Shoot' leaflet, *Justice* was insisting that there was 'practically no syndicalism' in Britain and that the 'Labour revolt' was a 'soldiers' battle' owing nothing to leaders or agitators. The *Labour Leader*, likewise, insisted that syndicalism was a 'new bogey' invented by the Tory press.[19] How far Tom Mann's standing in the eyes of *Justice* had declined in two years is suggested by the paper's headlining, in July 1912, of his claim that improvements in working-class conditions had been achieved in spite of rather than because of, political power: 'More Syndicalist Rubbish'.[20]

Justice continued to regard syndicalism as totally at variance with Social-Democracy – and even with democracy itself. Various ancestries – anarchist or impossibilist or both – were ascribed to it, although J. Hunter Watts gave a more original account of its provenance:

the Syndicalist proposes to make trade unionists dictators of the destinies of society by vesting in them the ownership of the means of life – a recrudescence of the theory of the Dictatorship of the Proletariat which may be traced to Robespierre, and which deluded Marx when he stated that the Paris Commune would 'serve as a lever' to overthrow capitalism.[21]

Such judgements should not surprise us. Reporting on the 1907 Russian Social-Democratic Labour Party conference held in exile in London in 1907, Elia Levin of the Whitechapel and Stepney SDF had described the 'majority', i.e. Bolshevik, wing of the party as 'saturated with Blanquist tendencies'.[22]

---

[15] *Justice*, 24 October 1908.   [16] See Holton, *British Syndicalism*, chapter 3.
[17] *Justice*, 21 May, 10 September 1910.   [18] *Justice*, 9 July 1910.
[19] *Justice*, 23 March 1912. *Labour Leader*, 5 April 1912.
[20] *Justice*, 27 July 1912.
[21] *Justice*, 8 March 1913.
[22] *Justice*, 15 June 1907, quoted in Walter Kendall, *The Revolutionary Movement in Britain 1900–1921. The Origins of British Communism* (London, 1969), p. 81.

And some Social-Democrats thought they detected something very similar in syndicalism. It was alleged by F. B. Sylvester that the BSP members supporting syndicalism were 'not trade unionists at all, but are either middle class people who would not be seriously put out by strikes, or are clerks and shop assistants who are too indifferent to join a trade union'. Moreover, his letter continued, if Leonard Hall and others really shared 'the heretical principles and impossibilist tactics of Tom Mann and Guy Bowman', they were 'honour bound to retire from the BSP, or should be compelled to do so'.[23] This correspondent was by no means alone in casting doubt upon the reality of working-class support for syndicalism. When the *Industrial Syndicalist* first appeared it was greeted by mock-incredulity from Victor Grayson writing in the *Clarion*:

Oh, Bowman! Bowman! how could you? [the title] . . . smacks of the *salon*. Fancy a hod-carrier asking his newsagent for 'The Industrial Syndicalist'. And imagine the newsagent looking it up in a list of horses for the next day's race!

Grayson, as political editor, did however go on to give a sympathetic welcome to Mann's 'calm and lucid exposition of the tenets of Industrial Unionism'.[24]

Much more potentially damaging than the claim that syndicalism was middle class, was the charge that it was anti-democratic in method, objective, or both. Later, in his post-1917 and anti-Bolshevik book, *Evolution of Revolution*, Hyndman described syndicalism as 'a scheme that has never been even partially thought out'. It is clear from the book that his major objection was to the direct action method of revolution rather than to industrial self-management in a socialist society.[25]

When efforts were made to 'think out' the implications of direct action, it became clear – to Social-Democrats at least – that to be successful such methods almost inevitably necessitated military-style leadership. This was true, not just of syndicalist-style general strikes, but of all forms of direct action including, for example, the forms adopted by the Suffragettes of the WSPU. As early as 1907, *Justice* had criticised their 'tactic of the hooligan'.[26] A leading article in 1912 asserted that socialists had always condemned 'riotous violence by whomsoever committed' and rejected the WSPU's attempts to legitimise their arson and other direct action campaigns by drawing parallels with past events, such as the reform agitations of the 1830s and 1860s. There was a crucial difference, *Justice* insisted, between spontaneous violence, which was usually in

---

[23] *Justice*, 2 November 1912.   [24] *Clarion*, 22 July 1910.
[25] H. M. Hyndman, *Evolution of Revolution* (London, 1920), p. 338.
[26] *Justice*, 3 November 1907.

response to provocation by the authorities, and deliberately planned campaigns. It gave its reason for protesting against the punishment of the *Don't Shoot* leafleters 'because their appeal was against violence, not for it'.[27]

There was an abundance of evidence to show that in the case of the WSPU, direct action methods and internal dictatorship went hand in hand. Was the same also true of syndicalism? Some justification for the Social-Democrats' belief that syndicalist direct action would entail less rather than more democracy could be found in syndicalist writings themselves. In an article on 'The Miner's Hope', W. F. Hay devoted a section to what he called 'Our Conception of Democracy': 'Our leaders must be elected by a ballot of the membership by direct vote, elected for a definite period with definite instructions, and *they must prove their competency by being successful*' (original emphasis). This had the right emphasis on directness and accountability to satisfy even *Clarion*-style notions of 'real democracy' – except that neither the acceptance of the need for leaders nor the unqualified emphasis on success as a yardstick were exactly Blatchfordian. But a few sentences later, Hay made the explicit parallel with military command:

Our democracy must be expressed in determining the object to be fought for, who shall lead in the fight, and what is a reasonable period to expect victory. For the rest, no General can consult with his troops when going into battle with the enemy. So with us.[28]

There had been many complaints, over a very long period, that political leaders tried to assume general-like rôles, tried to avoid discussion of strategy, and in general concentrated as much power as they could in their own hands. Would such critics of leadership really be prepared to adopt methods which enhanced the authority of leaders, even when democratically elected and subject to recall and even as a precondition of syndicalist success?

The problem of management and executive authority

Socialist doubts about the democratic credentials of syndicalism even extended to its version of the post-revolutionary society. Many socialist positions and values long pre-dated the advent of a syndicalist movement. Fabians, with the Webbs taking the lead, had from early on rejected the 'self-governing workshop'. In the introduction to his

---

27 *Justice*, 6 April 1912.
28 *The Industrial Syndicalist*, no. 5, November 1911, pp. 22–3.

Socialism in England, Sidney Webb contrasted consumer co-operation with producer co-operation. Consumer co-operation was, he said, making towards 'an idea of social organisation as much higher and sounder than that of the "self-governing workshop" as it is opposed to it'. It was 'essentially Collectivist in character, whereas the control of industry by selected little groups of profitmakers is but a variant of the existing industrial individualism'.[29] Webb regarded what he called 'Trade Sectionalism' as an 'insidious form of spurious collectivism . . . which makes, consciously or unconsciously, the trade and not the community the unit of administration and which is expressed in the cry of the land for the laborer [*sic*], the mine for the miner – I do not know whether we may add the school for the teacher and the sewer for the sewerman.'

His major objections were that, with the 'self-governing workshop', industries would be subject to no control by the community as a whole and that new generations of workers would find the ranks of the existing workforce closed against them. They would be admitted 'only as employees at competitive wages . . . thus creating at one stroke a new capitalist class and a new proletariat'. He insisted that socialism was a claim for the right of citizens – not occupational groups – to control.[30]

Social-Democrats shared with Fabians the view that socialism meant control by the community. The bone of contention between them was the degree of, and immediacy of, the accountability of the elected to their constituents and the desirability or otherwise of direct democracy. The Social-Democrats' conception involved a much more active rôle for the citizen and, as we have seen, they continually criticised the Fabians for conceding too much power and influence to the 'expert' whether elected politician or civil servant.

But both assumed that it was 'citizens', rather than 'workers', who should participate in democratic decision-making. If there was any significant difference between the Fabians and the Social-Democrats on this point it was that the Fabians had quickly grasped the importance of the issue and clarified their position. By contrast, the Social-Democrats

29 Sidney Webb, *Socialism in England*, 2nd edn (London, 1893), pp. xvii–xviii.
30 Sidney Webb, *Socialism: True or False*, Fabian Tract No. 51, July 1899, pp. 12–16. McBriar cites as other sources for Fabian opposition to 'workers' control', Beatrice Webb's (then still Beatrice Potter) *The Cooperative Movement in Great Britain* (1891) and the *Report on Fabian Policy* (1896). He traces the 'sewer for the sewermen' jibe to William Clarke's 'The Limits of Collectivism' in the *Contemporary Review*, February 1893. For another rejection of 'direct election of the manager and foreman by the employees', see Annie Besant's contribution to *Fabian Essays*, pp. 147–8.

– including SDF exiles in the Socialist League – had, in the early days of the movement, displayed a rather alarming confusion.

In 1885, *Justice*'s retort to the suggestion that nationalised railways should be managed by delegates of railwaymen and passengers was merely that 'A Democratic State department means no bureaucracy or class authority at all'. Even at this early stage, this breathtaking example of the instant solution of problems by means of definition probably had something to do with the fact that the correspondent who put forward the suggestion signed him (or her) self 'E. F. Tomkins (Fabian)'. When John Burns referred, in a report on that year's TUC a few months later, to the time when workers 'would own their own factories and decide by vote who their managers and foremen shall be' this triggered no debate, perhaps because it could be understood in two entirely different senses.[31]

William Morris in his 1893 essay on 'Communism', virtually waved aside the problem of management. Suppose, he suggested, that an opponent had posed the question of how a ship could be sailed in a socialist society.

> How? Why with a captain and mates and sailing master and engineer (if it be a steamer) and ABs and stokers and so on. *Only*, there will be no 1st, 2nd and 3rd class among the passengers; the sailors and stokers will be as well fed and lodged as the captain or passengers; and the stoker will have the same pay.
>
> There are plenty of enterprises which will be carried out as they are now (and, to be successful must probably remain under the guidance of one man). The only difference between then and now will be that he will be chosen because he is fit for the work . . .[32]

Morris slid over the problems, conflating socio-economic and political equality. Many questions he avoided posing, let alone answering. Given equality of pay and conditions, would not the continuing inequalities of power assume even greater significance? Would there not be a continual tendency for those with greater power to find ways of translating it into privileges amounting, more or less, to greater real pay? Would the stokers and ABs of Morris's ship be particularly concerned about whether the passengers were divided into separate classes or not? Significantly, Morris gave this aspect pride of place in his list of differences.

Who would decide who was best fitted to be captain, and how? Would there not be cases where there would be considerable and intractable

[31] *Justice*, 25 April, 12 September 1885.
[32] William Morris, 'Communism' (1893), in Henry Pelling (ed.), *The Challenge of Socialism* (A. & C. Black, 1954).

disagreement as to precisely which rôles, functions or tasks necessitated concentrating control into the hands of a single individual and which might be fulfilled without recourse to this expedient? Morris's own use of the word 'probably' shows us that this would in fact be the case.

Interestingly, Belfort Bax also used the ship's captain analogy in his essay on 'Democracy and the Word of Command', first published in the *Social-Democrat* in May 1898. He was more sensitive to the problems of executive authority than Morris. His belief was that one-person control always carried the dangers of autocracy. This could be avoided by substituting committees of three which would avoid such dangers while still being small enough to take effective decisions.[33] But when it came to saying precisely how such a model might be applied to industrial management – how the triumvirates might be elected and, crucially, whether they should be elected by workers or citizens – Bax was silent.

Earlier, in a *Commonweal* article, 'The Morrow of the Revolution' in 1887, Paul Lafargue had accused 'the English Socialists' in general, and Bax in particular of believing 'that the state will take the place of the capitalist property-owners and continue the exploitation of the great instruments of labour as in the past'. Their ideal, he said, was the 'capitalist public service'. He mentioned the post office, telegraphs, and police as examples of the services he had in mind. Though Morris, in an editorial footnote, denied vehemently that he would be prepared to 'walk across the street for such an ideal', he did little or nothing to clarify the real issues at stake. Lafargue's article ended by predicting how, rather than the revolutionary government imposing management, 'the workmen will come to an understanding among themselves as to the choosing of their engineers and foremen and sharing the gains of their business'.

In reply to this, Bax contrived to miss the point completely: 'I took it for granted that the revolutionary executive would be largely composed of really "representative" workers'. This response left unexamined Lafargue's contention that the revolutionary government – however composed – should not, in view of the colossal tasks confronting it, involve itself directly with the running of industry.[34]

The lack of any real debate on the management of industry seems particularly odd since the election of 'All Officers and Administrators' was the first 'plank' in the SDF programme. It also seems strange in

---

[33] E. Belfort Bax, 'Democracy and the Word of Command', in *The Social-Democrat*, May 1898, later reprinted in Bax's *Essays in Socialism: Old and New* (London, 1907).
[34] *Commonweal*, 16, 23 July 1887.

the light of the popularity, particularly in the mid 1880s, of Laurence Gronlund's book *The Co-operative Commonwealth* which predicted that administrators would be elected by their immediate subordinates.[35]

In the 1880s several editions of Gronlund's work were published, one of the first being edited by G. B. Shaw who was criticised both by *Justice* and Edward Aveling in the *Commonweal* for making a bad job of it. Both of these papers advertised *The Co-operative Commonwealth* from the end of 1884 and *Justice* promoted a cheap edition in 1888. Meanwhile, in May and June 1885, *Justice* had advertised readings of the book by Harry Quelch. Gronlund himself arrived in Britain about the same time, joined the Socialist League, spoke at its 1885 Conference, and was elected to the Executive Committee. He remained in Britain until 1887.

His view was that 'government over *things* rather than over men' would be secured as long as the Department Chiefs, collectively forming a 'nationalist' (significantly, his word for socialist) Board of Administration, were 'allowed to decree no laws'. According to Gronlund legislative power in the Co-operative Commonwealth would be exercised by means of the referendum, for the representative system and permanent political parties were 'unfit for a higher civilisation'. Such ideas were taken seriously enough at the time for Aveling to suggest that, together with the practice of the Paris Commune, Gronlund's book gave a broad model for the future socialist society.[36] It dealt in some detail with the question of executive authority or management. Holders of administrative posts would be elected by their own subordinates, but would have the power to sack those who had elected them: 'while subordinates elect, the *supervisors dismiss*', wrote Gronlund, 'This feature we hold will divide power between skill and numbers in proper proportion'[37] (original emphasis). Most surprisingly, in view of the attention given to *The Co-operative Commonwealth*, Social-Democrats chose virtually to ignore the whole issue of executive authority.

Apart, then, from the Fabians, little real consideration had been given to this crucial problem until syndicalism forced it to the attention of British Socialists. When at last this happened, Social-Democrats still tended to try to conjure away the management problem. Thus when, in 1912, a correspondent claimed that socialisation of the mines meant 'the miners owning and controlling them without being responsible to anyone for the good management of them', 'Tattler' tried to steer between, on

---

[35] Laurence Gronlund, *The Co-operative Commonwealth in its Outline: an Exposition of Modern Socialism* (1884; rpt Cambridge, MA, 1965).
[36] *Commonweal*, 15 May 1886.
[37] Gronlund, *The Co-operative Commonwealth*, p. 162.

the one hand, this version, which he contended would 'simply mean an extension of capitalism', and, on the other, what he called 'mere nationalisation' which might only result in a form of 'State capitalism'. The resulting formula, though it may have reassured some of *Justice*'s readers, can hardly have satisfied any who had come to realise the importance of the whole question of management:

complete socialisation can only be attained in a Social State, when the class State has been submerged, and the State has been democratised, has ceased to be that of a class, and has become that of the whole people – a Social-Democratic State.[38]

A few weeks later, in June 1912, there was more debate in the correspondence columns of *Justice*. Alf Barton thought that syndicalism was being misrepresented. There was an important difference between holding that the mines should be *owned* by the miners, which syndicalists did not propose, and holding that they should be *controlled* by them, which they did. Another correspondent, Edward G. Maxted, thought that this belief in community ownership but not community control was dangerously confused and insisted that 'we must make it clear that Socialism means public ownership and control and management'.

In between, J. Wendon insisted that many syndicalists were in fact socialists:

They advocate management of an industry by the workers engaged in it, not as an alternative to Socialism, but as an alternative to bureaucracy. In a Socialist community such management, subject to a general supervision by the community at large, would naturally obtain.[39]

Another Social-Democrat who saw merit in this aspect of syndicalism was J. W. Ellam, for whom syndicalist ideas provided an answer 'to *how* administration in the future communist society will be carried out'[40] (original emphasis). Similarly, George Simpson argued that 'We are rushing headlong into the system of slavery termed by Belloc "The Servile State" and the only thing that will save us is the adoption of Syndicalist methods.' This letter moved *Justice*'s editors to snap unhelpfully that 'The Socialist aims at the *socialisation* of wealth and the means of production, the Syndicalist . . . at syndicalising these things.'[41] Nevertheless, such exchanges focused some rare attention on a genuinely important issue of socialist theory and practice.

[38] *Justice*, 27 April 1912.   [39] *Justice*, 8, 15, 22 June 1912.
[40] *Justice*, 12 October 1912.   [41] *Justice*, 19 October 1912.

The Servile State

Simpson's reference to the *Servile State* pinpoints another important influence which, like syndicalism, was leading socialists to question their precise goals. Belloc was not a socialist, but his critique of the tendencies of modern capitalism struck a chord with those socialists who were most hostile to bureaucracy and most concerned to find ways to eliminate it from a future socialist society. In this respect, it reinforced the influence of syndicalism. Belloc was an opponent of a very special kind: in his introduction, he explicitly denied that his purpose was to attack socialism:

This book does not discuss the Socialist State. Indeed it is the very heart of my thesis that we are not, in fact approaching socialism at all, but a very different state of society: to wit, a society in which the Capitalist class shall be even more powerful and far more secure than it is at present: a society in which the proletarian mass shall not suffer from particular regulations oppressive or beneficient, but shall change their status, lose their present freedom and be subject to compulsory labour.

Such a state of affairs might not be altogether bad. It might prove more tolerable than capitalism. It was not what socialists wanted, yet it would probably result from the interaction between capitalism and the socialist critique: 'the Socialist idea, in conflict with and yet informing the body of Capitalism, produces a third thing very different from the Socialist idea – to wit, a Servile State.'[42]
There was a large measure of agreement between Belloc and many socialists about what needed to be resisted or avoided. In February 1911, both the *Clarion* and *Justice* gave favourable reviews to *The Party System* by Belloc and Cecil Chesterton. The *Clarion* cited with approval the book's ridicule of 'the fiction that the House of Commons is an instrument of representative Government' and quoted the authors' contention that 'The governing group is divided arbitrarily into two teams, each of which is, by mutual understanding, entitled to its turn of office and emoluments.'[43] In his review of the book in *Justice*, Hyndman warmly seconded the attack on the concentration of undemocratic power:

Possessed of complete control over the party funds and exercising absolute authority over ministerial and other appointments, the Liberal Party today, even more than the Tory Party yesterday, possesses a machinery for bribery from the Cabinet at the top to the smallest labour exchange manager at the bottom quite unprecedented in the history of this country.

---

[42] Hilaire Belloc, *The Servile State*, preface to the 2nd edition, 1913, 3rd edn (London, 1927), pp. ix–xi.
[43] *Clarion*, 3 February 1911.

Hyndman's only criticism was that the authors were less clear about what should be done to put this situation right. 'They approve of the break-up of the unconstitutional Cabinet, with its unconstitutional right of dissolution; and the substitution of heads of department as advocated by Mr Jowett in his pamphlet', but, Hyndman concluded, there was a need to start 'further down'. Here, he went on to rehearse part of the traditional Social-Democratic political reform package: 'proportional representation, the suppression of canvassing, the strict limitation of expenditure . . . on elections to an official maximum; the reduction of the numbers in the House of Commons'. All these the writers had unaccountably failed to suggest as countermeasures.[44]

At the 1911 ILP Conference, Belloc's warnings were cited by Lansbury against the policy of the Parliamentary Group. More strikingly, the South West London Federation of the ILP organised, a few weeks later, a debate between MacDonald and Belloc at the Memorial Hall on the motion 'That the unreality of the Collectivist ideal is apparent from the fact that the contemporary Collectivist effort is leading not to Collectivisim but to the Servile State.' MacDonald attacked Belloc's 'medieval individualism' as 'unscientific', while his opponent claimed to question not the *principle* but the practice of collectivism which meant, in reality, control by politicians: 'the community is an abstraction and the politician a reality'.

Not, Belloc further insisted, that collectivism was likely to be achieved: this could only come via confiscation, but collectivists 'had not the courage to confiscate'. The result was that 'all reform in the economic sphere which touched the proletariat without threatening monopoly tended, not to the collectivist state, but a servile state'. This was defined as a state in which the majority 'whilst dispossessed of the means of production were secure in sufficiency, although industry was still controlled by the capitalist class'.[45]

When the Belloc/MacDonald debate was published in pamphlet-form, Grayson urged socialists to take Belloc seriously and not just dismiss him as an anti-socialist. He continued:

we can see no means of securing sufficiency and security short of getting the instruments of production into the hands of the community.

Mr Belloc pulls us up at the word 'community' and excitedly interjects 'the politicians'. Under existing circumstances we confess we can find no very honest or effective answer to his interjection . . .

On the whole, Mr MacDonald claimed too much for Socialist propaganda and political action.[46]

[44] *Justice*, 25 February 1911.   [45] *Labour Leader*, 21 April, 11 May 1911.
[46] *Clarion*, 21 July 1911.

Early in 1913, Belloc took Blatchford to task when the latter ventured the opinion that there was nothing sufficiently original or important about the *Servile State* to justify the effect it had had on the socialist movement. It had, said Blatchford, 'shaken the ranks like a vehement and concentrated artillery fire'.[47] The book, its author insisted in reply, was not an attack on collectivism but a prediction about the future of capitalism. The accuracy of his predictions was, he went on, demonstrated by such recent developments as the Insurance Act which made for 'security of the wage-earner and at the same time for official control over his actions'. Similarly, the new labour exchanges registered and controlled an increasing number of wage-earners while leaving the owning class uncontrolled. Other projects in the wind, such as the legal minimum wage, labour colonies and compulsory arbitration of industrial disputes all had the same tendency.[48]

By this time, Belloc's notion of the Servile State – and still more the phrase itself – had become part of the currency of socialist debate. Arthur Rose, writing to the *Clarion* in March 1913, thought Belloc's argument 'unanswerable'. A true agitation for socialism – which Rose insisted meant economic freedom rather than merely the extinction of poverty – had yet to take place. Gaylord Wilshire, whose articles advocating syndicalism were still appearing with some regularity in the *Clarion*, drew from Belloc's argument that private property was a necessary precondition of individual freedom the conclusion that, for large-scale industries, this could only take the form of joint stock ownership through trade unions.[49]

The probability of the socialist project faltering and capitulating when faced with the necessity for confiscation seemed anyway all too great in the light of the behaviour of MacDonald and the Parliamentary Group. The thought that, even if this obstacle could be overcome, socialism would turn out to comprise rule by politicians and officials was a deeply troubling one for socialists. From the standpoint of the radical democrats of the movement, the differences between Belloc's capitalist Servile State and bureaucratic state socialism were far less significant than the similarities. The question was how both undesirable outcomes could best be avoided. Traditionally, the radical answer lay in the most direct and accountable forms of citizen democracy. But did these provide a credible solution to the problem of executive authority, particularly in industry? This left an important area open to the influence of syndicalist ideas of self-management. In the immediate pre-war years, more and

---

[47] *Clarion*, 28 February 1913.
[48] *Clarion*, 21 March 1913.   [49] *Clarion*, 4, 18 April 1913.

more socialists began to doubt whether even the strongest forms of citizen democracy could provide a total antidote to the dangers of bureaucracy.

Guild Socialism: the road to an answer?

George Lansbury was one socialist who made a fundamental reappraisal of his ideas and attitudes during these years. Writing in *Labour Leader* in May 1912, he explained how his views had changed:

A few years ago I should have sworn by a Socialist State dominated and organised by officials. To bring this about I should have declared for a disciplined party in Parliament . . . On this matter however my mind has undergone a great change. I no longer want a bureaucratic State, even if the boards are elected by the direct suffrage of the people. Labour exchanges, Insurance Acts have sickened me of [*sic*] the whole paraphernalia of State officialdom.[50]

Ironically, not so long previously, we have seen Lansbury himself being subjected to much criticism from Social-Democrats for supporting 'bureaucracy' as a signatory of the Minority Report on the Poor Law. The SDP had campaigned against the abolition of the locally elected Boards of Guardians for exactly the same reasons as it had defended the school boards. Now Lansbury was arguing that, for him, even the Social-Democrats' safeguard of the direct election of administrative bodies was inadequate as a protection against the dangers of bureaucracy.

And already, in *Labour Leader*, Fenner Brockway was beginning to draw conclusions which anticipated Guild Socialism. He argued that, by insisting so uncompromisingly on the dangers of bureaucracy, Belloc had rendered socialists a great service. The important thing was the awakening of the spirit of self-reliance in the working class. He drew the conclusion that in a socialist society 'much of the administration of the national industries will no doubt be placed in the hands of the Trade Unions themselves'.[51] Syndicalism had revived the militant trade union spirit and had 'awakened the intelligent working class to the dangers of bureaucratic State Socialism'.[52]

Guild Socialists made the most systematic attempt to reconcile the citizen democracy of 'traditional' socialism with the worker democracy of syndicalism. Guild Socialism originated in the *New Age*, developed by S. G. Hobson and A. R. Orage. Later, in his memoirs *Pilgrim to the Left*, Hobson described arriving in a position 'above and between' the Labour

---

[50] *Labour Leader*, 17 May 1912.
[51] *Labour Leader*, 4 July 1912.   [52] *Labour Leader*, 26 September 1912.

Party and the syndicalists.[53] In the summer of 1912 another important Guild Socialist – G. R. S. Taylor, the future author of *The Guild State* – summarised what he saw as the positive features of syndicalism in a *Clarion* article. Taylor applauded both the reaction against over-centralisation and the syndicalist emphasis on avoiding bureaucracy by preparing people to be their own administrators. 'It is a helpful suggestion,' he went on, 'to think of the citizen as being primarily a worker rather than a voter.'[54]

For Taylor, the real argument between syndicalists and orthodox socialists turned on the growing perception that 'unless we managed our reforms carefully we might easily be landed in a Collectivist State run by bureaucrats instead of a Collectivist State managed on democratic principles'. The apparently central issue of contention about 'political' or 'industrial' action was, he said, a side issue inflated in importance by 'extremists on either side (and still more by people who want to misrepresent either side)'.[55]

Taylor was writing regular editorial leaders for the *Clarion* at this time. He had ample opportunity to put forward his own ideas on solving this problem. He applauded Jowett's continuing efforts in support of the 'Bradford' policy, criticised the BSP Executive and *Justice* for their anti-syndicalism and insisted that there was 'no conflict between Socialism and Industrial Unionism'. The influence of 'traditional' radical democratic socialism in Taylor's thinking can be seen in his presenting, as the *central* question for socialists: 'whether society should be controlled by leaders, however efficient, or by the democracy, however slowly it may move'.

But syndicalists and industrial unionists were making 'a definite challenge to the hard and fast theory that the final aim of Socialism is the production of a highly centralised State in which the main industries will be under the control of central state departments'. They were putting forward the alternative of control via the unions. He believed that socialists should avoid narrowing the limits of the movement by 'excluding all who have not grasped the economics of democratic collectivism'. Rather, socialists should be prepared to work with anti-socialists like Belloc and G. K. Chesterton who were 'doing as

---

[53] S. G. Hobson, *Pilgrim to the Left: Memoirs of a Modern Revolutionist* (London, 1938), p. 171. See also M. Cole, *Life of G. D. H. Cole* (London, 1971); John D. Coates, *Chesterton and the Edwardian Cultural Crisis* (Hull, 1984); Wallace Martin, *The 'New Age' under Orage* (Manchester, 1967); Tom Steele, *Alfred Orage and the Leeds Art Club 1893–1923* (London, 1990).

[54] *Clarion*, 9 August 1912.

[55] *Clarion*, 13 September 1912.

much as any men in helping to dislodge autocracy from its seat of power'.[56]

Guild Socialism represented an attempt to reconcile the claims of citizen and worker democracy and to combine the 'lessons' of the radical version of socialist democracy, of syndicalism and of Belloc's *Servile State*. It was far more than merely a new name for co-operation, as *Justice* claimed.[57] A *Clarion* article, possibly by Hobson, argued in favour of creating one union or 'effective federation' in each industry. The state would act as trustee for the community, with ownership of industries vested in it. It would charter a guild, comprised of the appropriate industrial union plus the salariat and the administration to manage production. Such a system, the article insisted, would be socialist rather than syndicalist. It presumed that 'a man would be a citizen first and a guildsman second'.[58]

By the end of 1913, there were some signs of a softening of attitudes towards ideas of industrial self-management, even from *Justice* with its almost instinctive horror of anything smacking of syndicalism or anarchism. Reviewing *The World of Labour*, H. W. Lee saw some merits in the views of G. D. H. Cole:

> though he comes from the Fabian School, he is right up against the bureaucratic influence which has so long unfortunately dominated the Fabian Society, and at the same time he sees that, *however great may be the future functions of trade unions* [our emphasis] nevertheless a State, in some shape or form, must represent the interests of the community when once freed from capitalist domination.[59]

The stress, as one would expect from *Justice*, is on Cole's recognition of the continuing necessity for some kind of state, but the italicised phrase suggests a drift away from the old Social-Democrat line that the radical version of citizen democracy would alone be a sufficient safeguard against autocracy and bureaucracy in a socialist society.

Elsewhere too, the new stress on self-management in industry rejuvenated the more generalised opposition to what was seen as the bureaucratic version of socialism favoured by leading Fabians. As one letter in *Labour Leader* argued, their empowerment of experts gave

> a very narrow interpretation to the word expert, which [alienates] those who would otherwise be inclined to agree if a wider interpretation were given to it . . . Personally, I feel that until you get all the factors employed in your industry *represented* on the governing body of that particular undertaking you will never even have efficiency, leave alone democratic control.[60] (original emphasis)

---

[56] *Clarion*, 1, 8, 15 November, 6 December 1912.
[57] *Justice*, 11 January 1913.   [58] *Clarion*, 28 November 1913.
[59] *Justice*, 29 November 1913.   [60] *Labour Leader*, 10 April 1913.

Guild Socialist ideas were discussed more critically in the course of a *Clarion* series by the former Socialist Leaguer, Fred Henderson, on current socialist ideas and strategies. It appeared during the winter of 1913/1914. Henderson denied that there was a real distinction between 'economic' and 'political' power. He was concerned at the prospect of sectional claims taking precedence over those of the community. 'If they are forced to submit wholly to the occupational tie they will become more bricklayers than men, and will bare their teeth at the world because it does not lay bricks.'[61]

Responding to Henderson, T. E. Noble insisted that such an outcome was precisely what the *New Age* guild scheme was designed to avoid. Workers would elect their own officials and 'directly' manage their own guild, but the scheme also assumed 'a conscious unanimity of purpose in inter-guild policy, finding expression in an assembly or congress of guild representatives, exercising itself in matters economic'. And, in addition to this, individuals would continue to participate as citizens in the election of parliamentary representatives.[62]

In giving serious consideration to Guild Socialism, the *Clarion* was following its tradition of journalistic openness. No less predictably, *Justice* was ultra-cautious in entering an area of debate strewn, for older Social-Democrats, with the snares of anarchist heresy. More difficult would have been to predict the response of the ILP's official organ, now edited by A. Fenner Brockway. In the spring of 1914 Brockway asserted, in an article on 'The Free State of the Future', that 'The suggestion that merely by nationalisation democracy can be applied to industry is manifestly absurd.' Unfortunately, many had reacted into syndicalism after correctly seeing that such a course would lead inevitably to bureaucratic administration, because Parliament was not constructed in such a way as to make its control of industry a practicality. The trouble was, 'The Syndicalist Parliament would be a glorified Trades Union Congress.' Consumers' interests were overlooked by syndicalists and needed to be represented together with those of producers.[63]

In a second article, Brockway suggested that the future 'Free State' should be a synthesis of producer control, as per syndicalism, consumer control, as per co-operation, and state socialism. Industries could be owned by the nation and run by Boards of Management equally representative of consumer and producer interests. The former could form a sub-committee concerned with questions of the quantity and quality of goods and services: the producer representatives could form

[61] *Clarion*, 26 December 1913.
[62] *Clarion*, 9 January 1914.   [63] *Labour Leader*, 12 March 1914.

one to decide 'how production was to be carried out.' Distribution of the product would be the business of the national authority.[64]

Brockway's articles triggered a critical response both from those who complained that he had misrepresented syndicalism and from defenders of a more conventional state socialism. One correspondent, who thought that parliamentary appointment of the top management of nationalised industries was a sufficient degree of democratic control, rejected any notion of industrial self-management. 'It would never do for the workers to elect their own foremen, and these again to elect their own superintendents. The selection of controlling positions must be from above . . . '[65]

Brockway's 'Free State', with its special emphasis on the need for consumer representation, was clearly derived from G. D. H. Cole, who also contributed to the *Labour Leader* debate. The state's function, Cole argued, was to represent the general will of the community, but trade unions could legitimately claim to control industrial processes and conditions:

As the *New Age* in its brilliant articles and editorial notes has long been asserting, the solution lies in the free and equal industrial partnership of the State and the Unions. The Trade Union, or as the *New Age* calls it, the 'Guild', should be a great democratically-organised body of producers controlling the methods of production; but in matters of 'high policy' the State should be the deciding power. The State should own the means of production; the Trade Union should control the process. In some such partnership as the Guild Socialists advocate, and neither in pure Collectivism nor in pure Syndicalism lies the solution of the problem of industrial control.[66]

Differences continued, even among Guild Socialists. Later, in *Pilgrim to the Left*, Hobson was to be at pains to distinguish his own version from the later variant of Guild Socialism developed by Cole. He picked out the latter's 'ominous stress' on the rights of the consumer as the chief difference. 'Every economist knows that "capitalist" and "consumer", if not interchangeable, are complementary terms.' According to Hobson, Cole's stress on the consumer led him to

proclaim the state as the protector of the consumer vis-à-vis the Guilds as protector of the producer. This logically led to a dual sovereignty of the State and the Guilds. To this I offered an uncompromising negative. I held that the State is not primarily concerned with the consumer as such, but equally with producers and consumers as citizens.[67]

---

[64] *Labour Leader*, 19 March 1914.   [65] *Labour Leader*, 19 March 1914.
[66] *Labour Leader*, 26 March 1914.   [67] Hobson, *Pilgrim to the Left*, pp. 186–7.

But whatever differences continued to divide even Guild Socialist opinion, by this time the combined effect of the influence of syndicalism and the Guild Socialist hybrid had begun to shift the boundaries of the debate.

Significantly, even among some previously unequivocal supporters of central state control through appointed officials, their old tone of contempt towards any suggestion of self-management became less frequent. An excellent example is Beatrice Webb. Joining in the *Leader* debate on the 'Free State', she was far from taking a Guild Socialist position. But while insisting that consumers must be the 'ultimate controllers', she suggested that a degree of worker participation, with representation on management committees, should not be ruled out. She still doubted whether management by the workers in each industry would turn out to be an acceptable solution to 'the problem of partnership'. She predicted that the 'Free State of the Future' would find its equilibrium 'not in one form or type of partnership between consumer and producer, but in a mixture for different industries, different localities, and different purposes, of forms and methods, almost innumerable in their complexity and constantly shifting'.[68] When even so orthodox a Fabian was prepared to admit the existence of a 'problem of partnership', something important had changed.

Whatever doubts remained, there had clearly been a major shift in the terms of the debate. The possibility of workers' participation in industrial management – in some form – was no longer being dismissed out of hand as a 'primitive expedient'.

[68] *Labour Leader*, 30 April 1914.

13 1914: an emerging consensus on the eve of Armageddon

During what turned out to be the final year or so before the outbreak of war there were signs of a new consensus within the socialist movement. Crucial to this was a greater awareness than perhaps before or since that aim, strategy and organisation interact.

One factor tending to unify discussions was directly political: the BSP was preparing to seek affiliation to the Labour Party, removing a barrier to 'socialist unity' which had existed since the SDF's withdrawal from the LRC in 1901. When Harry Quelch fell ill, the editing of *Justice* was taken over by a 'Commission' consisting of H. W. Lee, Gorle, Swanson and Fred Knee. Quelch's last political efforts were devoted to vehement opposition to Labour Party affiliation, and such was his standing among the 'Old Guard' that it is possible that he would have tipped the balance in favour of staying outside Labour's ranks had he lived.[1] He died in September 1913. His comrades organised a magnificent funeral attended, *Justice* estimated, by 10,000 mourners. But along with the veteran Social-Democrat, the BSP buried its tradition of semi-isolation from Labour.

On its side, syndicalism, though it still attracted adherents, did not seem to so many as before to offer a credible alternative. Rather, its most important service had been to place the question of workplace democracy on the agenda at a time when the spectre of the 'Servile State' was leading to reappraisals of state socialism. Even in the Fabian Society the dominance of the ideas of the Webbs was being undermined by Cole and other younger members.

This book has argued that questions of internal democracy had long interacted with those of the direction in which MacDonald was seeking to lead the party: should activists adapt to existing power structures? The 'external' and 'internal' features of MacDonaldite ideas and practice were closely connected. Undeclared but effective coalition with the

---

[1] *Justice*, 9 July, 16 August 1913.

Liberals was a rational way of playing the parliamentary game according to conventional norms. A necessary condition for the success of this strategy was to turn Labour into a parliamentary grouping with a docile electoral and publicity machine outside. It was also part of a wider process by which Labour would become integrated into the British constitution rather than, as MacDonald's critics hoped, transforming that constitution in a radical-democratic direction.

In the long term, for these critics, such a transformation would entail the large-scale socialisation of industry, if ways could be found to avoid a gigantic growth in state bureaucracy. But this was likely to remain a long-term prospect until answers were found to the problem of a generally acceptable division of power between the workplace and the community. This presupposed credible machinery for democratically exercising such power.

In the sphere of citizen democracy there had long been substantial support for a decisive shift of legislative power towards direct popular sovereignty by means of the referendum and initiative. Something along these lines might have become a practical proposition had the Tories revived the position they had taken at the time of the second election of 1910, though their version of the referendum had been specifically and openly designed to put a brake on radical change. This was not going to satisfy A. M. Thompson and others of his persuasion. Nevertheless a window of opportunity would perhaps have been created.

Partial success for Jowett

The great strength of Jowett's 'Bradford Policy' was that it connected the daily practice of the Parliamentary Group with the long-term aim of democratic transformation, even if, in itself, it promised only to make a greater reality of 'representative government' rather than to replace it with 'popular government'. Adoption of 'Bradford' would at least halt the drift towards uncritical acceptance of the status quo. To many socialists, this drift was bound to seem the immediate problem.

Jowett's policy achieved a partial success at the 1912 ILP Conference: though the Bradford resolution was again defeated, a motion rejecting the single ministerial system was passed overwhelmingly. It asked the Parliamentary Group to press for all-party Standing Committees. Yet plainly, the prospects of achieving even such a relatively modest change were bleak if merely 'pressed' by the small number of Labour MPs. The *Labour Leader* responded with echoes of Hardie's old 'mere politics' sneer:

We should require to spend as much energy in abolishing the Cabinet system of government as in abolishing the capitalist system of industry, and we think it will pay us much better to put our energies into the latter channel. As Mr. Snowden said, our central grievance is that we ourselves are not the Cabinet. With the rise of Labour to power many of the Parliamentary difficulties would tend to adjust themselves.[2]

Anyway, without the anti-MacDonaldite 'voting on merits' policy, the committee system resolution could have little effect. In the *Clarion*, Jowett himself explained that Bradford ILP had placed the motion on Parliamentary policy first 'because if it were acted upon the system of Cabinet Government would be *punctured* in consequence' (original emphasis).[3]

He saw the results of the conference as a defeat. 'The issue was Cabinet Government versus Representative Government, and Cabinet Government won', he told *Clarion* readers. ILPers' loyalty to their leaders and to the Labour Party 'which conforms willingly to the Cabinet System', had more to do with the conference's decision than any of the arguments put forward in the debate. He dissociated himself from Snowden's contention that all would be well when Labour formed its own Cabinet, and he expressed the hope that the Cabinet system would have been destroyed before a Labour or Socialist majority in the Commons had been attained.[4]

Russell Smart, that other determined adversary of Cabinet government, had already reached this conclusion nearly five years before:

When shall we have a Socialist Cabinet? Let us hope never. I hope to see a Socialist majority in the House of Commons; but I hope I shall never see a Socialist Government, or, if I do, that it will only be formed for the express purpose of abolishing the present mode of government. All the functions now vested in single Ministers should be entrusted to committees. The very titles of Ministerial posts indicate how the Cabinet has encroached upon the common rights. There is a President of the Board of Trade, and there is a President of the Local Government Board. Where are the Boards over which they preside?[5]

In the summer of 1912, Jowett made a sustained effort to clarify the issues involved and to avoid obscuring them with attacks on his opponents. MacDonald, he insisted, had been 'much-maligned' for allegedly, 'pegging out a claim to office in a Liberal Government'. Rather

[2] *Labour Leader*, 31 May 1912. The 1912 BSP Conference similarly approved of 'the substitution of a Committee representative of all parties for the present Cabinet'. *Justice*, 1 June 1912.
[3] *Clarion*, 31 May 1912.
[4] *Clarion*, 7 June 1912.   [5] *Labour Leader*, 30 August 1907.

he was pursuing his ideal of building up the Labour Party within the Parliamentary system:

He believes in the Cabinet System, in Party leaders who when their followers are in a majority in the House of Commons, are to hold all the offices of State . . . He believes, in short, in the game of Party politics.

Jowett went on to criticise MacDonald's position not so much for being wrong in principle as for being unrealistic. It was, he contended, 'bound to remain for ever unrealised' since no Labour Parliamentary Group would ever be docile enough to conform to 'the old Party system'. Even if a socialist party with a majority formally supported the continuance of the Cabinet system, it was 'inconceivable that its members could be dragooned and disciplined to back up their leaders . . . if they were denied access to information and were not allowed to share the responsibilities of administration'.[6]

In Jowett's view, the path to socialism was via democracy. This entailed Labour totally changing its strategy and rejecting the Cabinet system. Participating in a *Clarion* debate on the failure of Labour 'in its appeal to the indifferent', he opposed the frequent view that the explanation lay in Labour's failure to appeal for support 'on the full Socialist programme':

I believe that the workers will be class-conscious before they are Socialists. I am as confident now as ever that a class-conscious working class party will and must (because it can't get wrongs redressed in any other way) develop into a Socialist Party. But it must be class-conscious first in order to sense its wrongs. To be successful, such a Party must be a democratic Party as well as a class-conscious Party. It must not merely seek to change one set of rulers for another, but it must assert the right of the people to control their own affairs – not through a self-appointed Cabinet, but through their elected representatives.[7]

Jowett was extremely sensitive – and with hindsight we can say prophetic – on the pressures to bring about the assimilation of Labour into the 'party system'. For he saw much wider implications in such developments:

MacDonald's election to the chairmanship of the Party was preceded by statements widely published in the Press, emanating from nobody knows where, to the effect that the Labour Party were [*sic*] about to follow the example of the Irish Party and have a permanent chairman who would be leader of his party as Mr. Redmond is [of the Irish Nationalists]. The Labour Party has never taken a decision on this point, but doubtless the majority will repeatedly elect him, at the invitation of influential members who hold the opinion that the Labour Party,

---

[6] *Clarion*, 9 August 1912.   [7] *Clarion*, 2 August 1912.

like other Parties in Parliament, should have a recognised leader and not merely a succession of different chairmen. Ever since MacDonald was elected chairman the leaders of both the great parties have encouraged this idea, and, with the exception of Mr. Bonar Law, whose vision is limited by bitterness and prejudice, they have magnified MacDonald's office, and by complimentary references as the occasion offered, tried to confirm his prestige.
. . .

Men such as Messrs Balfour and Asquith regard it as most important, if the present Parliamentary system is to be maintained, that the Labour Party should follow the example of the other Parties in having a recognised leader who believes in the Parliamentary system and who with full knowledge of its mysteries and outward forms and traditions – will work his party into the system. As I have often explained in these columns, I think the present Parliamentary system is a wonderfully effective contrivance for keeping the administrative departments of State in the hands of the governing classes and enabling Party leaders to arrange the agenda in the House of Commons to their own liking.

For his part, Jowett concluded, he had no desire at all to maintain the existing system, but Balfour, until recently the Conservative leader, had:

He is perfectly well aware that a Labour Party, even of forty or fifty, if it struck out a new line and declared that its members intended to press their own issues, give their votes in the division lobbies in accordance with the evidence, ignore the traditions of Party Government, could make Cabinet domination of public business impossible.[8]

This had some impact. In a *Clarion* leader the following week it was applauded by G. R. S. Taylor. He thought that Jowett's article might well 'become a historical document, for the case against the present Parliamentary system has never been better put in such a compact space; and further it is not the opinion of a theorist, it is the opinion of a practical "politician" '.[9]

Proportional representation

Another issue that came into prominence towards the end of 1912 was destined to be of great importance in the socialist debate on democratic government on the eve of the Great War. When the Liberal government included in their Home Rule legislation for Ireland a Senate elected by proportional representation, MacDonald opposed the proposal. The *Labour Leader* thought that he was right to insist on a unicameral parliament. Yet it insisted that proportional representation, which was supported, it said, almost unanimously by the international socialist

8 *Clarion*, 25 October 1912.   9 *Clarion*, 1 November 1912.

movement, at least deserved serious consideration. Further articles
exploring the whole question were promised.[10]

Proportional representation was not, of course, new. The SDF had
included it among its medley of political demands since the 1880s. But
it had seldom if ever been considered in any sustained or detailed way by
the British socialist press. John Humphreys, the tireless Secretary of the
Proportional Representation Society, seized the opportunity offered by
the *Labour Leader* to press his case.[11]

His advocacy was followed in the *Labour Leader*'s columns by
MacDonald's arguments against PR, summarising from his book
Socialism and Government. Parliament, MacDonald had argued, was a
legislative organ, not a 'debating society'. Before achieving parliamentary
representation, every body of opinion should 'have to stand the test of
public criticism', gain a substantial following and prove its staying power.
PR would favour wealthy candidates and increase caucus power, 'just
that part of our party system of government which is most open to
objection'. But this time it was clear that MacDonald was not going to
get his way without a serious struggle. The same issue of the *Labour
Leader* carried two letters arguing in favour of PR: it would enable
Labour to increase its parliamentary representation, regain its
independence from the Liberals and give an impetus to ILP propaganda
work.[12]

The debate continued into 1913. European socialists were amazed,
according to John Humphreys, at MacDonald's attitude to PR.
MacDonald's position, he claimed, implied 'a distrust of the capacity
of the electorate to choose wisely'. He seemed to believe that a more
representative House of Commons would be 'detrimental to good
Government' – an attitude highly reminiscent for Humphreys of the
Duke of Wellington's cry of '"How will the King's Government be
carried on?" against the abolition of the rotten boroughs'.[13]

Humphreys triggered some surprising reflections. Why, asked the
Labour Leader of all papers, was the Labour Party opposed to PR while
the TUC – which represented virtually the same body of opinion –
supported it? 'The unpalatable truth is that the question has not been
adequately discussed and the delegates were largely ignorant of the pros
and cons when they cast their votes.'[14]

[10] *Labour Leader*, 7 November 1912.
[11] *Labour Leader*, 28 November 1912. John Humphreys, a former civil servant, was
Secretary of the Proportional Representation Society from 1905 until his death in 1946.
[12] *Labour Leader*, 19 December 1912.
[13] *Labour Leader*, 2 January 1913.   [14] *Labour Leader*, 16 January 1913.

Labour and democracy: the conferences of 1913 and 1914

In 1913, with the question once more on the agenda of the Labour Party Conference, Humphreys organised an eve-of-conference meeting in support of PR. At the meeting Philip Snowden claimed that Labour's real support was in the region of 20 per cent of the electorate and that only with proportional representation could the party be fully independent of the Liberals.[15] In the event, motions for PR and the Alternative Vote were withdrawn from debate, pending a report on electoral systems to the 1914 Conference. 'Is this not a confession of inexcusable ignorance and negligence?' asked the *Leader*. 'It has for some years been apparent that the whole question of electoral reform must arise in the near future, and that the Labour Party ought long ere this to have decided upon its policy.'

Meanwhile the ILP gained a 'Magnificent victory' on the suffrage issue. It persuaded Labour to oppose any Franchise Bill in which women were not included. Furthermore, the Parliamentary Group was to take action against members acting 'contrary to the principles and policy of the party as embodied in conference resolutions' or persistently ignoring 'the collective decisions of the party.'[16] Commenting on this, Jowett argued that the Labour Party had failed to realise that the 'very first question' that needed to be decided was whether the Labour Group should be an addition to the party system or whether it should 'rely on honest voting and true speech'. If the former was the preferred option, 'the Labour Group must produce its own shadow Cabinet and follow it as other parties do'.[17]

Both the 'Bradford Policy' and PR were due to be considered by the ILP Conference. In the weeks between the annual conferences of the Labour Party and of the ILP, the *Labour Leader* concentrated on electoral reform. Egerton Wake and Dr Marion Phillips had been accused by *Justice* of misleading the Labour Party Conference about PR.[18] Wake argued against PR and in favour of the Alternative Vote (AV).[19] Most letters to the *Leader*, including one from J. H. Standring, the ILP Organiser for Lancashire and Cheshire, favoured PR.[20] The issue was widely recognised as lying between these two alternatives.

Moving the motion in favour of PR at the ILP Conference in March,

15 *Labour Leader*, 20 January 1913.   16 *Labour Leader*, 6 February 1913.
17 *Clarion*, 7 February 1913.   18 *Justice*, 8 February 1913.
19 *Labour Leader*, 27 February, 20 March 1913.
20 *Labour Leader*, 6, 13 March 1913.

Fred Hughes argued that, unlike the AV, it would avoid 'demoralising bargaining between parties'. Against him, Wake urged that PR would have precisely such an effect, leading to deals between parliamentary groups. It was also objectionable on grounds of complexity, expense and the loss of personal contact between elector and representative. Snowden, in supporting PR, made what the *Labour Leader* said was the 'most telling point' that proportional representation would make Labour MPs independent of Liberal support. An amendment favouring AV was decisively rejected and the conference endorsed PR overwhelmingly. The 'Bradford Resolution', for the Parliamentary Group to vote 'on the merits' of each issue, though again rejected, was lost more narrowly than at any previous conference: by 150 to 114 votes.[21]

Philip Snowden had played a crucial part in both debates, and in the *Clarion* Jowett challenged his contention that the Labour Group was already essentially acting on the Bradford basis.

The opposition to the Bradford resolution was remarkable in more ways than one. Obvious and well-understood facts concerning the votes given by Labour members were denied. The object of the Bradford resolution was misrepresented, and assumptions of the most extravagant nature as to the future of big Liberal measures which might disappear if the Government were pressed by Labour members to the point of defeat on some trumpery questions of no interest to the workers were seriously stated.[22]

The ILP's new commitment to PR raised the question of which form of proportional representation should be supported. John Humphreys favoured the Single Transferable Vote (STV) but J. Sachse entered a plea for the party list system. STV would, Sachse maintained, encourage 'faddists' and confuse voters. Under the List System voters could be allowed preferences within the list. 'And let those who are still afraid of strengthening the hands of the Party caucus address themselves to the democratisation of their party, and see to it that the members and supporters of the party obtain an effective voice in the selection of candidates'.[23]

Sachse enlarged later on his objections to STV and preference for the party list:

The single transferable vote would make the 'personal element' supreme in elections, and thus among other evils, penalise [people] who have not practised the gentle art of becoming shining stars. The list system would make the rivalry of contending principles the decisive factor in elections.[24]

---

[21] *Labour Leader*, 27 March 1913.   [22] *Clarion*, 28 March 1913.
[23] *Labour Leader*, 27 March 1913.   [24] *Labour Leader*, 8 May 1913.

More immediately important than the question of which form of PR to support was MacDonald's response to the ILP's new policy. Had he actually wished to promote hostility to his leadership and confirm doubts about his real motives he could hardly have done so more effectively. In a letter to the *Leader* early in May he asserted that the adoption of PR raised the question

of how far conference decisions on subjects which do not relate to Socialism have any binding or disciplinary value upon members. No doubt something depends upon the circumstances and upon the thoroughness of the examination which has preceded the decision. So far as I am concerned the conference vote leaves me exactly where I was . . .

Under PR, he went on, by-elections would become 'absolutely forbidden luxuries' for Labour candidates, and in Parliament 'the most objectionable kind of log-rolling' would take place.

It will also place a man in a position of independence over his party. Indeed that is why the founders of the Proportional Representation Society began their work. Proportional Representation is designed to put mugwumps into Parliament. Our old 'democratic' fraud, the Referendum, has been taken over by that politically vile body, the British Constitutional Association. It has also blessed Proportional Representation. And it knows its game.[25]

There were several features of MacDonald's letter that were bound to raise hackles. His attempt at guilt-by-association was quickly attacked by both J. H. Standring and John Humphreys.[26] The latter also resisted MacDonald's attempt to link PR with the Referendum:

in some respects the Referendum and P.R. are antagonistic. P.R. accepts the principles of representative government and endeavours to strengthen it by bringing representative assemblies into agreement with the electorate. The referendum asks for direct government by the electors on the ground that representative government has failed.[27]

Both Standring and Humphreys pointed out that by-elections were unnecessary under PR. MacDonald retorted that, if PR *had* to come, then the List System was the lesser of evils, though it would give 'the party such a recognised, and such a tyrannical place in our constitution that even I, who am supposed to believe in party far too much, decline to support such a mischievous proposal'.[28] Anyway by-elections were valuable indicators of shifts in public opinion.[29]

In the meantime, another correspondent had taken up what he saw as

[25] *Labour Leader*, 8 May 1913.
[26] *Labour Leader*, 15 May 1913.   [27] *Labour Leader*, 22 May 1913.
[28] *Labour Leader*, 29 May 1913.   [29] *Labour Leader*, 26 June 1913.

MacDonald's most contentious point. 'No matter whether a thing "relates to socialism" or not the highest authority in our Party is the National Conference'. Therefore, ILP members should now consider

how far the Party is to be financially responsible for the presence of men in Parliament who superciliously tell us that Conference resolutions are of smaller value than what is euphemistically termed 'pledges to their constituents'.[30]

The 1913 Labour Party Conference, it will be remembered, had postponed consideration of electoral reform until the following year. So, as the 1914 conference drew nearer, interest naturally revived. The *Labour Leader*, in line with ILP policy, backed the adoption by Labour of PR. It predicted that PR would be the 'most keenly debated question'. Of the sub-committee appointed by the 1913 conference to examine the rival merits of PR and the AV, G. H. Roberts, MP and W. C. Anderson favoured the former and MacDonald the latter.

The supporters of PR argued that whereas the AV would mean wiping out all Labour Party representation at the next election, PR would secure fair representation for the Labour vote. The AV, they urged, would necessitate 'understandings' with the capitalist parties, while PR could facilitate Labour independence in both the constituencies and Parliament. Furthermore, there was a tendency in other countries to reject the Second Ballot in favour of PR, and the Labour Party should not cut itself off from the international movement.

Against this, MacDonald argued that PR would entail additional expense, that it was supported mainly by opponents of Labour and that it would not necessarily result in votes of equal value. Moreover the Labour Party would be made more dependent on the Liberals since it would rely heavily on second preference votes from Liberal supporters and the tyranny of the 'party machine' would be increased. He also asserted that dissatisfaction with PR was growing among the socialist parties of the Continent. This was firmly denied by Humphreys, who admitted that some members of the Belgian Socialist Party opposed PR, but countered that the party as a whole was demanding its extension to local elections. In general, European socialists were in favour.

By now, Snowden had lost patience completely with MacDonald's arguments – and indeed with his leadership generally. In a pre-conference editorial in the *Labour Leader* he linked the adoption of PR to the accomplishment of Labour's independence from the Liberals. The ILP, he believed, was losing the confidence of members and supporters because of the Parliamentary Group's 'failure to maintain the strictly

[30] *Labour Leader*, 22 May 1913.

independent position and to adopt a more militant attitude to the Government'. Some trade union leaders and Labour MPs had 'in the most flagrant manner outraged the party's principles and broken their pledged word' by associating politically with the Liberals. A special conference should be held by the Labour Party 'to purge it of these Liberals'. The adoption by the conference of the Alternative Vote 'would aggravate all the evils of compromise and intrigue'. Should the Labour Conference reject Proportional Representation, it would have 'sealed the fate of the Labour party. It would have rejected the only electoral system by which independent Labour and Socialist members can be returned to Parliament.'[31]

For once Snowden and *Justice* were on the same side of the argument. On MacDonald's position on PR, *Justice* commented:

Why he should be so vehemently opposed to it is only explainable by the fact that Proportional Representation will put an end to most of the bargaining with other political parties which has such a disastrous effect on genuine independent Labour representation. Already he is at work finding fault, very likely with some amount of reason, with schemes of proportional representation that have been suggested. The supporters of this very necessary electoral reform at the Labour Party Conference will do well to avoid being dragged into all manner of details and stick to the main principle.[32]

It became clear that MacDonald was preparing to go to considerable lengths to prevent the Labour Party Conference coming out in support of PR. The Miners' delegates had supported PR at the TUC. MacDonald addressed them at a private meeting on the eve of Labour's conference. The result was – said the *Labour Leader* – inevitable, even after a 'star' debate during which Snowden and Anderson made powerful pleas in support of proportional representation. The Conference rejected both PR and the AV by majorities of nearly 2 to 1. A slightly larger minority supported PR than the AV – 704,000 to 632,000.[33] And it is quite certain', added *Justice* wryly, 'that had a resolution in favour of the present system been put to the delegates it would have been defeated by a still bigger majority.'[34]

But if MacDonald believed that was to be the end of the story he was soon disabused. Within a few weeks the *Labour Leader* was expressing surprise that an Electoral Reform Bill, introduced for Labour by Henderson, included a provision for the Alternative Vote which had just been rejected by the Conference.[35] An explanation was given by Hardie

[31] *Labour Leader*, 22 January 1914.
[32] *Justice*, 22 January 1914.   [33] *Labour Leader*, 5 February 1914.
[34] *Justice*, 1 February 1914.   [35] *Labour Leader*, 12 March 1914.

at the ILP Conference in answer to a question from 'Mr Attlee of Limehouse'. The inclusion of the AV provision, he said, was the consequence of the Bill's having been drafted before the Conference. For many this must have simply underlined the way in which the Parliamentary Group carried on with its own policies willy-nilly. Attlee criticised MacDonald for misrepresenting the views of Continental socialists on the PR issue and added 'his violent opposition to the system really arises from his policy which is essentially based on agreement, expressed or implicit, of the parties of the Left'. The future Labour prime minister went on to accuse MacDonald of being out of touch with the feeling among socialists against 'the present policy of supporting the Government'.[36]

One clear sign of the continuing consolidation of ILP opinion against MacDonald's parliamentary strategy and his conservative version of democracy on which it was predicated was the adoption by the 1914 ILP conference of the Bradford Resolution. For to some extent, the 'voting on merits' policy could be seen as an alternative, or complementary, method to PR for achieving Labour independence in Parliament. This in turn seemed to be a necessary condition for a greatly democratised governmental system.

Jowett himself was doubtful about the merits of PR. He believed that its adoption would tend to strengthen the 'Party caucus system'. He insisted that the Bradford policy must be given priority over electoral reform.[37] The triumph of his policy in the ILP had, as noted, been foreshadowed in the voting figures during the previous two years. But it also owed much to immediate circumstances.

Fenner Brockway describes these: he was approached by Hardie before the conference and urged to make every effort to defeat MacDonald's 'incredible proposal' for an electoral alliance with the Liberals.[38] The Liberals had offered what amounted to a coalition with Labour as the junior partner. David Marquand in his biography of MacDonald, and drawing on MacDonald's papers, gives a fascinating account of the incident. Apparently, Lloyd George approached MacDonald on 3 March and proposed, in the presence of Arthur Henderson and of Illingworth, the Liberal Chief Whip, an electoral arrangement with a substantial increase in the proportion of seats allotted to Labour, an agreed programme to be pursued by the Government after a successful election, and, if Labour wished, representation in

[36] *Labour Leader*, 30 April 1914.
[37] *Clarion*, 6 February 1914.
[38] A. Fenner Brockway, *Towards Tomorrow* (London, 1977), p. 30.

the Cabinet.[39] How much MacDonald revealed to the Labour Party Executive is unclear. We can assume, though, that it was enough, together with his attitude to the approach, to alarm Hardie.

At the conference, with the press excluded, MacDonald denied – or seemed to deny – that a Liberal–Labour alliance was being considered. But his position was completely undermined by Snowden's revelation that 'a definite proposal' had been made at the recent meeting of the Labour Party Executive. Hardie's insistence, from the chair, that there had been 'no proposition' and that 'the matter had been mentioned only' cut little ice and failed to mitigate the effect of Snowden's attack which had concluded with an announcement of his refusal to denounce the Liberals at by-elections while parliamentary colleagues sought to keep them in power. There must be 'a little more honesty'.[40]

After the conclusion of that 'secret session', the debate on the Bradford motion began. The mover quoted from MacDonald's *Socialism and Government* with 'destructive effect', according to the *Clarion* 'on that statesman's obsequious attitude towards the Premier and the Government's autocratic inner circle'. He asked delegates to imagine the Cabinet system transposed into local government with 'A mayor entrusted with the selection of chairman of committees from the ranks of his relatives and friends.' The resolution was carried by 233 to 78. It was, wrote Alex Thompson, 'the beginning of political honesty'.[41]

The mood of the conference was underlined in the elections for chairman. The candidates were Jowett, Burgess, and Wallhead. The first two were identified with the Bradford policy. Wallhead, who had opposed 'Bradford' in the debate, represented the 'official view of the NAC'. In the event, Wallhead was eliminated on the first ballot. In the run off, Jowett polled 205 votes to Burgess's 170.[42]

It is clear that Snowden's revelations about the Liberal alliance proposal were a factor in producing this result. MacDonald's apparently devious machinations behind the back of the ILP must have alarmed many. But Jowett's argument had always included the prediction that some such outcome was more or less inevitable if the Parliamentary Group did not adopt a 'voting on merits' policy.

In the same dismissive way in which he had reacted to the ILP's adoption of proportional representation the previous year, MacDonald was quick to belittle the significance of the Bradford Resolution. Both the

---

[39] David Marquand, *Ramsay MacDonald* (London, 1977), pp. 159–60.
[40] *Labour Leader*, 16 April 1914. See also Colin Cross, *Philip Snowden* (London, 1960), p. 117.
[41] *Clarion*, 17 April 1914.   [42] *Justice*, 16 April 1914.

Labour Leader and the *Clarion* quoted his dismissal of the new ILP policy: the Bradford Resolution was, said MacDonald, 'one of those strings of meaningless words that have no reference to any of the problems which the Parliamentary Party has to face.'

Both papers contrasted MacDonald's attitude with that of Snowden, also an opponent of the Bradford policy in previous years. The *Clarion* quoted from the *Leader*'s report of Snowden's speech in the 'secret session' of the Conference. He had declared that 'our policy in the House of Commons should be in conformity with our platform propaganda'. If Labour acted upon the Bradford policy 'it would not destroy the Cabinet system, and it would probably not destroy a Government. But it would make the tyranny of the Cabinet less oppressive, and it would raise the prestige of the Labour Party.'[43]

Meanwhile, while this near-revolution was taking place within the ILP, the BSP annual conference had agreed to hold a referendum of members on the question of Labour Party affiliation. Hyndman told the conference that he regretted the SDF's withdrawal in 1901. Had they remained affiliated they would have been able to 'stiffen the weak-kneed Lib-Labs'.[44] The result of the referendum was a majority of 3,263 to 2,410 in favour of affiliation.[45] Meanwhile, Dan Irving had drawn the attention of readers of *Justice* to the 'solid value' of the ILP's Bradford Resolution.[46]

Thus a broad consensus was emerging about the way forward for socialism. It would perhaps have broken up rapidly. No doubt MacDonald would have attempted to rally trade union support against 'Bradford', just as he had done successfully against PR. Whether he would have succeeded or not we can only conjecture. Certainly it was not a foregone conclusion that he would. And his task would have been made much harder by the reinforcements the ILP would have received from the BSP.

Had the war not intervened, it is reasonable to assume that the pursuit of MacDonald's parliamentary policy and the consolidation – or even the continuance of – his leadership would have been seriously threatened. The Bradford policy, or something very like it, had a fair prospect of becoming Labour Party, as well as ILP, policy. The combination of the ILP and BSP would also have had a reasonable chance of committing the Labour Party to proportional representation, probably on some variant of the party list system like the modern 'additional member' method, within a relatively short space of time.

---

[43] *Clarion*, 24 April 1914. *Labour Leader*, 23 April 1914.
[44] *Clarion*, 17 April 1914. *Justice*, 16 April 1914.
[45] *Justice*, 28 May 1914. *Labour Leader*, 4 June 1914.   [46] *Justice*, 23 April 1914.

Nor was 'votes for women' the divisive issue it had been among socialists in the earlier years of the century. Since the abortive Reform Bill of January 1913, it was evident that the practical task would now be to ensure that women were included in any extension of the franchise. Genuine 'adult suffragists' – and there were clearly a good many of them in spite of their opponents' attempts to portray them as secret adversaries of women's enfranchisement – and all those 'women's suffragists' who did not retain a doctrinaire insistence on women being enfranchised on the 'existing terms' *before* the advent of universal suffrage, could agree to combine against any attempt to introduce mere 'manhood' suffrage.

Much has sometimes been made of Asquith's statement to Sylvia Pankhurst and the delegation from the East London Federation of Suffragettes (ELFS) on 20 June 1914. 'If the change has to come', Asquith told the delegation, 'we must face it boldly, and make it thorough-going and democratic in its basis.' Andrew Rosen is surely right to argue that this did not necessarily reflect or presage any real change in the Government's position. But it did, and does, suggest that if and when the Liberals had been persuaded to enfranchise women, this would have been on the basis of 'adult' not 'limited' suffrage. The latter was seen by many Liberals as certain political suicide.[47] Sylvia Pankhurst's organisation had been forced out of the WSPU by Emmeline and above all by Christabel Pankhurst. Sylvia's efforts to persuade Asquith were welcomed by *Justice*, which noted the ELFS policy of 'adult suffrage' and commented: 'We are entirely of this opinion. Our opposition to the WSPU from the first has been due to the fact that their demand was not for universal suffrage . . . '[48] The WSPU's arson campaign had cooled the ardour of many former supporters in the ILP.

All these factors combined to remove, to a very large extent, an important division among British socialists. The Labour Party was now committed to resisting any franchise extension which excluded women.

In the longer term, even a cautious move in the direction of direct democracy – perhaps proposing to replace the Lords by some sort of Referendum arrangement – seemed during early 1914 to be a possible Labour Party policy. We have also seen something approaching a consensus beginning to emerge even on the tricky question of industrial

[47] Andrew Rosen, *Rise Up Women! The Militant Campaign of the Women's Social and Political Union, 1903-1914* (London, 1974), pp. 236–7.
[48] *Justice*, 25 June 1914. See Les Garner, *Stepping Stones to Women's Liberty – Feminist Ideas in the Women's Suffrage Movement, 1900–1918* (London, 1984) and 'Suffragism and Socialism: Sylvia Pankhurst 1903–1914', in Ian Bullock and Richard Pankhurst (eds.), *Sylvia Pankhurst: from Artist to Anti-Fascist* (London, 1992).

democracy, and the eventual acceptance by Labour of a Guild Socialist-like compromise between the claims of citizen and worker democracy was not by any means beyond the bounds of possibility.

But could it all have lasted? For *Justice*, the *Clarion* and the *Labour Leader* and their followings to be in broad agreement was unusual. Might it therefore have proved a fragile aberration? This, quite apart from the cataclysm that was about to overwhelm the protagonists for the rest of their lives! All that can be said with confidence is that the prospects for an advance towards some form of 'real democracy' on the basis of a broad consensus looked better in that early summer of 1914 than at any previous time in the history of the British socialism.

Coda: Home Rule and Ireland – the other July crisis of 1914

In a curious way the preoccupations of the socialist press in the immediate pre-war period resembled those of the mid-1880s more than those of any of the intervening years. The main reason was the revival of the Irish Home Rule issue.

The repercussions in Britain of the Irish question had played a major rôle in the foundation of the Democratic Federation at the very beginning of the 'socialist revival'. Point 7 of the Federation's original programme had called for the 'Legislative Independence of Ireland'. Hyndman was a 'close and personal friend' of Michael Davitt, leader of the Irish Land League, and was later to recall that: 'During the whole of 1881 the Irish question overshadowed all others, and our organisation, young as it was, took a very active part against Coercion, and supported the Irish cause to the fullest extent we could.'[49] This assistance had included setting up an election committee to support the Land League candidate in the Tyrone by-election in September 1881 against both Conservative and Liberal opponents, though this had led to the disaffiliation from the Federation of all but one of the Radical working men's clubs.[50]

In 1913 when the Irish issue came to a head once more, with Carson's Ulster Volunteers preparing to resist by force the Liberals' implementation of Home Rule, the 'Old Guard' of the SDF – or so says Chushichi Tsuzuki – 'now [took] a totally different view of the issue'. Quelch urged support of the Ulstermen on the ground that Socialists should stand up for every small nation. Hyndman, himself of Ulster stock, welcomed

[49] H. M. Hyndman, *Record of an Adventurous Life* (London, 1911), p. 255.
[50] C. Tsuzuki, *H. M. Hyndman and British Socialism* (Oxford, 1961), p. 47.

what he called 'the bold front shown by the Ulstermen'. Tsuzuki says that this approach 'smacked of the current policy of the Unionist Party' and was an issue on which Hyndman failed to carry the BSP with him.[51]

Yet, properly understood, there was nothing 'totally different' in this except the practical urgency of the Ulster problem: the SDF had recognised, nearly thirty years before, the right of the Ulster Protestants to opt out of Home Rule. The explanation of this stance lies not in Hyndman's family background but in the democratic principles that he and other SDFers attempted to apply to the Irish question, as they did to all others. Given, not least, such a mistake by so major an authority as Tsuzuki, the views of the SDF on this still all-too-relevant question are worth examining.

In the 1880s, SDF support for Home Rule was frequently justified in terms not of its intrinsic desirability but of the removal of an unnecessary obstacle to working class cooperation. In September 1885 *Justice* declared:

As we have said frequently before we are in favour of the fullest legislative independence for Ireland, not because we have the slightest belief in the advantage of a separate self-governing 'nationality' – as Social-Democrats and therefore International organisers with our fellows we can see the absurdity of the Nationalist cry – but because this is the only hope of an early understanding . . . between the workers of England and Ireland on a wider basis.[52]

Moreover, Irish independence could still be perceived at this stage as a temporary thing. Ulster, as late as December 1885, was not seen to be a problem.

The geographical and economical position of Ireland towards Great Britain is such that, as all her ablest men have admitted, her independence can never be permanent. But an arrangement between a Democratic Ireland and a Democratic England [*sic*] means something very different from the ruinous domination of today. Nor do we consider that there is any reason to fear real injustice to the minority when Legislative Independence is granted.[53]

Yet less than a month later *Justice* was much less optimistic about the position of the minority. 'If the Irish cannot come to a reasonable settlement with the Scotch and English settled in the northern part of their island, then we may secure for these a reasonable autonomy. Beyond that we have no right to go.'[54] Reiterating his support for Home Rule in a leading article in April 1886, Hyndman went on: 'Nor should we change

---

[51] Tsuzuki, *H. M. Hyndman*, pp. 188–9.   [52] *Justice*, 12 September 1885.
[53] *Justice*, 19 December 1885.   [54] *Justice*, 9 January 1886.

our opinion if it became necessary in order to avoid a conflict to establish a little local Parliament in Belfast, as well as in Dublin.'[55]

This was not simply a matter of expediency. As *Justice* explained the following week: 'We hold that the Irishmen of the South of Ireland have the fullest right to manage their own affairs; they have no more claim to dominate the Ulster Presbyterians than we have to dominate them.'[56] The next issue referred approvingly to the 'Separation of South and West Ireland of the completest kind' and criticised Irish Nationalist politicians for their reactionary views.[57] Soon even Michael Davitt, usually excluded from such criticism, was being taken to task for his support for 'subjugating Ulster'.[58]

It was not, as Tsuzuki maintains, that Hyndman subsequently changed his views. They remained exactly the same on the eve of the Great War. After *Justice*, in March 1914, had declared itself 'not at all keen'[59] on the Liberal proposal to exclude Ulster from Home Rule for a six year period, he restated his case. Hyndman began by describing himself as 'one of the oldest Home Rulers in Great Britain'. The Liberal Government, he went on to argue, had no mandate to introduce Home Rule since it had not put it to the electorate as a definite policy for 28 years. Nor was it worth provoking a civil war to force it through.[60]

Blatchford, in the *Clarion*, shared Hyndman's view and indeed went much further, becoming an apologist for the 'Curragh Mutiny' and seeing in this episode a warning to governments against using the army to break strikes.[61] This, as we might expect, triggered a great deal of criticism in which, incidentally, Jowett took a prominent part.[62] Blatchford defended his position, urging that 'my defence of the Ulster minority was not, as some suppose a sudden caprice. It was the logical result of the democratic philosophy which I have held for at least a quarter of a century.'[63]

At the same time, *Justice* was questioning Hyndman's position. It conceded that it would be right to exclude Ulster from the operation of Home Rule if the overwhelming majority there was anti-nationalist. The point was, it insisted, that this was not so.[64] Several *Clarion* correspondents put forward the same argument,[65] while Jowett raised the related question of how far Blatchford was prepared to insist on the rights of minorities.[66]

[55] *Justice*, 17 April 1886.   [56] *Justice*, 24 April 1886.
[57] *Justice*, 1 May 1886.   [58] *Justice*, 15 May 1886.
[59] *Justice*, 12 March 1914.   [60] *Justice*, 2 April 1914.
[61] *Clarion*, 27 March 1914.   [62] *Clarion*, 24 April 1914.
[63] *Clarion*, 1 May 1914.   [64] *Justice*, 2 April 1914.
[65] *Clarion*, 17 April 1914.   [66] *Clarion*, 24 April 1914.

The problem was and is a puzzle for those seeking to apply consistent democratic principles, but in 1914 whether there was great disagreement, as in *Justice* and the *Clarion*, or a more or less clear anti-exclusion line as in the *Labour Leader*[67] – it is crystal clear that this is what British socialists were facing up to, irrespective of the different conclusions they reached. There was general agreement that what counted was the wishes of the inhabitants of Ireland. The difficulties lay, then as now, in interpreting and reconciling them.

The evaluation of the conflict over Ireland had wider implications. Jowett saw the 'Curragh Mutiny' very differently from Blatchford:

A small but influential group of persons are unceasingly working for the establishment of a new oligarchy supported by the King and the Army. The governing classes are afraid. All their efforts to discredit elected bodies are part of a plan the object of which is to weaken, and if possible, destroy representative government so far as it exists in this country.[68]

Such suspicions of an authoritarian anti-democratic plot were heightened when George V 'commanded' an all-party conference on Ulster in July. The Labour Group protested against 'the undue influence of the Crown' as 'calculated to defeat the purposes of the Parliament Act'. The Parliamentary Group's 'bold attitude' was commended by the *Labour Leader* which asserted that 'the Conservatives having lost the power of veto which they exercised through the House of Lords, claim the right to resist the legislation of the Commons first by armed force, second by inspiring mutiny in the army, and third by the intervention of the Court and King.'[69]

Justice saw things in a very similar light:

Whether the Cabinet are responsible for the Buckingham Palace conference or whether they have bowed to the personal 'command' of the King, they have driven another nail into our so-called Parliamentary government . . .

Parliament is becoming more and more a machine for registering the desires and designs of Ministers who happen to be in office. Very few vestiges of Parliamentary independence now remain. Party government is fast becoming a by-word [among] all intelligent people of no matter what opinions. Confidence in the House of Commons is at a low ebb. The way is being prepared for the introduction of the personal power of the King in this country, as soon as a monarch arises vigorous and dexterous enough to wield and handle it.

. . .

The Parliamentary Labour Group, in conjunction with the Labour Party outside and all genuine democratic and socialist bodies have therefore a golden

---

67 *Labour Leader*, 12 March, 2 April, 23 July 1914.
68 *Clarion*, 27 March 1914.   69 *Labour Leader*, 23 July 1914.

opportunity before them. Let them take the initiative in summoning a great National Convention for the complete revision, reorganisation, and democratisation of our whole effete and chaotic system of Parliamentary government. We are choked up with 'precedents' that have grown up like noxious weeds in the course of centuries. A thorough root and branch revolution occasionally is of the utmost benefit to a people.

Such a National Convention seriously and determinedly undertaken at this critical period, with the object of letting the voice of the people be heard above the petty clamour of King and Cabinet, would furnish the means of bringing about such a political revolution in a peaceable manner. The Parliamentary Labour Group, if they will only take the lead in such an endeavour, will make history for themselves in the generations to come. They will gather around them the best of the nation.[70]

We began this book by drawing attention to the survival of Chartist assumptions in the 'socialist revival' of the 1880s in general and the SDF in particular. Appropriately, we can bring our story to an end – as always in the writing of history an artificial procedure – with this late echo of the Chartist device of the National Convention. It was made on 23 July 1914 and repeated again, now in the context of an approaching calamity that dwarfed the Home Rule issue, in a leading article by H. W. Lee, 'Drifting into Danger', a week later – just a few days before the outbreak of war. The convening of a National Convention was now urgent:

The secret diplomacy of the Foreign Office may be committing us to international obligations of which we shall have no knowledge until perhaps called upon to face the armed forces of nations with which we have not the slightest quarrel.[71]

[70] *Justice*, 23 July 1914.   [71] *Justice*, 30 July 1914.

Conclusions

At the broadest level, there were two views of democracy competing with each other in the socialist and trade union movements in Britain. These two views can be distinguished, most simply, as the 'strong' and the 'weak'.

The strong view established itself in the 1880s when socialist organisations and their direct influence were both very small. Consciously descended from a long British and European tradition of plebeian radical democracy, this strong version took the notions of the sovereignty of the people, political equality and self-government literally. Aspirations extended beyond universal suffrage and representative government to ensuring the power of electors over elected and the most direct participation possible by the citizen in decision-making: what was sometimes described as 'popular government'. Great emphasis was placed on the need for socialists to prepare and stimulate popular participation through 'education' and 'agitation'.

The proponents of such views recognised many obstacles. Those with power encouraged apathy and the related disease of 'Leadermania'. T. H. Hunt, writing in *Justice* in 1897 believed that 'Leadermania has now arrived at the stage when, if it is not utterly to subvert the power of democratic thought must be checked through . . . a drastic antidote'.[1] Such a remedy was hard to find, though socialist organisations, it was believed, might begin doing so by means of their own practice. Their standards of internal democracy were expected to prefigure those looked for in the future 'Socialist Commonwealth'.

Any perceived failure was severely criticised and could lead to long and acrimonious internal dissension. Thus, at a very early stage, the belief that Hyndman was seeking both to promote 'leadermania' to his own advantage and to compromise socialism through electoral participation in an essentially fraudulent political system led, in large measure, to the

[1] *Justice*, 13 November 1897.

290

formation of the Socialist League. After the League's effective demise, the *Clarion* became the most uncompromising advocate of the strong view of democracy and a major inspiration and support of those who battled for it in the interminable struggles within the ILP. Similarly, dissatisfaction with what was seen as manipulation by officials and other 'leaders' was a major theme within the 'federation' movements in the trade unions culminating in the ill-fated NIGFTLU.

Syndicalism later also drew on hostility to the idea of leadership. 'No man,' the authors of *The Miners' Next Step* warned, 'was ever good enough, or strong enough, to have such power at his disposal, as real leadership implies'.[2] But there was now less danger than had been the case thirteen to fifteen years previously, that the attack on leadership would degenerate into impotent – but for recipients still unpleasant – braying against individual opponents at any level, such as when P. J. King in his frustration had railed against the allegedly crushing powers available to even low-level officials.

His rhetoric was obviously selective. As we saw, so long as *some* leaders, even national ones, had been prepared to go along with him, he had been prepared to go along with them – and even to trumpet the fact. We can surely imagine many of his supporters being equally selective when the occasion suited them. Soon inconsistency was a matter not so much of opportunism as of confusion. Both amongst officials and elsewhere – indeed at all levels in the movement – people supported or opposed Federation and rival versions of it from perspectives which the syndicalists would rightly have seen as variegated to the point of chaos. As we noted, some people favoured deterrence and conciliation, others escalation and general strike; some favoured combination with political action while others did not. The NIGFTLU constitution encouraged the federating of existing organisations while also allowing individual supporters to come together irrespective of these.

On the latter issue, admittedly, the syndicalists in their period were by no means monolithic. A minority, mainly on Clydeside, did support what is now known as 'Dual Unionism'. Nor were syndicalist slogans without confusing, but very important, echoes among union officialdoms – as when the National Transport Workers' Federation was formed from existing organisations during late 1910, or when the Triple Alliance was arrived at during 1914–15 with all the ambiguities that were to become so fateful on Black Friday less than seven years later. But no less an informed contemporary than G. D. H. Cole was clear that the actual agitation for 'Amalgamation' itself 'became almost a synonym

---

[2] *The Miners' Next Step* (rpt London, 1972), p. 19.

for the militant New Unionism of the Syndicalists and Industrial Unionists'.[3]

What we have called the 'weak' view was to emerge clearly, among socialists, only in the 1890s. The Fabian Society became its most consistent and coherent advocate. The main thrust was to shift the definition of what was essential to democracy from active participation in decision-making to passive consent. It was forcefully argued that the active and initiatory rôle was, of necessity, confined to legislative and administrative 'experts': professional politicians, civil servants and other 'specialists'. The average citizen lacked the time, knowledge and experience necessary to initiate political decision-making, and public opinion was bound to lag far behind that of the enlightened minority. Public trust could be won, however, by the demonstration of beneficial results, and new general mandates to pursue further enlightened policies could be won on this basis.

Supporters of the strong view equated democracy with 'popular government'. By contrast, the Fabians conflated it with 'representative government'. Under the leadership of Keir Hardie and others, the ILP followed the latter path, albeit in a less explicit fashion and at the cost of constant and considerable internal dissent.

In the later 1890s, the gap between the strong and weak conceptions of democracy grew. On the one side was a deepening of SDF commitment to 'popular government' and denunciations of 'Fabian Caesarism'; these chimed with *Clarion* calls for 'real democracy'. On the other, was the explicit Fabian rejection of 'primitive expedients'; this harmonised with Hardie's exasperation with 'ultra-democratic' antics in his ILP.

The failure of the SDF and, more spectacularly, of those socialists associated with the *Clarion* to achieve what could be counted as concrete results – seen most clearly in the swift humiliation of NIGFTLU – contrasted with the apparent success of Hardie's strategy of the 'Labour alliance'. This contrast, together with the background of Boer War 'popular imperialism', went a long way to undermine the appeal of the 'strong' version. *De facto* acceptance of the existing political system by Labour tended gradually to turn into identification of that system as 'representative government' and of representative government as democracy. Such tendencies were reinforced by Ramsay MacDonald, in both his practice and his writings.

But there were counter-attacks. Fred Jowett took the lead in resisting

---

[3] G. D. H. Cole, *A Short History of the British Working-Class Movement 1789–1947* (London, 1948), p. 324.

MacDonald's attempts to 'work his party into the system'. Jowett argued that representative government, let alone democracy, was still to be achieved. It could not, he urged, be equated with Cabinet government. In the ILP, opposition increased to the course being pursued by parliamentary Labour, and MacDonald overreached himself by 'arrangements' with the Liberals. This cost him the support, at least temporarily, of even erstwhile allies like Snowden and Hardie. The result was the advance of the 'Bradford Resolution', a parliamentary strategy intended to undermine the operation of cabinet government and eventually to compel the substitution for it of the committee system. By 1914 this had become the policy of the ILP – Labour's main socialist affiliate and in effect its local organisation. The Bradford policy was also applauded by *Justice* and the *Clarion*.

There was still considerable support for replacing the House of Lords with a referendum system – thereby, as A. M. Thompson put it, 'grafting on' an element of 'popular government'. But there was less support for SDF defence of elected ad hoc administrative bodies like the School Boards – seen as more 'direct' and therefore more democratic than either appointed national government agencies or omnibus local authorities. Crucially, when a reaction set in against the corporatism of Liberal social reform – old-age pensions, the Insurance Act, labour exchanges – it came increasingly in forms influenced by syndicalist ideas of industrial self-management. The latter was seen as a means of avoiding bureaucracy and Belloc's 'Servile State'. The by now traditional Social-Democratic remedies were overshadowed.

The latter, in their 'strong' way, shared with the much reviled because (in our terms) 'weak' 'Fabian Democracy' the assumption that, whether as active participant or as passive giver of consent, the individual's democratic rights would be exercised as a *citizen*. Syndicalism reintroduced the alternative version of the 'strong' idea – *worker* democracy – and focused attention on the largely neglected problem of undemocratic industrial management. Guild Socialism was the clearest attempt to reconcile the claims of 'citizen' and 'worker' democracy. More important, the terms of the debate were shifting broadly in the same direction over a much wider spectrum of socialist opinion.

Throughout our period, attitudes to leaders and leadership were a kind of test question to separate radical from conservative, or strong from weak, democrats. The stances taken could verge on self-parody. Blatchford addressed the final meeting of the Hammersmith Socialist Society in January 1897 in a speech which, as reported by the admittedly unsympathetic *Labour Leader*, reads like a compendium of *Clarion* clichés:

He did not approve of putting men on a platform separated from the rest of the gathering to make speeches. To have a lot of men sat there all in rows as Superior Persons, and then for them to protest against leaders was absurd. (Hear, hear and laughter.) He would like to see one Socialist Party. If they thought more about Democracy and less about Socialism they would have it. Nearly all causes – good and bad – were wrecked by leaders. They did not want leaders – nor platforms.

Other contributors equally hurled themselves into their preferred and preordained ruts. Blatchford was followed at the same meeting by Bernstein who claimed that leaders were inevitable – even the anarchists had them. This calumny was then hotly denied by the anarchists present. Shaw then informed the gathering that 'He emphatically believed in leadership. If the Socialist Party would make him leader it would get on very much better'.[4] All good knockabout stuff, no doubt, but debates tended all too often to go round in circles like this, seldom getting beyond general statements of position or principle. Examples include the constant recurrence of the same imagery of 'post cards' and 'dancing dolls' on the one side of the delegation/representation debate, and of complaints about the 'never ending audacity of elected persons' on the other. Significantly, when the question was examined in even a little more detail, the apparent gulf between Blatchford's 'delegate' and the Webbs' – improved – 'representative' narrowed, as we have seen, to a difference of emphasis, verbally at least.

The similarity of view between the SDF and the *Clarion* partially obscured important differences in their approaches to 'popular government'. The *Clarion* insisted on direct democracy in the *legislative* sphere and generally on questions of broad choice. But the executive, administrative or managerial realm was quite another matter. Montagu Blatchford's cautionary tale, 'Tollington the Democrat', was intended to make a serious point. Tollington's 'most uncompromising' addiction to democracy finally alienated his comrades when he insisted that the captain of the cricket team 'was not allowed to change the bowling or move a fielder until the change had been voted on by a majority of the players.' The 'moral' was clear:

When there is something to enjoy, the popular vote can decide who shall enjoy it, but when there is something *to do* the unanimous vote of the largest assembly cannot get it done except by those who have the necessary ability for its accomplishment.[5] (original emphasis)

Complaints by critics that Blatchford made no attempt to apply 'real democracy' to the running of the *Clarion* therefore left him unmoved and

---

[4] *Labour Leader*, 30 January 1897.   [5] *Clarion*, 14 March 1902.

it is noticeable that in all Thompson's pamphlets and articles it is the 'professional politician' rather than the 'bureaucrat' who is seen as the great danger to democracy. It was left mainly to the SDF – and especially to Bax – to tackle the anti-democratic tendencies of official-dom: to rise against the never-ending audacity if *non*-elected persons. The obvious explanation of this difference is no doubt the correct one. The SDF was an organisation; the *Clarion* was a newspaper. One failing of the *Clarion* was that it did not seem to consider that there might just possibly be *other* special circumstances that justified some departure from simon-pure direct democracy. As a result, it was seen by opponents as not only unrealistic but also hypocritical: ever ready to denounce others in uncompromising terms for failing to be good democrats, while *a priori* excusing its own conduct.

However much they might proclaim the inseparability of democracy and socialism, there was, for socialists of all tendencies, at least a latent tension between commitment to democracy and to the socialisation – whatever form that might take – of the means of production. One way to try to resolve this conflict was to opt for a weak definition of democracy. This would leave the initiative with, potentially, socialist 'experts' who would have been put in place by Fabian 'permeation' or 'Labour representation' or some combination of both. Such was what we may call the 'legislativist' approach. It sought to achieve socially beneficial legislation not only for its own sake but also to promote or facilitate a radical change in consciousness.

The alternative was the 'educationist' approach with its priority of 'making socialists' over electoral politics, and with its stress on the importance of avoiding confusing or diversionary tactics, even if these might seem to promise immediate electoral advantage. This went with the strong version of democracy just as the logic of legislativism was to raise leaders above led.

Both assumed that public opinion in general always lagged behind the enlightened minority – themselves. 'Legislativists' believed that the 'masses' would eventually 'catch up' through a combination of expert example, enlightened social engineering and the continued, if mysterious, working of the evolutionary process. The 'educationists', on the other hand, had come to believe in the value of the 'discovery method' of learning, decades before the term was invented. The 'people' would only really learn by being allowed to make their own 'mistakes'. Although this might at first seem a longer road to socialism, it would prove shorter in the long run. But this could only happen to the extent that they were *really* able to exercise free choice. This depended on having the 'strongest' forms of democracy possible.

What about non-socialist democrats? The conventional view has been to see radicals and 'new Liberals' as somewhere just to the right of the Fabians in the political spectrum. But this obscures at least as much as it illuminates. Quite often, on issues of democracy, such non-socialists were to be found lined up with the SDF and the 'ultra-democratic' *Clarion* rather than with the Fabians or the ILP. The National Democratic League is a case in point. And, as Peter Clarke has reminded us, L. T. Hobhouse in the *Nation* during 1907 charged the Fabians with attempting to 'force progress by packing and managing committees instead of winning popular consent'. In 1904 he had commented, in words that can be regarded as all too prophetic, that 'as the expert comes to the front and "efficiency" becomes the watchword of administration all that was human in Socialism vanishes out of it'.[6] H. V. Emy has made much the same point:

Radicals disliked both the bureaucratic manifestations of socialism and Fabian assumptions that institutional reform was a solution in itself. Where Hobhouse emphasised that the democratic machinery had to be perfect before new powers devolved on it, MacDonald thought electoral reform 'a red herring'.[7]

On questions of democratic form, 'New Liberals', like Hobhouse, and that other 'Hob', J. A. Hobson, had more in common with SDFers and 'Clarionettes' than with the Fabians or the emerging Labour leadership. Clarke notes that both supported proportional representation and that Hobson also placed particular emphasis on the referendum: 'From 1907 he took every opportunity to advocate it, on the ground that "the theoretically 'good' idea must be stamped with the sort of 'goodness' required to secure the approval of the people".' Hobson, says Clarke, thought the referendum would allow people 'not only to make mistakes but to recognise that they have made them' and that it would foster 'a process of social learning'.[8] This is an excellent example of the 'educationist' approach.

Justice lost few opportunities to praise and support Radicals, including Hobson and Hobhouse, for taking a stand on democracy. Later, when *Justice* and the *Clarion* came to judge Belloc's *The Servile State* his anti-socialism was of less consequence to them than his hostility to bureaucracy and 'party' politicians.

---

[6] The first quotation is from the *Nation*, 20 March 1907 and the second from *Democracy and Reaction* (London, 1904), p. 228. See Peter Clarke, *Liberals and Social Democrats* (London, 1978), p. 71.
[7] H. V. Emy, *Liberals, Radicals and Social Politics* (London, 1973), p. 117.
[8] Clarke, *Liberals and Social Democrats*, p. 143, quoting Hobson's *The Crisis of Liberalism*, p. 65.

Yet the SDF seems to have had more problems than other socialist groupings in relating socialism and democracy. In principle, democracy was integral to socialism. If 'the people' really were to rule, two sorts of change were needed. We may think of these as 'vertical' and 'horizontal'. Earlier radical democrats – like the Chartists – had concentrated on the vertical axis: securing popular control of the state. But even if this object had been achieved, the narrow 'horizontal' confines of state activity would still, from the standpoint of Social-Democrats, have left society under the control of capitalists. Therefore, not only should the vertical axis be made as responsive as possible to the popular will, but the horizontal axis must be extended, bringing economic power under adequate state control.

In the Social-Democrat view, both of these were necessary and desirable. But, as Hyndman recognised in his 1897 article on 'Social Democrat or Socialist?', 'Democratic action might not by any means necessarily be collectivist and collectivist action might not by any means necessarily be democratic'. True, Hyndman was at pains to differentiate Social-Democracy from what he termed 'State or Bureaucratic Socialism'.[9] But in practice the SDF could be at odds with itself about whether to give *priority* to collectivism or to democracy.

This dilemma was most evident during 1900. The SDF was committed to both collectivist and democratic action – in each case in the strongest of senses. The newly founded Labour Representation Committee meant, from the SDF standpoint, weak collectivist action; the also newly founded National Democratic League weakish democratic action. SDFers toyed with both, but in the end gave real support to neither.

One consequence of the SDF leaving the LRC was to weaken the forces of *both* strong collectivism *and* democracy in the Labour Party during its crucial formative years. One consequence of turning its back on the NDL – an organisation committed to 'Adult Suffrage' – was that, when objecting to 'women's suffrage' as elitist, it had no adult suffragist campaigning to preen itself on more recent than the eighties or early nineties. This left the impression that it was only raising the cry of universal suffrage as a dishonest means of opposing the enfranchisement of women.

Fundamentally, although the SDF had its fair share of 'barricades men' and was quite capable of indulging in revolutionary rhetoric, on balance its commitment – strong in every sense – to democratic methods comes out much more strongly week by week from the pages of *Justice*.

---

[9] H. M. Hyndman, 'Social-Democrat or Socialist?', *The Social-Democrat*, no. 8, August 1897.

Hyndman especially, but others too, often wrote in ways which suggested at least a sort of *chronological* priority for democracy over collectivism: the greater the democracy achieved, the easier would be the achievement – ultimately at least – of the collective goals of socialism. Democracy was the only reliable path. As Fred Knee put it in a *Justice* article on 'Democracy *v* Demagoguery' in 1897, 'we are doubtful of getting socialism except by and through democracy, and as no other but a democratic basis for socialism would be a lasting one, our duty is clear'.[10] How this duty took precedence over possible party advantage was made clear in 1902:

We are democrats as well as Socialists, indeed it is because we are democrats that we are Socialists. True democracy is impossible without Socialism, and Socialism without democracy is unthinkable. But democracy means the most perfect political equality attainable between human beings: therefore Socialists demand universal adult suffrage, not as a mere piece of tactics, not as a measure which may be likely to be of advantage to the Socialist Party, but as a matter of principle. Consequently, while Liberals and Tories, in spite of their professed love of political enfranchisement, may and do strive to disfranchise known opponents and keep them off the register . . . for a Socialist to endeavour to get anyone struck off . . . is inconsistent with the principles of Socialism . . . [11]

Yet for all socialists, the problem of remaining both democratic and collectivist was a real one, however approached. Even if the question of democratic form was shelved in the manner of Hardie this meant, implicitly, accepting the status quo. Democratic issues concerning particular devices or procedures had, and have, a habit of jumping out suddenly and catching unawares those who disdained 'mere politics'. This seems to be what happened to Hardie and the ILP with the School Board issue at the beginning of the century, and with proportional representation just before the Great War.

A major complication was the question of the status of the existing political system. Could it be called democratic in even the most minimal sense? On the basis of the 1911 census, Neal Blewett has calculated that, allowing for plural voting, only 59 per cent of the male population was able to vote.[12] On the other hand there *was* a form of 'representative government' which, one could even argue, amounted to a rough approximation of democracy if looked at from a 'class' standpoint. If the working class accounted for far more than its 'fair share' of the

---

[10] *Justice*, 17 July 1897.   [11] *Justice*, 18 October 1902.
[12] Neal Blewett, 'The Franchise in the United Kingdom, 1885–1819', *Past and Present*, 32, December 1965, 31. For the complexities of the Edwardian electoral system, see Duncan Tanner, *Political Change and the Labour Party 1900–1918* (London, 1990), pp. 99–129.

unenfranchised, it still constituted at the very least the largest single group of voters. The male unenfranchised were a heterogeneous collection which included domestic servants, soldiers in barracks, Irish police, paid party agents, recipients of poor relief and peers of the realm (with the last of whom it has become traditional to link lunatics). This helped to reinforce the view that the last remaining great exclusion was that of women.

Responses to this situation varied enormously. On the one hand there were those who might, like MacDonald, support 'women's suffrage', but who nevertheless seemed willing to bestow the epithet democratic not only on Britain but on virtually all 'modern' states. This suggests the tendency of the 'weak' version of democracy to accept as democratic any form of representative government. On the other hand, the radicals' and socialists' uncertainty as to the status of the existing form of government facilitated their awareness of a wide range of more or less competing forms. These ranged from what was deemed genuine 'popular government' via 'representative government', to the status quo which was held by them to have met not even the basic requirements of representativeness.

As we have seen, the Webbs had identified 'primitive democracy' with the past rather than with the present or future of trade unionism. Yet its persistence, like the revival of the use of the referendum during NIGFTLU's brief hour of glory, suggests that Shaw's gibe that the SDF conception of democracy was that of an '*old-fashioned* trade unionist' (our emphasis) owed much to wishful thinking.

There is no shortage of other examples of the continuing attraction of the – allegedly – primitive. For example, a Ministry of Labour report to the Cabinet on 'The Labour Situation' early in 1920 began with a detailed consideration of 'Delegation versus Representation'. It noted that 'in several recent instances the rank and file have shown an inclination to challenge and over-rule the authority of their leaders'. It considered, as a question of 'fundamental importance', the status of trade union leaders: whether 'they should be delegates merely expressing the will of their followers or representatives chosen by their followers to guide and lead them'.[13] Many trade unionists have continued to display a stubborn tendency to regard general secretaries, presidents, executive committees and negotiators as delegates, spokespeople, servants or employees rather than to see themselves – in the manner of the authors of this report – as their 'followers'.

---

[13] *The Labour Situation. Report from the Ministry of Labour for the week ending 18 February 1920*, CP 690. We are grateful to Stephen Yeo for this reference.

In general we may conclude that weaker, status-quo-based versions of democracy were more likely to commend themselves to the elected than to the elector; to the powerful, than to the powerless; to the contented rather than to the dissatisfied. In so far as working-class people were more likely than their 'betters' to be among the unelected, powerless, and discontented, stronger notions of democracy were likely to attract their support, at least among the minority of activists. A countervailing process then often began. Some of the activists found themselves among the elected and began to see problems from this new standpoint. It became all too easy to label any commitment to radical notions of democracy as 'naive' and 'unrealistic' – yet as something, perhaps, to be looked back on with nostalgia, like Joseph Clayton's account of earlier days from the standpoint of the 1920s:

Political ambition was exceedingly rare. That men or women should want to be elected to City Councils or School Boards seemed as odd to the Socialists of the 'nineties as a desire to sit on a jury. It might be a duty, it was hardly an honour. To attend a committee was irksome enough. As for Parliament, it was incredible that any reason, save a willingness to promote the cause of Socialism and to serve mankind should be given for contesting an election.[14]

Once the transition had been made to seeing strong democratic commitments as part of the innocence of socialism before the Fall, it was easy to lose sight of the fact that 'realism' in this negative sense was no guarantee of a critical approach to the existing power structures. A naive opposition could simply be replaced by an equally unreflective acceptance. In any case, it was not only among the elected that personal experience and self-interest counted for something. A cynical explanation of the *Clarion*'s devotion to the referendum and initiative would be that this form of decision-making was the one most likely to maximise the paper's influence among socialists. Further, as Clifford Sharp argued in his Fabian pamphlet, if the referendum and initiative were to become a feature of national government, they would tend to enhance the power of the press generally.[15]

By the last few pre-war years, syndicalism had taken the centre of the stage. In some ways it represented a more consistent recasting of radical democracy. But syndicalism had an ambivalent relationship with earlier traditions. Thus it foreshadowed to some extent the contradictions of the post-1917 Bolshevik appeal. On the one hand it took the suspicion of

---

[14] Joseph Clayton, *The Rise and Decline of Socialism in Great Britain, 1884–1924* (London, 1926), p. 88.
[15] Clifford D. Sharp, *The Case Against the Referendum*, Fabian Tract No. 155 (London, 1911).

'elected persons' – whether politicians or union office holders credibly presentable as bureaucrats or, for De Leonists, 'labour fakirs' – to its extreme. Instead it emphasised a 'do-it-yourself' approach.

On the other, its very uncompromising militancy tended to inculcate a 'soldier of the revolution' mentality. The logic of large-scale ferociously-fought industrial actions, whether actual or hypothetical, led to co-ordination of effort by some *de facto* general staff. The despised 'leaders', defenestrated at the front of the house, marched back in through the back door.

One index of the success of Labour in 'working itself into the system' is that, in the early 1980s, amid the bitter wrangling over the question of how to elect leaders, the terms of the debate were quite different from those of the party's early years. No longer was it even remotely a question of whether or not there should *be* a leader.

There was an 'evolutionary' assumption, in Fabian – and MacDonaldite – theory and practice that public opinion was bound to lag far behind that of the enlightened minority. Such an assumption also found its way into ostensibly more radical and revolutionary varieties of socialism. It is therefore not surprising that, with few exceptions, socialist aspirations to 'popular government' have been muted, if never entirely silenced, for so much of the twentieth century. Leninism, in its various versions, tended no less than Fabianism to wear down notions of radical democracy on the Left. True, the Bolshevik approach was to generate incoherences of its own. But any exploration of these was soon cut short by Stalinisation and then overlaid by the urgency of the fight against fascism.

True, until about 1930, the National Minority Movement (NMM) did represent the most sophisticated and successful attempt till the present time at an agitation, linked to a perspective for radically democratising society, for rank-and-file control within existing organisations. In this – and whatever manipulations may have taken place under its aegis – it can also be seen as developing one of the potentials of the NIGFTLU agitation.

From another angle, though, the NMM's links with Bolshevism were precisely with that approach whose popularity on the Left of the Labour Party after 1918 helped almost to drown the earlier concerns with democratic form which this book has recorded. Of course, there were broader factors, not least the perplexity among wide swathes of Labour supporters about whether to hold, and how to hold on to, high office without ever having an overall Commons majority in a period of threatened or actual economic breakdown. In addition, Labour's need to continue squeezing the Liberals into third place was allowed to dampen

– or confuse – interest in proportional representation in any form. The confusion is exemplified in a November 1931 report in the *Manchester Guardian* of an analysis by the Proportional Representation Society which (as one historian has summarised it) concluded that the existing electoral system had 'worked strongly in favour of Labour in 1929, and drastically against it in 1931.'[16]

But what is also indicative is the silence on the subject in the ILP both during the 1920s, when it was still uneasily inside the Labour Party, and during the 1930s when it was outside it. At the top, veterans such as Jowett – let alone the relatively youthful Brockway – felt hemmed in by many tasks and dilemmas more urgent that any revision in the forms of the British constitution.[17] 'Fred's obsession', though not forgotten especially by Jowett himself, became eternally less urgent precisely – in part – because British political forms (centrally a 'first-past-the-post' electoral system which tends to smother third parties) freeze lesser urgencies into utter abstractions.

Communist ambiguity about democracy goes back to Lenin's 1902 pamphlet, *What is to be Done?* This had itself applauded the Webbs' and Kautsky's critique of 'primitive democracy'. His immediate targets were the critics of 'anti-democratic tendencies' in Russian Social-Democracy, but his arguments against internal democracy were applicable outside conditions of Tsarist repression. In attacking the notion that committee decisions should become effective 'only after they have been circulated among all the circles', Lenin comments: 'Observe that this proposal for a widely applied referendum is advanced *in addition* to the demand that *the whole of* the organisation be built on an elective basis!' (original emphasis).[18] Few of the socialists and trade unionists we have met in the course of this study – few even of those who would have resolutely opposed attempts to run their organisations by means of the referendum – would have understood the amazement signalled by these italics and exclamation mark at the proposal to establish democratic control over decision-making as well as to elect office-holders.

Of course, by the time Lenin wrote *The State and Revolution* (summer

---

[16] Ben Pimlott, *Labour and the Left in the 1930s* (London, 1977), p. 17.

[17] How confined they let themselves become is exemplified by Brockway's slowness during 1936–7 to back his Spanish comrades in the POUM against Stalinist pressure until weeks after their bloody suppression. See Sam Bernstein, Al Richardson, *Against the Stream: the History of the Trotskyist Movement in Britain, 1924–38* (London, 1986), pp. 226–7, quoting the experience of Harry Wicks. See also Harry Wicks, *Keeping My Head* (London, 1992), pp. 175–6.

[18] V. I. Lenin, *What is to be Done? Burning Questions of Our Movement* (1902, rpt. Peking, 1973), pp. 174–5.

1917) the stock of 'primitive democracy' had risen greatly. Now, instead of quoting the Webbs with approval, they were damned for having supplied arguments against 'primitive democracy' used by Bernstein in 'his renegade book, *The Premises of Socialism*'. On the contrary, Lenin went on to assert:

Under socialism much of the 'primitive' democracy will inevitably be revived, since for the first time in the history of civilised society the *mass* of the population will rise to the level of taking an *independent* part, not only in voting and elections *but also in the everyday administration of affairs.* Under socialism *all* will govern in turn and will soon become accustomed to no one governing.[19] (original emphasis)

The gap between such confident predictions and subsequent post-1917 realities is all too evident.[20] True, only tramline versions of history have Lenin as the sole major theorist of socialist revolution during the early twentieth century. But in practice, it was the Lenin of *What is to be Done?* who prevailed over all, not least over his other self. In the socialist movement, 'strong' democrats thus found themselves squeezed between the benevolent élitism and 'realism' of one sort of Fabianism and what in some ways was the re-importation of the same thing in the revolutionary guise of Leninism.

Nevertheless, strong, radical notions of democracy were of major importance in the British socialist and labour movements in the period preceding the Great War and the Russian Revolution. The roots of this went back to the very origins of the working-class movement. A number of forms or devices that seemed to be means of achieving such a democracy – delegation, the referendum and initiative, elected *ad hoc* authorities, industrial self-management, proportional representation and so on – were widely and persistently advocated by socialists. Disputes and disagreements about questions of democracy and democratic form played a much more important part in conflicts within and between the socialist groupings than historians have noticed.

More often than not, the particular nostrums selected were not explored in detail. Nor were their implications always worked out. Thus, for example, at one stage the SDF seems to have been quite happy to support *both* proportional representation and the second ballot. But if we sometimes permit ourselves to smile condescendingly at such

[19] V. I. Lenin, *The State and Revolution: The Marxist Teaching on the State and the Tasks of the Proletariat in the Revolution* (1917, rpt. Moscow, nd), p. 200.
[20] Carmen Sirianni, *Workers' Control and Socialist Democracy: the Soviet Experience* (London, 1982); Maurice Brinton, *The Bolsheviks and Workers' Control: the State and Counter-Revolution* (London, 1970).

confusions, the underlying determination to achieve the sturdiest democracy should surely, in this new age of alleged democratic revival, compel our attention. As Groucho Marx almost said, only condescension deserves condescension.

Appendix: Federation for local labour historians – and for national

One of the aims of the trade union side of this book is to send those historians with knowledge of specific industries and unions and local labour movements during the 1890s and 1900s, back to their sources. For, in the writing of it, uneven survival of documents along with complexity of data, rules out selecting particular areas or industries or unions as likelier fields than others. From their side, local historians have omitted at least as much as national (whom we have just sampled).

It is at the branch level that support for the *Clarion* scheme or for anything else may conceivably bear occasional long-term significance for later developments in at least local labour movements. Regional variations may also be significant here, though sometimes less so than branch ones. Unfortunately, the preservation of branch and local union records has been notoriously uneven, despite massive advances during the last decade. But occasional indications may be culled, though all too often indirectly. Many have already been mentioned during the course of this book. The following paragraphs amount merely to an opportune scraping of the files for the benefit, if any at all, of local specialists. Those occasions when branches from a number of areas agreed on a particular initiative have been omitted.

So, in the north-west, the Friendly Society of Ironfounders (FSI)'s district that included Salford and Wigan seems to have been particularly hot on national federation and seems mainly to have preferred the *Clarion*'s.[1] Within the ASRS, much sympathy for federation has already been noted, particularly for the *Clarion* and around Wigan. And a Wigan engineer claimed that the ASE branch and the Trades Council also 'supported the *Clarion* scheme – or at least . . . its main principles'.[2] Within the ASE, some support for the *Clarion* Scheme from Manchester

---

[1] FSI *Monthly Report*, February 1898, p. 1.
[2] ASE *Monthly Report*, May 1898, p. 13: 'Jaice'.

has been noted.[3] Locally, Horwich's no. 2 branch was to be one of the mere two from the Society as a whole to send delegates to the founding FLP.[4] Horwich also sent the only Gasworkers' representative.[5] King had earlier noted support from this branch and also from the Trades Council – though this body was not to be directly represented. Horwich's was also one of the ASRS branches that sent their own delegates.

In the Pennines, Huddersfield Trades Council was said to have 'practically adopted the Clarion scheme'.[6] This cannot be confirmed from the Council Minutes, though 'Ben Riley' (possibly the Clarionette) did represent it at the 1898 FLP.[7] The Leeds Cabinetmakers clearly did.[8] Leeds Trades Council was lukewarm at most, though it did organise a meeting for King.[9] In the ASE there were individual members expressing support.[10] Elsewhere in Yorkshire itself, we have already noted King's relationship with the North Yorkshire and Cleveland Miners. In non-Pennine Yorkshire, King claimed support from Mexborough Trades Council – though again, this body does not appear to have reached the 1898 FLP directly.[11]

From the outer north-west, Workington seems to have shown notable interest in federation, particularly in the *Clarion*'s. Its ASRS branch expected its delegates to be one of 'about five . . . from this town', and remembered 'the pleasure of having Mr King here twice': 'the Workington branch' seemed 'enthusiastic on the Clarion scheme'.[12] During the final ten days before the 1899 FLP convened, King had subheaded his claim that all but two union branches affiliated to the Workington Trades Council supported his scheme: 'Workington goes nap for the Clarion scheme'.[13] In the Parliament's Report, Workington's delegates, beside that of its ASRS branch, included two from the National Amalgamated Society of Enginemen, Cranemen, Boilermen and Firemen (NAS of ECBF), one from the much smaller branch of the 'National Steel Association Labour League', and two from the

3 E.g. William Pannell of Manchester no. 7 branch, ASE *Monthly Report*, 1898, elections, pp. 7–11.
4 FLP delegates list, p. 9. The other was the 140-strong Halifax no. 3 branch, p. 11.
5 A. Waring, representing 140 members, same page.
6 *Clarion*, 25 June 1898.
7 AU of Cabinetmakers, *Report* of District Meeting of 25–30 July 1898, p. 41.
8 Same, April 1898.
9 Leeds TLC *Monthly Bulletin*, 29 September 1897.
10 E.g. 'Worth, Bradford', ASE *Monthly Report*, September 1897, pp. 10f.
11 *Clarion*, 20 August 1898.
12 *Railway Review*, 1 July 1898.
13 *Clarion*, 9 July 1898. The other two, he claimed, had not voted. Whatever the truth of his general claims, his forecast of six Workington delegates was more than upheld.

Blastfurnacemen. Conceivably, therefore, the presence of J. Flynn from Cumberland's Iron Ore Miners' Association (representing 1,000 members) might owe something to encouragement from out of Workington. There was also W. Calvert, representing (or partially double-representing!) the 2,500 union members affiliated to the Trades Council.[14] He himself was on the EC of the NAS of Enginemen. He doubled as secretary to Workington lodge[15] which, the next year, presented him and his wife with 'combined presents valued at £20 . . . in recognition of the splendid services rendered to our Workington brethren.'[16] At the January 1899 TUC, it was to be Pete Walls of the West Coast Blastfurnacemen who, with Flynn, was to move unsuccessfully to discuss all schemes. Walls, too, was a pillar of the local labour movement.[17]

Identifiably from the north-east, there were three ASRS branches represented at the FLP (Bensham, Darlington and Gateshead). A 'J. Burns' represented Sunderland Trades Council (whose claimed membership of 15,000 was, by a factor of more than four, easily the largest among those of the trades councils, excluding the Yorkshire Federation's). Otherwise, there seems to remain only the elusive town of Stockton. A mere month before the FLP, King reported a meeting, under Trades Council auspices, that had resolved 'strongly in favour' of his scheme. The meeting had also elected a committee to persuade all union branches 'in this district . . . to approve of the Clarion Scheme, and [to elect] a delegate' to itself. Branches of societies which were not to be represented at the FLP, but which had a Stockton branch mentioned by King at the Trades Council's meeting, included the NAS of ECBF; the NAS of House and Ship Painters and Decorators; the Bricklayers' Society; the Amalgamated Society of Carpenters and Joiners (AS of C and J); British Steel Smelters' Amalgamated Association; the ASE (no. 3 branch); the Typographical Association; the Associated Iron and Steel Workers of Great Britain; 'the United Society of Brushmakers; the U O Plumbers of Great Britain and Ireland . . . the National Union of Gasworkers and General Labourers, etc., etc.'. Yet, apart from the Trades Council (representing 1,350), the FLP's list was to mention no delegates clearly from the 'district' of Stockton – unless one includes Guisborough, whose ironstone miners would presumably have been represented via the North Yorkshire and Cleveland Miners' and

[14] FLP *Report*, pp. 9ff.
[15] NAS of Enginemen . . . , *Annual Report* till 30 June 1898.
[16] Same, till 31 December 1899.
[17] See *Labour Annual*, 1907, p. 240. He had also been 'in ILP since formation'.

Quarrymen's Association. One cannot, therefore, say that nothing came
of this Stockton meeting. But one can hardly say, either, what did.[18]

In the English Midlands, the FSI's twelfth district, centred on Derby,
allegedly preferred the *Clarion* scheme to its rivals.[19] Back in 1897, the
Trades Council had heard King, apparently with cautious sympathy.[20]
But its subsequent doings on the matter are unclear. King also claimed
to have received a sympathetic hearing at the Leicester branch of
the Upholsterers.[21] From the neighbouring town of Loughborough, the
Trades Council seems to have held at least one meeting for King,
probably during the first half of 1897.[22] During the last two weeks before
the founding FLP, it voted (i.e., after receiving the news rather late) to
ask King for circulars to put before its affiliated branches and, later,
to send a delegate.[23] Nottingham Trades Council seems to have been
sympathetic at first,[24] though only mildly.[25] Mention has already
been made of the West Bromwich miners, in the context of the Knights
of Labour.

In the Woolwich area, the degree to which ASE branches focused
discussion on various schemes amongst at least fellow London ASEers
has been noted. Among individuals recommending the *Clarion* scheme
were the moderate Socialist J. T. Brownlie of Belvedere,[26] one member
of Woolwich 6th Branch[27] and, just north of the river, a member of
Blackwall 2nd Branch.[28] Within the FSE's no. 1 District which
encompassed this area, Erith branch also spearheaded for the *Clarion*
during February 1898.[29] And one member had recommended the
Clarion early the previous year, allegedly in his branch's name.[30] In
London itself, a 'Special Meeting' of 'the' Branch of the AU of Cabinetmakers supported the *Clarion* scheme from late 1897.[31]

In Scotland, Edinburgh and Aberdeen were centres of interest. Of

---

[18] *Clarion*, 18 June 1898. Names mentioned: D. R. Wright of the Bricklayers and Trades Council; Councillor A. Smith and J. Addison of the Carpenters and Joiners; D. C. Miller of the Painters; Clarke of the Steel Smelters; James Merryweather of the Committee.

[19] FSI *Monthly Report*, April 1898, p. 5.

[20] Derby and DTC *Annual Report* till 31 December 1897, pp. 5ff., 10f.

[21] *Clarion*, 20 August 1898.

[22] Loughborough TC Minutes. Retrospective decision undated, but taken between 13 July and 15 September 1897. (Many thanks to Mr J. V. Moran, Hon. Sec. of Loughborough Trades Council, for making these Minutes available.)

[23] Same.

[24] Nottingham TC *Monthly Bulletin*, 27 October and 8 December 1897.

[25] Same, 8 December 1897.   [26] E.g. ASE *Monthly Report*, June 1897, pp. 7f.

[27] W. F. Cliff, same.   [28] Same, May, p. 16; H. S. Woolley.

[29] FSI *Monthly Review*, May 1898, p. 11.   [30] Same, February 1897, p. 5; R. Davies.

[31] AU of Cabinetmakers, *Monthly Report*, December 1897.

course, they were not alone: we have already noted interest from the Central Ironmakers' Association of Scotland (CIAS) centred on Falkirk. On Edinburgh Trades Council, majority sympathy for a time for the *Clarion* scheme has already been noted. The Typographical Society declared for the scheme,[32] and moved for it at the 1898 Scottish TUC.[33] The support from the Edinburgh branch of the Bookbinders and Machine Rulers for the *Clarion* scheme began when its own Federation Committee recommended it over all others. However, the branch was too poor to send delegates to the Scottish TUC, let alone (as with some other Scottish societies and branches) to an FLP on the English side of the border.[34] Interest in federation and some support for the *Clarion* scheme have been noted from Edinburgh's no. 3 branch of the Cabinet and Chairmakers. The city's no. 7 branch of the Associated Carpenters and Joiners was cooler, though its junior section voted by 33 votes to none for the *Clarion*'s, even while the older members were coming down 12 to 26 against.[35]

As for Aberdeen, the Amalgamated Society of Woodworkers (ASW)'s no. 2 branch's support for the *Clarion* has already been mentioned. The branch was clearly an outward-looking one: it was also conspicuously prepared to levy itself for Bethesda and for the engineers; and it argued for the latter duty within its Society nationally.[36] An Aberdeen Cabinet and Chairmakers' branch, similarly, supported the ASE with cash, and later asked its general secretary to attend the FLP (apparently without success, to judge from the FLP's delegates' list); the branch 'generally favoured the Clarion scheme' as late as March 1899.[37] We have already noted the Trades Council's sympathy for the *Clarion* in the president's support for it at the 1898 Scottish TUC.[38]

Of other Scottish Trades Councils, Glasgow directly collected 'nearly £700' for the engineers and later supported the *Clarion* scheme.[39] As late as the end of 1898, King claimed that the city's Printing and Kindred Trades supported his scheme by an 'overwhelming majority' (though, as

[32] ETS, 'Minutes of Proceedings', 25 February and 23 May 1897.
[33] Scottish TUC Minutes, p. 40.
[34] Bookbinders and Machine Rulers' Consolidated TU Edinburgh branch, *Monthly Bulletin*, 30 June 1898.
[35] Associated Carpenters and Joiners, Edinburgh no. 1 branch, *Monthly Bulletin*, 11 October 1898.
[36] ASW Aberdeen no. 1 branch, *Monthly Bulletin*, 2 February 1887, 10 and 24 August, 28 December 1897.
[37] United Operative Cabinet and Chairmakers' Association of Scotland, branch no. 10, Aberdeen, *Monthly Bulletin*, 8 September and 3 December, 1897; 15 April, 12 July 1898; and 12 December 1899.
[38] Aberdeen TC *Monthly Bulletin*, March 1897, April 1898.
[39] Glasgow UTC *Annual Reports* for 1896–7, p. 14; 1897–8, p. 13.

we have already indicated, less effusively), and (some of?) its Brass-moulders 'unanimously'.[40] Dundee Trades Council held a 'special meeting' on 'the various schemes' where King's was 'unanimously adopted' as 'the most practicable and serviceable'.[41] At Greenock, on the other hand, a 'special meeting' on the 'several schemes' was 'postponed' after 'limited attendance' and 'especially the absence of the principle promoters'.[42] Another faithful or late supporter was the West of Scotland District Council of the BSSAA.[43] For some reason, lateness may have been a Scottish characteristic, when it came to *Clarion* schemes.

In many unions, Wales seems to have been traditionalist. But not in all: the ASRS[44] and the BSSAA[45] were among the organisations some of whose Welsh branches broke from any such pattern. And King mentioned one 'large public meeting' at Blaenavon where his scheme was 'enthusiastically' supported.[46]

The south of England (outside the London area) seems to have been not merely a sparse area for trades unionism at this time but also, specifically, one of the slowest areas for federation. Still, King claimed that Maidstone and Brighton Trades Councils supported his scheme.[47]

Sadly, research of any length whatever is more than what historians have accorded to the question of union federation. Rather, to search trade-union histories, both primarily and secondary, for the federation-discussion is to discover the glacial violence of hindsight: it teaches us how not to learn – let alone to remember.

Historians of specific unions have naturally tended to avoid abortive schemes which apparently lead nowhere. Why should 'history', or at least those who write it, care for circulars that are 'ordered to lie on the table' – or which, when supported, leave only silence or ambiguity behind in subsequent Minutes? Thus, to take some – including some of the best – histories of unions or groups of unions, Page Arnot[48] appears as if ignorant that Bob Smillie, leader of his Scottish Miners, had been prominent at the foundation of a National and International General

---

[40] *Clarion*, 31 December 1898.
[41] Dundee and DUTLC *Annual Report* till October 1898, p. 5.
[42] Greenock and UTC *Annual Report* till December 1899.
[43] BSSAA *Monthly Report* January 1899, p. 13.
[44] Bagwell agrees – at least in the context of Bell's election to the General Secretaryship and of support for Independent Labour Representation. He attributes this mainly to the 1898 South Wales Miners' struggle: same, pp. 192, 205.
[45] BSSAA, August 1898 MR; a confusingly wide spread of votes.
[46] *Clarion*, 20 August 1898. The meeting's main instigators included A. Mitchell of ASLEF and G. Lewis of the 'Steel Smelters'.
[47] *Clarion*, same.
[48] R. Page Arnot, *A History of the Scottish Miners* (London, 1955).

Federation of Trades and Labour Unions and had incurred odium among miners' leaders for his pains. Howe and Waite[49] leave a similar impression over the London Compositors' involvement in solidarity-activity during the 1897–8 engineers' crisis and in discussions over federation. Bagwell[50] notes the 'vast sea of indifference' among ASRS members towards federating with ASLEF during 1900 (and perhaps into 1903). But he does not mention the question of national federation which had very recently consumed almost as many column-inches and even branch meetings as the often related issue of Labour Representation, which he rightly treats at great length.[51] To an extent, these inches occurred even in the same or neighbouring columns.

Other historians, such as Fyrth and Collins[52] do at least mention general federation. But they telescope the matter even less alertly than in the secondary literature published before their book, as well as subsequently.[53] 'The militants', they write, were for 'political action and . . . a federation of all unions. In 1898, the TUC proposed such a GFTU.' This is a frequent format: it continues by summarising the scale of benefits and contributions. It notes that the union under discussion did or did not join. We then sweep on to grander matters.

Coincidentally – but embarrassingly for historians of Arnot's, Fyrth's or Collins' sympathies – a classic example of this kind of treatment occurs, not in a union history, but in the autobiography of Sir Ben Turner, Privy Councillor. As has emerged, Turner figured conspicuously, though not quite prominently, in the foundation of the NIGFTLU, and not only of the GFTU and the Labour Representation Committee. Sir Ben remembers how

After this [1894 Trades Union] Congress, there was an outside attempt to form a federation of trade unions. Mr P. J. King, backed by Blatchford in the Clarion, drew up a scheme of federation on a financial scientific basis. It was established at a Congress [1898] of unions favourable to it, held at Manchester, and my old friend Bob Smillie, then one of the most vigorous left-wingers, was appointed Chairman. I became Treasurer of the Congress – not of the Federation – and

49 F. Howe, H. E. Waite, *The London Society of Compositors* (London, 1948).
50 P. Bagwell, *The Railwaymen* (London, 1963), pp. 314ff.
51 P. Bagwell, same, particularly p. 205. Similarly, F. Bealey, H. Pelling, *Labour and Politics* (London, 1958), pp. 15, 23.
52 J. R. Fyrth, H. Collins, *The Foundryworker* (London 1958), p. 102. Similarly, J. E. Mortimer, *History of the Boilermakers' Society* (London, 1973), p. 136f.
53 E.g. H. A. Clegg, A. Fox, A. Thompson, *A History of British Trades Unions since 1889*, vol. 1 (1964), particularly p. 266; also pp. 304, 488. H. Pelling, *History of British Trades Unionism* (London, 1963), pp. 113f. The most sophisticated version is E. H. Phelps-Brown, *Growth of British Industrial Relations* (London, 1959), p. 257, which at least quotes a mention of the existence of other schemes.

have today a balance of 8¹/₂d. in hand over Congress expenditure. I have the
audited balance sheet among my trade union archives today.

The Federation did not function much . . .

The TUC had nothing to do with it, and later on [1897] Congress appointed
another committee to report on a scheme of federation, and as a consequence
[January 1899] the present GFTU came into being . . .

Another notable Congress was that held in Bristol [1898], when Sir James
O'Grady, then plain Jim O'Grady, delivered his biological and sociological
address.

Where notably – though Sir Ben, then plain Ben, forgets to tell us – what
would have been the main discussion of the Congress (on Federation)
was postponed for four months when the hall was reduced to rubble.[54]

We should never deny, even to a TUC knight and Privy Councillor,
the right to arrive at retirement age with his dates askew; but Turner's
omissions are more important than his jumblings. Though, as he stresses,
he might not have been the Treasurer of the actual *Clarion* Federation
once it had been set up, he had been elected to the Committee of this
federation with a total vote second only to that for his 'old friend Bob
Smillie'.[55] More important still, Turner forgets that, at the time many
believed – not always wildly – that the founding of the NIGFTLU
ratified the eclipse of a TUC scheme which had so far received an exceptionally rough reception. Admittedly, others did intend the TUC's to do
the eclipsing. And eventually it did – but not always as automatically as
had been hoped. The claim of another union historian, Higenbottam,
that 'whatever the merits of the Clarion scheme it was doomed to
extinction when the TUC decided to build an official scheme' is basically
true, but not quite so straightforward.

Of course, not all union histories are so mute. Higenbottam, in fact,
spends most of five pages on the issue, and ends with a summary of the
two main schemes.[56] None the less, the next historian of the same union
appears almost deaf to these passages.[57] Finally, even Postgate, a brilliant
pathbreaker, is so summary – even though writing (during the mid-
1920s) a mere quarter-century after the event – that he appears to
telescope the two schemes into each other. He does this partly by talking
of 'the new Socialist leaders who had captured the TUC.' (This
exaggeration, had it been perpetrated consciously, would have suggested

---

[54] Sir Ben Turner, *About Myself* (London, 1930), pp. 142f.
[55] *Report* of the Federal Labour Parliament held at the Cooperative Hall, Manchester,
1898. Trade Union Federation, compiled by P. J. King, General Secretary, p. 35
(IISH).
[56] S. Higenbottam, *Our Society's History* (London, 1939), p. 114.
[57] T. J. Connelly, *The Woodworkers, 1860–1960* (London, 1960).

more about the finer points of Postgate's Communism during the mid-1920s than about the late 1890s.) Admittedly, though, he does imply later that these two schemes were rivals. Fifteen years later, writing with G. D. H. Cole a work of far broader and more lasting appeal, he was more explicitly aware of this. But *The Common People* manages to give incorrect dates both for the publication of the TUC scheme and for the end of the ('gigantic') engineering lock-out.[58]

The world of trade-unionists' ideas was and perhaps always will be crucially more complex than merely those of its components which subsequent historians come to select on grounds of immediate familiarity (such as the pros and cons of parliamentary socialism): longer terms may also have their say, sooner or later and in whatever language. To minimise the confusions faced or suffered by innovators during earlier generations is no help to innovators during a later one. True, this book may be accused of doing more than mirror some earlier confusions: no doubt, it has added some of its own. But by reading very widely against the weave of the sources, it has at least opened important and increasingly topical dimensions – let alone the sources and itself – to informed attack.

---

[58] R. W. Postgate, *The Builders' History* (London, 1923), pp. 360f. G. D. H. Cole and R. W. Postgate, *The Common People, 1746–1946*, 4th edn (London, 1949) (original edition 1938), pp. 439, 713. The confusion continues; in 1986, Angela Tuckett (*The Scottish Trades Union Congress: the First Eighty Years, 1897–1977*, London, 1986, p. 48) speaks of 'the scheme by Philip King which had been pushed by the Independent Labour Party and was known as "the *Clarion* scheme"'.

Index